CRAFTER'S
MARKET 2016

HOW TO SELL YOUR CRAFTS AND MAKE A LIVING

Kerry Bogert, Editor

Fons&Porter

CINCINNATI, OHIO

Crafter's Market 2016. Copyright © 2015 by F+W Media. Manufactured in USA. All rights reserved. No part of this book may be reproduced in any form or by any electronic or mechanical means including information storage and retrieval systems without permission in writing from the publisher, except by a reviewer who may quote brief passages in a review. Published by Fons & Porter Books, an imprint of F+W, a Content + eCommerce Company, 10151 Carver Road, Blue Ash, Ohio 45242. (800) 289-0963. First Edition.

www.fwcommunity.com

Distributed in Canada by Fraser Direct
100 Armstrong Avenue
Georgetown, ON, Canada L7G 5S4
Tel: (905) 877-4411

Distributed in the U.K. and Europe by F+W MEDIA INTERNATIONAL
Brunel House, Newton Abbot, Devon, TQ12 4PU, England
Tel: (+44) 1626 323200, Fax: (+44) 1626 323319
E-mail: postmaster@davidandcharles.co.uk

Distributed in Australia by Capricorn Link
P.O. Box 704, S. Windsor NSW, 2756 Australia
Tel: (02) 4560-1600, Fax: (02) 4577-5288
E-mail: books@capricornlink.com.au

ISBN-13: 978-1-4402-4484-1
SRN: T8644

Edited by Kerry Bogert and Noel Rivera
Designed by Hanna Firestone
Production coordinated by Debbie Thomas

Attention Booksellers: This is an annual directory of F+W, a Content + eCommerce Company. Return deadline for this edition is December 31, 2016.

CONTENTS

MARKET LISTINGS

Photo by Jason Tennant

Photo by Danielle Spurge

Photo by Carter Seibels Singh

FROM THE EDITOR

I've been a crafter for as long as I can remember. Whether as an eight-year-old tying crate-paper ribbon to my Mom's mixer to twist it into rope, a middle schooler doodling Disney characters in the back of my Social Studies notebook, a teenager painting a portrait that would earn me a college scholarship to study design, melting glass as an artist for ten years, or now acquiring craft books, the act of creating has always been a part of my life. I know I'm not alone in this; I've heard from many artists and crafters that their experiences have been similar. Crafting is something ingrained in our beings. It's a passion we are called to do. How amazing is it when that passion can translate to supporting ourselves and our families?

No matter the craft, be it jewelry making, sewing, quilting, woodworking, knitting, crocheting, or papercrafting, you can turn your creative passion into a rewarding career. In the articles and interviews in this edition of *Crafter's Market*, makers from all walks of crafting share with you valuable advice on the business of crafting. Some share it through their personal creative journeys, showing you how the creative choices they made led to their successes and places in the craft community. Others share insights through explaining what works best for them. Each article has something richly unique to offer, which we hope will add something of value to your own path from crafter to business owner.

Turning your creativity into a rewarding business can be a craft in and of itself. Following the business articles, flip through the more than 1,400 listings of places you can market and sell your work. We're sure you're going to discover new opportunities in each section that will help you craft a business plan that's right for you. Will you be adding a new festival to your list of places to vend? Perhaps you're finally ready to submit your first project for publication. Or how about investing in a craft retreat, as a student or a teacher? There are so many possibilities!

Happy Crafting,

Kerry

HOW TO USE
THIS BOOK

//

If you're picking up this book for the first time, you might not know quite how to start using it. Your first impulse might be to flip through and quickly make a mailing list, submitting your work to everyone with hopes that *someone* might like it. Resist that urge. First you have to narrow down the names in this book to those who need your particular style. That's what this book is all about. We provide the names and addresses of places to sell your handmade creations and publish how-to instructions, along with plenty of business advice. You provide the hard work, creativity, and dedication to making and selling handmade goods.

Listings
The book is divided into market sections, from craft fairs to publishers. (See the Table of Contents for a complete list.) Each section begins with an introduction containing information and advice to help you break into that specific market. Listings are the meat of this book. In a nutshell, listings are names, addresses, and contact information for avenues through which you can sell your craft and hone your business.

Articles and Interviews
In this book, you will find helpful articles and interviews with working crafters, editors, and experts from the craft world. These articles give you a richer understanding of the marketplace by sharing the featured artists' personal experiences and insights. Their stories, and the lessons you can learn from other crafters' feats and follies, give you an important edge over competition.

How Crafter's Market Works

We suggest you follow the instructions in the listings and explore the different methods and avenues you can use to successfully sell your handmade goods. Whether your interest lies in publishing, craft fairs, or growing your online presence, you will find instructions in the listing on how to reach out to the correct people.

Working With Listings

1. **Read the entire listing to decide whether that publisher, craft fair, or website is a good fit.** Do not use this book simply as a mailing list of names and addresses. Reading listings carefully helps you narrow your list to select the most appropriate places to sell your work.
2. **Read the description of the company in the first paragraph of the listing.** Then jump to the Needs or Media heading to find out what type of artwork is preferred. Is it the type of craft you create? This is the first step to narrowing your target market. Only consider working with those places that need the kind of work you create.
3. **Send appropriate submissions.** It seems like common sense to research what kind of samples a listing wants before sending off just any artwork you have on hand. But believe it or not, some artists skip this step. Look under the First Contact & Terms heading to find out how to contact the market and what to send. Some companies

KEY TO SYMBOLS & ABBREVIATIONS

☘	Canadian market
☂	market located outside of the U.S. and Canada
⌂	market prefers to work with local artists/ designers
b&w	black & white (photo or illustration)
SASE	self-addressed, stamped envelope
SAE	self-addressed envelope
IRC	International Reply Coupon, for use when mailing to countries other than your own

and publishers are very picky about what kinds of samples they like to see; others are more flexible. Failure to follow directions in submissions may result in automatic rejection from a publisher or show.

4. **Be sure to read the Tips.** This is where editors and directors describe their pet peeves and give clues for how to impress them. The information within the Tips will help you get a feel for what a publisher might be like to work with or a show might be like to attend.

These steps are just the beginning. As you become accustomed to reading listings, you will think of more ways to mine this book for potential craft outlets.

Pay Attention to Copyright Information

If you are using this book to locate a publisher or find a magazine to work with, it's important to consider what rights publishing companies buy. It is preferable to work with companies that buy first or one-time rights. If you see a listing that buys "all rights," be aware you may be giving up the right to sell that particular craft in the future. See the "Copyright Basics" article in Business Basics for more information.

Look for Specialties and Niche Markets

Read listings closely. Most describe their specialties, clients, and products within the first paragraph. If you are primarily a knitter, it probably won't be beneficial for you to apply as a vendor to International Quilt Market. If you design plushie patterns, look for a magazine that caters to sewing or general craft, not scrapbooking. Make sure your submissions and applications are targeted to maximize the potential success of your craft endeavor.

COMPLAINT PROCEDURE

If you feel you have not been treated fairly by a company listed in *Crafter's Market*, we advise you to take the following steps:

- First, try to contact the company. Sometimes one e-mail or letter can quickly clear up the matter.
- Document all your correspondence with the company. If you write to us with a complaint, provide the details of your submission, the date of your first contact with the company, and the nature of your subsequent correspondence.
- We will enter your complaint into our files.
- The number and severity of complaints will be considered in our decision whether to delete the listing from the next edition.
- We reserve the right to not list any company for any reason.

Browse the listings for new information. A publisher you thought was only interested in quilting patterns may in fact have an imprint dedicated to cross stitch.

See You Next Year

Use this book for one year. Highlight listings, make notes in the margins, fill it with Post-it notes. In November of 2016, our next edition—the *2017 Crafter's Market*—starts arriving in bookstores. By then, we'll have collected hundreds of new listings and changes in contact information. It is a career investment to buy the new edition every year. (And it's deductible! See the "How to Stay on Track and Get Paid" article in Business Basics for information on tax deductions.)

Hang In There!

Building a professional business doesn't happen overnight. It's a gradual process. It may take two or three years to gain enough information and experience to be a true professional in your field. So if you really want to be a professional crafter, hang in there. Before long, you'll experience the exhilaration of seeing your name in print, your social media stats rise, your work pop up on Pinterest, and your sales steadily increase. If you really want it and you're willing to work for it, it will happen.

FREQUENTLY ASKED QUESTIONS

1. **How do companies get listed in the book?** No company pays to be included—all listings are free. Every company has to fill out a detailed questionnaire about their art needs. All questionnaires are screened to make sure the companies meet our requirements. Each year we contact every company in the book and ask them to update their information.

2. **Why aren't other companies I know about listed in this book?** We may have sent these companies a questionnaire, but they never returned it. Or if they did return a questionnaire, we may have decided not to include them based on our requirements.

3. **I applied to a show or sent a proposal to a company that stated they were open to reviewing the type of work I do, but I have not heard from them yet. What should I do?** At the time we contacted the company, they were open to receiving such submissions. However, things can change. It's a good idea to contact any company listed in this book to check on their policy before sending them anything. Perhaps they have not had time to review your submission yet. If the listing states that they respond to queries in one month, and more than a month has passed, you can send a brief e-mail to the company to inquire about the status of your submission. Some companies receive a large volume of submissions, so you must be patient.

4. **A company says they want to publish my artwork, but first they will need a fee from me. Is this a standard business practice?** No, it is not a standard business practice. You should never have to pay to have your work reviewed or accepted for publication. If you suspect that a company may not be reputable, do some research before you submit anything or pay their fees. The exception to this rule is craft fairs and shows. Most fairs and shows have an application fee, and usually there is a fee for renting booth space. Some galleries may also require a fee for renting space to exhibit your work.

HOW TO STAY ON TRACK AND GET PAID

As you launch your craft career, be aware that you are actually starting a small business. It is crucial that you keep track of the details, or your business will not last very long. The most important rule of all is to find a system to keep your business organized and stick with it.

YOUR DAILY RECORD-KEEPING SYSTEM

Every artist needs to keep a daily record of art-making and marketing activities. Before you do anything else, visit an office supply store and pick out the items listed below (or your own variations of these items). Keep it simple so you can remember your system and use it on automatic pilot whenever you make a business transaction.

What You'll Need:

- **a packet of colorful file folders or a basic Personal Information Manager on your smartphone, computer, or personal digital assistant (PDA).**
- **a notebook or legal pads to serve as a log or journal to keep track of your daily craft-making and craft-marketing activities.**
- **a small pocket notebook to keep in your car to track mileage and gas expenses.**

How to Start Your System

Designate a permanent location in your studio or home office for two file folders and your notebook. Label one red file folder "Expenses." Label one green file folder "Income." Write in your daily log book each and every day.

Every time you purchase anything for your business, such as envelopes or art supplies, place the receipt in your red Expenses folder. When you receive payment for a sale or other crafty job (such as writing an article for a magazine), photocopy the check or place the receipt in your green Income folder.

GETTING PAID

Be sure to factor in the value of your time and supplies, and then add 50 percent to arrive at your retail price. This 50 percent increase will allow you to sell wholesale without taking a loss.

For standard items offered in your inventory, be sure to receive payment upfront before sending the item to its new home. Once you have sent off the merchandise, you may have a problem collecting unpaid bills. If you are taking custom orders, consider how you'd like to handle payment. Will you require full payment before starting the work, or just a deposit? Decide how and when you need to be paid for custom work, and be sure to collect the final amount due before sending the final product.

When writing for magazines or working with a publisher, you will most likely be asked to submit an invoice with the finished work. Some book deals may include a small advance prior to beginning work, and others may not. Be sure to understand the terms of a publishing contract or agreement before starting work. Pay close attention to how and when you will receive payment, and ask if you need to submit an invoice or if you will be paid automatically upon completion of the work.

Take Advantage of Tax Deductions

You have the right to deduct legitimate business expenses from your taxable income. Art supplies, studio rent, printing costs, and other business expenses are deductible against your gross craft-related income. It is imperative to seek the help of an accountant or tax preparation service in filing your return. In the event your deductions exceed profits, the loss will lower your taxable income from other sources.

To guard against taxpayers fraudulently claiming hobby expenses as business losses, the IRS requires taxpayers to demonstrate a "profit motive." As a general rule, you must show a profit for three out of five years to retain a business status. If you are audited, the burden of proof will be on you to validate your work as a business and not a hobby. The nine criteria the IRS uses to distinguish a business from a hobby are:

- **the manner in which you conduct your business**
- **expertise**
- **amount of time and effort put into your work**
- **expectation of future profits**
- **success in similar ventures**
- **history of profit and losses**

- **amount of occasional profits**
- **financial status**
- **element of personal pleasure or recreation**

If the IRS rules that you sew for pure enjoyment rather than profit, they will consider you a hobbyist. Complete and accurate records will demonstrate to the IRS that you take your business seriously.

Even if you are a "hobbyist," you can deduct expenses such as supplies on a Schedule A, but you can only take craft-related deductions equal to craft-related income. If you sold two $500 quilts, you can deduct expenses such as fabric, patterns, books, and seminars only up to $1,000. Itemize deductions only if your total itemized deductions exceed your standard deduction. You will not be allowed to deduct a loss from other sources of income.

Figuring Deductions

To deduct business expenses, you or your accountant will fill out a 1040 tax form (not 1040EZ) and prepare a Schedule C, which is a separate form used to calculate profit or loss from your business. The income (or loss) from Schedule C is then reported on the 1040 form. In regard to business expenses, the standard deduction does not come into play as it would for a hobbyist. The total of your business expenses need not exceed the standard deduction.

There is a shorter form called Schedule C-EZ for self-employed people in service industries. It can be applicable to those who have receipts of $25,000 or less and deductible expenses of $2,000 or less. Check with your accountant to see if you qualify.

Deductible expenses include advertising costs, brochures, business cards, professional group dues, subscriptions to trade journals and magazines, legal and professional services, leased office equipment, office supplies, business travel expenses, etc. Your accountant can give you a list of all 100 percent and 50 percent deductible expenses. Don't forget to deduct the cost of this book!

As a self-employed "sole proprietor," there is no employer regularly taking tax out of your paycheck. Your accountant will help you put money away to meet your tax obligations and may advise you to estimate your tax and file quarterly returns.

Your accountant also will be knowledgeable about another annual tax called the Social Security Self-Employment Tax. You must pay this tax if your net craft business income is $400 or more.

The fees of tax professionals are relatively low, and they are deductible. To find a good accountant, ask colleagues for recommendations, look for advertisements in trade publications, or ask your local Small Business Administration.

Report All Income to Uncle Sam

Don't be tempted to sell your work without reporting it on your income tax. You may think this saves money, but it can do real damage to your career and credibility—even if you are never audited by the IRS. Unless you report your income, the IRS will not categorize you as a professional, and you won't be able to deduct expenses. And don't think you won't get caught if you neglect to report income. If you bill any client in excess of $600 (for example, if you are consistently writing for a magazine), the IRS requires the client to provide you with a Form 1099 at the end of the year. Your client must send one copy to the IRS and a copy to you to attach to your income tax return. Likewise, if you pay a freelancer over $600 to assist with any portion of your work, you must issue a 1099 form. This procedure is one way the IRS cuts down on unreported income.

Register With the State Sales Tax Department

Most states require a 2–7 percent sales tax on artwork you sell directly from your studio or at art/craft fairs, or on work created for a client. You must register with the state sales tax department, which will issue you a sales permit or a resale number and send you appropriate forms and instructions for collecting the tax. Getting a sales permit usually involves filling out a form and paying a small fee. Reporting sales tax is a relatively simple procedure. Record all sales taxes on invoices and in your sales journal. Every three months, total the taxes collected and send it to the state sales tax department.

In most states, if you sell to a customer outside of your sales tax area, you do not have to collect sales tax. However, this may not hold true for your state. You may also need a business license or permit. Call your state tax office to find out what is required.

Save Money on Craft Supplies

As long as you have the above sales permit number, you can buy craft supplies without paying sales tax. You will probably have to fill out a tax-exempt form with your permit number at the sales desk where you buy materials. The reason you do not have to pay sales tax on craft supplies is that sales tax is only charged on the final product. However, you must then add the cost of materials into the cost of your finished product or the final work for your client. Keep all receipts in case of a tax audit. If the state discovers that you have not collected sales tax, you will be liable for tax and penalties.

Some states claim "creativity" is a nontaxable service, while others view it as a product and therefore taxable. Be certain you understand the sales tax laws to avoid being held liable for uncollected money at tax time. Contact your state auditor for sales tax information.

Save Money on Postage

When you send out postcard samples or invitations to openings, you can save big bucks by mailing in bulk. Artists should send orders via first-class mail for quicker service and better handling. Package flat work between heavy cardboard or foam core, or roll it in a cardboard tube. Include your business card or a label with your name and address on the outside of the packaging material in case the outer wrapper becomes separated from the inner packing in transit.

Protect larger works—particularly those that are matted or framed—with a strong outer surface, such as laminated cardboard, Masonite, or light plywood. Wrap the work in polyfoam, heavy cloth, or bubble wrap, and cushion it against the outer container with spacers to keep it from moving. Whenever possible, ship work before it is glassed. If the glass breaks en route, it may destroy your original image. If shipping large framed work, contact a museum in your area for more suggestions on packaging.

The U.S. Postal Service will not automatically insure your work, but you can purchase up to $5,000 worth of coverage. Artworks exceeding this value should be sent by registered mail, which can be insured for up to $25,000. Certified packages travel a little slower but are easier to track.

Consider special services offered by the post office, such as Priority Mail, Express Mail Next Day Service, and Special Delivery. For overnight delivery, check to see which air freight services are available in your area. Federal Express automatically insures packages for $100 and will ship art valued up to $500. Their twenty-four hour computer tracking system enables you to locate your package at any time.

The United Parcel Service automatically insures work for $100, but you can purchase additional insurance for work valued as high as $25,000 for items shipped by air (there is no limit for items sent on the ground). UPS cannot guarantee arrival dates but will track lost packages. It also offers 2nd Day Air within the U.S. and Next Day Air in specific ZIP code zones.

Always make a quick address check by phone before putting your package in the mail.

CAN I DEDUCT MY HOME STUDIO?

If you freelance full time from your home and devote a separate area to your business, you may qualify for a home office deduction. If eligible, you can deduct a percentage of your rent or mortgage as well as utilities and expenses like office supplies and business-related telephone calls.

The IRS does not allow deductions if the space is used for purposes other than business. A studio or office in your home must meet three criteria:

- The space must be used exclusively for your business.
- The space must be used regularly as a place of business.
- The space must be your principle place of business.

The IRS might question a home office deduction if you are employed full time elsewhere and freelance from home. If you do claim a home office, the area must be clearly divided from your living area. A desk in your bedroom will not qualify. To figure out the percentage of your home used for business, divide the total square footage of your home by the total square footage of your office. This will give you a percentage to work with when figuring deductions. If the home office is 10 percent of the square footage of your home, deduct 10 percent of expenses such as rent, heat, and air conditioning.

The total home office deduction cannot exceed the gross income you derive from its business use. You cannot take a net business loss resulting from a home office deduction. Your business must be profitable three out of five years; otherwise, you will be classified as a hobbyist and will not be entitled to this deduction.

Consult a tax advisor before attempting to take this deduction, as its interpretations frequently change.

For additional information, refer to IRS Publication 587, Business Use of Your Home, which can be downloaded at www.irs.gov or ordered by calling (800)829-3676.

COPYRIGHT BASICS

As creator of your artwork, you have certain inherent rights over your work and can control how each one of your works is used, until you sell your rights to someone else. The legal term for these rights is called *copyright*. Technically, any original artwork you produce is automatically copyrighted as soon as you put it in tangible form.

To be automatically copyrighted, your artwork must fall within these guidelines:

- **It must be your original creation.** It cannot be a copy of somebody else's work.
- **It must be "pictorial, graphic, or sculptural."** Utilitarian objects, such as lamps or toasters, are not covered, although you can copyright an illustration featured on a lamp or toaster.
- **It must be fixed in "any tangible medium, now known or later developed."** Your work, or at least a representation of a planned work, must be created in or on a medium you can see or touch, such as paper, canvas, clay, a sketch pad, or even a website. It can't just be an idea in your head. An idea cannot be copyrighted.

Copyright Lasts for Your Lifetime Plus Seventy Years

Copyright is exclusive. When you create a work, the rights automatically belong to you and nobody else but you until those rights are sold to someone else.

Works of art created on or after January 1978 are protected for your lifetime plus seventy years.

The Artist's Bundle of Rights

One of the most important things you need to know about copyright is that it is not just a singular right. It is a bundle of rights you enjoy as creator of your artwork:

- **Reproduction right.** You have the right to make copies of the original work.
- **Modification right.** You have the right to create derivative works based on the original work.
- **Distribution rights.** You have the right to sell, rent, or lease copies of your work.
- **Public performance right.** You have the right to play, recite, or otherwise perform a work. (This right is more applicable to written or musical art forms than to visual art.)
- **Public display right.** You have the right to display your work in a public place. This bundle of rights can be divided up in a number of ways, so that you can sell all or part of any of those exclusive rights to one or more parties. The system of selling parts of your copyright bundle is sometimes referred to as divisible copyright. Just as a landowner can divide up his property and sell it to many different people, the artist can divide up his rights to an artwork and sell portions of those rights to different buyers.

Divisible Copyright: Divide and Conquer

Why is divisible copyright so important? Because dividing up your bundle and selling parts of it to different buyers will help you get the most payment for each of your artworks. For any one of your artworks, you can sell your entire bundle of rights at one time (not advisable!) or divide each bundle pertaining to that work into smaller portions and make more money as a result. You can grant one party the right to use your work on a greeting card and sell another party the right to print that same work on T-shirts.

Divisible Copyright Terms

Clients tend to use legal jargon to specify the rights they want to buy. The terms below are commonly used in contracts to indicate portions of your bundle of rights. Some terms are vague or general, such as "all rights." Other terms are more specific, such as "first North American rights." Make sure you know what each term means before signing a contract.

- **One-time rights.** Your client buys the right to use or publish your artwork on a one-time basis. One fee is paid for one use. Most magazine assignments fall under this category.
- **First rights.** This is almost the same as one-time rights, except that the buyer is also paying for the privilege of being the first to use your image. He may use it only once unless the other rights are negotiated. Sometimes first rights can be further broken down geographically. The buyer might ask to buy first North American rights, meaning he would have the right to be the first to publish the work in North America.
- **Exclusive rights.** This guarantees the buyer's exclusive right to use the artwork in his particular market or for a particular product. Exclusive rights are frequently ne-

gotiated by greeting card and gift companies. One company might purchase the exclusive right to use your work as a greeting card, leaving you free to sell the exclusive rights to produce the image on a mug to another company.

- **Promotional rights.** These rights allow a publisher to use an artwork for promotion of a publication in which the artwork appears. For example, if *The New Yorker* bought promotional rights to your cartoon, they could also use it in a direct mail promotion.
- **Electronic rights.** These rights allow a buyer to place your work on electronic media such as websites. Often these rights are requested with print rights.
- **Work-for-hire.** Under the Copyright Act of 1976, section 101, a "work-for-hire" is defined as "(1) a work prepared by an employee within the scope of his or her employment; or (2) a work specially ordered or commissioned for use as a contribution to a collective work, as part of a motion picture or other audiovisual work . . . if the parties expressly agree in a written instrument signed by them that the work shall be considered a work made for hire." When the agreement is "work-for-hire," you surrender all rights to the image and can never resell that particular image again. If you agree to the terms, make sure the money you receive makes it well worth the arrangement.
- **All rights.** Again, be aware that this phrase means you will relinquish your entire copyright to a specific artwork. Before agreeing to the terms, make sure this is an arrangement you can live with. At the very least, arrange for the contract to expire after a specified date. Terms for all rights—including time period for usage and compensation—should be confirmed in a written agreement with the company.

Since legally your artwork is your property, when you create a project for a magazine you are, in effect, temporarily "leasing" your work to the client for publication.

Chances are you'll never hear an editor ask to lease or license your work, and he may not even realize he is leasing, not buying, your work. But most editors know that once the magazine is published, the editor has no further claims to your work and the rights revert back to you. If the editor wants to use your work a second or third time, he must ask permission and negotiate with you to determine any additional fees you want to charge. You are free to take that same work and sell it to another buyer.

However, if the editor buys "all rights," you cannot legally offer that same image to another magazine or company. If you agree to create the artwork as "work-for-hire," you relinquish your rights entirely.

What Licensing Agents Know

The practice of leasing parts or groups of an artist's bundle of rights is often referred to as licensing, because (legally) the artist is granting someone a "license" to use his work for a limited time for a specific reason. As licensing agents have come to realize, it is the exclusivity of the rights and the ability to divide and sell them that make them valuable. Knowing exactly what rights you own, which you can sell, and in what combinations, will help you negotiate.

Don't Sell Conflicting Rights to Different Clients

You also have to make sure the rights you sell to one client don't conflict with any of the rights sold to other clients. For example, you can't sell the exclusive right to use your image on greeting cards to two separate greeting card companies. You can sell the exclusive greeting card rights to one card company and the exclusive rights to use your artwork on mugs to a separate gift company. You should always get such agreements in writing and let both companies know your work will appear on other products.

When to Use the Copyright © and Credit Lines

A copyright notice consists of the word "Copyright" or its symbol ©, the year the work was created or first published, and the full name of the copyright owner. It should be placed where it can easily be seen, on the front or back of a piece of work.

Under today's laws, placing the copyright symbol on your work isn't absolutely necessary to claim copyright infringement and take a plagiarist to court if he steals your work. If you browse through magazines, you will often see the illustrator's name in small print near the illustration, without the Copyright ©. This is common practice in the magazine industry. Even though the © is not printed, the illustrator still owns the copyright unless the magazine purchased all rights to the work. Just make sure the editor gives you a credit line.

Usually you will not see the artist's name or credit line next to advertisements for products. Advertising agencies often purchase all rights to the work for a specified time. They usually pay the artist generously for this privilege and spell out the terms clearly in the artist's contract.

How to Register a Copyright

The process of registering your work is simple. Visit the United States Copyright Office website at www.copyright.gov to file electronically. You can still register with paper forms,

---

COPYRIGHT RESOURCES

The U.S. Copyright website (www.copyright.gov), the official site of the U.S. Copyright Office, is very helpful and will answer just about any question you can think of. Information is also available by phone at (202)707-3000. Another great site, called the Copyright Website, is located at www.benedict.com.

but this method requires a higher filing fee. To request paper forms, call (202)707-9100 or write to the Library of Congress, Copyright Office-COPUBS, 101 Independence Ave. SE, Washington, DC 20559-6304, Attn: Information Publications, Section LM0455 and ask for package 115 and circulars 40 and 40A. Crafters should ask for package 111 and circular 44. They will send you a package containing Form VA (for visual artists).

You can register an entire collection of your work rather than one work at a time. That way you will only have to pay one fee for an unlimited number of works. For example, if you have created a hundred works between 2012 and 2014, you can complete a copyright form to register "the collected works of Jane Smith, 2012–2014." But you will have to upload digital files or send either slides or photocopies of each of those works.

Why Register?

It seems like a lot of time and trouble to complete the forms to register copyrights for all your artworks. It may not be necessary or worth it to you to register every artwork you create. After all, a work is copyrighted the moment it's created anyway, right? The benefits of registering are basically to give you additional clout in case an infringement occurs and you decide to take the offender to court. Without a copyright registration, it probably wouldn't be economically feasible to file suit, because you'd be entitled to only your damages and the infringer's profits, which might not equal the cost of litigating the case. If the works are registered with the U.S. Copyright Office, it will be easier to prove your case and get reimbursed for your court costs.

Likewise, the big advantage of using the Copyright © also comes when and if you ever have to take an infringer to court. Since the Copyright © is the most clear warning to potential plagiarizers, it is easier to collect damages if the © is in plain sight.

Register with the U.S. Copyright Office those works you fear are likely to be plagiarized before or shortly after they have been exhibited or published. That way, if anyone uses your work without permission, you can take action.

Deal Swiftly With Plagiarists

If you suspect your work has been plagiarized and you have not already registered it with the Copyright Office, register it immediately. You have to wait until it is registered before you can take legal action against the infringer.

Before taking the matter to court, however, your first course of action might be a well-phrased letter from your lawyer telling the offender to "cease and desist" using your work, because you have a registered copyright. Such a warning (especially if printed on your lawyer's letterhead) is often enough to get the offender to stop using your work.

ESTABLISHING A CAREER IN THE ARTS

....

by Jane Dávila

*Excerpted from Quilting Arts, *issue 45*

Define Your Goals

In order to achieve your career goals, first you have to define them. The more specific you can be when doing so, the more likely it is that you will attain what you are after. Where would you like your art career to go? What are your short-term goals? Your long-term goals? What would you like to be doing in three months? In a year? In five years?

Pokey Bolton, the founder of *Quilting Arts*, shares that "The first year, I was hopeful to make ends meet and not go into too much debt. The magazine business is probably one of the most difficult businesses to break into. I can't tell you the number of people who thought I was crazy to do this—even the consultant I hired, who at that time suggested it should be online only. I didn't think the time was right for an exclusively digital magazine and wanted it in print, on the newsstands."

When Alisa Burke, painter, mixed-media artist, teacher, and author, started, she set small goals. She notes that "Since much of my time was spent working a day job and juggling my art career at the same time, the goals I set at first (for years) were small. Often my goals were about focusing on one opportunity at a time since that was all I could handle. I would focus on applying and making art for a show or specific event, or I would set a goal of creating a strong body of work that I could use in my portfolio, marketing, and applications to art shows." Alisa found that "My little goals slowly opened up bigger opportunities, and over time I was setting more goals for the year: creating a website and blog, creating new art, applying to teach, etc. Finally I came to a place of generating income that matched what I was making at my day job, which was my ultimate goal: to support myself with art."

Come Up With a plan

Defining what you want and visualizing what you will be doing in both the long and short term will help you achieve your goals. When I asked Pokey if she had a definite map of where she wanted to go in her business when she first started, or if she played things by ear, she explained, "I had a business plan that I devised with the help of a consultant. Not planning is a mistake I think many people make—they have a passion for something, and rely on that passion alone to carry them through. I think any successful venture is about 10 percent passion and 90 percent hard work that deals with all of the nitty-gritty details and not-so-fun tasks. I never would have survived had I played it by ear. I was also very fortunate in that my husband left his business to join the staff and take over all publishing and financial responsibilities. It's imperative to realize and accept your weaknesses and get help from others who excel in those areas."

Alisa loves setting goals and has a very specific idea of where she wants to go with her creative business. She states, "While I know that I may not meet all of them, I keep a comprehensive list of both short-term goals, which can be daily or weekly, and long-term goals, which are monthly and yearly." She also notes, "I am not very good at playing things by ear, but I try to keep myself open to changes and unexpected opportunities."

Work Hard

Both women attribute their successes to hard work and devotion. Alisa says that her accomplishments have required "really, really hard work, long days, discipline, learning and improving as much as I can, and never ever giving up on my passion to make art." Ultimately, she says, "All I know is that you have to be loyal to your passion, and in my opinion, if your heart is at the core of what you are doing, you will make time, take risks, be productive, find patience, keep learning, and eventually create your own success."

Pokey admits, "I am a workaholic, and truthfully, this is a labor of love. I have made sacrifices for *Quilting Arts*, but they have been well worth the cause. It's a good question to ask: In order to make sure your art venture is a success, are you willing to put in the time and effort required, and to really give it your all?"

Be Patient

Try to think long term when setting goals. Practice patience and build your career slowly and consistently. The keyword here is "consistently." Constant forward motion, no matter the pace, leads to achieving your goals. Waiting for the perfect moment in your life to set things in motion will get you nowhere fast. Expecting instant success, fame, and fortune will lead to disappointment and self-doubt. Nibble away at your tasks a little bit every day and you'll be surprised at how quickly even something seemingly overwhelming can get done. Once you move yourself onto the path toward your goals, you'll start a chain of events that will bring you closer to achieving them.

Jane Dávila

Jane Dávila is the popular author of the "Minding Your Business" series that has appeared in *Quilting Arts* magazine since 2009. She is a fiber artist, a media mixer, and a collector of found objects. Jane is the editor of *Quilting Arts In Stitches*, the author of *Surface Design Essentials*, and the co-author of *Art Quilt Workbook* and *Art Quilts At Play*. She has appeared on "Quilting Arts TV" and has a *Quilting Arts Workshop*™ DVD, "Mixed-Media One-Page Book." Jane lives in Ridgefield, Connecticut, with her husband Carlos, an oil painter and sculptor. Find more about Jane by visiting her website at janedavila.com.

NEWSLETTER KNOW-HOW

by Abby Glassenberg

Photo by Lisa Neighbors

Most artists and makers I talk to know that they should have an e-mail list. They've heard about how effective e-mail marketing can be, they feel guilty for not buckling down and doing it themselves, and yet they don't do it. When I ask why, the most common answer I hear is, "I don't want to bother people. Everyone's inbox is already so full! Won't my e-mail just be annoying?"

It's true that we're all bombarded, these days, with aggressive sales e-mails from big companies. Shop once online at The Gap and you know what I'm talking about. But you're creative business is not one of those big companies, and your e-mail newsletter doesn't have to be irritating and pushy. In fact, your e-mail newsletter can be just the opposite. When you do it well, an e-mail newsletter is a treat you create for your favorite fans, and it can help you accomplish your business goals more effectively than almost anything else.

E-mail is the oldest and most long lasting way to communicate online, and it's certainly the most familiar. Nearly everyone has an e-mail address no matter his or her age or level of familiarity with the Internet. Most people check their e-mail first thing in the morning and then multiple times throughout the day, especially if they have a smartphone. Unlike social media, e-mail feels private. When you check your e-mail, you're opening your personal inbox, and if you choose to respond, nobody sees your response but the recipient. All of this means that, when you choose to use e-mail to communicate with your customers and fans, you have the opportunity to reach out to them personally in a way they're sure not to miss.

Once you begin building an e-mail list you'll come to see it as one of your business's most valuable assets. Although it's nice to build an audience on Facebook or Instagram, when you depend on those platforms you're ultimately putting access to your fan base in the hands of another company. If Facebook changes its algorithm so that your friends no longer see all of your posts, or if Instagram were to shut down, you're stuck losing all your followers. Businesses that build their own mailing lists own those lists wholly and forever.

Getting started with an e-mail newsletter is easier than you might think. If you haven't been collecting e-mail addresses, start now. Bring a clipboard to classes and workshops you teach, craft fairs you do, and exhibitions you're in, and invite people to add their first and last name and e-mail address. When you get home, don't let those names just sit there. Lists go stale after a while. You don't want people to forget about you. Instead, sit down and spend a few hours setting up an e-mail newsletter.

The first step is to choose newsletter software. There are several good options available, including Mad Mimi, Constant Contact, AWeber, TinyLetter, and MailChimp, and many of them are free until you hit a subscriber threshold (MailChimp, for example, is free until you have 2,000 subscribers). Using software is a smart way to manage an e-mail newsletter for several reasons. First, anti-spam laws prohibit you from adding people to your mailing list without their permission. E-mail software helps you to create a "double opt-in" form so that your online subscribers have to enter their e-mail addresses to sign up and are then sent a confirmation. It also makes it easy for you to create a nice-looking e-mail without having to do any coding or formatting on your own. You choose a template and then just drag and drop images and type in your text. And finally, e-mail software gives your subscribers the option of unsubscribing at any time, which is both lawful and courteous.

Photo by Lisa Neighbors

Second to worrying that they might annoy people, the next question many artists and crafters have about starting an e-mail newsletter is, "What would I put in it?" Start by identifying a single broad goal for your newsletter. If, through writing to your customers and fans each week, you could achieve one thing, what would it be? Here are a few ideas to get your goal-setting juices flowing:

I want my newsletter readers to know that . . .

- I draw beautifully and can draw for hire.
- I'm a go-to source for new graphic novel book recommendations.
- I write funny stories that will make you laugh out loud.
- I'm an excellent quilting teacher who travels to teach nationally.
- I predict fashion trends.
- I'm highly knowledgeable about how to use social media.
- I'm an expert on the home sewing industry. (Hey! That's my goal.)

Truly, your goal can be anything, but it should be big enough that you can work towards it week after week for years to come. Notice that these goals do not include, "I want to sell as many sewing patterns as possible," or, "I want to get three new freelance writing gigs a month." The goal is more conceptual. It's focused on helping you to develop a deeper relationship with your subscribers so they understand what drives you, they come to trust you, and they learn to look to you for help when they need it (and eventually buy whatever products or services you have to sell). This is a long-haul goal that you'll use when you plan content for your newsletter.

One of the best ways to gather concrete ideas for your newsletter is to take a look at what other artists and makers are doing. Do some research by subscribing to the e-mail lists of five people you admire and see what appeals to you in their newsletters. Jot down some ideas to get you started.

Think about your newsletter as a value exchange; you're giving your subscribers valuable information in exchange for their attention. Give them something interesting to think about. Invite them to join you in your creative explorations and recommend things you've come across recently like new books, techniques, or websites. Show them a glimpse behind the scenes in your studio. Remember that it's okay to experiment with your newsletter, especially at the beginning. You don't have to have it all figured out for when you get started. After a few issues you'll begin to realize what belongs there.

Your newsletter subscribers are a very special group. I view my subscribers as my most devoted supporters and most loyal customers. They're the ones who gave me their e-mail addresses and said, "Send me something interesting, won't you?"

And so I treat them well. When I've got big news to share, I tell them first. When I'm having a sale, they get the coupon code before everyone else. If I'm wondering about something, I ask them for input. They are my VIPs and my inner circle.

When you first start an e-mail newsletter your mailing list will be very small. It's okay to wait a little while until you have a certain minimum number of subscribers before spending time and energy writing your first newsletter as long as you're doing some active marketing to grow your list while you're waiting.

What can you do to build your list? Marketers have come up with all kinds of creative strategies to encourage people to sign up for their mailing lists. Not every strategy will feel right to you. As you look through this list, think about which marketing technique appeals to you and how you might incorporate it into what you're already doing, both online and off. It's okay to experiment with different techniques and see how they go.

- Create an opt-in form and add it in a prominent place on your website. (Use clear, confident language on your form: "Enter your e-mail and get started today.")
- Add a link to your newsletter sign-up form in your bio when you guest post on blogs or if you're featured in a magazine.
- Include a link to your sign-up form in your e-mail signature.
- Ask people to sign up when you do in-person events like craft fairs, workshops, and gallery shows.
- Add the link to your sign-up form on your social media sites.
- Go back to your most popular blog posts and add a blurb about your newsletter and a link to sign up.
- Ask your subscribers to forward your newsletter to their friends.

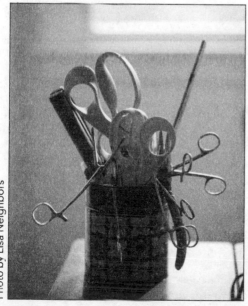

Photo by Lisa Neighbors

Every single time you send out a newsletter, a few people will unsubscribe. Don't worry! Keep working to build your list. The people who open, read, and respond to your newsletter are your devoted fans, and they are truly golden.

Choose a regular schedule for your newsletter (once a week, once every two weeks, or once a month are all good choices) and then stick to sending out interesting e-mails on that schedule. Your subscribers will start looking forward to hearing from you. Like anything in business, it helps to have a thick skin when authoring a newsletter.

Through my own trial and error, and a lot of reading, research, and planning, I came up with an e-mail strategy for my business that works. I know it works because I love writing my newsletter each week, I hear rave reviews from dozens of subscribers every time they get a new issue, and it's become a tremendous driver of both blog traffic and sales for my business.

As an artist or crafter with a business it's well worth your time to build your community through an e-mail newsletter. When you do it well, your fans will feel that they are part of something larger that you're building. The curtain is pulled back and they are right there, on the inside with you. They're rooting for you, they're buying from you, and you're all on the same team.

Abby Glassenberg
Abby Glassenberg is a sewing pattern designer, craft book author, teacher, and writer. On her blog, WhileSheNaps.com, she writes about the sewing industry, running a creative business, and the online culture of craft. Abby has an undergraduate degree in history from Johns Hopkins and a master's degree in education from Harvard. She taught middle school social studies in Mississippi through Teach For America, and sixth grade in the Newton Public Schools. She's the author of two sewing books, with a third due out in July. Abby lives in Wellesley, Massachusetts, with her husband and three daughters.

COLLABORATION IS KEY

....

by Heather Zoppetti

Knitwear design is a tough business. The problem with designing knitwear full-time is that you are either reliant on contracts from publishing houses, or dependent on other knitters downloading your patterns online. It's a saturated and unpredictable market that is, in most cases, unable to provide a living wage. One way to expand your market and become more profitable is through collaboration; by working together with yarn stores and yarn companies, everyone in the industry benefits.

Photo by Heather Zoppetti

Yarn Shops

Collaborating with a yarn shop isn't an intuitive step, but that's not to say it's not a beneficial one. Yarn stores are always looking to attract customers. You, as a designer, are an attraction. What ways can you work with a yarn shop?

By teaching, you build an audience. Pass on your knowledge and gain more confident and more proficient customers in return. Meeting customers is also a great way to learn about the market. What kinds of projects are knitters making? What designs do they wish existed but don't? Designing is often a solitary and sheltered occupation. By teaching and getting "out there" in person, you will learn more about the industry and will perhaps be able to find your place within it.

While teaching, try to promote yarns and tools that the store carries. This is part of your cross promotion with the shop. The storeowner has promoted you and filled your class with eager students. Help her out in return by suggesting that the students patronize the shop for their supplies. A talented teacher is often asked back to a yarn shop for more classes, for special events like book signings, or even for retreats that the shop may sponsor.

Trunk Shows

If you aren't into teaching or cannot take the time to travel, think about sending your designs via a traveling trunk show. This gets your name and work out there and still creates an event for the yarn shop. Everyone loves seeing designs in person so they can feel the yarn and check out the details. Seeing it in person will encourage them to buy the pattern, yarn, or both.

Be sure to promote your yarn store collaborations through your social media outlets. Write a blog post, keep a list of events on your website, and post pictures of your events online. Remember to tag the yarn shop, ask them to share your posts, and share theirs in return. A successful event will lead to future events, so do everything you can to make it a success.

Yarn Companies

Forming a relationship with a yarn company is like having a sponsor. It's a symbiotic relationship. You are helping to promote the company by displaying their yarns in your beautiful designs. They are providing you with the materials you need to work your magic as well as offering more predictable and steady contract work. Both parties help each other by reaching audiences that

Photo by Heather Zoppetti

the other did not have prior to the relationship. Everyone wins. How do you form these relationships?

In Person

Shows like TNNA bring yarn companies and designers together in person and provide the perfect arena for collaboration. This show is for wholesalers to sell to retail stores, but designers also attend to line up yarn support and other work. Designers should only approach the yarn company when the booth is empty; remember that you are not the customer at this show.

You may want to schedule an appointment to meet so that you have the company's full attention. When you meet, feel free to share your portfolio, design concepts, and future ideas. Be professional, leave your business card, and follow up after the show.

Virtually

If you cannot get to TNNA, think about sending your proposal to the yarn company directly via e-mail. Make this a professional proposal and not just a request for free yarn. A professional proposal contains your plans for the yarn in the form of a sketch, swatch, and even a mood board. Be sure to include other information such as a link to your website, portfolio, and when you expect to have your project completed. It's fine to request a specific color and quantity, but your request should be polite and reasonable. For example, don't ask for 2,000 yards of yarn to make a hat.

By reaching out in these ways, perhaps you will get yarn support for a personal project or be asked to create a collection for the yarn company, but, more than that, you are building the foundation for a strong alliance. Maintaining this partnership can lead to brand-building benefits such as steady commissions.

When you publish your design, always talk about the yarn. Also, let the company know about your design so they can help promote it on their site/page/feed. This type of cross promotion is part of why the company gives you yarn. It's mutually beneficial; they promote you, and you promote them. If you drop the ball (or skein, as the case may be), they may choose not to work with you in the future.

The knitwear industry is tough, but by working together with other segments, designers, yarn shops, and yarn companies can all grow to success. The key is collaboration.

Heather Zoppetti
Heather Zoppetti is a knitwear designer, teacher, and author of *Everyday Lace* (Interweave, 2014) and *Unexpected Cables* (Interweave, 2015). She lives in Lancaster, Pennsylvania, with her husband and yarn collection. Her patterns have been published in many Interweave publications and by yarn companies such as Manos del Uruguay, Baah, Reywa Fibers, The Alpaca Yarn Company, and Universal Yarn. She is the owner and founder of Stitch Sprouts, a company dedicated to helping your stitches grow. Stitch Sprouts is a distribution and service company offering access to the highest-quality yarns to fill your shelves, hundreds of patterns and books by the most popular designers, and dozens of handmade stitch markers. They also offer professional services to designers and yarn store owners such as logo and graphic design, technical editing, and copywriting.

TIME SUCKS

....

by Meighan O'Toole

Photo by Meighan O'Toole

How often have you experienced this scenario: you sit down at your computer, intending to spend a few minutes to check e-mail and social media. Two to three hours later, you realize you're stuck in a Facebook rabbit hole with not one shred of work done. Sound familiar? If so, welcome to one of the frustrating aspects of utilizing social media to promote a business online!

A big part of our business today is using social media to generate interest, increase sales, and build a following around what we make. While incredibly rewarding at times, it can be an immediate time suck if one is not carefully disciplined with time management. The Internet does not stop: never-ending articles are churned out, videos, comments, photographs, and notifications ring and ding left, right, and center to keep you dialed in. It can feel like a giant juggernaut of procrastination on steroids!

We're all guilty of getting sucked in and wasting time online; it happens to everyone. However, not everyone owns a small business. When you're the boss, every minute counts. The age-old adage "time is money" certainly applies here.

But getting sucked in online doesn't have to be the norm every time you log on. It is possible to stay focused in a noisy world and keep one's social media updated without wasting hours of time. Through discipline, perseverance, and the help of tools and productivity hacks, there are ways to stay focused online, get things done, and get back to the work you love to do.

Let's discuss a handful of tips and resources to help you get back on the road of focused sanity.

- **Silence Notifications:** This is probably one of the easiest and most important productivity tips—turn off social media e-mail notifications! Most sites like Facebook, Twitter, and Pinterest send e-mails out to alert their users of notifications such as likes, comments, new followers, etc. Not only do they needlessly fill up your inbox, but they're an unnecessary distraction keeping you in a never-ending loop online. We already check our accounts often, and have notifications on our smartphones, so there's no real need to have another indicator letting us know we should check in online. These e-mails can be disabled within the "settings" area on each platform. If you have trouble finding them (they tend to make this a bit difficult for a reason), the e-mails you receive will give you a link to opt out of future communication. Stop the madness!

- **Try Pocket:** We are drowning in content online. Reading articles and checking out what everyone is sharing seems almost unavoidable these days (see previous juggernaut of procrastination reference). It's also easy to understand that one enjoyable article can turn into a multitude of clicks, and five hours later you have no work to show for it. This is where Pocket comes in. Pocket is an online bookmarking tool that saves anything you find online with the click of a button. It is also multi-device compatible, which means you can view everything you've saved to your account on a laptop, smartphone, or tablet. Utilize Pocket to save all of the enticing articles that are begging you to click on them (and waste hours of time you could be making) and read them later, perhaps at night or over coffee in the morning. What I love about Pocket is it not only assures me I'll be able to find that article later, but I know I can choose the best time to read it.

- **Use the Pomodoro Technique/Set a Timer (pomodorotechnique.com):** This is a productivity hack in which you choose a task, set a timer for twenty-five minutes, and work until the timer goes off. I like to recommend this as a tool to use when posting to social media because it gives you a dedicated time frame to get your social media up and, once the timer goes off, you know it's time to get back to making, sewing, and creating! Concurrently, use the Pomodoro Technique while doing other tasks that may feel daunting; when the timer goes off, give yourself five minutes to goof around online. This is a great way to treat yourself and still stay on task. The hardest part here is staying disciplined and starting or stopping with the timer. I like to think of it as owing it to my business to dedicate allotted time to your work and social media.

- **Schedule Social Media:** Make it easy on yourself by planning out what to post on social media. Sites like Hootsuite (hootsuite.com) and Buffer (buffer.com) offer pub-

lishing dashboards that allow you to schedule social media for days and weeks in advance. Plan out what you are going to share and schedule it instead of dropping into Facebook, Twitter, and LinkedIn to post individually. Both offer the option to use one post for all three platforms! This allows the ability to kill a bunch of birds with one stone, organizing your workflow on one site, and all the while navigating the social media quicksand. Scheduling social media is a huge time saver, and both Hootsuite and Buffer offer the ability to post everything you need to do in one fell swoop. Both offer free and paid plans. Use Pocket to pick and choose great content you've saved throughout the week, and set your timer to get it done quickly.

- **Turn Off Your Ringer:** Most smartphones now have a Do Not Disturb mode (Android refers to it as Priority mode) that stops all calls and notifications from getting through to you. Turn this on when you are working for a few hours, or heck maybe the whole day! How wild would that be? What's great about this feature is that both Android and iPhone allow "Starred" contacts to be able to get through even if this setting is on. If there's an emergency, the right people can get through, otherwise you don't need to check your phone while working.

- **Utilize To-Do Apps:** Stay focused with free to-do apps like Trello (trello.com) or Wunderlist (www.wunderlist.com). Each allows you to create multiple lists, making it easy to divide and conquer everything you need to get done daily within your business. Both are multi-device compatible, so once you have created an account download the apps to stay on task. After you've completed a few tasks, set that Pomodoro timer and have a little fun online!

- **Dedicate Calendar Time:** One of the great things about being a business owner is that you set your own schedule. Set aside time either daily or weekly to plan out what you are going to post. Create a detailed list of how many posts each platform will receive, such as Instagram: 1 post everyday M-F, Facebook: 2 posts M-W-F, Twitter: 3-4 updates M-F, etc. Deciding when to post and how often to post is all up to you, but use your engagement and native stats to decide when the best times are. By setting aside time each week (or day) this gives you control over when and how much time you will be spending online during your work week. You're the boss. Own it!

While maintaining social media accounts can be an overwhelming experience, it doesn't have to be that way. Use these sites, apps, and productivity hacks to give yourself some breathing room, allow the maximization of your time, and get back to work!

Meighan O'Toole

Meighan O'Toole is a Digital Strategist who works with creative individuals to help define and build their voices and communities online. She's passionate about connecting people and technology, especially apps and resources that help make their work and personal lives easier and more enjoyable. In her spare time, she hosts a podcast called What's Your Story, where she interviews artists and makers about their journey. When she's not fiddling around on the Internet, she's learning more about plants and diving deeper into her passion of fiber arts through sewing, quilting, embroidery, and block printing. She lives in Boston, Massachusetts, with her two cats and one dog.

PERSPECTIVES FROM AN ONLINE VISUAL ARTIST

··

by Jason Tennant

Photo by Jason Tennant

I am compelled to make art, and have been since I was a boy. Later in my life, while I was teaching, I was still a very active artist; however, I was in a cycle of extreme engagement, producing art on weekends and evenings, then experiencing the melancholy of my work piling up in the studio attic. Through the years, I didn't have the time to find representation as I was also busy immersing myself in outdoor passions when given the opportunity.

After ten years of teaching at the secondary level, I quit my job on the first day of school. I had wanted to work part-time to pursue my art, but the inflexibility of the school led to a drastic and humiliating change, so I suddenly quit. That was eleven years ago.

I had a series of nature-based wood sculptures that I had experimented with for years, so I jumped into the arts and craft shows, full of the excitement of being newly liberated and eager to begin this new quest with the encouragement of my wife, Terri. I had some outside income as an adjunct professor and discovered wholesale outlets for the art as well.

Photo by Jason Tennant

Prior to the Internet and websites like Etsy, artists had limited options for selling their art and making a living. Options included art and craft shows, opening your own physical shop, selling at a craft store, acquiring gallery representation, or if you were lucky, finding a benefactor who committed large sums of money to the future of your art. With the exception of the last option, total expenses involved in the above were, and still are, high and extremely prohibitive. Expenses could minimally eat into 50–60 percent of your sales.

Then there was the advent of the Internet and online art stores like Etsy. I heard about Etsy through a few vendors at art shows and was unsure about selling my work online. In 2008, I created an Etsy storefront and, over the years through Etsy sales, I was able to begin making a living as an artist on a full-time basis. There are pros and cons, however, to any artist's choice, a choice that always involves maintaining the integrity of your work and your vision. Certainly, in the fine art world, there are distinct opinions about fine artists having an Etsy site, and as I initially developed my site, I worried about backlash. Some of the cons of selling on Etsy seem to directly oppose the path of the fine artist, yet some of the Etsy positives were very liberating and supportive of a visual artist's path. Here are some of the pros and cons to consider as a fine artist:

Etsy Pros

- Currently, Etsy takes only 3.5% commission on sales.
- Etsy is open to everyone.
- You receive immediate compensation (paid in full prior to shipping).
- You're able to have zero inventory and work on a commission basis (this could also be considered a negative).
- You receive exposure among many types of people, including curators, editors, ranchers, cosmonauts, and celebrities, which can lead to solo exhibitions, videos, book opportunities, magazine articles, and guest blogging.
- You have organized and independent control over your work.
- You have low overhead (for example, no need for employees).
- You have independence to manage your own time. You could go fishing on Monday morning and stay up all night working, if you choose.

Etsy Cons

- You're in a solitary work environment.
- Other tasks must be accomplished that often pull you out of the studio, such as shipping, writing e-mails, sending estimates, and making proposals.
- Because Etsy is a nonjuried site, I have experienced negative reactions from colleagues in more traditional gallery relationships. It's possible that it may have affected outcomes from jurors for grants and residencies as well.
- Due to sales (which isn't a bad thing) it is very challenging to maintain a set body of work to exhibit.

Photo by Jason Tennant

The evolving nature of the art business has brought me to a crossroads. The demand to produce works from designs that I have already created leaves little time for research and development, which raises questions as far as artistic growth. Does the success of my nature and spirit-based handmade designs hinder my artist's hunger to ask questions? My earlier work was much edgier and dealt directly with biology, ecology, society, and the human condition. This is an especially important question for me to ask myself in light of the world's current events.

To resolve this, I will gratefully continue to maintain my online art business with nature-based handcrafted designs. Then, through better time management, I will experiment with a new series of work. I realize my personal reality as an artist. My work must sustain me financially, but my artistic sense to create freely needs more sustenance. This new direction will have less restrictive parameters.

Jason Tennant

Jason Tennant primarily carves wooden masks and motifs of native plants and animals. He uses only domestic woods, most of which he has collected himself. His intent with these works is to express a certain gesture or characteristic that he has experienced or envisioned. These works are a celebration of nature's resilience to human stresses and are Jason's interpretation of the essence of wildness. You can see Jason Tennant artwork by visiting www.jasontennant.com or www.etsy.com/shop/jasontennant.

TIPS FOR A SUCCESSFUL FIRST CRAFT SHOW

....

by Kerry Bogert

When you take your creative passions by the reigns and consider it a business, rather than a hobby, there will come a time when you wonder if you should apply to be a vendor at a street fair or craft show. "Doing shows," as many vendors call it, can be just one aspect of your creative business or the primary focus; it's really dependent on your willingness to invest in them. Investment in shows isn't just monetary. There's a considerable time investment and emotional investment to consider as well.

I was an artist who decided to make that investment in doing shows. After more than a decade of vending at local and national shows, I've learned so many things I wish someone had shared with me sooner. I think those insider tips and tales would have led to more successful show experiences and, in one case, a much dryer show, but we'll get to that.

There are a few different stages of doing a show that I'll walk you through, using each stage as an opportunity to share firsthand accounts of experiences when things worked for me and when they didn't. Remember, no two show experiences are ever the same, but there are general rules of thumb to follow that can help make it a more successful one.

Long before you arrive at the venue for your show, there are things you need to do to set yourself up for success. In this preliminary stage of a craft show, you need to know how to choose shows that are right for you, understand the investment, know how to successfully apply, plan a booth, and prep for the event.

Choosing the Right Shows

The most critical advice I can give for knowing if a show is right for you is to physically attend the show as a visitor before being a vendor. Whether you're taking your business to a large industry trade show or a small canal-side festival, the message is the same: research the show.

You need to walk the show, get a sense for the audience attending (are they affluent buyers or families with tight budgets?), and identify the types of vendors showing (how many vendors are there working in your medium, for example?) to know for sure if it's right for you.

On several occasions, I've not taken my own advice, and it's come back to haunt me. Very early on in my career, I decided I wanted to try showing my handmade jewelry at a bridal show, thinking it would be a great way to drum up custom order business. At the time, I had shown at a few local street fairs and thought a bridal show probably wasn't much different. Wrong! It was hugely different. Had I attended a bridal show before deciding to vend there, I would have learned what poor lighting the venue had, and I would have known that the brides tend to go booth to booth grabbing business cards to look at later rather than taking time to actually talk with the vendors.

Understanding the Investment

Another key tip I learned about shows is that the cost to be a vendor can have a huge impact on your sales potential. When paying $30 for a table at a craft show in the high school gym, I wouldn't expect to make more than a couple hundred dollars. When paying $500 for a 10' × 10' space at a craft fair, I've found my sales fall in the $4,000–5,000 range. It's great to start out at smaller shows to earn the capital needed to invest in a larger show, but it's important to know what to expect from them financially.

The cost to vend at the show is just a fraction of the cost you'll actually be investing. You need to consider the cost of your display materials, travel expenses (if the show is out of driving distance), and the materials cost of making more of your craft so you have enough products in the booth. Not to mention, you need to consider your meals at the show, payment for helpers who attend the show and support you, and any purchases from other vendors you might make.

Fair warning, there are occasions where the cost of the show isn't a solid indication of what you can expect to earn. One year, after finally earning booth space in a show I had been wait-listed for three years in a row, I invested over $6,000 to sell there in a major city during the Christmas holiday rush. I had sales totaling less than $3,000. I blame my financial loss on myself because I ignored my first rule; I didn't research the show by physically attending. Had I done so, I would have discovered that the show I had imagined to be a well-respected event based on their advertising was actually not what it was cracked up to be.

How to Successfully Apply

So you've visited the show, you know you want to make the financial investment to attend, and now you're ready to apply. Most shows provide an online application, and it's important to follow the directions in detail. One thing to pay extra attention to is the application due date. Many applications are due nine to twelve months in advance of the show. You might be wondering why these are due so early, and the answer is most often advertising. At prestigious shows, the marketing team will want to promote the artists who are attending. They need time to create the print, online, and TV ads that will be shared with the public. That means their advanced planning is going to take planning on your part as well. Look at your overall schedule and plan accordingly.

In almost all cases, you'll need to provide images of the work you intend to sell; this is your ticket through the door. To understand the types of images that have earned artists spots in the past, take the time to do a bit more research and look at the websites of previous vendors. You can also look at the marketing materials that shows send out or post on their websites. Oftentimes, the images they use are pulled from the applications they receive. You'll have to decide for yourself if you should invest in professional product photos to submit for applications or if you'll take them yourself. Either way, the images you share should show your range as an artist, a cohesive body of work, and be indicative of what you plan on selling at the show.

Personally, I decided to take my own photos rather than hiring a photographer. I spent time online reading about ways to take product photos and, over the years, my photos improved to the point that they were selected for show advertising.

Planning Your Booth

I refer to your space at a show as your booth. This could be as small as a 2' × 8' table or as large as a 10' × 20' outdoor space. Either way, for the length of the show, this is *your* area

Photo by Kerry Bogert

and you want to use it as efficiently as possible. That's going to take planning. I'm sure many vendors could easily devote an entire article just to the psychology of planning a booth, but for me it comes down to two main things: visual appeal and traffic flow.

When I attend a show as a visitor, the booths that draw me in have visual appeal. They're inviting, often colorful, and show off the crafts they support. If you know your clientele and your product, a vision for your booth will take hold early on. If you're into shabby chic home décor, I doubt you'll plan to have a minimalist black-and-white booth. If you're short on ideas, though, I recommend spending time on Pinterest. Using search terms like "creative craft display" or something more specific like "jewelry show displays ideas" will have inspiration striking in no time.

Before falling in love with any one concept, however, you'll want to ask yourself a few questions:

- How portable is the design?
- Is it easy to set up and take down?
- Will you need more than yourself to set it up?
- How will it be transported? Does it fit in your vehicle or will you have to rent a truck to get it to the show?
- Do you need a canopy or pop-up tent? (If yes, be sure to waterproof the seams! I bought a "waterproof" pop-up tent only to discover that the fabric was waterproof, but the seams leaked like a sieve during a September downpour.)
- How secure is it? Are the tables at pick pocket height? If so, should you have glass enclosures?

Traffic flow is the way people attending the show move in and out of your booth. Don't expect to get a corner booth without paying a hefty fee. Most of the time, vendors who have frequented the show for many years reserve their spots from the year before, and end spaces are prime real estate they aren't likely to let go of. This means you either put your product on a table at the front of your booth (with lots of open space for yourself behind the table), or you lay out your tables in a way that allows people to walk in and through the space.

I've experimented with all manner of table layouts, from Z-shaped to L-shaped, and what worked best for me was a U-shape. As the flow of traffic moves by the front of my booth, people could easily enter my space, look at my offerings, and just as easily leave the space without causing a traffic jam.

Prepping for the Show

The prep work that goes into a show might be one of the most fun, yet stressful, times as a crafter. If this is your first show, questions will roll through your thoughts that range from "how will I know how many to make?" to "how much petty cash should I bring for the till?" The answer is, who knows! Until you have a few shows under your belt, there's no way to know which pieces people are going to respond to and which ones they won't. Some years, I've sold out of necklaces at a show and the next year only sold a handful, with bracelets suddenly the popular item. The same goes for your cash box. Some years, people seem to have cash on hand and others they want to pay with a credit card.

Photo by Kerry Bogert

The best way to prep for a show is to find a way to enjoy the process. I typically spend 6–8 weeks getting ready for a show and pour countless hours into my making. Why spend that time miserable and stressed? I've found that my most successful shows happen when I create and sell from a place of authenticity. I don't make what I think will sell or what I think I can get the most money for. No, I'm most successful personally and professionally when I'm making what I enjoy creating. When I've prepped for a show in a stressful, hurried, frantic pace, it shows. When I've slowed down and gotten more excited about the things I'm making rather than how much money I'll be making, I've had better results.

When the show finally arrives, if you've done your research, selected an event that fits your work, made an informed decision about your investment, and enjoyed the process of preparing to share your crafts with a community, I promise you it will be a rewarding experience. Take pride in what you've created and show it off with a positive attitude, rain or shine (or epic wind storm with golf-ball-sized hail). And remember, after the show, if it wasn't what you hoped for, you don't have to apply the following year.

Kerry Bogert
Kerry Bogert has been in creative arts for more than a dozen years. Her primary focus has always been colorfully combining metal and glass, with a side love for fiber arts—her yarn stash is almost as big as her bead stash. She is the author of *Totally Twisted* (Interweave, 2009) and *Rustic Wrappings* (Interweave, 2012). The majority of her days are now spent developing books with authors at Interweave while yearning for more torch and jewelry time. Visit her online at kabsconcepts.com.

25 LESSONS LEARNED FROM FILLING 2,500 CUSTOM ORDERS

by Danielle Spurge

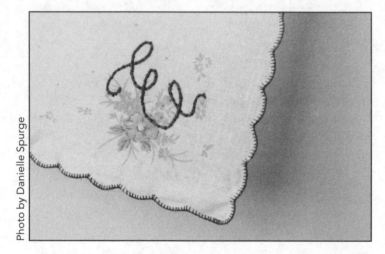

Photo by Danielle Spurge

In the past five years, I've filled thousands of custom and personalized orders, and I've learned a ton! It's a whole different ball game to do custom or personalized work than it is to batch-produce something and ship it once it's ordered (though that sort of work has a whole other set of challenges and nuances, I'm sure). Here are a few lessons I've learned from doing primarily custom work for the past five years:

1. People like options. The one color you don't offer is the one they're going to want.
2. But not too many options. So you'll add a few new colors to your rotation (because if you're going to add one, you may as well add three, right?), and then people will say they can't decide which one they want.
3. They will likely defer to your opinion. Customers might ask what you think looks best, and you'll suggest a few combinations or variations. They'll likely pick from those options. It happens 9.9 out of 10 times for me.

4. Or choose a color palette or option you show as a sample. Because your customers trust you more than they trust themselves, and they can see what the end result will look like when they see your sample.

5. People will pay extra for custom or personalized items. Sometimes they'll pay *a lot* extra. They expect to pay more and they expect to be taken care of for the additional expense. So be accommodating. You know how we hand makers are always saying "I'm not Target" when we can't do things the way people are used to them being done in the regular retail world? Well step on up to your "Not Target" standard and deliver something exceptional. (Not that I don't like Target because, amen, I do.)

6. Personalized is not the same as custom. Personalized means there is a base product and the color, motif, shape, or other elements can be chosen by the customer. Custom is the sort of thing that takes elements you work with and reconfigures them into a new project that you haven't really tried before.

7. Personalized is made to order but made to order can be anything. Obviously, if something is personalized, you have to wait for the order to be finalized to know what you are making. The customer sees it, orders it, and tells you how they want it, then you make it and ship it. But you can have standard made-to-order items as well. In that case, you have a sample, and people order it with an expected lead time but no customization or change to the product. They see it, they order it, then you make it and ship it.

8. You'll be handling a lot of e-mails. If you're dealing with personalized or custom orders, you'll likely be communicating with your buyers more often than if they ordered something ready to ship. So be prepared for that extra bit of time, and account for it in your pricing.

9. You need to have strict deadlines (but also some flexibility). Particularly in the case of Christmas, the period of time between when people start thinking about gifts and shopping for them versus when they need to be shipped in order to reasonably expect them to arrive on time is very short. Your lead times need to be definitive, but you want to try to stay flexible as well, add more work that you normally would prefer not to, because this is a time when you can make a lot of money if you go about it correctly.

10. Proofs are essential for custom orders. If someone wants something totally custom, send them a sketch to make sure you're on the same page. It will save a lot of time and headache down the line.

11. But not for personalized orders. There's no need to send a proof of something personalized. It's a waste of time. Be sure your item descriptions are clear so people understand what they are buying and be up front about the options with images. Trust me.

12. If people want to work with you, it's because of your style. Which is awesome! You've attracted people with the way you design, work, and present your product, and they

Photo by Danielle Spurge

got a good vibe from your style. They get a sense that you might be the person who can make a specific vision come to life.

13. So don't ditch your style just because it's custom. I repeat: do not change your style just because it's a custom piece. No one will be happy with that.

14. You determine how much personalization is allowed, not them. This is *your* business. If you don't do what they're asking for, let them know. It's okay to stand up for yourself if someone is milking you for all you're worth.

15. Seriously, you're the boss. You need to be clear about what you do, how you do it, and what it costs. No one is going to advocate for you. You have to be realistic and please, please, don't undercharge or sell yourself short.

16. You *do* know best what will work and what won't, so don't be shy in letting them know. If someone is asking for something that you can't do, or don't think will logistically work, let them know. They will appreciate that. You're the designer. If they could DIY this (or wanted to), they would. They've involved you in this because of your expertise, whether you want to believe or recognize that or not (but you should).

17. You can turn down custom work. It's okay to say no. Don't feel bad about it. You can't do everything, and you can't help everyone. That's why we have a lot of people in the world who do similar things with different flair.

18. You can refer work to other people. This is a really nice way to build some karma stock and release yourself from work you aren't interested in. If you know someone

else who you think would be a better fit for a proposed project that you aren't all that interested in, by all means, refer and defer.

19. If you're going to do shows, you need some *on hand* stuff. Custom is wonderful, and it's really a moneymaker, but if you want to do shows or fairs, you'll need to have some things on hand to sell. So leave time in your schedule to make these sorts of products if you'd like to apply or present at shows.

Photo by Danielle Spurge

20. But custom items can generate new ideas. I love custom projects because they always tap into a little part of my creativity that I haven't tapped before, and I get new ideas for other projects. Custom work is great for expanding your horizons and knowing what you're capable of.

21. So take on a few custom projects you aren't quite sure about. Be realistic but also be daring.

22. But don't agree to do things you really have no experience with. Yeah, that's not a good idea.

23. Weddings are moneymakers, but they're also a really big deal. You don't want to be the person provoking the bride two weeks before a wedding, so get a firm outline for your lead time and stick with your policies. Get all the details in writing, up front, as soon as possible. Trust me.

24. And send that wedding order priority. Nothing is worse than waiting on a wedding order to arrive—on either end! Ship it with a little extra time, care, and insurance.
25. Just know you're never going to be ahead. Custom work is rewarding and fun, but you're always behind. There is no getting ahead of it, unless you're a mind reader. You just have to wait for someone to order before you can work on it, so there's no way to preschedule it. This is neither good nor bad. It's just something to be aware of.

Danielle Spurge
Danielle is a crafter and craft business consultant to handmade shop owners who want to up-level and leverage their work, and build better brands and businesses. On her blog, The Merriweather Council Blog, Danielle writes to inspire and support makers in business and share insights from her five years of experience selling handmade work online. Danielle believes that a creative life is a happy life and works to empower creatives to share their work with confidence. More info can be found at merriweathercouncil.com.

HOW TO OBJECTIVELY PRICE YOUR ART QUILTS

....

by Jamie Fingal

*Excerpted from Quilting Arts, *issue 25*

I'm currently organizing an art quilt collection that will travel the country for three years, and as I began to review the artist statements and the pricing, I noticed that the prices varied greatly. The artists in this group are at all levels and stages in their art-quilting paths, yet some who are new to this medium are asking really high prices while others who are not new, but possibly emerging, have priced their work very low (though some in this group are priced high). If this seemingly random price structure was confusing to me, imagine what it must be like for a potential buyer.

This got me thinking about how I could help artists come to an understanding of how to price their work. Should the price be based on materials? Time spent on the piece? The artist's reputation (or lack thereof)? I e-mailed a few of my knowledgeable art quilt friends to see what they thought of my idea. Herewith is the collective wisdom of these artists and myself.

Guidelines for Pricing Your Art Quilts

The best way to price your art quilt is to get it appraised in writing by a certified art quilt appraiser. (Note that an insurance value is totally separate from a fair market value.) However, if you do not have a certified appraiser in your area or for some other reason don't want to go that route, you can determine the price by making a fact-based case for the value of your art quilt. To do this you need to be able to document your current body of work with an objective eye.

First, research the current price of similar work by going to galleries, shows, exhibits, and viewing work on the Internet. Be sure to find out the prices of quilts that sold; you

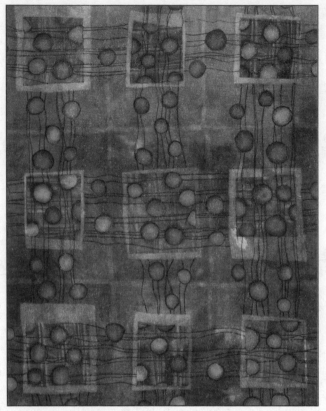

I'VE GOT RHYTHM by Jamie Fingal • 22" × 18" • $400
You can almost hear the beat of the music in the dance of the dots—simply fun and uplifting. Hand-dyed and commercial cottons; inks (shadows); fusing, free-motion machine quilting.

want to know what buyers are willing to pay, not what other quilters think their work is worth. This will give you a guideline—nothing set in stone—but an overall idea of what the market is like so beginning and emerging artists can start to assess what might be a reasonable price for their work.

It is also helpful to join one or more art quilt or ganizations or small art groups. If your work has to be juried in, the feedback provided will give you an idea of where you are as a fiber artist in terms of the market. As you get to know people, you can also get an idea of what others with a similar level of experience and quality charge for their quilts. Again, this is not a hard-and-fast rule of thumb, but it gives you an idea of where you might fit on the pricing continuum and can only help you in your overall growth.

Next, honestly answer the questions below, writing down your comments as you go. Your answers will help you determine if you are a beginner, emerging, established, or master fiber artist.

1. How long have you been making art quilts? How many have you made?
2. Are your art quilts original, unique, and is your style clearly recognizable?
3. Are your art quilts finished in a way that allows them to hang properly? Do you use the same care and quality in the execution that you find in art quilts priced in the same range? It's better if you have been able to make this comparison in person rather than online.

4. Do you have a body of work? (Example: do you have enough quilts in your portfolio from the last three years to enter four to five national shows in one year, plus another four to five for any subgroups that you are in or for other challenges?) Or, if you have chosen not to enter your art quilts into shows, how many quilts do you make a year?

5. Have your art quilts been accepted into national or international juried art quilt shows, mixed-media, or fine art shows? More than twice?

6. Have you exhibited your art quilts in an art gallery or museum?

7. Have you received awards for your art quilts at national or international quilt shows?

8. Have you sold your art quilts? What is the size range of your art quilts? And for what prices have you sold them in the last three years?

9. Have you sold your art quilts online? What percentage of the quilts you have made available to the public have sold?

10. Do you take commissions? How do you price your commission work? In general, what do you get for your commissions and how many commissions have you done in the last three years? What are the ranges of sizes and their prices?

11. Have your art quilts been published in a book or featured in a magazine?

12. Have you published any art quilt patterns? Have you written a book or books about art quilts?

13. Are you sought after as a teacher of art quilt techniques? Not everyone has a desire to teach, but teaching can add to your reputation, depending on the prestige of the class. For example, teaching at your local quilt store does not add much weight to your résumé, but teaching at the regional, national, or international level may. Make a list of the venues and the dates of the workshops/classes you have taught.

14. Are any of your art quilts part of a corporate and/or private collection?

15. Do you have a website or a blog that features your quilts? It is important to have a web presence in order to get your name and your work out there, but a website or blog alone does not make your quilts more valuable. You need to have the experience, sales, reputation, and level of quality to ask medium to top rates for your work.

16. Are you able to look at your quilts objectively, from a marketing point of view, or do your emotions get in the way? This can happen to art quilters of any level or experience, but when you find you can't set a realistic price on a quilt, perhaps it is best to keep it in your private collection.

17. Finally, where will you be selling your quilts? In most cases, you will be able to ask more for your work if it hangs in a gallery in New York than at a craft fair in a small, out-of-the-way town.

As you can see, a number of things go in to pricing a quilt; sentimental value is not one of those things. Artists need to be honest with themselves when answering the above questions and refer to them again over time as sales, reputation, and technique change.

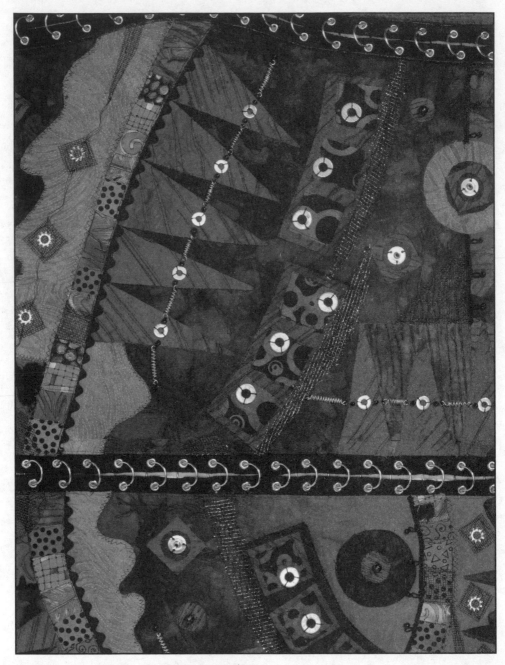

HEAVY METAL by Jamie Fingal • 29½" × 20½" • $600
A complex self-portrait; part of a series. Hand-dyed and commercial cottons, tulle; trim, hardware, screen, netting, beads, rickrack; free-motion quilting. "I consider myself to be a professional artist and generally charge $150 per square foot for my work. This price is based on a documented record of sales from commissions."

Armed with your research among other artists and an objective evaluation of yourself, you can begin to price your quilts. Note that this is not an exact science. Someone who has never won a national award might still have the quality, sales, and track record to be considered an established artist, while another artist who took first place in a national quilt show may still be considered a beginner or emerging artist. In general, however, we recommend the following guidelines:

- **Beginner:** Is still learning many of the finer techniques and has made and/or sold relatively few quilts, but may have received some attention locally. Pricing starts at $50 per square foot.
- **Emerging artist:** Ongoing art quilter who has won some competitions, exhibited in shows and galleries, locally and regionally, and has begun to sell work. May also have achieved recognition nationally, had work featured in a magazine, and/or been asked to teach outside the local community. Pricing starts at $75–100 per square foot.
- **Established artist:** Has a proven record of sales, enters multiple competitions and shows each year and has received recognition nationally and perhaps internationally, has been featured in magazines or may have written articles, may take commissions or have work in private and corporate galleries, and is sought after to teach. Pricing starts at $150–250 per square foot.
- **Master artist:** Is known throughout the world and can command her price—something to which we all can aspire.

The following artsts contributed to this article:

Pamela Allen: www.pamelart.homestead.com
Anne Copeland
Peg Keeney: pegkeeney.com
Holly Knott: hollyknott.com
Jeri Riggs: jeririggs.com
Michelle Verbeeck: michelleverbeeck.com

To learn more about the author, Jamie Fingal, visit jamiefingaldesigns.com.

HOSTING CREATIVE RETREATS

···

by Heather Powers

When it comes to creating a craft career, the best advice I can give is to diversify. This might include selling products directly, while writing projects for magazines or books, while licensing designs, and/or teaching. If you're a natural teacher and love sharing your craft, hosting workshops and retreats can add a nice boost to your income.

Photo by Kerry Bogert

With a little planning, you can create a memorable event that will have your fans returning year after year. I started hosting bead-themed cruise retreats ten years ago. I partnered with a travel agent to handle the registration and book the cabins. I manage the classes and instructors. This has grown into an event that attracts bead enthusiasts from all over the United States and even a few international students with fifty to seventy participants a year. Partnering with other instructors for a retreat has the added benefit of tapping into their fans and social media networks as they share the event.

Five years ago I began offering a smaller event inspired by my book, *Jewelry Designs From Nature*. I created the Inspired by Nature retreat that offers three days of jewelry and beadmaking classes in a woodland setting in the fall. The projects are themed and inspired by nature. For this intimate event, I'm the host and instructor. I've since added a one-day spring workshop, too, that is catered more to students within driving distance.

The larger and more expensive the event, the longer the lead time should be for registration. We plan our cruise a year in advance. My three-day retreats have registration open five to six months before the event.

Here a few tips to keep in mind for a successful retreat:

- **Location:** Research what's available in your area. I've rented vacation homes for events, retreat centers, and church halls. Some retreat centers are all inclusive and include lodging, classroom areas, and meals. Add local flavor and field trips to your retreat to inspire your students. We've visited woodland trails, farmers' markets, the beach, bead shops, and galleries during my fall retreat.
- **Housing and Meals:** Decide if your retreat will include housing and meals. You can rent a retreat center or hotel conference center and have everything in one location. But if that's not available, call a hotel or bed and breakfast and work out a deal for your students. You may decide to offer one or two meals during your retreat. Keep meals super easy and make sure there is a vegetarian option. I usually offer lunch at my retreats and then we go out together as a group for dinner. Arrange group dinners in advance so the restaurant can be prepared with extra staff. If your group is large, they may offer a limited menu.
- **Dates:** Every craft has major retreats and conventions. Make sure your event isn't in conflict with a large national event. Also, avoid holidays when picking your retreat date.
- **Budget and Pricing:** Figure out all of your expenses—all of them—from coffee, paper towels, lunch, instructor accommodations and lodging, instructor fees, project materials, etc. I use an Excel sheet where I fill in all of my expenses and then what the cost is per student. Don't undercharge for your event—make sure to cover your expenses, your time teaching, and the time it takes to host the event. And always add 10 percent more to your budget to cover incidentals or the unexpected.

- **Getting the Word Out:** If you're planning a large event with several instructors, create a website to share all the details and for registration and payment. Make sure the photos of your projects are eye-catching. Show photos of your location and lodging.

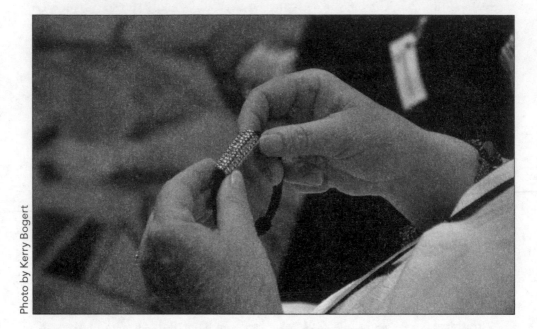

Photo by Kerry Bogert

Create ads and banners for your event for instructors to share. Create a Facebook group for your event. Use social media to share your event; create an event on Facebook and invite your friends. I use Facebook ads that are targeted to my craft and area. Send out an invite to your e-mail list. You could do a giveaway to encourage sharing the event. Have postcards made to give out at shows, events, and to post at art centers or the library in your area.

- **Little Touches:** I also package the class supplies and kits in creative ways, so every aspect of my event is inspiring. I like to start out the event with an icebreaker and encourage students to let go of judgment for the event and enjoy the creative process. Consider contacting a few sponsors to put together a gift bag for your students.
- **Don't Go It Alone:** Offer free registration to a friend in exchange for being your assistant for the day. Pairing up with another teacher in your field is another way to spread out the work and ensure a successful event.

Heather Powers

Heather Powers is the organizer of the Bead Cruise, a popular beadmaker, and a jewelry designer. She writes a column for *Step by Step Wire Jewelry* magazine and is currently working on her third bead book. You can view Heather's work and learn more at her website www.humblebeads.com.

CRAFTING A BOOK

....

by Diane Gilleland

///

Writing a craft book is a dream many creative people share, and with good reason. There are few things more exciting than holding a beautiful finished book that has your name on the cover, or happening upon your very own book in a local bookstore! I've written three books and I never, ever get tired of those moments. Not to mention, being an author can open interesting new business opportunities for you.

But those benefits come at a pretty hefty price. I've seen many an aspiring author follow the dream of book writing, assuming it will lead to fame and fortune, only to discover that—surprise!—writing a craft book actually costs the author quite a bit of money, and it's a much larger project than most people realize. So if you have the craft-book dream, let's talk about the realities of that dream and how to prepare for them. The more prepared you are, the more worthwhile your book-writing experience will be.

Reality #1: Can You Afford to Write a Book?

"What?" you may be wondering. "Why do I need to worry about affording anything? Doesn't the publisher pay me to write the book?" Well, yes, but frankly less than you might think.

As you may know, there are two ways an author can be paid to write a book: via an advance or via royalties. An advance is an agreed-upon sum you receive before the book comes out. Royalties are small payments you get each time a copy of your book is sold. Most book contracts give you a combination of these two, but there's a bit of a catch: in order to earn those royalties, your book has to sell enough copies to cover the advance you were paid. So if your book never sells enough to reach that advance amount (and most craft books don't), then you never receive any royalties.

Now, a book advance may seem like a big chunk of cash, but it's important to remember that several things have to come out of that advance:

- Taxes, which take up to a third of your advance.
- Agent fees, if you have a literary agent. These are usually 15 percent.
- Supplies for writing your book, which might include craft supplies, but also include things like equipment, software, and any illustration or photography services you hire.

So, by way of example, a $10,000 advance might seem like a great payday, but by the time you take out taxes and agent fees, you're left with about $5500. Now, take out the cost of the supplies you'll need to make all the projects for that book, and any special equipment you might need, then divide what's left by the number of hours you'll actually spend creating that book. You'll probably find yourself making very little an hour. And what if your advance is smaller, like $5000? How much per hour would you earn then?

Photo by Diane Gilleland

If you're wondering how many hours it takes to write a craft book, well, it's difficult to determine a precise number because every book is different. Even so, it's important to know that the writing and making aren't the only jobs involved. There will also be several rounds of edits and proofing, lots of research and fact-checking, and once the book is released, there's a lot of marketing. It's safe to assume that a project like this will consume hundreds of hours.

The other problematic thing about advances is that they aren't always paid out "in advance." Most publishers want to split an advance into two or more payments, and some of those payments could happen after you've turned in the work. So you're likely to have even less advance money while you're writing. This brings me to the next important reality:

Reality #2: How Will You Stay Afloat Through the Project?

We've established that writing a book consumes a great deal of time and doesn't pay a whole lot. Given that, it's smart to think about how you'll pay your bills while you're doing all this work.

The process of bringing a book to life takes an average of eighteen months. As we've just discussed, the advance money your publisher may have paid you isn't likely to cover your living expenses for that entire time. Not to worry. During some of that period, you'll be able to work part time on the book and earn other income on the side. But there will also be times, like the last few weeks of your manuscript deadline and the weeks surrounding your book launch, where you'll be working full time (or more) on the project. That's when things get financially tricky. If you have some kind of steady paycheck coming in, you can weather these full-time periods pretty easily. But if you depend on irregular income, like shop sales, wholesaling, or freelancing, then those periods of all-consuming book work will squeeze out your ability to earn your living, which can create some lean times. If your business income is irregular, I highly recommend putting some money in a savings account ahead of time so you can bridge those gaps in income.

Reality #3: What Do You Need This Book to Do For You?

So, with that financial picture looking a little grim, you may be wondering, "Why should I write a book at all?" Well, having a book to your name is still a very good thing. As an author, you'll find new doors of opportunity open to you, like media appearances, large-scale teaching opportunities at trade shows and conferences, and book signings at major stores around the country. All that newfound attention can be very exciting, and I recommend having some idea of how you'll use it when it happens.

I think authoring a book can benefit you most if you already have some kind of related business established. That way, the book becomes an excellent marketing tool, and that really makes up for how little you'll be paid to write it. If you sell craft patterns, for example, a book can introduce you to a whole new audience of buyers. If you design items, like fabric or paper goods, a book is a lovely way to get people excited about your work. If you're a freelance designer or blogger, a book can help you meet editors and other gatekeepers who might hire you in the future. In other words, think of book writing not as a career in itself, but as a way to boost another creative career. As you're thinking about what kind of book you might like to write, think about what kinds of opportunities you're seeking, and consider what kind of book would best help you get there.

Reality #4: Do You Have Enough Audience to Get a Book Deal?

Of course, before you can write that book, you'll need a book deal with a publisher. (The ins and outs of landing a publisher were covered in Margot Potter's excellent article, "Write and Publish a Craft Book," in *Crafter's Market 2015*).

The fact is, the advent of Internet sharing has created a general decline in craft book sales over the past ten years. And that means publishers are more cautious than ever about what books they publish. Keep in mind that it costs a publisher a lot of money to produce a craft book, with all the photography, illustration, editing, design, and other services they provide. So if that publisher is going to invest in your book, they'll want to feel confident that you already reach a sizeable audience of potential book buyers.

Most audience building is done online these days. You might keep a blog, an e-mail newsletter list, or a Twitter, Facebook, Tumbler, Pinterest, or Instagram account. More than likely, you use some combination of those tools. However you use these online tools, you should be an active, regular participant, and you should have at least 10,000 readers/followers in most places. (Sometimes you can convince a publisher to take a chance on smaller audience numbers, but in these cases, that audience should be very actively commenting on and participating with the content you share.) Your publisher will want to know your audience numbers for any online tool you're currently using, and keep in mind that these numbers are publicly visible, so don't fudge!

Photo by Diane Gilleland

If you don't yet have an online audience, don't despair. Just get started learning everything you can about blogging and social media. It takes quite a bit of time and energy to build up an audience, but it's absolutely worth the effort. A sizeable audience will not only make it significantly easier to find a publisher, it makes marketing your book a bit easier, and marketing is the last reality we'll discuss.

Reality #5: Are You Prepared to Market That Book...Forever?

Many new authors make the mistake of thinking that once a book is released, the work is done, but in fact, it's just beginning! If you want your book to sell well, plan to invest a great deal of time in marketing, not just the week the book is released, but for as long as it's in print. Here are some marketing tasks that may fall to you:

- Building and maintaining a book website.
- Looking for opportunities to propose book events at stores or organizations, in your town and other towns.
- Planning and organizing those events, not to mention being the presenter!
- Looking for opportunities to propose local media appearances.
- Proposing book signings, demonstrations, or classes at trade shows and conferences.
- Traveling to out-of-town events.
- Making promotional videos, PDF excerpts, postcards, buttons, online graphics, etc.
- Organizing online promotions like blog tours, blog hops, and social media campaigns.
- Contacting bloggers and website editors about reviewing your book.
- Contacting print magazines about reviewing your book.
- Proposing and writing guest posts for other websites.
- Proposing and writing magazine articles to promote your book.

In other words, you'll need to be constantly on the lookout for ways to get your book in front of new audiences. Many new authors believe that their publisher will handle marketing tasks, but the truth is, the amount of marketing your publisher will do on your behalf varies wildly from publisher to publisher. Some will assist you with getting reviews on major blogs and websites. Some will only send press releases to traditional media outlets. Some will help you plan and pay for travel. Some will expect you to fund your own travel. And a few publishers don't even have marketing departments anymore, so they won't do anything to promote you! When you're considering working with a publisher, it's very important to ask for details on how they plan to help you market your book.

The great news is, if you've planned your book as a marketing tool for another business, then the two can market each other synergistically. Every piece of marketing you do for the book can mention your business and vice versa. Every time you visit a store or club meeting to teach a class based on your book, be sure to carry postcards that promote your business. If you sell items at craft shows or online, always have copies of your book for sale, too.

It's easy to work out a calendar of complementary promotions so you're always marketing. Try a monthly focus. Decide, for each month of the year, what aspect of your book you want people to know about. Maybe it's a certain project in the book, or maybe it's a special technique you developed. Maybe it's the overall visual mood of the book, or the kind of crafter it's written for. Once you know what element of the book you're promoting each month, then you can think about your other business through that same lens. What kinds of promotions suggest themselves around that theme? By way of example, let's say you have a PDF pattern business and you also want to promote how easy your book projects are for beginners. You could approach a few bloggers who are abject beginners at your craft. Ask them to try one project in your book and then blog about the experience. Then you might design a special coupon code for any of their readers who are also abject beginners, so they can get a discount on one of your PDF patterns. See what I mean? You can gain a lot more marketing value when your book and business relate well to each other.

So, Should You Write a Craft Book?

I realize that I haven't exactly presented the dreamiest side of craft book authoring here. But I'm still a big fan of authoring them! Writing a craft book will challenge you like few other creative projects can. You'll grow your craft skills and gain all kinds of new writing, editing, and organizing talents. The pride and accomplishment of having a book published will stay with you always, and in the process of making a book, you'll likely end up with a whole slew of new ideas you can use for future business and creative endeavors.

So, yes, you should absolutely write that craft book. Just make sure you prepare for the tougher realities of the process and have a business direction in mind. Then you can really enjoy the creative parts.

Diane Gilleland
Diane Gilleland is a writer and crafter based in Portland, Oregon. Her three books are *Kanzashi In Bloom*, *Quilting Happiness*, and *All Points Patchwork*. You can visit her online at CraftyPod.com.

GROWING YOUR PINTEREST FOLLOWING

by Emma Lamb

Photo by Emma Lamb

About Pinterest

Over the last five years, Pinterest has become one of the most important social media tools for businesses out there. For small craft businesses, it offers a free and easy way to market

Photo by Emma Lamb

your products to a vast, global audience. It also gives you an unprecedented way in which to tell the story of your brand alongside your own story.

Pinterest is a tool for saving beautiful and inspirational images and videos you find across the web by collating them into virtual mood boards in your Pinterest account. Many websites have already installed the "pin it" button or share functions to allow and encourage their customers and followers to pin their images as a means of viral marketing. Once an image has been pinned to Pinterest, it can be repinned thousands of times by other Pinterest users, meaning that the image and its content can be seen by tens of thousands, if not millions, of potential customers (Pinterest has around seventy million active users globally!). No business, no matter how big or small, can afford to ignore this new marketing platform.

Creating a Pinterest Account for Business

While Pinterest gives small businesses the potential to reach a vast audience for little investment, it pays to spend time ensuring that your Pinterest account and website or blog are optimized to be as pin friendly as possible. There are a number of things you can easily do to make the process of pinning as smooth as possible for your customers while ensuring that all your key business and product information accompanies each pin.

The first thing to do is to set up a Pinterest for Business account. If you already have a personal Pinterest account you can easily convert to a business account from the link on this web page: business.pinterest.com. The Getting Started link on the same page will take you to a wealth of information about Pinterest.

The main benefit of having a business account is having access to their analytics tool—analytics.pinterest.com—which will give you invaluable statistics on your most popular pins and boards and will show an array of demographics detailing your audience engagement. An invaluable resource for any business is understanding its audience and how they interact with its content.

Optimizing Your Website or Blog for Easy Pinning

Once you have a business account set up, it's time to install the Pin It button on your website or blog. There are a number of different Pin It buttons that you can add, which will appear either on top of your images or beside them. It's up to you to choose which is the most aesthetically pleasing for your brand. While Pinterest offers some visual customization options, it is possible to create your own graphic. To add the Pin It button, you will need to add a small piece of code to your website or blog. Your web developer can easily do this for you. There are also many online tutorials that will guide you through adding it to various blogging platforms (useful if this is your main web presence, and you have a shopfront on a shopping platform such as Etsy).

The next thing to implement is Rich Pins, which is essential for promoting your brand visibility on Pinterest. Rich Pins are the most effective method for ensuring that all your brand and product information accompanies each pin regardless of how many times it is repinned or if the caption information is subsequently removed or not included in the original pin. You may have already noticed pins that have a website's icon and title embedded directly below the image? This information is a live feed from the original website, and if you click through to the pin, you may well see more information. If it's an article, there may be a snippet of text. A recipe can have the ingredients listed, and a product can show a price in real time. The information that's included can be customized to suit your needs, and Pinterest offers five main types of Rich Pin that you can apply for: product, recipe, movie, article, and place. Choose which best suits your business or the website you wish to install the function on. For example, a blog would be best suited to article pins. Pinterest will guide you or

your web developer through installing Rich Pins here: http://developers.pinterest.com/docs/rich-pins/. The great thing about Rich Pins is that once you've set up the relevant meta tags and code on your website, Pinterest will apply it retrospectively to all pins on the site that have come from the same website URL. I found this to be especially effective for blog posts! The last thing you can do is to verify your website or blog to show your followers on Pinterest that you are the official owner. Pinterest has a handy walkthrough for how to add another meta tag or small piece of html code to your site with detailed steps for the more popular host sites here: http://help.pinterest.com/en/articles/verify-your-website. Verifying your website will place a "tick" next to your website link in your profile, and this small symbol will add credibility and a mark of trust to your Pinterest account.

Something to keep in mind when optimizing your website for Pinterest is that vertically orientated, also called portrait, images both look and perform better on Pinterest than horizontal landscape images. This is simply because of the way Pinterest renders the pins in columns; if you look at your home feed (all the pins from boards and people you follow) you will notice that vertical images will always appear larger than horizontal ones because of the way they are scaled to fit into those columns. By quickly scanning over the page you will instantly notice that it's the vertical images that capture your attention most. This is certainly worth bearing in mind when producing and cropping imagery for your website. It's a simple trick that can make your images instantly more pin-worthy!

Setting Up Great Pinterest Boards

Another key aspect of successful pinning and growing your Pinterest audience is how you showcase your brand's ethos and the story behind your products. Your customers will definitely want to get to know more about you and your story! They will want to see behind the scenes of your products and will be curious about what goes into making them—everything from where you draw your inspiration to your favorite materials, and even what you like to eat when you're working or the music you listen to! This is where you can come into your own and really engage your audience because the more they care about the backstory of your products the more they will be interested in buying your products and sharing them with their friends and above all their Pinterest following!

If you are already blogging about these aspects of your creative process then you will already have a bunch of themes to draw ideas from for creating a collection of Pinterest boards. Take a look at your post tags and see which ones are featured the most and think about which have been your most popular blog posts so far; read through the comments to find out what it was that your followers engaged with the most. If you do this you should start to see some key themes and words emerge. You can also do the same with any of your social media channels to gather your ideas.

However, if you are starting from scratch and are just about to embark on creating your online presence, now is the time to do a little brainstorming session (if you haven't already!) and really examine your products and creative process. Again, jot down lots of keywords that relate to your inspiration, creative process, materials, and general brand ethos as well as anything else you love outside of your business—maybe you collect vintage pressed glass bowls or enjoy doodling geometric patterns in sketchbooks? Include those too and you will start to build a collection of ideas that will be the inspiration for your collection of Pinterest boards.

Now that you have gathered together a variety of keywords to play with you will start to see possible board titles jumping out at you, which is great! With those in mind try to think of ways to make those titles and themes more niche, more specific to you and your brand so that your pins and boards will stand out from the crowd. For example, I adore pinning images with beautiful color, but rather than group everything under one color board, I have eighteen different boards that divide my color pins by the spectrum and seasons! Think of how you can apply this to your boards. If you are an embroidery artist why not devote a collection of boards to different embroidery techniques, styles, and genres of embroidery art or even your favorite materials to work with? Maybe you like to use vintage carved mother-of-pearl buttons in your work? The more niche you can get the better; the more niche you get, the more boards and pins you are likely to add which will ultimately mean more followers too!

Ready, Steady, Start Pinning!

Now comes the best bit of all, pinning pretty pictures and filling up your boards with great collections that will inspire both your followers and yourself!

Set aside some time in your schedule to pin every day, once or twice a day at different times to ensure that you keep your followers engaged. Remember that the Pinterest audience is global and yours will be, too, so pinning at different times of day will give you a better chance of your pins showing prominently in your followers' home feed. Aim for around ten pins at a time and try to spread them across different boards so your followers don't feel like you're spamming their feed with too much of the same imagery; however, don't be afraid of adding several pins at once that are based around a single theme. For example, if you're feeling inspired by chevron patterns, pin ten chevron-inspired pins onto different boards. Your followers will be able to see that you're inspired, and they'll be excited to see how you develop designs and products from that inspiration. You will have engaged your followers from the beginning of your creative process!

When pinning your own products and imagery, there is no need to keep it all confined to your own brand boards. Repin those great images into any other boards they will fit into, this will help to strengthen your brand identity and ethos. For example, if you make children's clothing using ethically sourced organic fabrics and have eco-friendly themed boards, mix your pins in there! Since all of your Pinterest followers aren't likely to be following all of your boards this is a great way to showcase your wares to a larger portion of your following.

Pinning with Integrity/Pinning Etiquette

One of my biggest bugbears in using Pinterest is how often improperly credited content crops up in my feed, pins that either have dead links (links that no longer link to the original source because the web page is no longer active) or aren't credited or linked to the original creator. Some pinners don't see the harm in these pins and will happily repin with complete disregard to their followers or the original creators of the content. Imagine if one of these pins was for your product or work and was being repinned hundreds of times without credit to you. How frustrated would you feel? Think about how many potential customers and sales you could be missing out on every time your work was repinned without your vital information. Not only is it frustrating for you, but also to your potential customers, who are unable to find their way to your products, unable to buy and wear that necklace they love so much, and unable to share it with their friends and followers! All it takes is a little thought and integrity when pinning and you will build up your Pinterest Karma!

Dead links do happen regularly, especially from shopping sites where product pages aren't permanent; however, rather than repinning a dead link, there are a few things you can do to continue pinning with integrity. First, you could simply save the pin in your "likes," although other Pinterest users are able to view your likes and could still pin the dead link from there. An alternative could be to use a private board to save dead pins that you find beautiful and really don't want to forget about. However, my favorite option is to visit that shopping site, especially when it's another small business or artist, and see what new things they have for you to love and pin. Not only will you be adding fresh new content for your Pinterest followers, but you could also be providing invaluable support to a fellow small business—win, win!

Worse than dead links are completely uncredited pins, repinned without a source, description, or explanation. As a seasoned pinner, I have learned two ways of dealing with such pins, and the first solution is the simplest. If you don't completely love it, forget it and move on. There are always plenty of other pretty pins out there just waiting for you to find them! My second option is for truly beautiful pins that I don't want to give up on so easily, or for pins that I know belong to great artists or fellow small businesses to whom I want to give proper credit and find the original source. With a little detective work, the Google image search tool can be very useful here. Using your mouse, right-click on a pin and select "view image info" in the dialogue box that pops up. Copy the URL after "Location." Next, go to Google Images (www.google.com/imghp) and click the small camera icon to "search by image," paste the URL you copied into the field, and hit search. Google will then bring up links to all instances of that image (or similar) it can find across the web. If you're lucky, the link you're looking for will come up right away and you can pin with integrity!

Promoting Your Pinterest Activity

Once you've begun pinning all this great content, there are still a few tricks you can use to make them work for you and your business. Why not blog, tweet, and share your pins through your social media channels? If you've created a beautiful collection of pins, people will want to know about it, especially your customers and followers who, in turn, will want to share it with their friends, too. With every share and repin you receive, you will be reaching out to new potential customers. If you blog regularly, collate some of your favorite pins into a weekly post to share them. Remember to include links to each of your pins and boards as well as the original source. Pinterest also has a handy widget builder that will generate a few lines of code that you can include at the end of a blog post, whch will embed one of your boards or even your main Pinterest feed into that post. The great thing about these widgets is that they show a live feed of your latest pins, so once your blog post becomes weeks, months, and years old, it will still contain current content—nifty!

Throughout your pinning adventures, the more traffic you can drive to your Pinterest account, the more opportunity you will have to share your work and products with potential new customers. And since Pinterest is one of the most fun social media platforms to use, it almost doesn't feel like work!

Emma Lamb

Emma Lamb is a British crochet designer, blogger, and avid pinner. She lives in the beautiful city of Edinburgh, Scotland, with her Man and dog (Spanner the English Cocker Spaniel) and spends her days dreaming in beautiful color. With an exceptional eye for detail, Emma's crochet designs explore playful and pretty combinations of color, pattern, and texture with a nod to retro styles. She draws inspiration from the Scandinavian aesthetic, mid-century design, and her everyday life.

CARTER SEIBELS SINGH OF WOMAN SHOPS WORLD

Interview with Carter Seibels Singh

Photo by Carter Seibels Singh

Q: Tell me a little about your evolution as an artist and crafter. Have you been creative since a young age? When did you know you needed creativity as part of your everyday life?

A: I was definitely born with a creative streak. I went to Montessori before I went to K-5, and I think that fueled my creative fire. I have really vivid early memories of learning about patterns, puzzles, colors, and being fascinated with it all. As a child, I would spend my time playing with beads and fabric, and I remember having obsessions with color. The excitement of a full box of crayons would literally send me bouncing around the house.

Q: I've really enjoyed watching your transition from glass artist to creative goods shop owner, and the success of Woman Shops World is amazing. What made you decide to make the switch? When did you officially open shop?

A: Opening an Etsy shop wasn't really in my master plan; it just sort of happened. I was creating glass beads, and also working a lot for my husband's wholesale beads business, Beads Forever, and doing a lot of computer work and paperwork. One day I had this revelation that I had gotten really far away from the beads, so I hatched a plan to start selling some of my favorite beads on Etsy. I came up with a shop name and officially opened shop December 10, 2010. It was just a hobby until sales really started picking up, and pretty quickly I transitioned from doing it part time to doing it full time (and then some!). So, I guess I can say that it wasn't a plotted decision; it was more like me letting the world show me the way. I felt fulfilled creatively and inspired as a business owner, and that combination was too good to pass up. I feel like there was a natural pull for me to focus on Woman-ShopsWorld, so that's what I did!

Photo by Carter Seibels Singh

Q: When you started Woman Shops World, did you write a formal business plan?

A: Business Plan? What's that?! I have always been more of a "fly by the seat of my colorful pants" kind of gal. I know that a business plan could be quite helpful, but I can't bring myself to sit down and do things like that. I am more of a right-brained thinker, so my instincts and interests lead me. I follow my heart and mind, and so far I haven't been led astray! I will say that I learned a lot about business by working with Beads Forever, so I do apply that knowledge and experience to WomanShopsWorld.

Q: Can you tell us about the types of goods you sell in your shop? How do you decide what to sell in your shop, and do you have a hand in the design of any of the goods you sell?

A: I sell a colorful selection of what I like to call "Crafty Global Goods." I think of WomanShopsWorld as my personal supplies shop that I am sharing with the rest of the world. I only sell things that I would love to create myself, which I think is a large part of why it's been so successful. Coming from a background of selling anything and everything related to beads, it is refreshing and liberating to focus on the goods that I love.

When it comes to adding new lines and products to my line, I choose things that make my heart skip a beat, that give me butterflies in my stomach. It's all about color, texture, history, and a bit of mystery. Things with a history enchant me, and oftentimes I don't know the history of a piece, but I can feel the magic in it.

I realize that I am in a uniquely beautiful position in that I am a jewelry designer and a supplier, with manufacturing connections. So I have been able to fill a void in the market when I see it. For example, I have developed a full line of tassels that are perfect for jewelry making. It's such a beautiful reality that I get to fulfill my creativity in the designing of the product, and I get to share the magic with others by selling the finished products.

Q: Etsy is your primary storefront. What made you decide to focus on Etsy over a traditional website?

A: I have learned that it's best to focus on what you do best. I have a good bit of experience with trying to market my own website. And it's not easy work! Etsy is such a powerful marketplace, and they handle so much of the SEO and marketing, that it frees me up to focus on my shop.

Q: What do you find works best for you when it comes to marketing and promoting your shop? Do you have a marketing plan? How do you get people to your shop?

A: I use social media a lot to market my shop, and I use the tools that Etsy provides, like keywords and tags. I think staying fresh and active is a crucial ingredient to success, with your own website or Etsy. I don't have an official marketing plan, and I am always trying new things. I learn a lot from watching other successful small business owners. With the Internet, you can learn so much from observing your contemporaries. I also have an active mailing list, and use newsletters to let customers know about new products and things that I have going on.

Q: What's your favorite thing about having a creative business?

A: Sharing the magic. I love that my customers are just as excited over my goods as I am. Nothing makes me happier than when I get a message from a customer or even a browser, telling me how inspired they are just from entering my shop. It makes me feel like someone else "gets" my magic.

Q: Is there anything you'd do differently if you started over?

A: Amazingly, no! This has been such a perfect and beautiful ride; I can truly say that I wouldn't change a thing. I am so fulfilled every day, and so happy, and have enjoyed every moment in the evolution of my business, that it makes me think that it had to have happened exactly the way it did! It hasn't been an easy evolution, but every step was a necessary one.

Carter Seibels Singh
Carter resides in Charlotte, NC, when she's not traveling around the world sourcing crafty global goods. Some of her favorite activities are yoga, long walks with her golden retriever Gypsy, and exploring ethnic grocery stores. You can find Carter online at www.womanshopsworld.etsy.com.

INDUSTRY SHOWS

//

Attending an industry trade show can be an eye-opening experience. For the craft industry, there are niche trade shows that take place multiple times a year in various parts of the country, each with potentially hundreds of top-name exhibitors. Attend one of these shows and you'll see just how popular sewing, quilting, scrapbooking, jewelry making, needlearts and craft in general continue to be. This section includes listings of major industry shows in different niches of the craft industry, as well as some that are not craft specific but still may be good places to exhibit your handmade goods.

Simply attending one of these shows and walking the floor as a new business owner can be helpful. You'll be able to see the wide variety of items produced in your industry, and identify major competitors or those that you might want to work with down the line. You will certainly have the chance to network within your chosen craft with your peers and those who inspire you. All trade shows have different restrictions on who can attend the show. Most are open only to buyers or industry professionals, not the general public, so be sure to find out if you are eligible to attend a show before showing up. You may be required to submit your business identification number, wholesale receipts, tax information, or other paperwork showing that you are indeed a professional in the industry.

A major step for any professional crafter is to exhibit at an industry show. Doing so can be expensive and time consuming, but the benefits are great. Exhibiting as a vendor at one of these shows puts you in contact with retailers from around the world who are at the show specifically to place wholesale orders and stock their store. Depending on the items you sell, exhibiting at one of the major trade shows could provide you with a major increase in sales. If you are interested in exhibiting at a trade show in your industry niche, be sure to do your research. There will most likely be a lengthy application process to complete. You will also want to know how large your booth is so you can dress it well. Many booths are decorated to the gills at these events to draw in potential buyers. Make sure you are able to put your best foot forward if you choose to exhibit. Also, think through your sales process for these types of events. You'll need order sheets, sales slips, receipts, the ability to take payment information, etc. Read Heather Zoppetti's article "Collaboration Is Key" for more information on trade shows and the wholesale process. Also, reach out to someone who's "been there, done that" before you exhibit for the first time. They will be able to provide you with invaluable insight as you gear up for your first show.

KEY TO SYMBOLS & ABBREVIATIONS

○	Canadian market
○	market located outside of the U.S. and Canada
○	market prefers to work with local artists/ designers
b&w	black & white (photo or illustration)
SASE	self-addressed, stamped envelope
SAE	self-addressed envelope
IRC	International Reply Coupon, for use when mailing to countries other than your own

ALASKA WHOLESALE GIFT & FOOD SHOW

Alaska Genesis Productions, P.O. Box 200846, Anchorage AK 99520. (907)929-2822. E-mail: info@alaskagiftshow.com. Website: www.alaskagiftshow.com. Annual wholesale/cash & carry show held in January. Indoors. Open to trade only. Accepts handmade craft merchants, pattern, magazine, book publishers, and other mediums. Number exhibitors: see website. Number attendees: see website. Admission: see website. Apply online. Deadline for entry: see website. Application fee: none. Space fee: varies. Exhibition space: 10×10. For more information, exhibitors should e-mail, visit website, or call.

○ ALBERTA GIFT FAIR

42 Voyager Court S., Toronto, Ontario M9W5M7 Canada. (416)679-0170. Fax: (800)611-6100. E-mail: alberta@cangift.org. Website: www.albertagiftfair. org. Annual wholesale show held in spring/fall. Indoors. Open to trade only. Accepts handmade craft merchants, gifts, collectibles, and other mediums. Number exhibitors: 800. Number attendees: 16,000. Admission: see website. Apply online. Deadline for entry: see website. Application fee: none. Space fee: varies. Exhibition space: 10×10. For more information, e-mail, visit website, or call.

AMERICAN BEAD & JEWELRY SHOWS

P.O. Box 490803, Atlanta GA 30349. (770)739-0057. Fax: (866)311-7774. E-mail: info@americangemexpo.com. Website: www.americanbeadshows.com. Wholesale show held multiple times per year. Indoors. Open to public. Accepts handmade craft merchants, beads, jewelry, gems, gifts, body products, and more. Number exhibitors: see website. Number attendees: varies. Admission: see website. Apply online. Deadline for entry: varies by date. Application fee: none. Space fee: varies. Exhibition space: varies. For more information, e-mail, visit website, or call.

AMERICAN CRAFT
RETAILER EXPO—LAS VEGAS

P.O. Box 4597, Mooresville NC 28117-4597. (888)427-2381. E-mail: service@wholesalecrafts.com. Website: www.acrelasvegas.com. Currently boasting 1,200 artists and 16,000 retailer members, Wholesalecrafts.

com is the only successful online trade show of its kind. See website for details.

AMERICAN CRAFT
RETAILER EXPO—ORLANDO

Website: www.wholesalecrafts.com. Currently boasting 1,200 artists and 16,000 retailer members, Wholesalecrafts.com is the only successful online trade show of its kind. See website for details.

AMERICAN MADE SHOW

(410)889-2933, ext. 227. E-mail: jenm@rosengrp. com. Website: www.americanmadeshow.com. Contact: Jen Menkhaus, exhibits manager. Estab. 1983. Annual wholesale show held in winter. Indoors. Open to trade only. Accepts handcrafted artist-made goods. Awards/prizes: Merit Awards. Number exhibitors: 800. Number attendees: 4,500. Admission: see website. Apply online. Deadline for entry: see website. Application fee: none. Space fee: varies. Exhibition space: 6×10; 10×10. For more information, e-mail, visit website, or call.

ATLANTA INTERNATIONAL
GIFT & HOME FURNISHINGS

Website: www.americasmart.com. "We know your time is money, so we strive to make your experience at AmericasMart productive and profitable. As the leading international source for consumer goods, AmericasMart remains unmatched in convenience, amenities, and professionalism. Experience AmericasMart for yourself and make it your business advantage. We've got an edge over our national competitors: nation's largest single product collection. By design, the airport connects to rapid rail that takes you directly to the heart of downtown, where AmericasMart is located." See website for more information.

THE ATLANTIC CRAFT
TRADE SHOW (ACTS)

(902)492-2773. Fax: (902)429-9059. E-mail: acts@ craftalliance.ca. Website: www.actshow.ca/EN/. Estab. 1977. Annual wholesale show held in February. Indoors. Open to trade only. Accepts handmade craft merchants, giftware. Juried. Number exhibitors: see website. Number attendees: see website. Admission: see website. Apply online. Deadline for entry: see website. Application fee: none. Space fee: see website. Exhibition space: see website. For more information, e-mail, visit website, or call.

BEAD & BUTTON SHOW

Website: www.beadandbuttonshow.com. Over 300 vendors will be selling one-of-a-kind finished jewelry plus precious gems, pearls, art beads, gold and silver, beading supplies, and books. The show will also feature a juried exhibit of inspiring bead art and over 700 bead and jewelry classes. See website for more information.

BEAD FEST

(513)531-2690. Fax: (610)232-5754. E-mail: mkralle@interweave.com. Website: www.beadfest.com. Contact: Morgan Kralle, event planner. Estab. 2001. Annual cash & carry show held in spring/summer. Indoors. Open to public. Accepts handmade craft merchants, pattern, magazine, book publishers, and other mediums. Awards/prizes: Bead Show Winner. Number exhibitors: 150. Number attendees: 3,000-5,000. Admission: $8 for expo; workshop prices vary. Apply online. Deadline for entry: see website. Application fee: none. Space fee: $850-995. Exhibition space: 10×10. For more information e-mail, visit website, call, or check social media.

BILOXI WHOLESALE GIFT SHOW

E-mail: biloximarket@gmail.com. Website: www.wmigiftshows.com. "Buyers attending the Biloxi Wholesale Gift Show will experience over 300 booths with manufacturers from 22 states and a huge selection of new and trendy merchandise including holiday, home décor, tabletop, garden accessories, souvenirs, gourmet, jewelry, apparel, floral, gift wrap, and much more." See website for more information.

BOSTON GIFT SHOW

(800)318-2238. Fax: (678)285-7469. E-mail: info@urbanexpositions.com. Website: www.bostongiftshow.com. Contact: Erica Davidson, show director. Cash & carry/wholesale show held annually in March. In-doors. Open to trade only; must show business ID to enter. Accepts handmade craft merchants, pattern, magazine, book publishers, functional & decorative accessories, fashion. Juried. Number exhibitors: 500. Number attendees: 4,000. Admission: no fee, open to trade only. Apply online. Deadline for entry: August. Application fee: none. Space fee: $1,690. Exhibition space: 10×10. For more information, e-mail, visit website, or call.

🌏 BRITISH CRAFT TRADE FAIR

E-mail: info@bctf.co.uk. Website: www.bctf.co.uk. "The British Craft Trade Fair (BCTF) is a three-day event that takes place in April each year at the scenic Great Yorkshire Showground in beautiful Harrogate, Yorkshire. The fair is strictly trade-only and showcases work from exclusively British and Irish makers. BCTF differs from other trade fairs in that no mass-manufactured products or products made overseas are allowed. Visitors can be confident that they will be presented with a selection of the best handmade British giftware available from more than 500 talented makers." See website for more information.

BUYER'S CASH & CARRY—MADISON

E-mail: mktsqr@epix.net. Website: www.marketsquareshows.com. Select from a large variety of unusual gift items, handcrafted furniture, gourmet food products, jewelry, as well as handcrafted quality reproductions. All for immediate inventory needs. See website for more information.

BUYER'S CASH & CARRY—MARLBOROUGH

E-mail: mktsqr@epix.net. Website: www.marketsquareshows.com. Select from a large variety of unusual gift items, handcrafted furniture, gourmet food products, jewelry, as well as handcrafted quality reproductions. All for immediate inventory needs. See website for details.

BUYER'S CASH & CARRY—VALLEY FORGE

E-mail: mktsqr@epix.net. Website: www.marketsquareshows.com. Hand pick holiday collectibles, folk art, handcrafted furniture, and speciality foods.

All available for immediate inventory needs. See website for more information.

◎ BY HAND

(888)773-4444. Fax: (613)241-5678. E-mail: info@byhand.ca. Website: www.byhand.ca. "Canada's premier wholesale marketplace allows buyers the opportunity to discover the very best in Canadian handmade products. Buyers who visit By Hand will see the finest in handmade glass, ceramics, mixed media, fashion, jewelery, leather, art, wood, metal, raku, home décor, stone, pottery, photography, sculpture, toys, and more. At By Hand you will find new and exciting product designs that will delight your customers and separate you from your competition. By Hand is a juried show where you will meet the designers and makers of the products and come to understand the joy and passion artisans have for their work." See website for more information.

CALIFORNIA GIFT SHOW

Website: www.californiagiftshow.com. See website for more information and to apply.

CHICAGO GIFT MARKET

Website: www.chicagogiftmarket.com. Wholesale show that takes place 4 times a year. See website for more information and to apply.

COLUMBUS MARKETPLACE

Website: www.thecolumbusmarketplace.com. "The Columbus MarketPlace is a permanent wholesale market center offering the newest and finest lines of gifts, collectibles, home furnishings, accessories, housewares, stationery, and floral items. This array of trend-setting merchandise is displayed in permanent showrooms in an easy-to-shop, single-floor layout." See website for more information.

◎ CRAFT

Website: www.craft-london.com. "Covering basketry, blacksmithing, book art, ceramics, enamelling, fashion accessories, furniture, glass, interiors, non-precious and precious jewelery, knitwear, leather, lettering, metalwork, wood, millinery, mosaic, pa-per, printmaking, product design, sculptural, recycled, stone carving, textiles, traditional, and more, CRAFT fills a gap in the UK market for a high-quality, juried trade event which enables over 150 leading makers and artisans to meet a substantial audience of international retailers, galleries, museums, professional buyers, and collectors within a dedicated trade event in London."

CRAFT AND HOBBY ASSOCIATION CONFERENCE & TRADE SHOW

E-mail: nschwartz@craftandhobby.org. Website: www.craftandhobby.org. See website for more information.

◎ CRAFT HOBBY & STITCH INTERNATIONAL

E-mail: info@chsi.co.uk. Website: www.chsi.co.uk. "Europe's No. 1 trade show for the creative craft sector provides suppliers of creative art, craft, needlecraft, and hobby products with a fantastic platform to showcase their products to a worldwide audience."

DALLAS TEMP SHOW

Website: www.dallasmarketcenter.com. See website for more information.

DALLAS TOTAL HOME & GIFT SHOW

Website: www.dallasmarketcenter.com. "The premier product destination offering more than 20,000 gift and home décor lines within a convenient, easy-to-shop marketplace."

GALVESTON GIFT & RESORT MERCHANDISE SHOW

(800)318-2238. Fax: (678)285-7469. E-mail: info@urbanexpositions.com. Website: www.galvestongiftshow.com. Contact: Christina Bell, show director. Wholesale show held annually in October. Indoors. Open to trade only. Accepts handmade craft merchants, pattern, magazine, and book publishers. Number exhibitors: see website. Number attendees: see website. Admission: none. Apply online. Deadline for entry: see website. Application fee: none. Space fee:

$645. Exhibition space: 10×10. For more information e-mail cbell@urban-expo.com.

GEM AND LAPIDARY WHOLESALERS SHOW

E-mail: info@glwshows.com. Website: www.glwshows.com. G&LW trade shows are produced in many major trade centers across the United States for the convenience of retail dealers.

HAWAII MARKET MERCHANDISE EXPO

Website: www.douglastradeshows.com. Featured products are: jewelry, gift, apparel, fashion accessories, leather goods, art, and collectibles in addition to products manufactured in Hawaii. The expos are designed specifically to serve Hawaii's business buyers and sellers. The expos are not open to the public. The cash & carry format of immediate release of merchandise encourages thousands of business owners, managers, and professional trade buyers to purchase hundreds of products for use or resale in their businesses.

INTERNATIONAL QUILT MARKET

Website: www.quilts.com. See website for more information.

LAS VEGAS MARKET

Website: www.lasvegasmarket.com. "Las Vegas Market is the most comprehensive furniture, home décor, and gift market in the US, presenting a unique cross-section of 2,000+ resources in an unrivaled market destination. With two markets each year, retailers and designers can shop a broad assortment of product from thousands of manufacturers of furniture, mattress, lighting, decorative accessories, floor coverings, home textiles, tabletop, general gift, and more delivering the most complete, cross-category wholesale trade show for the furniture, home décor, and gift industries in the US"

LAS VEGAS SOUVENIR & RESORT GIFT SHOW

(800)318-2238. Fax: (678)285-7469. E-mail: info@urbanexpositions.com. Website: www.lvsouvenirshow.com. Contact: Lisa Glosson, show director. Wholesale show held annually in September. Indoors. Open to trade only. Accepts handmade craft merchants, pattern, magazine, book publishers. Number exhibitors: see website. Number attendees: see website. Admission: none. Apply online. Deadline for entry: see website. Application fee: none. Space fee: $1,950. Exhibition space: 10×10. For more information e-mail lglosson@urban-expo.com.

LOUISVILLE GIFT SHOW

(513)861-1139. Fax: (513)861-1557. E-mail: lpharris42@hotmail.com. Website: www.stlouisgiftshow.com. Contact: Larry Harris, president. Estab. 1960s. Wholesale show (some cash & carry and order writing) held semi-annually in February & August. Indoors. Not open to public. Accepts handmade craft merchants, pattern, magazine, book publishers, USA made, imports. Number exhibitors: 70. Number attendees: 800. Admission: none. Apply online. Deadline for entry: open until filled. Application fee: none. Space fee: $525 (10×8); $625 (10×10). Exhibition space: 10×8; 10×10. For more information e-mail or visit website.

TIPS "Product presentation."

🌀 MAKE IT!—EDMONTON

Website: www.make-it.org.uk. "Make it! continues to be one of the biggest and most popular paper crafting events in the South of England, attracting the most celebrated companies in the craft world and thousands of enthusiastic visitors each year. Make it! brings you the best in paper and card craft from over a hundred exhibiting companies."

🌀 MAKE IT!—VANCOUVER

Website: www.make-it.org.uk. "Make it! continues to be one of the biggest and most popular paper crafting events in the South of England, attracting the most celebrated companies in the craft world and thousands of enthusiastic visitors each year. Make it! brings you the best in paper and card craft from over a hundred exhibiting companies."

MINNEAPOLIS MART GIFT HOME & ACCESSORY SHOW

(952)932-7200 or (800)626-1298. Fax: (952)932-0847. E-mail: mart@mplsmart.com. Website: www.mplsmart.com. Wholesale show held 4 times a year (see website for dates). Indoors. Open to trade only. Accepts home decor, accessories and apparel merchandise. Number exhibitors: see website. Number attendees: see website. Admission: see website. Apply online. Deadline for entry: see website. Application fee: see website. Space fee: varies. Exhibition space: varies. For more information e-mail, visit website, call.

MJSA EXPO

(508)316-2132 or (800)444-6572. Fax: (508)316-1429. E-mail: corrie.silvia@mjsa.org. Website: www.mjsa.org. Contact: Corrie Silvia Berry. Annual wholesale show held in spring (check website for dates). Indoors. Open to trade only. Accepts jewelry machinery, supplies, components, services, and finished product. Number exhibitors: see website. Number attendees: see website. Admission: see website. Apply online. Deadline for entry: see website. Application fee: none. Space fee: varies. Exhibition space: varies. For more information, e-mail, visit website, or call.

NAMTA ART MATERIALS WORLD

(704)892-6244. Fax: (704)892-6247. E-mail: rmunisteri@namta.org. Website: www.namta.org. Contact: Rick Munisteri, director of meetings. Annual conference & wholesale show held in spring. Indoors. Open to trade only. Accepts art & craft materials. Number exhibitors: see website. Number attendees: see website. Admission: see website. Apply online. Deadline for entry: see website. Application fee: see website. Space fee: varies. Exhibition space: 10×10. For more information e-mail, visit website, or call.

THE NATIONAL NEEDLEARTS ASSOCIATION TRADESHOW

(800)889-8662; (740)455-6773. E-mail: info@tnna.org. Website: www.tnna.org. Wholesale show held winter, spring, and fall. Indoors. Open to trade only. Accepts needle arts. Number exhibitors: see website. Number attendees: see website. Admission: see website. Apply online. Deadline for entry: see website.

Application fee: none. Space fee: varies. Exhibition space: see website. For more information e-mail, visit website, or call.

THE NEW YORK INTERNATIONAL GIFT FAIR

(914)421-3395. E-mail: paula_bertolotti@glmshows.com. Website: www.nynow.com. Contact: Paula Bertolotti. Estab. 2001. Semiannual wholesale market. Indoors. Open to trade only. Accepts home, lifestyle, and gift vendors. Number exhibitors: 2,800. Number attendees: 35,000. Admission: see website. Apply online. Deadline for entry: see website. Application fee: none. Space fee: varies. Exhibition space: varies. For more information e-mail, visit website, or call.

NORTHEAST MARKET CENTER

(800)435-2775. E-mail: info@northeastmarketcenter.com. Website: www.northeastmarketcenter.com. Wholesale marketplace open several times a year. Indoors. Open to trade only. Accepts gifts, decorative accessories. Number exhibitors: see website. Number attendees: see website. Admission: see website. Apply online. Deadline for entry: see website. Application fee: see website. Space fee: varies. Exhibition space: see website. For more information e-mail, visit website, or call.

OASIS GIFT SHOWS

(602)952-2050 or (800)424-9519. Fax: (602)445-6936. E-mail: information@oasis.org. Website: www.oasis.org. Estab. 1976. Semiannual wholesale show, not open to public, held in January & September. Indoors. Accepts giftware. Number exhibitors: see website. Number attendees: 3,000-5,000. Admission: see website. Apply online. Deadline for entry: see website. Application fee: see website. Space fee: varies. Exhibition space: 10×10. For more information e-mail, visit website, or call.

OCEAN CITY RESORT & GIFT EXPO

(800)318-2238. Fax: (678)285-7469. E-mail: info@urbanexpositions.com. Website: www.oceancitygiftshow.com. Contact: Russ Turner, show director. Wholesale show held annually in October/November.

Indoors. Open to trade only. Accepts handmade craft merchants, pattern, magazine, and book publishers. Number exhibitors: 200. Number attendees: see website. Admission: none. Apply online. Deadline for entry: see website. Application fee: none. Space fee: $890. Exhibition space: 10×10. For more information e-mail rturner@urban-expo.com.

OFFINGER'S MARKETPLACES

(888)878-GIFT (4438). Fax: (740)452-2552. E-mail: OffingersMarketplaces@Offinger.com; gfleming@offinger.com. Website: www.offingersmarketplaces.com. Estab. 1930. Wholesale show held 4 times a year (see website for dates). Indoors. Open to trade only. Accepts handmade craft merchants, giftware, home decor, and other mediums. Number exhibitors: see website. Number attendees: see website. Admission: see website. Apply online. Deadline for entry: see website. Application fee: see website. Space fee: varies. Exhibition space: 12×10; 24×20. For more information, e-mail, visit website, or call.

ORLANDO GIFT SHOW

(800)318-2238. E-mail: kcunningham@urban-expo.com. Website: www.orlandogiftshow.com. Contact: Kristi Cunningham, show coordinator. Annual wholesale and cash & carry show held in summer. Indoors. Open to trade only. Accepts handmade craft merchants, general giftware, home and garden accents, gourmet gifts, party and paper goods, tabletop, holiday/seasonal, collectibles, stationery, souvenir/resort merchandise, bed, bath, linen, and other mediums. Number exhibitors: see website. Number attendees: see website. Admission: see website. Apply online. Deadline for entry: see website. Application fee: none. Space fee: varies. Exhibition space: 10×10. For more information, e-mail, visit website, or call.

THE PHILADELPHIA GIFT SHOW

(800)318 2238. Fax: (678)285-7469. E-mail: manderson@urban-expo.com. Website: www.philadelphiagiftshow.com. Contact: Marilyn Anderson, show director. Estab. 1996. Wholesale show held semi-annually in January & July. Indoors. Open to trade only. Accepts pattern, magazine, and book publishers. Number exhibitors: see website. Number attendees:

see website. Admission: none. Apply online. Deadline for entry: see website. Application fee: none. Space fee: $1,785 plus a $100 show promotional fee for the first booth. Exhibition space: 10×10. For more information, e-mail manderson@urban-expo.com.

PIEDMONT CRAFTSMEN'S FAIR

(336)725-1516. E-mail: craftsfair@piedmontcraftsmen.org. Website: www.piedmontcraftsmen.org/programs/crafts-fair. Contact: Deborah Britton, fair coordinator. Estab. 1963. Annual showcase held 3rd weekend in November. Indoors. Open to public. Accepts clay, wood, glass, fibers, leather, metal, photography, printmaking, and mixed media. Number exhibitors: see website. Number attendees: see website. Admission: $7 adults; $6 students/seniors; children 12 & under free; weekend pass $11. Apply online. Deadline for entry: mid-April. Application fee: $35. Space fee: starts at $625. Exhibition space: see website. For more information, e-mail, visit website, or call.

✪ QUEBEC GIFT FAIR

(416)679-0170; (800)611-6100. Fax: (416)385-1851 or (877)373 7555. E-mail: quebec@cangift.org. Website: quebecgiftfair.org. Wholesale show held semiannually in spring/fall. Indoors. Open to trade only. Accepts giftware merchants. Awards/prizes: Best Booth Awards. Number exhibitors: see website. Number attendees: see website. Admission: see website. Apply online. Deadline for entry: see website. Application fee: none. Space fee: varies. Exhibition space: varies. For more information, e-mail, visit website, or call.

THE SEATTLE GIFT SHOW

(800)318-2238. Fax: (678)285-7469. E-mail: info@urbanexpositions.com. Website: www.seattlegiftshow.com. Contact: Lisa Glosson, show director. Cash & carry/wholesale show held semi-annually in January & August. Indoors. Open to trade only. Accepts handmade craft merchants, pattern, magazine, and book publishers. Number exhibitors: see website. Number attendees: see website. Admission: no fee for retail buyers; $30 guest fee. Apply online. Deadline for entry: see website. Application fee: none. Space fee: see website. Exhibition space: 10×10. For more information, e-mail lglosson@urban-expo.com.

STITCHES EXPOS

(800)237-7099. Fax: (605)338-2994. E-mail: stitches-registration@xrx-inc.com. Website: www.knittinguniverse.com/STITCHES/. Conference and market held 4 times a year. Indoors. Open to public. Accepts fiber. Number exhibitors: see website. Number attendees: see website. Admission: $10/1-day pass; $15/2-day pass; $20/3-day pass. Apply online. Deadline for entry: see website. Application fee: none. Space fee: see website. Exhibition space: see website. For more information, e-mail, visit website, or call.

ST. LOUIS GIFT SHOW

(513)861-1139. Fax: (513)861-1557. E-mail: lpharris42@hotmail.com. Website: www.stlouisgiftshow.com. Contact: Larry Harris, president. Estab. 1970s. Wholesale show (some cash & carry and order writing) held semi-annually in January & August. Indoors. Not open to public. Accepts handmade craft merchants, pattern, magazine, book publishers, USA made, imports. Number exhibitors: 80. Number attendees: 800. Admission: none. Apply online. Deadline for entry: open until filled. Application fee: none. Space fee: $525 (10×8); $625 (10×10). Exhibition space: 10×8; 10×10. For more information, visit website.
TIPS "Presentation of product."

⊘ TORONTO GIFT FAIR

(416)679-0170 or (800)611-6100. Fax: (416)679-0175; (800)496-2966. E-mail: toronto@cangift.org. Website: torontogiftfair.org. Wholesale show held semiannually in spring/fall. Indoors. Open to trade only. Accepts innovative tabletop, housewares, gourmet food, garden accessories, collectibles, handmade, stationery, home decor, bath, bed, and linen products. Number exhibitors: 900. Number attendees: 26,000. Admission: see website. Apply online. Deadline for entry: see website. Application fee: none. Space fee: see website. Exhibition space: see website. For more information, e-mail, visit website, or call.

WHOLESALECRAFTS.COM

(888)427-2381. E-mail: ACREinfo@wholesalecrafts.com. Website: www.wholesalecrafts.com. Estab. 1998. Wholesale show held 3 times a year. Indoors. Open to trade only. Accepts handmade craft merchants. Number exhibitors: see website. Number attendees: see website. Admission: see website. Apply online. Deadline for entry: see website. Application fee: none. Space fee: see website. Exhibition space: see website. For more information, e-mail, visit website, or call.

WINTER SEATTLE MARKET WEEK: GIFT & HOME ACCESSORIES SHOW

(206)767-6800 or (800)433-1014. Fax: (206)767-5449. E-mail: info@pacmarket.com. Website: www.pacific-marketcenter.com. Wholesale show held semiannually. Indoors. Number exhibitors: see website. Number attendees: see website. Admission: see website. Apply online. Deadline for entry: see website. Application fee: none. Space fee: see website. Exhibition space: see website. For more information, e-mail, visit website, or call.

SHOWS AND FAIRS

//

What better way to sell your handmade wares than to attend a craft or art fair? Craft fairs are found in most cities throughout the year. Some are specifically geared toward holiday handmades, while others are indie shows that trend a bit cooler. From traditional to modern, yarn to paper, and quilting to woodworking, crafts of all kinds can find a home at a craft fair. The listings in the following pages are for craft and art fairs that might be a good fit for you and your artisan product.

Peruse the listings in the following pages to find the fairs that are most interesting to you. Perhaps there's a show that takes place just a few miles away from your home, or perhaps there's a show dedicated to your style of craft. After selling at a few fairs, you will learn even more about which type of show is best suited to your craft, attracts your demographic, and is most valuable for you to attend. Be sure to read Kerry Bogert's article "Tips for a Successful First Craft Show" for tips in deciding which craft show is best for you and what to consider when planning for your show.

Each listing includes the basic information about the show, but visiting the show will always give you a better sense of the market, and if your wares fit in that particular venue. Over time, you'll develop an instinct for knowing what market will work for your business. Selling in person at craft shows is not only a way to make money, but it provides invaluable firsthand contact with your customer. That firsthand feedback is key to developing your brand and your business. Are certain colors more popular? Do you need to expand the sizes you have on offer? Do attendees at different markets want different things, and how can that help you develop your focus?

Attending craft shows can also be a way of marketing your online store. Many exhibitors note that, while they may see only a handful of sales at a particular show, they'll often see a spike in orders through their online shop from that area. That being the case, make a point to advertise your online shop. Print your website name on your packaging, of course, and have business cards and brochures available.

Whether you focus on in-person selling at craft fairs or online through sites like Etsy.com, you will find benefits to both. Meeting your customers face-to-face is invaluable for building lifelong customers, and creating a beautiful online shop allows you to craft a story through photos that your customers will want to come back to time and again.

As you become a regular exhibitor at craft shows, you'll develop a schedule, your booth's look and feel, a set plan for handling payment, and a routine for setting up and breaking down. If this is your first time out, check out the regional craft show index in order to focus on shows nearby. Over time, you can consider expanding your reach to markets in other regions.

KEY TO SYMBOLS & ABBREVIATIONS

☺	Canadian market
☻	market located outside of the U.S. and Canada
☺	market prefers to work with local artists/ designers
b&w	black & white (photo or illustration)
SASE	self-addressed, stamped envelope
SAE	self-addressed envelope
IRC	International Reply Coupon, for use when mailing to countries other than your own

6TH STREET FAIR

Bellevue Downtown Association, 400 108th Ave. NE, Suite 110, Bellevue WA 98004. (425)453-1223. E-mail: tyler@bellevuedowntown.org. Website: www.bellevuedowntown.org. Art & crafts fair held annually in July. Outdoors. Accepts sculpture, jewelry, home décor, wood, glass, fabrics, and more. Juried. Awards/prizes: Best in Show, Best Booth, Best Newbie. Exhibitors: 120. Number of attendees: 45,000. Free to public. Apply online.

ADDITIONAL INFORMATION Deadline for entry: March 20. Application fee: $25. Space fee: varies. Exhibition space: varies. For more information, call, e-mail, or visit, website.

TIPS "Sales are best for items under $100."

57TH STREET ART FAIR

1507 E. 53rd St., PMB 296, Chicago IL 60615. (773)234-3247. E-mail: info@57thstartfair.org. Website: www.57thstreetartfair.org. Estab. 1948. Fine art & craft show held annually in June. Outdoors. Accepts painting, sculpture, photography, glass, jewelry, leather, wood, ceramics, fiber, printmaking. Juried. Free to public. Apply via Zapplication.org.

ADDITIONAL INFORMATION Deadline for entry: January 15. Application fee: $35. Space fee: $300. Exhibition space: 10×10. For more information, e-mail or visit website.

AFFORDABLE ARTS FESTIVAL

P.O. Box 1634, Boulder CO 80306. (303)330-8237. E-mail: jdphotos@earthlink.net. Website: www.affordableartsfestival.com. Contact: Jim DeLutes, director. Fine art & craft show held annually in August. Outdoors. Accepts painting, jewelry, glass, sculpture, photography, wood, fiber, pottery, mixed media, drawing, pastels, and more. Juried. Admission: $5. Apply via Zapplication.org.

ADDITIONAL INFORMATION Deadline for entry: see website. Application fee: $30. Space fee: $195. Exhibition space: 10×15. For more information, e-mail, call, or visit website.

AIKEN'S MAKIN'

121 Richland Ave. E., Aiken SC 29801. (803)649-1200, ext. 224. Fax: (803)641-4174. E-mail: dphillips@aiken-chamber.net. Website: www.aikensmakin.net. Contact: Diane Phillips, director. Estab. 1976. Annual arts & crafts show held in September the Friday & Saturday after Labor Day. Outdoors. Accepts handmade crafts, photography, art, needle crafts, pottery, wood. Juried. Exhibitors: 205. Number of attendees: 30,000. Free to public. See website for application.

ADDITIONAL INFORMATION Deadline for entry: February 28. Space fee: $200-225. Exhibition space: 13×10. For more information, e-mail, call, or see website or Facebook page.

TIPS "Follow instruction. Include good quality photos and all items requested."

ALASKA-JUNEAU PUBLIC MARKET

(907)586-4072. Fax: (907)586-1166. E-mail: metcom@gci.net. Website: www.juneaupublicmarket.com. Contact: Peter Metcalfe, owner/manager. Estab. 1983. Seasonal/holiday show held annually Thanksgiving weekend (November). Indoors. Accepts handmade crafts. Exhibitors: 175. Number of attendees: 10,000 (all 3 days). Admission: $7 for weekend pass. Apply via website.

ADDITIONAL INFORMATION Deadline for entry: July 31. Space fee: $125-980. Exhibition space: 8×8. Average sales: $5,000. For more information, see website.

TIPS "Basic salesmanship: look the customer in the eye and draw them in."

ALEXANDRIA KING STREET ART FESTIVAL

270 Central Blvd., Suite 107B, Jupiter FL 33458. (561)746-6615. Fax: (561)746-6528. E-mail: info@artfestival.com. Website: www.artfestival.com. Contact: Malinda Ratliff, communications manager. Estab. 2003. Fine art & craft fair held annually in late September. Outdoors. Accepts photography, jewelry, mixed media, sculpture, wood, ceramic, glass, painting, digital, fiber, metal. Juried. Number exhibitors: 230. Number attendees: 150,000. Free to public. Apply online via www.zapplication.org. Deadline: see website. Application fee: $35. Space fee: $575. Exhibition space: 10×10 and 10×20. For more information, artists should e-mail, call, or visit website.

TIPS "You have to start somewhere. First, assess where you are, and what you'll need to get things off the ground. Next, make a plan of action. Outdoor street art shows are a great way to begin your career and lifetime as a working artist. You'll meet a lot of other artists who have been where you are now. Network with them!"

ALLEY ART FESTIVAL

E-mail: downtownauroran@gmail.com. Website: www.facebook.com/pages/Alley-Art-Festival/107654222593659; www.downtownauroran.com/alley-art-festival/. Art & craft show held annually the last Saturday in August. Outdoors. Apply via e-mail.

ADDITIONAL INFORMATION Deadline for entry: July 1. Application fee: none. Space fee: see website. Exhibition space: 10×10. For more information, e-mail or visit website.

⌂ AMAGANSETT FINE ARTS FESTIVAL

David Oleski Events, 977 Broad Run Rd., West Chester PA 19380. (610)864-3500. E-mail: davidoleski@gmail.com. Website: www.amagansettfinearts.com. "The cutting edge of individual artistic expression and the communities of the Hamptons go hand in hand, and this festival will provide a rare opportunity for the public to meet these talented visonaries in an up close and personal experience for one remarkable weekend." See website for more information.

AMERICAN FINE CRAFT SHOW NYC

P.O. Box 480, Slate Hill NY 10973. (845)355-2400 or (845)661-1221. Fax: (845)355-2444. E-mail: show.director@americanartmarketing.com. Website: www.americanfinecraftshownyc.com. Contact: Richard Rothbard, director. Fine art & craft show held annually in October. Indoors. Accepts handmade crafts, basketry, ceramics, decorative fiber, furniture, glass, jewelry, leather, metal, mixed media, paper, wearable art, wood. Juried. Apply online.

ADDITIONAL INFORMATION Deadline for entry: April 30. Application fee: $35. Space fee: $200. Exhibition space: varies. For more information, e-mail or visit website.

AMERICAN FOLK ART FESTIVAL

(707)246-2460. E-mail: gavitee@aol.com. Website: www.americanfolkartfestival.com. Contact: Susan Bartolucci. Arts & crafts show held annually in Sep-

tember. Indoors. Accepts handmade crafts, one-of-a-kind folk art, Americana, & folk art antiques. Admission: $10. Apply online.

ADDITIONAL INFORMATION Deadline for entry: see website. Application fee: see website. Space fee: see website. Exhibition space: see website. For more information, e-mail or visit website.

TIPS "We are looking for outside of the norm, so feel free to experiment."

ANDERSON ORCHARD APPLE FESTIVAL & CRAFT FAIR

369 E. Greencastle Rd., Mooresville, IN 46158. (317)831-4181. E-mail: erin@andersonorchard.com. Website: www.andersonorchards.com/apple_festival.php. Contact: Erin. Arts & crafts show held annually in September. Indoors & outdoors. Accepts handmade crafts and other items. Apply online.

ADDITIONAL INFORMATION Deadline for entry: see website. Application fee: none. Space fee: $100. Exhibition space: varies. For more information, e-mail, visit website, or call.

THE ANNA MARIA ISLAND ARTS & CRAFTS FESTIVAL

270 Central Blvd., Suite 107B, Jupiter FL 33458. (561)746-6615. Fax: (561)746-6528. E-mail: info@artfestival.com. Website: www.artfestival.com. Fine art & craft fair held annually in mid-November. Outdoors. Accepts photography, jewelry, mixed media, sculpture, wood, ceramic, glass, painting, digital, fiber, metal. Juried. Number exhibitors: 106. Number attendees: 10,000. Free to public. Apply online via zapplication.org. Deadline: see website. Application fee: $15; free to mail in paper application. Space fee: $250. Exhibition space: 10×10 and 10×20. For more information, artists should e-mail, call, or visit website.

TIPS "You have to start somewhere. First, assess where you are, and what you'll need to get things off the ground. Next, make a plan of action. Outdoor street art shows are a great way to begin your career and lifetime as a working artist. You'll meet a lot of other artists who have been where you are now. Network with them!"

ANNUAL ARTS AND CRAFTS FESTIVAL- FAIRHOPE

(251)928-6387. E-mail: lroberts@eschamber.com. Website: www.annualartsandcraftsfestivalfairhope. com. Contact: Liz R. Thomson, director of tourism & special events. Estab. 1952. Arts & crafts show held annually in March. Outdoors. Accepts handmade crafts, fine art, painting, sculpture, jewelry, watercolor, graphics & drawing, woodworking, pottery & ceramics, photography. Juried. Awards/prizes: $10,750 in prize money. Exhibitors: 200+. Number of attendees. 300,000. Free to public. Apply online.

ADDITIONAL INFORMATION Deadline for entry: September 30. Application fee: $30. Space fee: $300 (single); $600 (double). Exhibition space: 10×10. For more information visit website, send e-mail, or call.

ANNUAL BOCA FEST

270 Central Blvd., Suite 107B, Jupiter FL 33458. (561)746-6615. Fax: (561)746-6528. E-mail: info@ artfestival.com. Website: www.artfestival.com. "Boca Fest is the longest-running show presented by Howard Alan Events and has become considered Boca's no. 1 event to attend. Over two decades since its inception, this esteemed community art festival continues to highlight the talents of more than 150 exhibitors displaying a wide range of works from life-size sculptures to photography, paintings, and jewelry. The festival offers many opportunities to appreciate—and purchase—art during this weekend of visual inspiration. This phenomenal art festival brings together an affluent customer base with an exceptional eye for great art, the aesthetic beauty of Boca Raton, and an abundant mix of fine art." See website for more information.

ANNUAL DOWNTOWN HYATTSVILLE ART FESTIVAL

(301)683-8267. Website: www.hyattsvilleartsfestival. com. Contact: Stuart Eisenberg, executive director. "See over 70 exhibiting and performing artists, enjoy live entertainment and eat some great food on the happening streets of Hyattsville, in the Gateway Arts District of Prince George's County." See website for more information.

ANNUAL HERITAGE FESTIVAL & CRAFT SHOW

Attn: Heritage Festival, P.O. Box 6015, Columbia MO 65205. (573)874-7460. E-mail: klr@gocolumbiamo. com. Website: www.gocolumbiamo.com. Contact: Karen Chandler, director. Estab. 1976. Arts & crafts show held annually in September. Outdoors. Accepts handmade crafts and fine art. Juried. Exhibitors: 80. Number of attendees: 20,000. Free to public. Apply online.

ADDITIONAL INFORMATION Deadline for entry: September 1. Application fee: none. Space fee: $80; $85 after Sept. 1. Exhibition space: 12×12. For more information visit website, send e-mail, or call.

ANNUAL SHADYSIDE—THE ART FESTIVAL ON WALNUT ST.

270 Central Blvd., Suite 107B, Jupiter FL 33458. (561)746-6615. Fax: (561)746-6528. E-mail: info@ artfestival.com. Website: www.artfestival.com. "The annual Shadyside—The Art Festival on Walnut Street, which started out as a neighborhood street fair, is now regarded as one of the top shows in Pittsburgh. Shadyside features boutiques, shops, and galleries mingled with national retailers in a neighborhood of tree-lined streets, historic homes, hip events, and distinctive restaurants." See website for more information.

ANNUAL SIESTA FIESTA

270 Central Blvd., Suite 107B, Jupiter FL 33458. (561)746-6615. Fax: (561)746-6528. E-mail: info@artfestival.com. Website: www.artfestival.com. "Hosted in an exquisite venue seated along the beautifully lush Ocean Boulevard and Beach Road, you can stroll along the beach as you take in art from 250 of the nation's most talented artists & crafters out there. Showcasing an extensive collection of work ranging from life-size sculptures, spectacular paintings, one-of-a-kind jewels, photography, ceramics, and much, much more, this show truly has something for anyone. Complete with an additional green market, this spectacular show also features plants, orchids, body products, and tasty dips." See website for more information.

ANNUAL ST. ARMANDS CIRCLE FESTIVAL

270 Central Blvd., Suite 107B, Jupiter FL 33458. (561)746-6615. Fax: (561)746-6528. E-mail: info@

artfestival.com. Website: www.artfestival.com. "Year after year, the Annual St. Armands Circle Art Festival makes the list of *Sunshine Artist Magazine*'s top art shows in the country. For two days, festival-goers will enjoy works from the nation's best talent and long-time festival favorites, along with the newest names on the contemporary art scene. Come see some of America's best artists displaying one-of-a-kind jewelry, pottery, paintings, and much, much more. Festival patrons and art collectors alike can meet and visit with their favorite artists—having the opportunity to view and purchase original art." See website for more information.

APPLE COUNTRY CRAFT FAIR

(603)437-8333. E-mail: saintpeterscraftfair@gmail.com. Website: www.stpeterslondonderry.org. Estab. 1999. Arts & crafts show held annually in May. Outdoors. Accepts handmade crafts. Juried. Exhibitors: 50. Number of attendees: varies. Free to public. Apply online.

ADDITIONAL INFORMATION Deadline for entry: early May. Application fee: none. Space fee: $65. Exhibition space: 10×10. For more information visit website, send e-mail, or call.

TIPS "High-quality, unique crafts are bestsellers."

APPLEWOOD ARTS

(303)797-9656. Fax: (303)797-9656. E-mail: knessso@aol.com. Website: www.applewoodartsandcrafts.com. Contact: Kathleen Ness. Estab. 1977. Arts & crafts show held annually 3 times in November. Indoors. Accepts original fine art & handmade crafts. Juried. Awards/prizes: 9 Most Original Booth prizes. Exhibitors: 100. Number of attendees: 4,000. Admission: $4. Artists should apply via website.

ADDITIONAL INFORMATION Deadline for entry: mid-June. Application fee: none. Space fee: $300. Exhibition space: 10×10; 12×12. For more information, artists should visit website.

TIPS "Present a creative, well-done booth."

ARLINGTON FESTIVAL OF THE ARTS

270 Central Blvd., Suite 107B, Jupiter FL 33458. (561)746-6615. Fax: (561)746-6528. E-mail: info@artfestival.com. Website: www.artfestival.com. Con-

tact: Malinda Ratliff, communications manager. Estab. 2013. Fine art & craft fair held annually in mid-April. Outdoors. Accepts photography, jewelry, mixed media, sculpture, wood, ceramic, glass, painting, digital, fiber, metal. Juried. Number exhibitors: 140. Number attendees: 50,000. Free to public. Apply online via zapplication.org. Deadline: see website. Application fee: $25. Space fee: $395. Exhibition space: 10×10 and 10×20. For more information, artists should e-mail, call or visit website. Festival located at Highland St. in the Clarendon district of Arlington, VA.

TIPS "You have to start somewhere. First, assess where you are, and what you'll need to get things off the ground. Next, make a plan of action. Outdoor street art shows are a great way to begin your career and lifetime as a working artist. You'll meet a lot of other artists who have been where you are now. Network with them!"

ART & APPLES FESTIVAL

407 Pine St., Rochester MI 48307. (248)651-4110. Fax: (248)651-4757. E-mail: festivals@pccart.org. E-mail: lbates@pccart.org. Website: www.artandapples.com. Contact: Laura Bates, festival director. Estab. 1965. Fine arts & crafts show held annually in September. Outdoors. Accepts handmade crafts and fine art. Juried. Exhibitors: 290. Number of attendees: 125,000. Admission: $5. Apply online.

ADDITIONAL INFORMATION Deadline for entry: see website. Application fee: see website. Space fee: see website. Exhibition space: see website. For more information, e-mail or visit website.

ART & CRAFT MARKETPLACE AT THE COLUMBUS OKTOBERFEST

4275 Fulton Rd. NW, Canton OH 44718. (330)493-4130. Fax: (330)493-7607. E-mail: shows@huffspromo.com. Website: www.huffspromo.com. Estab. 1965. Arts & crafts show held annually in September. Outdoors (covered). Accepts handmade crafts and other items. Juried. Exhibitors: varies. Number of attendees: 30,000. Free to public. Apply online.

ADDITIONAL INFORMATION Deadline for entry: see website. Application fee: none. Space fee: $190 (single); $380 (double). Exhibition space: 10×14. For more information, e-mail, visit website, or call.

ART & CRAFT SHOWCASE AT
THE AKRON HOME & FLOWER SHOW

4275 Fulton Rd. NW, Canton OH 44718. (330)493-4130. Fax: (330)493-7607. E-mail: shows@huffspromo.com. Website: www.huffspromo.com. Estab. 1965. Arts & crafts show held annually in February. Indoors. Accepts handmade crafts. Juried. Exhibitors: varies. Number of attendees: 30,000. Free to public. Apply online.

ADDITIONAL INFORMATION Deadline for entry: see website. Application fee: none; $100 space deposit required at time of application. Space fee: $395. Exhibition space: 8×12. For more information, e-mail, visit website, or call.

ART-A-FAIR

P.O. Box 547, Laguna Beach CA 92652. (949)494-4514. E-mail: marketing@art-a-fair.com. Website: www.art-a-fair.com. Estab. 1967. Fine arts show held annually in June-August. Outdoors. Accepts painting, sculpture, ceramics, jewelry, printmaking, photography, master crafts, digital art, fiber, glass, pencil, wood. Juried. Exhibitors: 125. Number of attendees: see website. Admission: $7.50 adults; $4.50 seniors; children 12 & under free. Apply online.

ADDITIONAL INFORMATION Deadline for entry: see website. Application fee: $40 (per medium). Space fee: $200 + $35 membership fee. Exhibition space: see website. For more information, e-mail, visit website, or call.

ART AT THE GLEN

P.O. Box 550, Highland Park IL 60035. (847)926-4300. Fax: (847)926-4330. E-mail: info@amdurproductions.com. Website: www.amdurproductions.com. Arts & crafts show held annually in August. Outdoors. Accepts handmade crafts, ceramics, fiber, furniture, glass, jewelry, metal, mixed media, paintings, drawings, photography, and wood. Juried. Exhibitors: 185. Number of attendees: 50,000. Free to public. Apply online.

ADDITIONAL INFORMATION Deadline for entry: see website. Application fee: $35. Space fee: $525. Exhibition space: see website. For more information, e-mail, visit website, or call.

ART BIRMINGHAM

118 N. Fourth Ave., Ann Arbor MI 48104. (734)662-3382. Fax: (734)662-0339. Website: www.theguild.org. Estab. 1981. Arts & crafts show held annually in May. Outdoors. Accepts handmade crafts, painting, ceramics, photography, jewelry, glass, wood, sculpture, mixed media, fiber, metal, and more. Juried. Exhibitors: 150. Number of attendees: see website. Free to public. Apply online.

ADDITIONAL INFORMATION Deadline for entry: see website. Application fee: see website. Space fee: see website. Exhibition space: see website. For more information, visit website or call.

ART FAIR AT JUNCTION CITY

4275 Fulton Rd. NW, Canton OH 44718. (330)493-4130. Fax: (330)493-7607. E-mail: shows@huffspromo.com. Website: www.huffspromo.com. Estab. 1965. Arts & crafts show held annually in September. Outdoors (covered). Accepts handmade crafts and other items. Juried. Exhibitors: varies. Number of attendees: 30,000. Free to public. Apply online.

ADDITIONAL INFORMATION Deadline for entry: see website. Application fee: none. Space fee: $190 (single); $380 (double). Exhibition space: 10×14. For more information, artists should send e-mail, visit website, or call.

ART FAIR AT LAUMEIER SCULPTURE PARK

(314)615-5278. E-mail: artfair@laumeier.org. Website: www.laumeier.org. Contact: Sara Matthew, special events manager. Estab. 1987. Arts & crafts show held annually in May during Mother's Day weekend. Outdoors. Accepts fine handmade crafts, ceramics, fiber/textiles, glass, jewelry, mixed media 2D, printmaking/drawing, painting, photography/digital, sculpture, wood. Features regional food vendors, a wine garden, and live music. Juried. Awards/prizes: $5,000 in cash awards. Number of exhibitors: 150. Number of attendees: 15,000. Admission: $10 adults 12+; $5 children 6-11; children 5 and under free. Apply via www.zapplication.org or visit www.laumeiersculpturepark.org/programs_events/art_fair/artists.

ADDITIONAL INFORMATION Deadline for entry: January 10. Application fee: $35 (per category). Space fee: $350 (open booth); $450 (tented booth). Exhibition space: 10x10. Average sales: $5,000. For more information, see website.

ART FAIR AT QUEENY PARK

GSLAA-Vic Barr, 1668 Rishon Hill Dr., St. Louis MO 63146. (636)724-5968. Website: www.artfairatqueenypark.com. Arts & crafts show held annually in August. Indoors. Accepts handmade crafts, clay, digital (computer) art, drawing/print, fiber (basketry, paper, wearable, woven), glass, jewelry, 2D/3D mixed media, oil/acrylic, photography, sculpture, water media, wood. Juried. Exhibitors: 140. Number of attendees: see website. Free to public. Apply online.

ADDITIONAL INFORMATION Deadline for entry: see website. Application fee: $25; $50 for late application. Space fee: $225. Exhibition space: 10×8. For more information, visit website or call.

ART FAIR JACKSON HOLE

Art Association of Jackson Hole, P.O. Box 1248, Jackson WY 83001. (307)733-6379. Fax: (307)733-6694. E-mail: artistinfo@jhartfair.org. Website: www.jhartfair.org. Estab. 1965. Arts & crafts show held annually in July & August. Outdoors. Accepts handmade crafts, ceramic, drawing, fiber, furniture, glass, graphics & printmaking, jewelry, leather, metalwork, 2D/3D mixed media, painting, photography, sculpture, toys & games, wearable fiber, wood. Juried. Exhibitors: 135. Number of attendees: 30,000. Free for art association members; $5 per day for non-members. Apply via Zapplication.org.

ADDITIONAL INFORMATION Deadline for entry: see website. Application fee: $35. Space fee: varies. Exhibition space: varies. For more information, e-mail, visit website, or call.

ART FAIR OFF THE SQUARE

P.O. Box 1791, Madison WI 53701-1791. E-mail: wiartcraft@gmail.com. Website: www.artcraftwis.org/AFOS.html. Estab. 1965. Arts & crafts show held annually in July. Outdoors. Accepts handmade crafts, ceramics, art glass, painting, fiber, sculpture, jewelry, graphics, papermaking, photography, wood, and more. Juried. Awards/prizes: Best of Category. Exhibitors: 140. Number of attendees: see website. Free to public. Apply via Zapplication.org.

ADDITIONAL INFORMATION Deadline for entry: see website. Application fee: $25. Space fee: $300. Exhibition space: 10×10. For more information, e-mail, visit website, or call.

ART FAIR ON THE SQUARE

227 State St., Madison WI 53703. (608)257-0158, ext 229. E-mail: artfair@mmoca.org. Website: www.mmoca.org. Contact: Annik Dupaty. Estab. 1958. Arts & crafts show held annually in July. Outdoors. Accepts handmade crafts, ceramics, fiber, leather, furniture, jewelry, glass, digital art, metal, sculpture, 2D/3D mixed media, painting, photography, printmaking/graphics/drawing, wood. Juried. Awards/prizes: Best of Show; Invitational Award. Exhibitors: varies. Number of attendees: 150,000+. Free to public. Apply via www.zapplication.org.

ADDITIONAL INFORMATION Deadline for entry: see website. Application fee: $35. Space fee: $510 (single); $1,050 (double). Exhibition space: 10×10 (single); 10×20 (double). For more information, e-mail, visit website, or call.

ART FEST BY THE SEA

270 Central Blvd., Suite 107B, Jupiter FL 33458. (561)746-6615. Fax: (561)746-6528. E-mail: info@artfestival.com. Website: www.artfestival.com. Contact: Malinda Ratliff, communications manager. Estab. 1989. Fine art & craft fair held annually in early March. Outdoors. Accepts photography, jewelry, mixed media, sculpture, wood, ceramic, glass, painting, digital, fiber, metal. Juried. Number exhibitors: 340. Number attendees: 125,000. Free to public. Apply online via zapplication.org. Deadline: see website. Application fee: $25. Space fee: $415. Exhibition space: 10×10 and 10×20. For more information, artists should e-mail, call, or visit website. Fair located along A1A Between Donald Ross Rd. and Marcinski in Juno Beach, FL.

TIPS "You have to start somewhere. First, assess where you are, and what you'll need to get things off the ground. Next, make a plan of action. Outdoor street art shows are a great way to begin your career and lifetime as a working artist. You'll meet a lot of other artists who have been where you are now. Network with them!"

ARTFEST FORT MYERS

1375 Jackson St., Suite 401, Fort Myers FL 33901. (239)768-3602. E-mail: info@artfestfortmyers.com. Website: www.artfestformyers.com. Fine arts & crafts fair held annually in February. Outdoors. Accepts handmade crafts, ceramics, digital, drawing/graphics, fiber, glass, jewelry, metal, 2D/3D mixed media, painting, photography, printmaking, sculpture, wearable, wood. Juried. Awards/prizes: $5,000 in cash. Exhibitors: 200. Number of attendees: 85,000. Free to public. Apply online.

ADDITIONAL INFORMATION Deadline for entry: September 15. Application fee: $35. Space fee: $460.50. Exhibition space: 10×10. For more information, e-mail, visit website, or call.

ART FESTIVAL OF HENDERSON

P.O. Box 95050, Henderson NV 89009-5050. (702)267-2171. Website: www.hendersonlive.com/special-events/art-festival-of-henderson#New_Artist. Arts & crafts show held annually in May. Outdoors. Accepts handmade crafts, paintings, pottery, jewelry, photography, and much more. Juried. Exhibitors: varies. Number of attendees: 25,000. Free to public. Apply online.

ADDITIONAL INFORMATION Deadline for entry: see website. Application fee: see website. Space fee: see website. Exhibition space: see website. For more information, visit website or call.

ARTFEST MIDWEST—"THE OTHER SHOW"

Stookey Companies, P.O. Box 31083, Des Moines IA 50310. (515)278-6200. Fax: (515)276-7513. E-mail: suestookey@att.net. Website: www.artfestmidwest.com. Fine art fair held annually in June. Indoors & outdoors. Accepts handmade fine art, ceramic, fiber, drawing, glass, jewelry, metal, 2D/3D mixed media, painting, photography, wood. Juried. Exhibitors: 240. Number of attendees: 30,000. Free to public. Apply via www.zapplication.org.

ADDITIONAL INFORMATION Deadline for entry: March. Application fee: $30. Space fee: varies. Exhibition space: see website. For more information, e-mail suestookey@att.net, visit website at www.artfestmidwest.com, or call (515)278-6200.

ARTIGRAS FINE ARTS FESTIVAL

5520 PGA Blvd., Suite 200, Palm Beach Gardens FL 33418. (561)748-3946. Fax: (561)745-7519. E-mail: info@artigras.org; artists@artigras.org. Website: www.artigras.org. Estab. 1985. Fine arts & crafts fair held annually in February. Outdoors. Accepts handmade crafts, ceramics, fiber (wearable and non-wearable), digital art, drawing & printmaking, glass, jewelry, metal, mixed media, painting, photography, sculpture, and wood. Juried. Awards/prizes: $17,000 in cash awards and ribbons. Exhibitors: 300. Number of attendees: 85,000. Admission: $8 advance; $10 at gate; children 12 & under free. Apply online.

ADDITIONAL INFORMATION Deadline for entry: September. Application fee: $40. Space fee: $450 +tax (single); $900+ tax (double). Exhibition space: 12×12 (single); 12×24 (double). For more information, e-mail, visit website, or call.

ART IN BLOOM—CATIGNY PARK

EM Events, LLC, P.O. Box 4332, Naperville IL 60567. (630)536-8416. E-mail: emelloy@emevents.com. Website: www.cantigny.org/calendar/signature-events/art-in-bloom. Fine arts & crafts show held annually in June. Outdoors. Accepts handmade crafts, ceramics, drawing, fiber nonfunctional, fiber wearable, paper nonfunctional, furniture, glass, jewelry, acrylic, oil, watercolor, pastel, sculpture, wood, mixed media, collage, photography, and printmaking. Juried. Exhibitors: 80. Number of attendees: 8,000. Free to public. Apply online.

ADDITIONAL INFORMATION Deadline for entry: see website. Application fee: $10. Space fee: $285. Exhibition space: 10×10. For more information, e-mail, visit website, or call.

ART IN THE BARN—BARRINGTON

Advocate Good Shepherd Hospital, Art in the Barn Artist Committee, 450 W. Highway 22, Barrington IL 60010. (847)842-4496. E-mail: artinthebarn@comcast.net. Website: www.artinthebarn-barrington.com. Estab. 1974. Fine arts & crafts show held annually in September. Indoors & outdoors. Accepts handmade crafts, ceramics, painting, jewelry, glass, sculpture, fiber, drawing, photography, digital media, printmaking, scratchboard, mixed media, wood. Juried. Awards/prizes: Best of Show; Best of Medium;

Purchase Awards. Exhibitors: 185. Number of attendees: 8,500. Admission: $5; children 12 & under free. Apply online.

ADDITIONAL INFORMATION Deadline for entry: see website. Application fee: $20. Space fee: $100 (indoors); $85 (outdoors). Exhibition space: varies. For more information, e-mail, visit website, or call.

ART IN THE BARN—FITCHBURG

5927 Adams Rd., Fitchburg WI 53575. (608)835-0454. Website: www.site.artinthebarnwi.org. "Art in the Barn is dedicated to bringing quality visual and performing arts for people of all ages, in a serene and natural rural setting for life-enriching experiences and pure enjoyment. Art in the Barn is a series of performances featuring local, national, and international performers and visual artists. The series takes place in an 1870s restored barn in a rural setting outside of Madison, Wisconsin."

ART IN THE GARDENS

9400 Boerner Dr., Hales Corners WI 53130. (414)525-5656. Fax: (414)525-5668. E-mail: jschmitz@fbbg.org. Website: www.boernerbotanicalgardens.org. Contact: Jennifer Schmitz, gift shop manager. Estab. 2009. Arts & crafts show held annually in May. Indoors & outdoors. Accepts handmade crafts, photography, painting. Juried. Number of exhibitors: 40. Number of attendees: 1,000. Free to public. Apply online.

ADDITIONAL INFORMATION Deadline for entry: April 3. Application fee: $5 before February 3; $10 after February 3. Space fee: $75. Exhibition space: 8×8 inside; 10×10 outside. Average sales: $500-2,000. For more information, e-mail or visit website.

TIPS "We look for quality and variety."

ART IN THE PARK (ELMHURST)

Website: www.rglmarketingforthearts.com/elmhurst-art-in-the-park. Estab. 1996. Fine arts & crafts show held annually in May. Outdoors. Accepts handmade crafts and other items. Juried. Exhibitors: varies. Number of attendees: 10,000. Free to public. Apply online.

ADDITIONAL INFORMATION Deadline for entry: see website. Application fee: see website. Space fee: see website. Exhibition space: see website. For more information, visit website.

ART IN THE PARK (KEARNY)

Kearney Artist Guild, P.O. Box 1368, Kearney NE 68848-1368. (308)708-0510. E-mail: artintheparkkearney@charter.net. Website: www.kearneyartistsguild.com. Estab. 1971. Fine arts & crafts show held annually in July. Outdoors. Accepts handmade crafts, ceramics, drawing, fiber, mixed media, glass, jewelry, painting, photography, sculpture. Juried. Exhibitors: 90. Number of attendees: varies. Free to public. Apply online.

ADDITIONAL INFORMATION Deadline for entry: early June. Application fee: $10. Space fee: varies. Exhibition space: varies. For more information, e-mail, visit website, or call.

ART IN THE PARK (PLYMOUTH)

P.O. Box 702490, Plymouth MI 48170. (734)454-1314. Fax: (734)454-3670. E-mail: info@artinthepark.com. Website: www.artinthepark.com. Estab. 1979. Arts & crafts show held annually in July. Outdoors. Accepts handmade crafts, paintings, sculpture, ceramics, jewelry, fiber, fine glass, woodwork, mixed media, photography, and folk art. Juried. Exhibitors: 400. Number of attendees: 300,000. Free to public. Apply online.

ADDITIONAL INFORMATION Deadline for entry: see website. Application fee: $20. Space fee: $580. Exhibition space: 10×10. For more information, e-mail, visit website, or call.

ART IN THE PEARL FINE ARTS & CRAFTS FESTIVAL

P.O. Box 5906, Portland OR 97228-5906. (503)722-9017. E-mail: info@artinthepearl.com. Website: www.artinthepearl.com. Estab. 1996. Arts & crafts show held annually Labor Day weekend. Outdoors. Accepts handmade crafts, fine art, ceramics, fiber, glass, drawings, computer-generated media, 2D/3D mixed media, jewelry, metal, painting, photography, printmaking, sculpture, wood. Juried. Exhibitors: 130. Number of attendees: varies. Free to public. Apply online at www.zapplication.org.

ADDITIONAL INFORMATION Deadline for entry: February15; late deadline February 28. Application fee: $35; late fee $45. Space fee: varies. Exhibition space: varies. For more information, visit www.artinthepearl.com or www.zapplication.org.

ART IN THE VILLAGE WITH CRAFT MARKETPLACE

270 Central Blvd., Suite 107B, Jupiter FL 33458. (561)746-6615. Fax: (561)746-6528. E-mail: info@artfestival.com. Website: www.artfestival.com. Contact: Malinda Ratliff, communications manager. Estab. 1991. Fine art & craft fair held annually in early June. Outdoors. Accepts photography, jewelry, mixed media, sculpture, wood, ceramic, glass, painting, digital, fiber, metal. Juried. Number exhibitors: 150. Number attendees: 70,000. Free to public. Apply online via zapplication.org. Deadline: see website. Application fee: $25. Space fee: $450. Exhibition space: 10×10 and 10×20. For more information, artists should e-mail, call, or visit website. Show located at Legacy Village in Cleveland, OH.

TIPS "You have to start somewhere. First, assess where you are, and what you'll need to get things off the ground. Next, make a plan of action. Outdoor street art shows are a great way to begin your career and lifetime as a working artist. You'll meet a lot of other artists who have been where you are now. Network with them!"

ART IN THE WILDS

214 Chemical Works Rd., Kane PA 16735. (814)837-7167. E-mail: mab@penn.com. Website: www.artinthewilds.org. Contact: Marilyn Blackmore. Estab. 2006. Arts & crafts show held annually in September. Outdoors. Accepts handmade crafts, drawing/pastels, metal, glass, clay/porcelain, photography, printmaking/graphics, mixed media, fabric/fiber, wood, leather, and jewelry. Juried. Awards/prizes: Best of Show; Excellence Award. Exhibitors: varies. Number of attendees: varies. Free to public. Apply online.

ADDITIONAL INFORMATION Deadline for entry: see website. Application fee: $20. Space fee: varies. Exhibition space: varies. For more information, e-mail, visit website, or call.

ART IN YOUR EYE FESTIVAL

4½ W. Wilson St., Batavia IL 60510. (630)761-3528. E-mail: info@artinyoureye.com. Website: www.artinyoureye.com. Estab. 2004. Fine arts & crafts show held annually in September. Outdoors. Accepts handmade crafts and other items. Juried. Awards/prizes:

over $4,000 in cash. Exhibitors: varies. Number of attendees: varies. Free to public. Apply online.

ADDITIONAL INFORMATION Deadline for entry: see website. Application fee: $20. Space fee: $285. Exhibition space: see website. For more information, e-mail, visit website, or call.

ARTISPHERE

16 Augusta St., Greenville SC 29601. (864)271-9398. E-mail: kerry@greenvillearts.com. Website: www.artisphere.us. Estab. 2004. Fine arts & crafts fair held annually in May. Outdoors. Accepts handmade crafts, ceramic, digital art, fiber, drawing, furniture, glass, jewelry, metal, 2D/3D mixed media, painting, photography, printmaking, sculpture, wood. Juried. Awards/prizes: Best in Show, 2nd place, 3rd place, 4 merit awards, Mayor's Choice Award. Exhibitors: 130. Number of attendees: varies. Free to public. Apply via www.zapplication.org.

ADDITIONAL INFORMATION Deadline for entry: early January. Application fee: $30. Space fee: $350. Exhibition space: 12×12. For more information, e-mail, visit website, or call.

ARTMARKET SAN FRANCISCO

109 S. Fifth St., Suite 407, Brooklyn NY 11249. (212)518-6912. Fax: (212)518-7142. E-mail: info@artmrkt.com. Website: www.artmarketsf.com. Estab. 2011. "Since 2011, Art Market Productions has produced a different type of art fair that focuses on creating the highest-quality fair experience by connecting collectors with dealers in the most optimal settings and contexts. Art Market Productions is dedicated to improving the art world by creating platforms and expanding networks of connection."

ART ON THE CHATTAHOOCHEE

(678)277-0920. E-mail: brian.r.bentley@gwinnettcounty.com. Website: www.gwinnettcounty.com. "Art on the Chattahoochee is a delightful, fine art event at a unique venue along the Chattahoochee River in Jones Bridge Park. The event brings together outstanding artists throughout North Georgia in a fine art market highlighting their talent. The event also features a shaded food court area, a fun, interactive kids craft corner, as well as all the park amenities!"

ART ON THE MALL

The Office of Alumni Relations, Mail Stop 301, The University of Toledo, 2801 W. Bancroft St., Toledo OH 43606-3390. (419)530-2586. E-mail: artonthemall@utoledo.edu. Website: www.toledoalumni.org. Art & craft show held annually in July. Outdoors. Accepts handmade crafts, ceramics, fiber, glass, jewelry, mixed media, photography, wood. Juried. Awards/prizes: Best of Show, 1st place, 2nd place, 3rd place, Purchase Award. Number exhibitors: see website. Number attendees: 12,000. Free to public. Apply online.

ADDITIONAL INFORMATION Deadline for entry: late April. Application fee: $25. Space fee: $100. Exhibition space: 10×10. For more information, e-mail, call, or visit website.

ART ON THE SQUARE

P.O. Box 23561, Belleville IL 62223. (800)677-9255; (618)233-6769. E-mail: artonthesquarecompetition@gmail.com. Website: www.artonthesquare.com. Estab. 2002. Fine arts & crafts show held annually in May. Outdoors. Accepts handmade crafts, photography, glass, jewelry, clay, sculpture, fine craft, mixed media, wood, and digital art. Juried. Awards/prizes: over $30,000 in cash. Exhibitors: 105. Number of attendees: varies. Free to public. Apply online.

ADDITIONAL INFORMATION Deadline for entry: see website. Application fee: see website. Space fee: see website. Exhibition space: see website. For more information, e-mail, visit website, or call.

ART RAPIDS!

P.O. Box 301, Elk Rapids MI 49629. (231)264-6660. E-mail: art@mullalys128.com. Website: www.artrapids.org. Contact: Barb Mullaly. Arts & crafts fair held annually last Saturday in June. Outdoors. Accepts handmade crafts, ceramic, drawing, fiber, glass, jewelry, painting, photography, printmaking, sculpture, wood, metal, paper, or mixed media. Juried. Awards/prizes: Best of Show, Honorable Mention, People's Choice. Exhibitors: 70. Number of attendees: 4,000. Free to public. Apply online.

ADDITIONAL INFORMATION Deadline for entry: early April. Application fee: $20. Space fee: varies. Exhibition space: 10×10. For more information, e-mail, visit website, or call.

ARTS, BEATS & EATS

Arts, Beats & Eats, 301 W. Fourth St., Suite LL-150, Royal Oak MI 48067. (208)792-2726. Fax: (208)792-2850. E-mail: lisa@artsbeatseats.com. Website: www.artsbeatseats.com. Contact: Lisa Konikow, art director. Estab. 1997. Fine arts & crafts fair held annually in September. Outdoors. Accepts handmade crafts, ceramic, digital art, fiber, drawing, glass, jewelry, metal, 2D/3D mixed media, painting, photography, printmaking, wood. Juried. Awards/prizes: $7,500 in cash awards. Exhibitors: 145. Number of attendees: 400,000. Free to public. Apply online.

ADDITIONAL INFORMATION Deadline for entry: March. Application fee: $25. Space fee: $490. Exhibition space: 10×10. For more information, artists should send e-mail, visit website, or call.

ARTSCAPE

Dallas Arboretum, 8525 Garland Rd., Dallas TX 75218. (214)515-6615. Website: www.dallasarboretum.org/visit/seasonal-festivals-events/artscape. Arts & crafts show held annually in April. "The beauty of art meets the beauty of nature at the Dallas Arboretum's annual fine art and fine craft show and sale in the garden. This juried art fair features art that is of or about nature by artists from around the country. Guests will also enjoy artist demonstrations, entertainment, food, and fun for all ages! Don't miss the chance to see and buy from your favorite artists set amid a garden that has been listed as one of the top three most beautiful display gardens in the nation." See website for more information.

ARTSFEST

13480 Dowell Road, P.O. Box 99, Dowell MD 20629. (410)326-4640. Fax: (410)326-4887. E-mail: info@annmariegarden.org. Website: www.annmariegarden.org. Estab. 1984. Fine arts & crafts fair held annually in September. Indoors & outdoors. Accepts handmade crafts, ceramic, digital art, fiber, drawing, furniture, glass, jewelry, metal, 2D/3D mixed media, painting, photography, printmaking, wood. Juried. Awards/prizes: Best of Show, Best Demonstration, Wooded Path Award, Best New Artsfest Artist Award. Exhibitors: 170. Number of attendees: varies. Admission: $6 adults; children 11 & under free; members free. Apply online.

ADDITIONAL INFORMATION Deadline for entry: March. Application fee: $25. Space fee: varies. Exhibition space: varies. For more information, artists should send e-mail, visit website, or call.

ARTSPLASH

Sioux City Art Center, 225 Nebraska Street, Sioux City IA 51101-1712. (712)279-6272, ext. 232. Fax: (712)255-2921. E-mail: ewebber@sioux-city.org. Website: www.siouxcityartcenter.org/artsplash. Contact: Erin Webber-Dreeszen, development coordinator. Fine arts & crafts fair held annually over Labor Day weekend. Outdoors. Accepts handmade fine art and fine craft. Juried. Exhibitors: see website. Number of attendees: see website. Admission: $5; kids 11 & under free. Apply online.
ADDITIONAL INFORMATION Deadline for entry: see website. Application fee: see website. Space fee: see website. Exhibition space: see website. For more information, artists should send e-mail, visit website, or call.

ARTSPLOSURE - THE RALEIGH ART FESTIVAL

313 W. Blount St., Ste 200B, Raleigh NC 27601. (919)832-8699. Fax: (919)832-0890. E-mail: info@artsplosure.org. Website: www.artsplosure.org. Contact: Sarah Wolfe, art market coordinator. Estab. 1979. Arts & craft show held annually 3rd weekend of May. Outdoors. Accepts handmade crafts, 2D/3D, glass, jewelry, ceramics, wood, metal, fiber, photography, painting. Juried. Awards/prizes: $3,500 in cash. Exhibitors: 175. Number of attendees: 75,000. Free to public. Apply via Zapplication.org.
ADDITIONAL INFORMATION Deadline for entry: January 16. Application fee: $22 (early registration); $32 (regular registration). Space fee: $240 (single); $480 (double). Exhibition space: 12×12 (single); 12×24 (double). For more information, artists should e-mail.
TIPS "We use entrythingy.com for processing applications. The site will be updated for 2015 by October."

ARTSQUEST FINE ARTS FESTIVAL

Cultural Arts Alliance of Walton County, Bayou Arts Center, 105 Hogtown Bayou Lane, Santa Rosa Beach FL 32459. (850)622-5970. E-mail: info@culturalartsalliance.com. Website: www.artsquestflor-

ida.com. Estab. 1988. Fine arts & crafts fair held annually in May. Outdoors. Accepts handmade crafts, ceramic, digital art, fiber, drawing, glass, jewelry, metal, 2D/3D mixed media, painting, photography, printmaking, sculpture, wood. Juried. Awards/prizes: Best in Show, Awards of Excellence, and Awards of Merit. Exhibitors: 125. Number of attendees: varies. Free to public. Apply online.
ADDITIONAL INFORMATION Deadline for entry: February. Application fee: $40. Space fee: $300. Exhibition space: 10×10. For more information, artists should send e-mail, visit website, or call.

ART STAR CRAFT BAZAAR

E-mail: info@artstarphilly.com. Website: www.artstarcraftbazaar.com. Estab. 2003. Arts & crafts fair held annually in May. Outdoors. Accepts handmade crafts, fabric, clay, glass, wood, paper, paintings/drawings, sculpture, and more. Juried. Exhibitors: varies. Number of attendees: varies. Free to public. Apply online.
ADDITIONAL INFORMATION Deadline for entry: see website. Application fee: see website. Space fee: see website. Exhibition space: see website. For more information, artists should send e-mail or visit website.

ARTSTREET

130 E. Walnut St., Suite 509, Green Bay WI 54115. (920)435-5220. Fax: (920)435-2787. E-mail: info@mosaicartsinc.org. Website: www.mosaicartsinc.org/artstreet. Estab. 1981. Fine arts & crafts fair held annually in August. Outdoors. Accepts handmade crafts and other mediums. Juried. Awards/prizes: $5,000 in cash awards. Exhibitors: 200. Number of attendees: 80,000. Free to public. Apply online.
ADDITIONAL INFORMATION Deadline for entry: March. Application fee: $35. Space fee: $225. Exhibition space: 10×10. For more information, artists should send e-mail, visit website, or call.

ART UNDER THE ELMS

Art Under the Elms, 415 Main St., Lewiston ID 83501. (208)792-2726. Fax: (208)792-2850. E-mail: defitzgerald@lcsc.edu. Website: www.lcsc.edu/ce/aue/. Contact: Debi Fitzgerald, director. Estab. 1984. Fine arts & crafts fair held annually in April. Outdoors. Accepts handmade crafts, ceramic, digital art, fiber, drawing, furniture, glass, jewelry, metal, 2D/3D mixed media, painting, photography, prepackaged food, printmaking, wood. Juried. Awards/prizes: announced after jury. Exhibitors: 100. Number of attendees: varies. Free to public. Apply online.

ADDITIONAL INFORMATION Deadline for entry: early January. Application fee: $20. Space fee: varies. Exhibition space: 10×10. For more information, artists should send e-mail, visit website, or call.

ARVADA CENTER FOR THE ARTS HOLIDAY CRAFT FAIR

(720)763-9013. E-mail: misty@eventsetc.net. Website: www.arvadacenter.org/galleries/special-events/call-for-entries. Estab. 1979. Fine arts & crafts fair held annually in November. Indoors. Accepts handmade crafts and other mediums. Juried. Exhibitors: see website. Number of attendees: varies. Free to public. Apply online.

ADDITIONAL INFORMATION Deadline for entry: August. Application fee: $35. Space fee: varies. Exhibition space: varies. For more information, artists should send e-mail, visit website, or call.

ATLANTA ARTS FESTIVAL

P. O. Box 724694, Atlanta GA 31139. (770)941-9660. Fax: (866)519-2918. E-mail: info@atlantaartsfestival. com. Website: www.atlantaartsfestival.com. Estab. 2006. Fine arts & crafts fair held annually in September. Outdoors. Accepts handmade crafts, ceramic, digital art, fiber, drawing, glass, jewelry, metal, 2D/3D mixed media, painting, photography, printmaking, wood. Juried. Awards/prizes: Best in Category, Best in Show. Exhibitors: 200. Number of attendees: varies. Free to public. Apply online.

ADDITIONAL INFORMATION Deadline for entry: April. Application fee: $25. Space fee: varies. Exhibition space: 10×10. For more information, artists should send e-mail, visit website, or call.

ATLANTA FINE CRAFT SHOW

American Craft Council Shows, 155 Water St., 4th Floor, Unit 5, Brooklyn NY 11201. (800)836-3470. Fax: (612)355-2330. E-mail: shows@craftcouncil.org. Website: www.craftcouncil.org. Art & craft show held annually in March. Indoors. Accepts handmade crafts,

ceramics, fiber, metal, and other mediums. Juried. Awards/prizes: Awards of Excellence. Number exhibitors: 250. Number attendees: varies. Free to public. Apply online.

ADDITIONAL INFORMATION Deadline for entry: August. Application fee: $30 + $10 handling/processing fee for each set of images. Space fee: varies. Exhibition space: varies. For more information, artists should e-mail, call, or visit website.

ATOMIC HOLIDAY BAZAAR

801 N. Tamiami Trail, Sarasota FL 34236. E-mail: atomicholidaybazaar@gmail.com. Website: www. atomicholidaybazaar.com. Contact: Adrien Lucas, event producer. Estab. 2006. Arts & Crafts show held annually the 1st or 2nd weekend of December. Indoors. Accepts handmade crafts, vintage clothing, kitsch, vintage jewelry, art, paper products, body products & makeup, homemade canned goods, fine jewelry, silversmiths, shoe cobblers, t-shirt screen printing, artists, and plushie makers. Exhibitors: 150. Number of attendees: 1,000. Admission: $5 adults; 12 & under free. Apply via website.

ADDITIONAL INFORMATION Deadline for entry: mid-September. Space fee: $90 table; $280 booth. Exhibition space: 8×3 (table); 12×8 (booth). For more information e-mail or see website.

TIPS "First and foremost this show is all about handmade items made with your two hands or your hands using tools. Supplies are necessary to build our objects of desire, however, products will be scrutinized for lack of revision, upcycling, repurposing, etc., so get creative! Atomic encourages vintage clothing, kitsch, vintage jewelry, art, paper products, body products & makeup, canned yummy goods, fine jewelry, silversmiths, shoe cobblers, t-shirt screen printing, artists, and plushie makers. Hopefully that helps you out a bit!"

AUSTIN CRAFT RIOT

E-mail: austincraftriot@gmail.com. Website: www. austincraftriot.com. Estab. 2011. Arts & crafts show held annually in August. Indoors. Accepts handmade crafts and vintage items. Exhibitors: see website. Number of attendees: varies. Admission: $2 adults; children free. Apply online.

ADDITIONAL INFORMATION Deadline for entry: June. Application fee: $25. Space fee: varies. Exhibition space: 8×8. For more information, artists should send e-mail, or visit website.

AUTUMN CRAFTS FESTIVAL AT LINCOLN CENTER FOR THE PERFORMING ARTS

American Concern for Artistry and Craftsmanship, P.O. Box 650, Montclair NJ 07042. (973)746-0091. Fax: (973)509-7739. E-mail: acacinfo@gmail.com. Website: www.craftsatlincoln.org. Fine art & craft show held annually in October. Outdoors. Accepts handmade crafts. Juried. Number exhibitors: 250. Number attendees: varies. Free to public. Apply online or via Zapplication.org.

ADDITIONAL INFORMATION Deadline for entry: June. Application fee: none. Space fee: varies. Exhibition space: varies. For more information, artists should call, e-mail, or visit website.

AUTUMN FESTIVAL: AN ARTS & CRAFTS AFFAIR

P.O. Box 655, Antioch IL 60002. (402)331-2889. E-mail: hpifestivals@cox.net. Website: www.hpifestivals.com. Estab. 1985. Fine arts & crafts fair held annually in November. Indoors. Accepts handmade crafts and other mediums. Juried. Exhibitors: 500. Number of attendees: 60,000. Admission: $9 adults; $8 seniors; children 10 & under free. Apply online.

ADDITIONAL INFORMATION Deadline for entry: see website. Application fee: none. Space fee: see website. Exhibition space: 10×10. For more information, artists should send e-mail, visit website or call.

AVANT-GARDE ART & CRAFT SHOWS

Avant-Garde Art & Craft Shows, Rebecca Adele Events, Solon OH 44139. (440)227-8794. E-mail: becki@ag-shows.com. Website: www.avantgardeshows.com. "The Avant-Garde Art & Craft Shows are based around Ohio year-round. They feature an eclectic selection of the area's most talented handmade artisans & crafters." See website for more information.

BALTIMORE FINE CRAFT SHOW

American Craft Council Shows, 155 Water St., 4th Floor, Unit 5, Brooklyn NY 11201. (800)836-3470. Fax: (612)355-2330. E-mail: shows@craftcouncil.org.

Website: www.craftcouncil.org. Art & craft show held annually in February. Indoors. Accepts handmade crafts, ceramics, fiber, metal, and other mediums. Juried. Awards/prizes: Awards of Excellence. Number exhibitors: 300. Number attendees: varies. Free to public. Apply online.

ADDITIONAL INFORMATION Deadline for entry: August. Application fee: $30 + $10 handling/processing fee for each set of images. Space fee: varies. Exhibition space: varies. For more information, artists should e-mail, call, or visit website.

BARRINGTON ART FESTIVAL

Amdur Productions, P.O. Box 550, Highland Park IL 60035. (847)926-4300. Fax: (847)926-4330. E-mail: info@amdurproductions.com. Website: www.amdurproductions.com. Estab. 2009. Fine arts & crafts fair held annually in May. Outdoors. Accepts handmade crafts, ceramics, fiber, glass, jewelry, metal, photography, watercolors, and wood. Juried. Awards/prizes: announced at awards party. Exhibitors: 125. Number of attendees: 122,000. Free to public. Apply online.

ADDITIONAL INFORMATION Deadline for entry: early January. Application fee: $25. Space fee: $415. Exhibition space: see website. For more information, artists should send e-mail, visit website, or call.

BARTLETT FESTIVAL OF THE ART

118 W. Bartlett Ave., Suite 2, Bartlett IL 60103. (630)372-4152. E-mail: art@artsinbartlett.org. Website: www.artsinbartlett.org. Estab. 2002. Fine arts & crafts fair held annually in June. Outdoors. Accepts handmade crafts, paintings, photography, fiber, sculpture, glass, jewelry, wood, and more. Juried. Exhibitors: see website. Number of attendees: 3,000. Free to public. Apply online.

ADDITIONAL INFORMATION Deadline for entry: April. Application fee: see website. Space fee: $150. Exhibition space: 10×10. For more information, artists should send e-mail, visit, website or call.

BASS RIVER ARTS AND CRAFTS FESTIVAL

38 Charles St., Rochester NH 03867. (603)332-2616. E-mail: info@castleberryfairs.com. Website: www.castleberryfairs.com. Contact: Terry & Chris Mullen. Fine arts & crafts fair held annually in July. Outdoors.

Accepts handmade crafts and other mediums. Juried. Exhibitors: see website. Number of attendees: varies. Free to public. Apply online.

ADDITIONAL INFORMATION Deadline for entry: see website. Application fee: see website. Space fee: $225. Exhibition space: 10×10. For more information, artists should send e-mail, visit website, or call.

BAYOU CITY ART FESTIVAL

(713)521-0133. E-mail: info@bayoucityartfestival. com. Website: www.artcolonyassociation.org/bayou-city-art-festival-memorial-park. Fine arts & crafts fair held annually in March. Outdoors. Accepts handmade crafts, ceramic, digital art, fiber, drawing, furniture, glass, jewelry, metal, 2D/3D mixed media, painting, photography, printmaking, sculpture, wood. Juried. Awards/prizes: Best of Show, 2nd Place, 3rd Place, Best Booth, Award of Excellence. Exhibitors: see website. Number of attendees: varies. Admission: $15 adults; $3 children 4-12; children 3 & under free. Apply online.

ADDITIONAL INFORMATION Deadline for entry: November. Application fee: see website. Space fee: varies. Exhibition space: varies. For more information, artists should send e-mail, visit website, or call.

SAN FRANCISCO BAZAAR

E-mail: sf_info@bazaarbizarre.org. Website: www. sanfranciscobazaar.org. Estab. 2001. "Each year San Francisco Bazaar features hundreds of juried artists and designers. Shoppers can expect to find the crème de la crème of indie goods: handbags, pottery, letterpress stationery, silk-screened t-shirts, baby clothes, zines, posters, body products, and more!"

BEAVER CREEK ART FESTIVAL

270 Central Blvd., Suite 107B, Jupiter FL 33458. (561)746-6615. Fax: (561)746-6528. E-mail: info@ artfestival.com. Website: www.artfestival.com. Contact: Malinda Ratliff, communications manager. Estab. 1988. Fine arts & crafts fair held annually in August. Outdoors. Accepts handmade crafts, clay, digital, fiber, glass, jewelry, mixed media, painting, photography, printmaking/drawing, sculpture, wood. Juried. Awards/prizes: announced after jury. Exhibitors: 150. Number of attendees: varies. Free to public. Apply online.

ADDITIONAL INFORMATION Deadline for entry: see website. Application fee: $35. Space fee: $475. Exhibition space: 10×10 and 10×20. For more information, artists should send e-mail, visit website, or call. Festival located at Beaver Creek Village in Avon, CO.

TIPS "You have to start somewhere. First, assess where you are, and what you'll need to get things off the ground. Next, make a plan of action. Outdoor street art shows are a great way to begin your career and lifetime as a working artist. You'll meet a lot of other artists who have been where you are now. Network with them!"

BELLEVUE ARTS MUSEUM ARTSFAIR

E-mail: meredithl@bellevuearts.org. Website: www. bellevuearts.org. "For more than 60 years, BAM ARTSfair has been celebrating the connection between our community and the world of art, craft, and design. Devoted to bringing some of the nation's most talented artists to our region, the Fair features thousands of original artworks, including painting, sculpture, fashion, and jewelry. With over 300 exhibiting artists, both emerging and well-known, BAM ARTSfair is one the region's largest gatherings and a unique opportunity to acquire art directly from the makers. Also join us for live music, artist demonstrations, community art projects, KIDSfair, and complimentary admission to BAM. - See more at: http://www.bellevuearts.org/fair/index.html#sthash.2lzYtAjm.dpuf.

BELLEVUE FESTIVAL OF THE ARTS

Craft Cooperative of the Northwest, 1916 Pike Place, Suite 146, Seattle WA 98101-1013. (206)363-2048. E-mail: info@bellevuefest.org. Website: www.bellevuefest.org. Contact: Ann Sutherland, fair coordinator. Fine arts & crafts fair held annually in June. Outdoors. Accepts handmade crafts, and other mediums. Juried. Exhibitors: 200. Number of attendees: 75,000. Free to public. Apply online.

ADDITIONAL INFORMATION Deadline for entry: February. Application fee: $40. Space fee: varies. Exhibition space: varies. For more information, artists should send e-mail, visit website, or call.

BELL ROCK PLAZA ART & CRAFT SHOW

Donna Campbell, P.O. Box 20039, Sedona AZ 86341. (928)284-9627. E-mail: ohdarnitall@yahoo.com. Website: www.bellrockartshows.com. Contact: Donna Campbell. Fine arts & crafts fair held annually several times a year. Outdoors. Accepts handmade crafts and other mediums. Juried. Exhibitors: see website. Number of attendees: varies. Free to public. Apply online.

ADDITIONAL INFORMATION Deadline for entry: varies per show. Application fee: see website. Space fee: $125. Exhibition space: 10×10. For more information, artists should send e-mail, visit website, or call.

BERKELEY ARTS FESTIVAL

E-mail: fabarts@silcon.com. Website: www.berkeley-artsfestival.com. Month-long arts festival in Berkeley. See website for details.

BERKSHIRE CRAFTS FAIR

E-mail: paulgib@mapinternet.com. Website: www.berkshirecraftsfair.org. Contact: Paul Gibbons. Estab. 1974. Fine arts & crafts fair held annually in August. Indoors. Accepts handmade crafts, jewelry, furniture, ceramics, textiles, glassware, woodwork, and more. Juried. Exhibitors: 90. Number of attendees: varies. Admission: $7; children 12 & under free. Apply online.

ADDITIONAL INFORMATION Deadline for entry: April. Application fee: $25. Space fee: $450. Exhibition space: 10×6. For more information, artists should send e-mail, or visit website.

BERKSHIRES ARTS FESTIVAL

P.O. Box 480, Slate Hill NY 10973. (845)355-2400. Fax: (845)355-2444. E-mail: show.director@americanart-marketing.com. Website: www.berkshiresartsfestival.com. Estab. 1984. Fine arts & crafts fair held annually in July. Indoors & outdoors. Accepts handmade crafts, ceramic, digital art, fiber, drawing, encaustic, furniture, glass, jewelry, metal, 2D/3D mixed media, painting, photography, sculpture, wood. Juried. Exhibitors: see website. Number of attendees: varies. Admission: $13 adults; $11 seniors; $5 students; $14 weekend pass; children 10 & under free. Apply online.

ADDITIONAL INFORMATION Deadline for entry: early January. Application fee: $35. Space fee: varies. Exhibition space: varies. For more information, artists should send e-mail, visit website or call.

BEST OF THE NORTHWEST FALL ART & FINE CRAFT SHOW

Northwest Art Alliance, 7777 62nd Ave. NE, Suite 103, Seattle WA 98115. (206)525-5926. E-mail: info@nwartalliance.com. Website: www.nwartalliance.com. Fine art & craft show held annually in October & November. Indoors. Accepts handmade crafts, ceramics, paintings, jewelry, glass, photography, wearable art, and other mediums. Juried. Number exhibitors: 110. Number attendees: varies. Admission: $5 online; $6 at door; children 12 & under free. Apply via Zapplication.org.

ADDITIONAL INFORMATION Deadline for entry: May. Application fee: $35. Space fee: varies. Exhibition space: varies. For more information, artists should call, e-mail, or visit website.

BEST OF THE NORTHWEST SPRING ART & FINE CRAFT SHOW

Northwest Art Alliance, 7777 62nd Ave. NE, Suite 103, Seattle WA 98115. (206)525-5926. E-mail: info@nwartalliance.com. Website: www.nwartalliance.com. Fine art & craft show held annually in March. Indoors. Accepts handmade crafts, ceramics, paintings, jewelry, glass, photography, wearable art, and other mediums. Juried. Number exhibitors: 110. Number attendees: varies. Admission: $5 online; $6 at door; children 12 & under free. Apply via Zapplication.org.

ADDITIONAL INFORMATION Deadline for entry: January. Application fee: $35. Space fee: varies. Exhibition space: varies. For more information, artists should call, e-mail, or visit website.

THE BIG CRAFTY

E-mail: crafty@thebigcrafty.com. Website: www.thebigcrafty.com. "The Big Crafty revives the tradition of the community bazaar, a lively celebration of handmade commerce, featuring local food, beer, music, and fine wares from a juried group of select indie artists and crafters. Our free and fun-for-all-ages events are held semiannually in the heart of beautiful Asheville, NC." See website for more information.

THE BIG HEAP VINTAGE & HANDMADE FESTIVAL

The Big Heap, P.O. Box 4373, Cave Creek AZ 85327. (480)329-6118. E-mail: info@thievesmarketvintage-flea.com. Website: www.thebigheap.com. "The Big Heap Vintage & Handmade Festival, a juried event featuring the most exciting vintage furniture and decor, fashion, adornment, and hand-wrought and hand-rendered items in the West. Our focus is beyond avoiding tetanus and lead poisoning, our focus is on style. The Big Heap will support you with the raw elements to make your own unique statement in your home, your garden, and in the way you express yourself. We are not a flea market, not an antique show, and we sure as he_ _ aren't a craft show. Come see us. Gon' be good." See website for more information.

THE BIG ONE ART & CRAFT FAIRS

The Big One Art & Craft Fair LLC, 101 22nd Street SW, P.O. Box 1276, Minot ND 58701. (701)837-6059. Fax: (701)839-0874. E-mail: info@thebigone.biz. Website: www.thebigone.biz. "THE BIG ONE Art & Craft Fair consists of four shows in North Dakota with over 350 different exhibitors showcasing their handmade items to thousands of consumers. Items you will see at each show are handcrafted wood furniture and decorative pieces; photography; pottery; jewelry; variety of floral arrangements to accommodate all tastes; flavorful foods including baked goods, soups, dips, jams, jellies, breads, salsa, spices, candies, and wonderful desserts; creative and comfortable clothing pieces for all ages; handmade soaps and lotions made from various natural resources; unlimited baby items from blankets to bibs and everything in between; handwoven rugs; homesewn quilts and blankets; wind chimes; 3D photography and artwork; and handmade toys." See website for more information.

BIRMINGHAM HOLLYDAZZLE CRAFT AND GIFT MARKET

E-mail: hollydazzlemarket@gmail.com. Website: www.hollydazzlemarket.com. Holiday arts and craft show in Birmingham. See website for details.

BIRMINGHAM WOMEN'S SHOW

Southern Shows, Inc., P.O. Box 36859, Charlotte NC 28236. (800)849.0248, ext. 107. E-mail: banderson@southernshows.com. Website: www.southernshows.com. Contact: Beth Anderson, show manager. Exhibitor fair held annually in October. Indoors. Accepts handmade crafts and other items. Exhibitors: see website. Number of attendees: varies. Admission: $10 adults; $5 youth; children 6 & under free. Apply online. **ADDITIONAL INFORMATION** Deadline for entry: see website. Application fee: see website. Space fee: varies. Exhibition space: varies. For more information, artists should send e-mail, visit website, or call.

BITCHCRAFT TRADING POST

E-mail: btchcrafttradingpost@gmail.com. Website: www.facebook.com/btchcrafttradingpost. "Bitchcraft Trading Post is a vintage & art collective event. We host a variety of vendors who sell handmade goods, vintage items, jewelry, artwork, records, food, beverages, & more." See website for more information.

BLACK SWAMP ARTS FESTIVAL

Bowling Green, OH 43402. Website: www.blackswampfest.org/. E-mail: info@blackswamparts.com. Estab. 1992. Fine arts & crafts fair held annually in September. Outdoors. Accepts handmade crafts and other mediums. Juried. Awards/prizes: Best of Show, Best 2D, Best 3D, 2nd Place, 3rd Place, Honorable Mention, Community Purchase Award. Exhibitors: 112. Number of attendees: varies. Free to public. Apply online. **ADDITIONAL INFORMATION** Deadline for entry: April. Application fee: $35. Space fee: $275 (single); $550 (double). Exhibition space: 10×10 (single); 10×20 (double). For more information, artists should send e-mail, visit website.

BLISSFEST MUSIC FESTIVAL

(231)348-7047. E-mail: jennifer@blissfest.org. Website: www.blissfest.org. Contact: Jennifer Ferguson. "The arts & craft fair is open to amateur and professional artists and craftspeople who create their own works of arts/crafts. Our goal is to provide opportunities for these creators and innovators of traditional and contemporary arts and crafts to present their respective talents in a festival atmosphere of music and dance that affirms and honors our shared cultural heritage and diversity." See website for more information and to apply.

BLUEGRASS FESTIVAL & ARTIST MARKET

922 Main St., Stone Mountain GA 30083. (404)873-1222. E-mail: lisa@affps.com. Website: www.stonemountainvillage.com/ssim.html. Contact: Lisa Windle, festival director. Estab. 2011. Arts & crafts show held annually late March. Outdoors. Accepts handmade crafts, painting, photography, sculpture, leather, metal, glass, jewelry. Juried by a panel. Awards/prizes: ribbons. Number of exhibitors: 150. Number of attendees: 7,500. Free to public. Apply online at www.zapplication.com.

ADDITIONAL INFORMATION Deadline for entry: February 14. Application fee: $25. Space fee: $200. Exhibition space: 10×10. For more information, see website.

BOCA FEST

270 Central Blvd., Suite 107B, Jupiter FL 33458. (561)746-6615. Fax: (561)746-6528. E-mail: info@artfestival.com. Website: www.artfestivalc.com. Contact: Malinda Ratliff, communications manager. Estab. 1988. Fine art & craft fair held annually in January. Outdoors. Accepts photography, jewelry, mixed media, sculpture, wood, ceramic, glass, painting, digital, fiber, metal. Juried. Number exhibitors: 210. Number attendees: 80,000. Free to public. Apply online via www.zapplication.org. Deadline: see website. Application fee: $25. Space fee: $395. Exhibition space: 10×10 and 10×20. For more information, artists should e-mail, call, or visit website. Festival located at The Shops at Boca Center in Boca Raton, FL.

TIPS "You have to start somewhere. First, assess where you are, and what you'll need to get things off the ground. Next, make a plan of action. Outdoor street art shows are a great way to begin your career and lifetime as a working artist. You'll meet a lot of other artists who have been where you are now. Network with them!"

BOCA RATON MUSEUM OF ART OUTDOOR JURIED ART FESTIVAL

Boca Museum of Art, 501 Plaza Real, Mizner Park, Boca Raton FL 33432. (561)392-2500. Fax: (561)391-6410. E-mail: info@bocamuseum.org. Website: www.bocamuseum.org. Estab. 1986. Fine arts & crafts fair held annually in February. Outdoors. Accepts handmade crafts and other mediums. Juried. Awards/prizes: Best in Show, Merit Awards. Exhibitors: 200. Number of attendees: varies. Free to public. Apply online.

ADDITIONAL INFORMATION Deadline for entry: see website. Application fee: see website. Space fee: see website. Exhibition space: see website. For more information, artists should send e-mail, visit website, or call.

BONITA SPRINGS NATIONAL ART FESTIVAL

Bonita Springs National Art Festival, P.O. Box 367465, Bonita Springs FL 34136-7465. (239)992-1213. Fax: (239)495-3999. E-mail: artfest@artinusa.com. Website: www.artinusa.com/bonita. Contact: Barry Witt, director. Fine arts & crafts fair held annually 3 times a year. Outdoors. Accepts handmade crafts, paintings, glass, jewelry, clay works, photography, sculpture, wood, and more. Juried. Awards/prizes: Best of Show, Best 2D, Best 3D, Distinction Award. Exhibitors: see website. Number of attendees: varies. Free to public. Apply online.

ADDITIONAL INFORMATION Deadline for entry: early January. Application fee: $30. Space fee: $400. Exhibition space: 10×12. For more information, artists should send e-mail, visit website, or call.

BOSTON MILLS ARTFEST

Website: www.bmbw.com. Estab. 1971. Fine arts & crafts fair held annually in June & July. Outdoors. Accepts handmade crafts, ceramic, digital art, fiber, drawing, furniture, glass, jewelry, metal, 2D/3D mixed media, painting, photography, printmaking, wood. Juried. Awards/prizes: First in Category, Award of Excellence. Exhibitors: see website. Number of attendees: varies. Free to public. Apply online.

ADDITIONAL INFORMATION Deadline for entry: see website. Application fee: see website. Space fee: see website. Exhibition space: see website. For more information, artists should send e-mail, visit website, or call.

BOULDER MOUNTAIN HANDMADE

1905 Linden Dr., Boulder CO 80304. (303)997-8319. E-mail: bmhart@bouldermountainhandmade.com. Website: www.bouldermountainhandmade.com. Estab. 1973. "Boulder Mountain Handmade is a fine art, craft, and baked goods tradition since 1973. We invite you to sip complimentary cider, chat with the artists, and browse unique creations in all price ranges."

BRECKENRIDGE MAIN STREET ART FESTIVAL

Mountain Art Festivals, P.O. Box 3578, Breckenridge CO 80424. E-mail: info@mountainartfestivals.com. Website: www.mountainartfestivals.com. Estab. 2001. Fine arts & crafts fair held annually in July. Outdoors. Accepts handmade crafts and other mediums. Juried. Exhibitors: 120. Number of attendees: varies. Free to public. Apply online.

ADDITIONAL INFORMATION Deadline for entry: April. Application fee: $35. Space fee: $500. Exhibition space: 10×10. For more information, artists should send e-mail, visit website, or call.

BROAD RIPPLE ART FAIR

Indianapolis Art Center, Marilyn K. Glick School of Art, 820 E. 67th St., Indianapolis IN 46220. (317)255-2464. Website: www.indplsartcenter.org/events/braf. Estab. 1971. Fine arts & crafts fair held annually in May. Outdoors. Accepts handmade crafts and other mediums. Juried. Exhibitors: 225. Number of attendees: varies. Admission: $13 adult presale; $15 adult day of; $3 children. Apply online.

ADDITIONAL INFORMATION Deadline for entry: see website. Application fee: see website. Space fee: varies. Exhibition space: see website. For more information, artists should visit website or call.

BROOKINGS SUMMER ARTS FESTIVAL

Brookings Summer Arts Festival, P.O. Box 4, Brookings SD 57006. (605)692-2787. E-mail: generalinfo@bsaf.com. E-mail: artbooths@bsaf.com. Website: www.bsaf.com. Estab. 1972. Fine arts & skilled crafts festival held annually in July. Outdoors. Accepts original art & handcrafted work. Juried. Exhibitors: 200 art booths. Number of attendees: 75,000. Free to public. Apply online. Festival held in historic Pioneer Park.

Features free entertainment, children's art area, over 40 food booths, regional, and historic areas. Vendor social the Friday evening before festival. Free vendor parking.

ADDITIONAL INFORMATION Deadline for entry: March 1. Application fee: $25. Space fee: $200. Exhibition space: 12×12. For more information, artists should send e-mail, visit website, or call.

BROOKSIDE ART ANNUAL

Brookside Business Association, 6814 Troost Ave., Kansas City MO 64131-1509. (816)523-5553. Fax: (816)333-1022. E-mail: brooksideartannualkc@gmail.com. Website: www.brooksidekc.org. Estab. 1984. Fine arts & crafts fair held annually in May. Outdoors. Accepts handmade crafts and other mediums. Juried. Awards/prizes: Best of Show, Best in Category. Exhibitors: 180. Number of attendees: 70,000. Free to public. Apply online.

ADDITIONAL INFORMATION Deadline for entry: see website. Application fee: see website. Space fee: see website. Exhibition space: see website. For more information, artists should send e-mail, visit website, or call.

BROWNWOOD PADDOCK SQUARE ART & CRAFT FESTIVAL

270 Central Blvd., Suite 107B, Jupiter FL 33458. (561)746-6615. Fax: (561)746-6528. E-mail: info@artfestival.com. Website: www.artfestival.com. Contact: Malinda Ratliff, communications manager. Estab. 1997. Fine art & craft fair held annually in mid-April. Outdoors. Accepts photography, jewelry, mixed media, sculpture, wood, ceramic, glass, painting, digital, fiber, metal. Juried. Number exhibitors: 205. Number attendees: 20,000. Free to public. Apply online via www.zapplication.org or visit website for paper application. Deadline: see website. Application fee: $15. Space fee: $265. Exhibition space: 10×10 and 10×20. For more information, artists should e-mail, call, or visit website. Festival located at Brownwood in The Villages, FL.

TIPS "You have to start somewhere. First, assess where you are, and what you'll need to get things off the ground. Next, make a plan of action. Outdoor street art shows are a great way to begin your career and lifetime as a working artist. You'll meet a lot of other artists who have been where you are now. Network with them!"

BRUCE MUSEUM OUTDOOR ARTS FESTIVAL

1 Museum Drive, Greenwich CT 06830-7157. (203) 869-6786, ext. 336. E-mail: sue@brucemuseum. org. Website: www.brucemuseum.org. Contact: Sue Brown Gordon, festival director. Estab. 1981. Fine arts & crafts fair held annually in October. Outdoors. Accepts handmade crafts, painting, sculpture, mixed media, graphics/drawing (including computer-generated works), photography. Juried. Exhibitors: see website. Number of attendees: varies. Free to public. Apply online.

ADDITIONAL INFORMATION Deadline for entry: June. Application fee: $20. Space fee: $350. Exhibition space: 10×12. For more information, artists should send e-mail, visit website, or call.

BUCKHEAD SPRING ARTS & CRAFTS FESTIVAL

4469 Stella Dr., Atlanta GA 30327. (404)873-1222. E-mail: lisa@affps.com. Website: www.buckheadartsfestival.com. Contact: Lisa Windle, festival director. Estab. 2009. Annual arts & crafts show. Held mid-May. Outdoors. Accepts handmade crafts, paintings, photography, sculpture, leather, metal, glass, jewelry. Juried. Awards/prizes: ribbons. Number of exhibitors: 185. Number of attendees: 40,000. Free to public. Apply online at www.zapplication.com.

ADDITIONAL INFORMATION Deadline for entry: March 14. Application fee: $25. Space fee: $200. Exhibition space: 10×10. For more information, artists should visit website.

BUCKTOWN ARTS FEST

Bucktown Arts Fest, c/o Holstein Park, 2200 N. Oakley Ave., Chicago IL 60647. E-mail: inquiries@bucktownartsfest.com. Website: www.bucktownartsfest. com. Estab. 1984. Fine arts & crafts fair held annually in August. Outdoors. Accepts handmade crafts and other mediums. Juried. Exhibitors: 200. Number of attendees: 40,000. Free to public. Apply online.

ADDITIONAL INFORMATION Deadline for entry: March. Application fee: $45. Space fee: $300; $200

(seniors 60 and over). Exhibition space: 10×10. For more information, artists should send e-mail, visit website, or call.

BUFFALO GROVE INVITATIONAL ART FESTIVAL

Amdur Productions, P.O. Box 550, Highland Park IL 60035. (847)926-4300. Fax: (847)926-4330. E-mail: info@amdurproductions.com. Website: www.amdurproductions.com. Estab. 2002. Fine arts & crafts fair held annually in July. Outdoors. Accepts handmade crafts, ceramic, digital art, fiber, drawing, furniture, glass, jewelry, metal, 2D/3D mixed media, painting, photography, printmaking, wood. Juried. Exhibitors: 120. Number of attendees: 20,000. Free to public. Apply online.

ADDITIONAL INFORMATION Deadline for entry: see website. Application fee: $25. Space fee: $450. Exhibition space: 10×10. For more information, artists should send e-mail, visit website, or call.

BUFFALO RIVER ELK FESTIVAL

Jasper AR 72641. (870)446-2455. Website: www.theozarkmountains.com. Contact: Patti or Nancy, vendor coordinators. Estab. 1997. Arts & crafts show held annually in June. Outdoors. Accepts fine art & handmade crafts, photography, on-site design. Exhibitors: 60. Number of attendees: 6,000. Free to public. Artists should apply via website.

ADDITIONAL INFORMATION Deadline for entry: June 1. Application fee: none. Space fee: $75. Exhibition space: 10×10. For more information, artists should visit website.

BUST MAGAZINE'S HOLIDAY CRAFTACULAR

E-mail: craftacular@bust.com. Website: www.bust. com. Fine arts & crafts fair held annually in June. Indoors. Accepts handmade crafts and other mediums. Exhibitors: see website. Number of attendees: varies. Admission: $3 adults; children 12 & under free. Apply online.

ADDITIONAL INFORMATION Deadline for entry: May. Application fee: $20. Space fee: see website. Exhibition space: see website. For more information, artists should send e-mail, visit website, or call.

CABIN FEVER CRAFT SHOW

(215)850-1888. E-mail: frommyhand@gmail.com. Website: www.craftsatmolandhouse.com. Contact: Gwyn Duffy. "Chase away the winter blahs! We have gathered over 50 talented local crafters to lift your spirits with their creativity. Find the perfect gift, tasty treat, or decoration for your home and leave here knowing that spring is just around the corner. Spend some time wandering around the beautiful historic setting that was once the headquarters for General George Washington. $1 admission benefits the Moland House Restoration Project."

CANTIGNY PARK
JEWELRY & ACCESSORIES SHOW

1s151 Winfield Rd., Wheaton IL 60189. (630)260-8216. Fax: (630)260-8284. E-mail: aanderson@cantigny.org. Website: www.cantigny.org. Contact: Alicia Anderson, visitors center & Cantigny shop manager. Estab. 2011. Arts & crafts/jewelry show held in September. Indoors. Accepts handmade crafts. Exhibitors: 30. Number of attendees: 1,200. Admission: $5/car. Apply online.

ADDITIONAL INFORMATION Deadline for entry: August 31. Application fee: $50. Space fee: see website. Exhibition space: 8ft. table. For more information e-mail or visit website.

CANTIGNY PARK MISTLETOE MARKET

1s151 Winfield Rd., Wheaton IL 60189. (630)260-8216. Fax: (630)260-8284. E-mail: aanderson@cantigny.org. Website: www.cantigny.org. Contact: Alicia Anderson, visitors center & Cantigny shop manager. Estab. 2012. Arts & crafts/holiday show held in December. Indoors. Accepts handmade crafts. Exhibitors: 30. Number of attendees: 2,500. Admission: $5. Apply online.

ADDITIONAL INFORMATION Deadline for entry: mid-November. Application fee: $50. Space fee: see website. Exhibition space: 8ft. table. For more information e-mail or visit website.

CAPE CORAL FESTIVAL OF THE ARTS

Cape Coral Festival of the Arts Committee, P.O. Box 101346, Cape Coral FL 33910. (239)699-7942. E-mail: info@capecoralfestival.com. Website: www.capecoralfestival.com. Estab. 1985. Fine arts & crafts fair held annually in January. Outdoors. Accepts handmade crafts and other mediums. Juried. Exhibitors: see website. Number of attendees: see website. Free to public. Apply online.

ADDITIONAL INFORMATION Deadline for entry: October 1. Application fee: $20. Space fee: $306. Exhibition space: see website. For more information, artists should send e-mail, visit website, or call.

CAROLINA ONE STOP SHOP HOP

Hubbard Dr., Lancaster SC 29720. (803)273-3834. E-mail: dusawyer@comporium.net. Website: carolinaonestopshophop.blogspot.com. Contact: Donna Sawyer, co-chair. Estab. 2006. Annual shop hop held last Saturday in February. Indoors. Accepts handmade crafts, fabric, yarns, thread, patterns, quilting tools and gadgets, vintage linens, buttons, quilting supplies. Awards/prizes: door prizes. Exhibitors: 25. Number of attendees: 300. Admission: $3. See website for application.

ADDITIONAL INFORMATION Deadline for entry: November. Space fee: $60-200. Exhibition space: classroom, 10×10. For more information send e-mail.
TIPS "Reasonably priced and quality work."

CAROUSEL FINE CRAFT SHOW

OCA Renaissance Arts Center & Theatre, 1200 E. Center St., Kingsport TN 37660. (423)392-8414. E-mail: stephanos@kingsporttn.gov. Website: www.engagekingsport.com. Contact: Will Stephanos, show director. Estab. 2012. Fine art show held annually in March. Indoors. Accepts fine art & handmade crafts, photography, clay, fiber, paintings, furniture, wood, metal, jewelry, glass. Juried. Exhibitors: 38. Number of attendees: 5-8,000. Admission: $5 (day pass); $7 (2 day pass). Artists should apply online.

ADDITIONAL INFORMATION Deadline for entry: December 1. Application fee: none. Space fee: $250. Exhibition space: 10×10. For more information, artists should e-mail, visit website, or call.
TIPS "Start with good work, photos, display, and personal connections."

CASA GRANDE HOLIDAY ARTS & CRAFTS FESTIVAL

7225 N. Oracle Rd., Suite 112, Tucson AZ 85704. (520)797-3959, ext. 0. Fax: (520)531-9225. E-mail: lauren@saaca.org. Website: www.saaca.org. Fine arts & crafts fair held annually in December. Outdoors. Accepts handmade crafts and other mediums. Exhibitors: 60. Number of attendees: see website. Free to public. Apply online.

ADDITIONAL INFORMATION Deadline for entry: December. Application fee: see website. Space fee: $185 (single); $310 (double). Exhibition space: 12×12 (single); 12×24 (double). For more information, artists should send e-mail, visit website, or call.

CASTLEBERRY FAIRE

38 Charles St., Rochester NY 03867. (603)332-2616. E-mail: info@castleberryfairs.com. Website: www.castleberryfairs.com. Contact: Terry & Chris Mullen. Estab. 1995. Fine arts & crafts fair held annually in November, Thanksgiving weekend. Indoors. Accepts handmade crafts and other mediums. Juried. Exhibitors: see website. Number of attendees: see website. Admission: $8 adults; children 12 & under free. Apply online.

ADDITIONAL INFORMATION Deadline for entry: see website. Application fee: see website. Space fee: $375 (10×6); $475 (10×10). Exhibition space: 10×6; 10×10. For more information, artists should send e-mail, visit website, or call.

CENTERFEST: THE ART LOVERS FESTIVAL

Durham Arts Council, 120 Morris St., Durham NC 27701. (919)560-2787. E-mail: centerfest@durhamarts.org. Website: www.centerfest.durhamarts.org. Estab. 1974. Fine arts & crafts fair held annually in September. Outdoors. Accepts handmade crafts, clay, drawing, fibers, glass, painting, photography, printmaking, wood, jewelry, mixed media, sculpture. Juried. Awards/prizes: Best in Show, 1st place, 2nd place, 3rd place. Exhibitors: 140. Number of attendees: see website. Admission: $5 donation accepted at gate. Apply online.

ADDITIONAL INFORMATION Deadline for entry: May. Application fee: see website. Space fee: $195 (single); $390 (double). Exhibition space: 10×10 (single); 10×20 (double). For more information, artists should send e-mail, visit website, or call.

CENTRAL OREGON WILD WEST SHOW, THE

Central Oregon Shows, P.O. Box 1555, Sisters OR 97759. (541)420-0279. E-mail: centraloregonshows@gmail.com. Website: www.centraloregonshows.com. "This event is a theatrical production similar to the famous Buffalo Bill Wild West Show. There are only 10 vendor spaces available for this show. Attendance: 26,000 paid attendees. Contact to apply ($150, 10×10)." See website for more information.

CENTRAL PENNSYLVANIA FESTIVAL OF THE ARTS

403 S. Allen St., Suite 205A, P.O. Box 1023, State College PA 16804. (814)237-3682. Website: www.arts-festival.com. Estab. 1966. Fine arts & crafts fair held annually in July. Outdoors. Accepts handmade crafts and other mediums. Exhibitors: see website. Number of attendees: see website. Admission: Free to public. Apply online.

ADDITIONAL INFORMATION Deadline for entry: June. Application fee: see website. Space fee: see website. Exhibition space: see website. For more information, artists should visit website or call.

CHARLEVOIX WATERFRONT ART FAIR

Charlevoix Waterfront Art Fair, P.O. Box 57, Charlevoix MI 49720. (231)547-2675. E-mail: cwaf14@gmail.com. Website: www.charlevoixwaterfrontartfair.org. "The Annual Charlevoix Waterfront Art Fair is a juried and invitational show and sale. Categories are: ceramics, glass, fiber; drawing; wood; painting; mixed media 2D and 3D; jewelry, fine and other; printmaking; photography; sculpture. To apply, each entrant must submit 4 digital images (3 images of your artwork and booth image) sized 1920 × 1920 pixels at 72 dpi for consideration by the jury (ZAPP images are acceptable). A nonrefundable processing fee of $25 plus $15 for each additional category entered, must accompany the artist's application."

CHASTAIN PARK FESTIVAL

4469 Stella Dr., Atlanta GA 30327. (404)873-1222. E-mail: lisa@affps.com. Website: www.chastain-parkartsfestival.com. Contact: Lisa Windle, festival director. Estab. 2008. Arts & crafts show held annually early November. Outdoors. Accepts handmade crafts, painting, photography, sculpture, leather, metal, glass, jewelry. Juried by a panel. Awards/prizes: ribbons. Number of exhibitors: 175. Number of attendees: 45,000. Free to public. Apply online at www.zapplication.com.

ADDITIONAL INFORMATION Deadline for entry: August 28. Application fee: $25. Space fee: $300. Exhibition space: 10×10. For more information, send e-mail or see website.

TIPS "Offer a variety of price ranges, have a professional setup and display materials, greet guests."

CHEROKEE TRIANGLE ART FAIR

Cherokee Triangle Association, P.O. Box 4306, Louisville KY 40204. (502)459-0256. E-mail: cherokeetriangle@bellsouth.net. Website: www.cherokeetriangleartfair.org. "The Cherokee Triangle Art Fair is a juried fair with more than 200 artists' booths. The outdoor event is in Louisville's historic Cherokee Triangle neighborhood on tree-lined Cherokee Pkwy. between Willow Ave. and Cherokee Rd. adjacent to the Gen. John Breckinridge Castleman statue." See website for more details.

CHERRY CREEK ARTS FESTIVAL

2 Steele Street, Suite B-100, Denver CO 80206. (303)355-2787. E-mail: management@cherryarts.org. Website: www.cherrycreekartsfestival.org. "The Cherry Creek Arts Festival (CCAF) weekend event is a world-class and award-winning celebration of the visual, culinary, and performing arts, and enjoys an attendance of 350,000 visitors over the course of the three-day event. The Arts Festival features artists in 13 different media categories including: ceramics, digital art, drawing, fiber, glass, jewelry, metalworks, mixed media, new media, painting, photography, printmaking, sculpture, and wood. The CCAF's year-round 501c3 nonprofit mission is to provide access to art experiences and to support education."

CHERRYWOOD ART FAIR

Cherrywood Art Fair, P.O. Box 4283, Austin TX 78765. E-mail: cherrywoodartfair@gmail.com. Website: www.cherrywoodartfair.org. Estab. 2001. Cherrywood Art Fair is an art-filled 2-day event showcasing local artists, live music, kids activities, and great food in a free, family-friendly environment. More than 8,000 visitors stroll through the fairgrounds looking at art, listening to beautiful music, and sampling some of Austin's finest food trailer cuisine. Since its inception, the Fair has served as a destination for discerning holiday shoppers seeking unique and artful items from Texas artists.

CHESTER CRAFT SHOWS

P.O. Box 613, Madison NJ 07940. (973)377-6600. Website: www.chestercraftshow.com. "Rated no. 1 in New Jersey and one of the Top 50 'Best Crafts Show in the Nation' by America's Premier Art and Craft Show Magazine, *Sunshine Artist*, previous shows have set all-time attendance records, with crafters and artisans from throughout the region offering an array of select, handcrafted furniture, jewelry, apparel, ornaments, home accessories, and more."

CHESTERTON ART FAIR

The Chesterton Art Fair, P.O. Box 783, Chesterton IN 46304. (219)926-4711. E-mail: gallery@chestertonart.com. Website: www.chestertonart.com. Fine arts & crafts fair held annually. Outdoors. Accepts handmade crafts and other mediums. Exhibitors: see website. Number of attendees: see website. Admission: Free to public. Apply online.

ADDITIONAL INFORMATION Deadline for entry: July. Application fee: $25. Space fee: single- $190.00 (non AACPC member); $180.00 (member); double- $350.00 (non-member); $295.00 (member). Exhibition space: see website. For more information, artists should visit website, or call.

CHICAGO BOTANIC ART FESTIVAL

E-mail: info@amdurproductions.com. Website: www.amdurproductions.com. Fine arts & crafts fair held in July. Outdoors. Accepts handmade crafts and other mediums. Exhibitors: 95. Number of attendees: 30,000. Free to public. Apply online.

ADDITIONAL INFORMATION Deadline for entry: January. Application fee: $35. Space fee: $625. Exhibition space: see website. For more information, artists should email, visit website, or call.

CHRISTKINDL MARKT

Canton Museum of Art, 1001 Market Ave. N., Canton OH 44702. (330)453-7666, ext. 105. E-mail: carol@cantonart.org. Website: www.cantonart.org/christ-kindl. Contact: Carol Paris, assistant. Estab. 1972. Fine arts & crafts show held annually in November. Indoors. Accepts handmade crafts, ceramics, drawing, pastel, fiber, leather, glass, graphics, printmaking, jewelry, metalwork, mixed media, painting, photography, sculpture, wearable art, wood. Juried. Awards/prizes: Best in Show; 1st Place Fine Art; 1st Place Fine Craft; 2nd Place Fine Art; 2nd Place Fine Craft; Best Booth; honorable mentions, ribbons. Exhibitors: 106. Number of attendees: 4,500. Admission: $6 advance; $7 at the door. Apply online.

ADDITIONAL INFORMATION Deadline for entry: June 15. Application fee: $25. Space fee: $300 (single); $550 (double). Exhibition space: 8×10 (single); 8×20 (double). For more information visit website.

TIPS "All work must be original and handcrafted by the artist. No buy/sell or imports. The artist must be present during the show."

CHRISTMAS CONNECTION

Renaissance Arts Center, 1200 E. Center St., Ste. 223, Kingsport TN 37660. (423)392-8415. E-mail: bethestep@kingsporttn.gov. Website: www.engagekingsport.com. Contact: Beth Estep, show director. Estab. 1978. Arts & crafts show held annually in November. Indoors. Accepts fine art & handmade crafts. Juried. Exhibitors: 148. Number of attendees: 10,000. Free to public. Artists should apply online.

ADDITIONAL INFORMATION Deadline for entry: August 1. Application fee: none. Space fee: $195. Exhibition space: 10×10. For more information, artists should e-mail, visit website, or call.

CHRISTMAS IN SEATTLE GIFT & GOURMET FOOD SHOW

Washington State Convention Center, 800 Convention Place, Seattle WA 98101. (800)521-7469. Fax: (425)889-8165. E-mail: seattle@showcaseevents.org. Website: www.showcaseevents.org. Contact: Dena Sablan, show manager. Estab. 1992. Seasonal holiday show held annually in November. Indoors. Accepts handmade crafts, art, photography, pottery, glass, jewelry, clothing, fiber. Juried. Exhibitors: 300. Number of attendees: 15,000. Admission: $14.50 (for all 3 days); 12 & under free. Apply via website or call or e-mail for application.

ADDITIONAL INFORMATION Deadline for entry: October 31. Space fee: see website. Exhibition space: 10×10. For more information send e-mail, call, send SASE, or visit website.

TIPS "Competitive pricing, attractive booth display, quality product, something unique for sale, friendly & outgoing personality."

CHRISTMAS IN THE COUNTRY ARTISAN MARKET

(910)799-9424. E-mail: wnypremier@ec.rr.com. Website: www.wnypremierpromotions.com/christmas-in-the-country. Christmas in the Country has been recognized as the No. 2 Contemporary and Classic Artisan Market in the nation by *Sunshine Artist*, the leading publication in the art and craft event industry. The event has been ranked either no. 1 or no. 2 in the nation for the past 10 years. Now, drawing almost 60,000 visitors over 4 days, the event is widely recognized as the preeminent holiday artisan market in the United States. Christmas in the Country is held in November at the Hamburg Fairgrounds. Christmas in the Country will welcome over 400 artisans spread out over 5 buildings. Attendees to Christmas in the Country will find unique and only handcrafted creations including home décor, gourmet foods and wine, original music, trendsetting jewelry, handpoured aromatic candles, children's toys and clothing, stylish pottery, original wall art, gifts for pets, and holiday gift items galore.

CHURCH ON THE HILL ANNUAL FINE ARTS AND HANDMADE CRAFTS FAIR

55 Main St., Lenox MA 01240. (413)637-1001. Fax: (413)637-3395. E-mail: ucclenox@verizon.net. Website: www.churchonthehilllenox.org. Estab. 1987. Arts & crafts show held annually in July. Outdoors. Accepts handmade crafts and other mediums. Juried. Exhib-

itors: 60. Number of attendees: 800. Free to public. Apply online.

ADDITIONAL INFORMATION Deadline for entry: mid-April. Application fee: none. Space fee: $250. Exhibition space: 11×11. For more information send e-mail or visit website.

CITYPLACE ART FAIR

270 Central Blvd., Suite 107B, Jupiter FL 33458. (561)746-6615. Fax: (561)746-6528. E-mail: info@artfestival.com. Website: www.artfestival.com. Contact: Malinda Ratliff, communications manager. Estab. 2011. Fine art & craft fair held annually in early March. Outdoors. Accepts photography, jewelry, mixed media, sculpture, wood, ceramic, glass, painting, digital, fiber, metal. Juried. Number exhibitors: 200. Number attendees: 40,000. Free to public. Apply online via www.zapplication.org. Deadline: see website. Application fee: $25. Space fee: $395. Exhibition space: 10×10 and 10×20. For more information, artists should e-mail, call, or visit website. Fair located in CityPlace in downtown West Palm Beach, FL.

TIPS "You have to start somewhere. First, assess where you are, and what you'll need to get things off the ground. Next, make a plan of action. Outdoor street art shows are a great way to begin your career and lifetime as a working artist. You'll meet a lot of other artists who have been where you are now. Network with them!"

CLEVELAND HANDMADE

E-mail: info@clevelandhandmade.com. Website: www.clevelandhandmade.com. Contact: Lori Paximadis, cofounder/membership director. "Cleveland Handmade brings together artists and craftspeople from northeast Ohio and promotes the value of buying and selling handmade goods. We foster relationships and provide opportunities for education, socializing, and networking among creators. We bring together resources that benefit our members and share our members' stories with the public."

COARSEGOLD CHRISTMAS FAIRE

P.O. Box 1514, Coarsegold CA 93614. (559)683-3900. E-mail: events@coarsegoldhistoricvillage.com. Website: www.coarsegoldhistoricvillage.com. "Get into the Christmas Spirit mountain style. Listen to carol-

ers, visit with Father Christmas, and do some Christmas shopping at the craft booths in the park." See website for more information and to apply.

COCONUT GROVE ARTS FESTIVAL

3390 Mary St., Suite 128, Coconut Grove FL 33133. (305)447-0401. E-mail: katrina@cgaf.com. Website: www.coconutgroveartsfest.com. Contact: Katrina Delgado. The Coconut Grove Arts Festival showcases the works of 360 internationally recognized artists who are selected from nearly 1,300 applicants. Jurors evaluate the artist's work and displays to select participants in such categories as mixed media, painting, photography, digital art, printmaking & drawing, watercolor, clay work, glass, fiber, jewelry & metalwork, sculpture, and wood.

COCONUT POINT ART FESTIVAL

270 Central Blvd., Suite 107B, Jupiter FL 33458. (561)746-6615. Fax: (561)746-6528. E-mail: info@artfestival.com. Website: www.artfestival.com. Contact: Malinda Ratliff, communications manager. Estab. 2007. Fine art & craft fair held annually in late December/early January & February. Outdoors. Accepts photography, jewelry, mixed media, sculpture, wood, ceramic, glass, painting, digital, fiber, metal. Juried. Number exhibitors: 200-280. Number attendees: 90,000. Free to public. Apply online via www.zapplication.org. Deadline: see website. Application fee: $25. Space fee: $395-425. Exhibition space: 10×10 and 10×20. For more information, artists should e-mail, call, or visit website. Festival held at Coconut Point in Estero, FL.

TIPS "You have to start somewhere. First, assess where you are, and what you'll need to get things off the ground. Next, make a plan of action. Outdoor street art shows are a great way to begin your career and lifetime as a working artist. You'll meet a lot of other artists who have been where you are now. Network with them!"

COLLEGE HILL ARTS FESTIVAL

College Hill Arts Festival, P.O. Box 544, Cedar Falls IA 50613. Website: www.collegehillartsfestival.com. The College Hill Arts Festival is a juried art show held on the campus of the University of Northern Iowa featuring 75 artists in a variety of media.

COLORADO COUNTRY CHRISTMAS GIFT SHOW

Denver Mart, 451 E. 58th Ave., Denver CO 80216. (800)521-7469. Fax: (425)889-8165. E-mail: denver@showcase.events.org. Website: www.showcaseevents.org. Contact: Kim Peck, show manager. Estab. 2003. Annual holiday show held early November. Indoors. Accepts handmade crafts, art, photography, pottery, glass, jewelry, fiber, clothing. Juried. Exhibitors: 400. Number of attendees: 25,000. Admission: see website. Apply by e-mail, call, or website.

ADDITIONAL INFORMATION Deadline for entry: see website. Space fee: see website. Exhibition space: 10×10. For more information e-mail, call, send SASE, or see website.

TIPS "Competitive pricing, attractive booth display, quality product, something unique for sale, friendly & outgoing personality."

COLUMBIANA ARTIST MARKET

104 Mildred St., P.O. Box 624, Columbiana AL 35051. (205)669-0044. E-mail: info@shelbycountyartscouncil.com. Website: www.shelbycountyartscouncil.com. Member artists gather to offer their original artwork. Work available includes oil paintings, acrylic paintings, photography, jewelry, fabric arts, printmaking, pottery, and more.

THE COLUMBUS ARTS FESTIVAL

100 E. Broad St., Suite 2250, Columbus OH 43216. (614)221-8531. Fax: (614)224-7461. E-mail: shuntley@gcac.org. Website: www.columbusartsfestival.org. Contact: Scott Huntley, director. Estab. 1962. Fine art show held annually in early June. Outdoors. Accepts fine art, 2D/3D mixed media, ceramics, digital art, drawing, fiber, glass, jewelry, leather, painting, metal, photography, printmaking, sculpture, wood. Juried. Awards/prizes: Best in Show, Jurors' Choice, Merit Award, Best Presentation, Best Emerging Artist. Exhibitors: 300. Number of attendees: 450,000. Free to public. Apply via Zapplication.org.

ADDITIONAL INFORMATION Deadline for entry: mid-January. Application fee: $35. Space fee: $495. Exhibition Space: 10×10; double booths available by invitation. Average sales: $8,000. For more information send e-mail.

COMMONWHEEL ARTISTS ANNUAL LABOR DAY ARTS & CRAFTS FESTIVAL

(719)577-7700. E-mail: festival@commonwheel.com. Website: www.commonwheel.com/festival. Contact: Festival committee (by e-mail). Estab. 1975. Arts & crafts show held annually in September. Outdoors. Accepts original fine art & handmade crafts in all mediums. Juried. Awards/prizes: ribbons in all categories and free booth for following year. Exhibitors: 110. Number of attendees: 15,000. Free to public. Artists should apply via website.

ADDITIONAL INFORMATION Deadline for entry: June 1. Application fee: $25. Space fee: $300 (artists); $350 (food). Exhibition space: 10×10 (artists); 12×14 (food). For more information, artists should e-mail or visit website.

CORAL SPRINGS FESTIVAL OF THE ARTS

270 Central Blvd., Suite 107B, Jupiter FL 33458. (561)746-6615. Fax: (561)746-6528. E-mail: info@artfestival.com. Website: www.artfestival.com. "The Coral Springs Festival of the Arts has grown considerably over the years into a 2-day celebration of arts and culture with a fine art show, contemporary craft festival, theatrical performances, and full lineup of live music. Held in conjunction with the Coral Springs Art Festival Committee and the City, this event brings 250 of the nations best artists and crafters to south Florida. Stroll amidst life-size sculptures, spectacular paintings, one-of-a-kind jewels, photography, ceramics, a separate craft festival, Green Market, and much more. No matter what you're looking for, you'll be sure to find it among the array of various artists and crafters participating in this arts and crafts fair."

CORN HILL ARTS FESTIVAL

133 S. Fitzhugh St., Rochester NY 14608-9956. (585)262-3142. E-mail: chna@cornhill.org. Website: www.cornhillartsfestival.com. Fine arts & crafts fair held annually in July. Outdoors. Accepts handmade crafts and other mediums. Exhibitors: see website. Number of attendees: see website. Admission: Free to public. Apply online.

ADDITIONAL INFORMATION Deadline for entry: March 15. Application fee: $35. Space fee: $275 (single); $530 (double). Exhibition space: 10×10 (single);

10×20 (double). For more information, artists should visit website, send e-mail, or call.

CORVALLIS FALL FESTIVAL

(541)752-9655. E-mail: director@corvallisfallfestival. com. Website: www.corvallisfallfestival.org. Corvallis Fall Festival is a not-for-profit event with the mission to help sustain local arts and crafts while serving, supporting, and showcasing the Corvallis community.

COTTONWOOD ART FESTIVAL

Cottonwood Art Festival, 2100 E. Campbell Rd., Suite 100, Richardson TX 75081. (972)744-4582. E-mail: serri.ayers@cor.gov. Website: www.cottonwoodart-festival.com. Contact: Serri Ayers. "The semiannual Cottonwood Art Festival is a juried show. Jurors have selected over 240 artists from 800 submissions to exhibit their museum-quality work at the festival. The artists compete in 14 categories: 2D mixed media, 3D mixed media, ceramics, digital, drawings/pastels, fiber, glass, jewelry, leather, metalwork, painting, photography, sculpture, and wood. Rated as one of the top art festivals in the United States, the prestigious show is the premier fine art event in north Texas."

COUNTRY FOLK ARTS AND CRAFTS SHOW

E-mail: shows@countryfolkart.com. Website: www. countryfolkart.com. Country Folk Art Shows has grown to 17 shows in 5 states. Every participant is juried and hand selected for their outstanding workmanship and integrity of creative design. Some of the more popular decorating items found at our shows are handcrafted furniture, home and garden decor, jewelry, textiles, holiday decor, wearable art, handmade candles and soaps, quilts, paintings, framed art, florals, iron work, wood carvings, baskets, stained glass, and much more.

COUNTRYSIDE VILLAGE ART FAIR

Countryside Village Art Fair, 11004 Prairie Brook Road, Omaha NE 68144. (402)391-4745. E-mail: artfair@countryside-village.com. Website: www.countryside-village.com. Contact: Juanita Galvan. Estab. 1969. "A mix of styles, perspectives, and media, the Countryside Village Art Fair takes place the first Saturday and Sunday in June. The incredible array of artwork inspires casual visitors to start art collections, and connoisseurs to add to existing collections."

COVINGTON ART FAIR

The Covington Art Fair, C/O Asher Agency, 535 W. Wayne Street, Ft. Wayne IN 46802. (800)900-7031. E-mail: covingtonartfair@asheragency.com. Website: www.facebook.com/CovingtonArtFair. The Covington Art Fair is a high-quality 2-day community event featuring fine arts. The fair is located at Covington Plaza, Fort Wayne's most prestigious shopping plaza featuring high fashion, specialty large shops, gourmet restaurants, a spa, and much, much more.

CRAFT & FINE ART FESTIVAL AT THE NASSAU COUNTY MUSEUM OF ART

American Concern for Artistry and Craftsmanship, P.O. Box 650, Montclair NJ 07042. (973)746-0091. Fax: (973)509-7739. E-mail: acacinfo@gmail.com. Website: www.craftsatlincoln.org. Fine art & craft show held annually in September. Outdoors. Accepts handmade crafts. Juried. Number exhibitors: 90. Number attendees: varies. Free to public. Apply online or via Zapplication.org.

ADDITIONAL INFORMATION Deadline for entry: June. Application fee: none. Space fee: varies. Exhibition space: varies. For more information, artists should call, e-mail, or visit website.

CRAFT & SPECIALTY FOOD FAIR (NEW HAMPSHIRE)

38 Charles St., Rochester NH 03867. (603)332-2616. E-mail: info@castleberryfairs.com. Website: www. castleberryfairs.com. Art & craft show held annually in November. Indoors. Accepts handmade crafts and other mediums. Juried. Number exhibitors: see website. Number attendees: varies. Admission: $7 adults; children 12 & under free. Apply online.

ADDITIONAL INFORMATION Deadline for entry: see website. Application fee: see website. Space fee: $350 (10×6); $450 (10×10). Exhibition space: 10×6; 10×10. For more information, artists should e-mail, call, or visit website.

CRAFT ALASKA ARTS AND CRAFTS SHOW

Website: www.yelp.com/events/anchorage-craft-alaska-arts-and-crafts-show. CraftAlaska features live entertainment and dozens of Alaska-made arts and crafts vendors.

CRAFTAPALOOZA & FABULOUS VINTAGE MARKET-ABILENE

E-mail: montagefestivals@earthlink.net. Website: www.montagefestivals.com. Arts & Crafts show held twice a year (see website for dates). Indoors. Accepts handmade crafts, artisan designs, antique & vintage, home decor & inspiration, and more. Exhibitors: varies. Number of attendees: varies. Admission: $3 adults; under 12 free. Apply via website.
ADDITIONAL INFORMATION Deadline for entry: see website. Application fee: see website. Space fee: $95 (10×10); $165 (10×20). Exhibition space: 10×10; 10×20. For more information send e-mail or visit website.

CRAFTAPALOOZA & FABULOUS VINTAGE MARKET-SALINA

E-mail: montagefestivals@earthlink.net. Website: www.montagefestivals.com. Arts & Crafts show held in March. Indoors. Accepts handmade crafts, artisan designs, antique & vintage, home decor & inspiration, and more. Exhibitors: varies. Number of attendees: varies. Admission: $3 adults; under 12 free. Apply via website.
ADDITIONAL INFORMATION Deadline for entry: see website. Application fee: see website. Space fee: $70 (10×10); $105 (10×20). Exhibition space: 10×10, 10×20. For more information send e-mail or visit website.

CRAFTAPALOOZA & FABULOUS VINTAGE MARKET-WICHITA

E-mail: montagefestivals@earthlink.net. Website: www.montagefestivals.com. Arts & Crafts show held twice a year (see website for dates). Indoors. Accepts handmade crafts, artisan designs, antique & vintage, home decor & inspiration, and more. Exhibitors: varies. Number of attendees: varies. Admission: $3 adults; under 12 free. Apply via website.
ADDITIONAL INFORMATION Deadline for entry: see website. Application fee: see website. Space fee: $95 (8×10); $165 (8×20). Exhibition space: 8×10; 8×20. For more information send e-mail or visit website.

CRAFTBOSTON

The Society of Arts & Crafts, 175 Newbury St., Boston MA 02116. (617)266-1810. Fax: (617)266-5654. E-mail: show@craftboston.org. Website: www.societyofcrafts.org. "Presented by The Society of Arts and Crafts, CraftBoston Spring and Holiday are New England's premiere juried exhibitions and sales of contemporary craft. This twice annual, well-established show features the most outstanding artists of our time, showcasing one-of-a-kind and limited-edition pieces in baskets, ceramics, decorative fiber, wearables, furniture, glass, jewelry, leather, metal, mixed media, paper, and wood."

CRAFT FAIR OF THE SOUTHERN HIGHLANDS

Website: www.southernhighlandguild.org. Nearly 200 juried artists of the Southern Highland Craft Guild will be selling works of clay, metal, wood, jewelry, fiber, paper, natural materials, leather, and mixed media. With styles ranging from traditional to contemporary, the Fairs showcase the rich talent, diversity, and craft mastery of Guild members.

CRAFT LAKE CITY DIY FESTIVAL

351 Pierpont Ave., 4B, Salt Lake City UT 84101. (801)487-9221. Fax: (801)487-1359. Website: www.craftlakecity.com. Fine arts & crafts fair held annually in June. Outdoors. Accepts handmade crafts and other mediums. Exhibitors: 200. Number of attendees: see website. Admission: Free to public. Apply online.
ADDITIONAL INFORMATION Deadline for entry: early May. Application fee: $15. Space fee: varies. Exhibition space: varies. For more information, artists should visit website or call.

CRAFTLAND

235 Westminster St., Providence RI 02903. (401)272-4285. E-mail: info@craftlandshop.com. Website: www.craftlandshop.com/pages/show. Craftland Show is an annual holiday craft show featuring the work of 170 artists from Rhode Island and nationwide. It celebrates all kinds of handmade objects and the people who make them.

CRAFTOBERFEST

E-mail: chelsiehellige@gmail.com. Website: www.craftoberfest.com. "Craftoberfest is St. Louis's first lantern-lit outdoor night market featuring local beer, live music, and some of the best handmade & vintage finds our fair city has to offer."

CRAFTS AT MOLAND HOUSE

1641 Old York Rd., Warminster/Hartsville PA 18974. (215)850-1888. E-mail: frommyhand@gmail.com. Website: www.craftsatmolandhouse.com. Contact: Gwyn Duffy, event coordinator. Estab. 2010. Arts & crafts show held biannually in March & November. Indoors. Accepts handmade crafts. Juried. Exhibitors: 55. Number of attendees: 5,000. Admission: $1. E-mail for application.

ADDITIONAL INFORMATION Deadline for entry: rolling. Application fee: $50. Space fee: 25% of sales. Exhibition space: varies. For more information e-mail or visit website.

CRAFTS IN THE BARN

4130 Thistlewood Rd., Hatboro PA 19040. (215)850-1888. E-mail: frommyhand@gmail.com. Website: www.craftsinthebarn.com. Contact: Gwyn Duffy, show coordinator. Estab. 1985. Arts & crafts show held biannually in May & October. Indoors. Accepts handmade crafts. Exhibitors: 75. Number of attendees: 6,000. Free to the public. E-mail for application.

ADDITIONAL INFORMATION Deadline for entry: rolling. Application fee: $50. Space fee: 25% of sales. Exhibition space: varies. For more information e-mail or visit website.

CRAFTY BASTARDS ARTS & CRAFTS FAIR

E-mail: craftybastards@washingtoncitypaper.com. Website: www.washingtoncitypaper.com/craftybastards. Crafty Bastards Arts & Crafts Fair is an exhibition and sale of handmade goods from independent artists presented by the *Washington City Paper*. Crafty Bastards is held outdoors at Union Market and features 175+ vendors.

CRAFTY SUPERMARKET

Cincinnati OH. E-mail: craftysupermarket@gmail.com. Website: www.craftysupermarket.com. Contact: Chris Salley Davis & Grace Dobush, co-organizers. Estab. 2009. Semiannual indie arts & crafts show held late April & late November. Indoors. Accepts handmade crafts, art & design, occasionally accepts edible gifts. Juried. Exhibitors: spring show 50; holiday show 90. Number of attendees: spring show, 2,000; holiday show 4,000. Free to public. Apply online.

ADDITIONAL INFORMATION Deadline for entry: check website. Application fee: $10. Space fee: $100 (spring); $140 (holiday). Exhibition space: varies. For more information see website.

TIPS "Our shows are very competitive (usually less than a quarter of applications are accepted), but we aim to make sure at least a third of the vendors at each show are new to us. We draw modern artists, crafters, and designers from all over the Eastern US and bring in shoppers from Ohio, Indiana, Kentucky, and beyond. Attend one of our shows or check out the lists of past vendors on our website to get an understanding of our style. We're a modern indie craft show with a serious eye for design."

CRAFTY WONDERLAND

E-mail: craftywonderland@yahoo.com. Website: www.craftywonderland.com. "Crafty Wonderland is the place to go to find the best handmade goods in the NW, as well as affordable work from talented visual artists. It's an event meant to bring together crafty people with those who appreciate cool handmade items, to support artists, and to spread the joy of craft throughout our community. The show even offers a kids' area where budding young artists can set up and sell their work! Each Crafty Wonderland features a free DIY area where local artists share their talent and teach visitors how to make a craft of their own to take home."

CREATIVE HAND

E-mail: info@creativehandkc.org. Website: www.creativehandkc.org. "Handcrafted fiber show sponsored by the Kansas City Fiber Guild and the Kansas City Weavers Guild. Artists from both groups come together for the Creative Hand Show and Sale. The show is both exhibition and sale of art-to-wear that members of both groups have created by hand."

CRESTED BUTTE ARTS FESTIVAL

P.O. Box 324, Crested Butte CO 81224. (970)349-1184. E-mail: juliette@crestedbutteartsfestival.com. Website: www.crestedbutteartsfestival.com. Estab. 1972. The Crested Butte Arts Festival, Crested Butte's signature cultural event and one of Colorado's top 5 fine art and fine craft shows, features 175 well-known, established artists from around the world and is recognized as a top-quality, juried show. See website for more information.

CROCKER PARK FINE ART FAIR
WITH CRAFT MARKETPLACE

270 Central Blvd., Suite 107B, Jupiter FL 33458. (561)746-6615. Fax: (561)746-6528. E-mail: info@artfestival.com. Website: www.artfestival.com. Contact: Malinda Ratliff, communications officer. Estab. 2006. Fine art & craft fair held annually in mid-June. Outdoors. Accepts photography, jewelry, mixed media, sculpture, wood, ceramic, glass, painting, digital, fiber, metal. Juried. Number exhibitors: 125. Number attendees: 50,000. Free to public. Apply online via www.zapplication.org. Deadline: see website. Application fee: $25. Space fee: $395. Exhibition space: 10×10 and 10×20. For more information, artists should e-mail, call, or visit website. Fair located in Crocker Park in Westlake/Cleveland, OH.

TIPS "You have to start somewhere. First, assess where you are, and what you'll need to get things off the ground. Next, make a plan of action. Outdoor street art shows are a great way to begin your career and lifetime as a working artist. You'll meet a lot of other artists who have been where you are now. Network with them!"

CROSBY FESTIVAL OF THE ARTS

(419)536-5588. E-mail: info@toledogarden.org. Website: www.toledogarden.org. Fine arts & crafts fair held annually in June. Outdoors. Accepts handmade crafts and other mediums. Exhibitors: 200. Number of attendees: see website. Admission: $8, general admission; Free Toledo Botanical Gardens Members, children 12 & under. Apply via Zapplication.org.

ADDITIONAL INFORMATION Deadline for entry: late February. Application fee: $25. Space fee: varies. Exhibition space: 10×10, $250 (standard); 10×10, $400 (corner); 10×20, $500 (double); 10×20, $650 (corner). For more information, artists should visit website or call.

CUSTER'S LAST STAND
FESTIVAL OF THE ARTS

P.O. Box 6013, Evanston IL 60204. (847)328-2204. E-mail: office@custerfair.com. Website: www.custerfair.com. Fine arts & crafts fair held annually in June. Outdoors. Accepts handmade crafts and other mediums. Exhibitors: 350. Number of attendees: 70,000. Admission: Free to public. Apply online.

ADDITIONAL INFORMATION Deadline for entry: mid-May. Application fee: $10. Space fee: varies. Exhibition space: varies. For more information, artists should visit website or call.

DELAND OUTDOOR ART FESTIVAL

E-mail: delandoutdoorartfestival@cfl.rr.com. Website: www.delandoutdoorartfest.com. "This annual festival is held in March. Admission is free. Fine artists from throughout the Southeast will be competing for thousands of dollars in cash prizes and awards. The DOAF attracts 95 juried artists and 70 traditional crafters. The festival offers a craft section with items for sale ranging from handmade jewelry, carved wooden toys to Adirondack lawn furniture. More than 5,000 spectators visit the festival." Appy online. For more information contact Martie Cox (386-736-7855) or Patty Clausen (386-717-1888).

DELRAY MARKETPLACE
ART & CRAFT FESTIVAL

270 Central Blvd., Suite 107B, Jupiter FL 33458. (561)746-6615. Fax: (561)746-6528. E-mail: info@artfestival.com. Website: www.artfestival.com. Contact: Malinda Ratliff, communications manager. Estab. 2013. Fine art & craft fair held annually in November. Outdoors. Accepts photography, jewelry, mixed media, sculpture, wood, ceramic, glass, painting, digital, fiber, metal. Juried. Number exhibitors: 100. Number attendees: 40,000. Free to public. Apply online via www.zapplication.org. Deadline: see website. Application fee: $25. Space fee: $350. Exhibi-

tion space: 10×10 and 10×20. For more information, artists should e-mail, call, or visit website. Festival located at Delray Marketplace off West Atlantic Ave. in Delray Beach, FL.

TIPS "You have to start somewhere. First, assess where you are, and what you'll need to get things off the ground. Next, make a plan of action. Outdoor street art shows are a great way to begin your career and lifetime as a working artist. You'll meet a lot of other artists who have been where you are now. Network with them!"

DES MOINES ARTS FESTIVAL

601 Locust St., Suite 700, Des Moines IA 50309. (951)735-4751. Website: www.desmoinesartsfestival. org. "The Des Moines Arts Festival features the nation's top professional artists and emerging Iowa artists in a juried exhibition of artwork in a variety of mediums. Providing guests with the unique opportunity to meet artists from around the world and purchase their artwork, the Des Moines Arts Festival has become a signature event for the community."

DETROIT LAKE STREET FESTIVAL

Central Oregon Shows, P.O. Box 1555, Sisters OR 97759. (541)420-0279. E-mail: centraloregonshows@ gmail.com. Website: www.centraloregonshows.com. "Detroit Lake is a resort area which attracts thousands of visitors year after year. There will be a variety of arts, crafts, antiques, food, and entertainment with a special fundraiser benefiting the local Fire Department." See website for more information.

DETROIT URBAN CRAFT FAIR

E-mail: vendors@detroiturbancraftfair.com. Website: www.detroiturbancraftfair.com. "The Detroit Urban Craft Fair (DUCF) is a 2-day alternative craft fair held annually in the city of Detroit. The fair features 100 handmade crafters and indie artists. DUCF is a community market that encourages the interaction of maker and buyer. It is unique opportunity for shoppers to find one-of-a-kind items and meet the people who made them. Participating crafters have the chance to connect with a large, supportive audience. The Detroit Urban Craft Fair's mission is to elevate handmade goods as an alternative to mass-produced

items, support and elevate small craft business by providing a place for them to sell during the busy holiday shopping season, and raise awareness of handmade craft." See website for more information.

DICKENS HOLIDAY CRAFTS FAIR

Finley Community Center, Attn: Crafts Fair, 2060 W. College Avenue, Santa Rosa CA 95401. (707)543-3755. E-mail: craftsfair@srcity.org. Website: www.http:// ci.santa-rosa.ca.us/departments/recreationandparks/ programs/specialevents/craftfair/Pages/default.aspx. Craft fair held annually in December. Indoors. Accepts handmade crafts. Exhibitors: 70. Number of attendees: see website. Admission: $2; children 12 & under free. Apply online.

ADDITIONAL INFORMATION Deadline for entry: July. Application fee: $25. Space fee: varies. Exhibition space: varies. For more information, artists should visit website or call.

DILLON ART FESTIVAL

CCM Events, 4214 E. Colfax Ave., Denver CO 80220. (720)941-6088. Website: www.summitcountyartfestival.com. Fine arts & crafts fair held annually in July. Outdoors. Accepts handmade crafts and other mediums. Exhibitors: see website. Number of attendees: see website. Admission: Free to public. Apply online.

ADDITIONAL INFORMATION Deadline for entry: mid-April. Application fee: $35. Space fee: see website. Exhibition space: see website. For more information, artists should visit website or call.

DIYPSI - AN INDIE ART FAIR

Website: www.diypsi.com. Indie art fair. See website for more information and to apply.

DIY STREET FAIR

E-mail: info@diystreetfair.com. Website: www.diystreetfair.com. "The DIY Street Fair is a free 2-day, 3-night event in Ferndale, Michigan, where local artists, crafters, businesses, groups and organizations, musicians, restaurants, food trucks, brewers, and others whose lives and work adhere to do-it-yourself ethic converge for one big celebration. The event, which launched its first weekend fair in 2008, showcases the immense creative energy, independent spirit, and innovative talent that can be found throughout the area. Open to the public, free to attend, and all are welcome." See website for more information and to apply.

DOLLAR BANK THREE RIVERS ARTS FESTIVAL

803 Liberty Ave., Pittsburgh PA 15222. (412)471-6070. E-mail: trafmarket@trustarts.org. Website: www.trustarts.org/traf. Contact: Melissa Franko, artist market manager. Estab. 1960. Fine art show held annually in June. Outdoors. Accepts fine art & handmade crafts, photography, clay, ceramics, fiber, paintings, furniture, wood, metal, leather, mixed media, jewelry, glass, sculpture, drawing, digital art, printmaking. Juried. Awards/prizes: $10,000 in awards/prizes given away. Exhibitors: 360. Number of attendees: 600,000. Free to public. Artists should apply via Zapplication.org.

ADDITIONAL INFORMATION Deadline for entry: February 1. Application fee: $35. Space fee: $360-485. Exhibition space: 10×10. For more information, artists should visit website.

TIPS "The only way to participate is to apply!"

DOWNTOWN ASPEN ART FESTIVAL

270 Central Blvd., Suite 107B, Jupiter FL 33458. (561)746-6615. Fax: (561)746-6528. E-mail: info@artfestival.com. Website: www.artfestival.com. Contact: Malinda Ratliff, communications manager. Estab. 2003. Fine art & craft fair held annually in July. Outdoors. Accepts photography, jewelry, mixed media, sculpture, wood, ceramic, glass, painting, digital, fiber, metal. Juried. Number exhibitors: 150. Number attendees: 80,000. Free to public. Apply online via www.wzapplication.org. Deadline: see website. Application fee: $35. Space fee: $475. Exhibition space: 10×10 and 10×20. For more information, artists should e-mail, call, or visit website. Festival located at Monarch Street in Aspen, CO.

TIPS "You have to start somewhere. First, assess where you are, and what you'll need to get things off the ground. Next, make a plan of action. Outdoor street art shows are a great way to begin your career and lifetime as a working artist. You'll meet a lot of other artists who have been where you are now. Network with them!"

DOWNTOWN DELRAY BEACH FESTIVAL OF THE ARTS

207 Central Blvd., Suite 107B, Jupiter FL 33458. (561)746-6615. Fax: (561)746-6528. E-mail: info@artfestival.com. Website: www.artfestival.com. Contact: Malinda Ratliff, communications manager. Estab. 2000. Fine art & craft fair held annually in mid-January. Outdoors. Accepts photography, jewelry, mixed media, sculpture, wood, ceramic, glass, painting, digital, fiber, metal. Juried. Number exhibitors: 305. Number attendees: 100,000. Free to public. Apply online via www.zapplication.org. Deadline: see website. Application fee: $25. Space fee: $395. Exhibition space: 10×10 and 10×20. For more information, artists should e-mail, call or visit website. Festival located at Atlantic Ave. in downtown Delray Beach, FL.

TIPS "You have to start somewhere. First, assess where you are, and what you'll need to get things off the ground. Next, make a plan of action. Outdoor street art shows are a great way to begin your career and lifetime as a working artist. You'll meet a lot of other artists who have been where you are now. Network with them!"

DOWNTOWN DELRAY BEACH THANKSGIVING WEEKEND ART FESTIVAL

207 Central Blvd., Suite 107B, Jupiter FL 33458. (561)746-6615. Fax: (561)746-6528. E-mail: info@artfestival.com. Website: www.artfestival.com. Contact: Malinda Ratliff, communications manager. Estab. 2000. Fine art & craft fair held annually in November. Outdoors. Accepts photography, jewelry, mixed media, sculpture, wood, ceramic, glass, painting, digital, fiber, metal. Juried. Number exhibitors: 150. Number attendees: 80,000. Free to public. Apply online via www.zapplication.org. Deadline: see website. Application fee: $25. Space fee: $395. Exhibition space: 10×10 and 10×20. For more information, artists should e-mail, call, or visit website. Festival located at 4th Ave. & Atlantic Ave. in downtown Delray Beach, FL.

TIPS "You have to start somewhere. First, assess where you are, and what you'll need to get things off the ground. Next, make a plan of action. Outdoor street art shows are a great way to begin your career and lifetime as a working artist. You'll meet a lot of other artists who have been where you are now. Network with them!"

DOWNTOWN DOWNERS GROVE FESTIVAL

Downers Grove Downtown Management Corp., Attn: Fine Arts Festival, 933A Curtiss St., Downers Grove IL 60515. (630)725-0991. Website: www.juriedartservices.com/index.php?content=event_info&event_id=903. Fine arts & crafts fair held annually in September. Outdoors. Accepts handmade crafts and other mediums. Exhibitors: see website. Number of attendees: 10,000. Admission: Free to public. Apply online. **ADDITIONAL INFORMATION** Deadline for entry: mid-March. Application fee: $20. Space fee: $200 (single); $400 (double). Exhibition space: 10×10 (single); 10×20 (double). For more information, artists should visit website or call.

DOWNTOWN DOWNERS GROVE FESTIVAL (ILLINOIS)

Amdur Productions, P.O. Box 550, Highland Park IL 60035. (847)926-4300. Fax: (847)926-4330. E-mail: info@amdurproductions.com. Website: www.amdurproductions.com. Art & craft show held annually in September. Outdoors. Accepts handmade crafts and other mediums. Juried. Awards/prizes: given at festival. Number exhibitors: 100. Number attendees: 30,000. Free to public. Apply online. **ADDITIONAL INFORMATION** Deadline for entry: early January. Application fee: $20. Space fee: $335. Exhibition space: 10×10. For more information, artists should e-mail, call, or visit website.

DOWNTOWN DUNEDIN ART FESTIVAL

270 Central Blvd., Suite 107B, Jupiter FL 33458. (561)746-6615. Fax: (561)746-6528. E-mail: info@artfestival.com. Website: www.arfestival.com. Contact: Malinda Ratliff, communications manager. Estab. 1997. Fine art & craft fair held annually in January. Outdoors. Accepts photography, jewelry, mixed media, sculpture, wood, ceramic, glass, painting, digital, fiber, metal. Juried. Number exhibitors: 130. Number attendees: 40,000. Free to public. Apply online via www.zapplication.org. Deadline: see website. Application fee: $25. Space fee: $395. Exhibition space: 10×10 and 10×20. For more information, artists should e-mail, call, or visit website. Festival located at Main St. in downtown Dunedin, FL.
TIPS "You have to start somewhere. First, assess where you are, and what you'll need to get things off the ground. Next, make a plan of action. Outdoor street art shows are a great way to begin your career and lifetime as a working artist. You'll meet a lot of other artists who have been where you are now. Network with them!"

DOWNTOWN DUNEDIN CRAFT FESTIVAL

270 Central Blvd., Suite 107B, Jupiter FL 33458. (561)746-6615. Fax: (561)746-6528. E-mail: info@ArtFestival.com. Website: www.artfestival.com. "If Tampa is on your travel agenda this June, you can't miss out on this terrific craft event in the city's most desirable suburb of Dunedin. It is here, a short drive from Tampa, along Dunedin's Main Street, you will meet some of the country's finest crafters with products all handmade in the U.S.A. Botanical hotplates, ceramic planters, functional pottery, hair accessories, handmade one-of-a-kind jewelry pieces, and an expansive Green Market offer something for every taste & budget."

DOWNTOWN FESTIVAL AND ART SHOW

302 NE Sixth Ave., Gainesville FL 32601. (352)393-8536. Fax: (352)334-2249. E-mail: piperlr@cityofgainesville.org. Website: www.gvlculturalaffairs.org. Contact: Linda Piper, events coordinator. Estab. 1981. Fine art show held annually in November. Outdoors. Accepts handmade crafts and fine art. Juried. Awards/prizes: $16,700 in cash awards. Exhibitors: 240. Number of attendees: 100,000. Free to public. Apply online . **ADDITIONAL INFORMATION** Deadline for entry: May 4. Application fee: $23.50. Space fee: $272. Exhibition space: 12×12. Average sales: $5,000. For more information, send e-mail.

DOWNTOWN SARASOTA CRAFT FAIR

270 Central Blvd., Suite 107B, Jupiter FL 33458. (561)746-6615. Fax: (561)746-6528. E-mail: info@ArtFestival.com. Website: www.artfestival.com. Contact: Malinda Ratliff, communications manager. "This popular annual craft festival has garnered crowds of fine craft lovers each year. Behold contemporary crafts from more than 100 of the nation's most talented artisans. A variety of jewelry, pottery, ceramics, photography, painting, clothing, and much more—all handmade in America—will be on display, ranging from $15 to $3,000. An expansive Green Market with plants, or-

chids, exotic flora, handmade soaps, gourmet spices, and freshly popped kettle corn further complements the weekend, blending nature with nurture."

DOWNTOWN SARASOTA FESTIVAL OF THE ARTS

270 Central Blvd., Suite 107B, Jupiter FL 33458. (561)746-6615. Fax: (561)746-6528. E-mail: info@ artfestival.com. Website: www.artfestival.com. Fine art & craft fair held annually in mid-February. Outdoors. Accepts photography, jewelry, mixed media, sculpture, wood, ceramic, glass, painting, digital, fiber, metal. Juried. Number exhibitors: 305. Number attendees: 80,000. Free to public. Apply online via zapplication.org. Deadline: see website. Application fee: $25. Space fee: $395. Exhibition space: 10×10 and 10×20. For more information, artists should e-mail, call or visit website. Festival located at Main St. at Orange Ave. heading east and ending at Links Ave. in Downtown Sarasota FL.

TIPS "You have to start somewhere. First, assess where you are, and what you'll need to get things off the ground. Next, make a plan of action. Outdoor street art shows are a great way to begin your career and lifetime as a working artist. You'll meet a lot of other artists who have been where you are now. Network with them!"

DOWNTOWN STEAMBOAT SPRINGS ART FESTIVAL ON YAMPA STREET, THE YAMPA ART STROLL

270 Central Blvd., Suite 107B, Jupiter FL 33458. (561)746-6615. Fax: (561)746-6528. E-mail: info@ artfestival.com. Website: www.artfestival.com. Contact: Malinda Ratliff, communications manager. Estab. 2015. Fine art & craft fair held annually in August. Outdoors. Accepts photography, jewelry, mixed media, sculpture, wood, ceramic, glass, painting, digital, fiber, metal. Juried. Number exhibitors: see website. Number attendees: see website. Free to public. Apply online via www.zapplication.org. Deadline: see website. Application fee: $35. Space fee: $350. Exhibition space: 10×10 and 10×20. For more information, artists should e-mail, call, or visit website. Festival located at Yampa Ave. in Steamboat Springs CO.

TIPS "You have to start somewhere. First, assess where you are, and what you'll need to get things off the

ground. Next, make a plan of action. Outdoor street art shows are a great way to begin your career and lifetime as a working artist. You'll meet a lot of other artists who have been where you are now. Network with them!"

DOWNTOWN STUART ART FESTIVAL

270 Central Blvd., Suite 107B, Jupiter FL 34458. (561)746-6615. Fax: (561)746-6528. E-mail: info@ artfestival.com. Website: www.artfestival.com. Contact: Malinda Ratliff, communications manager. Estab. 1991. Fine art & craft fair held annually in February. Outdoors. Accepts photography, jewelry, mixed media, sculpture, wood, ceramic, glass, painting, digital, fiber, metal. Juried. Number exhibitors: 200. Number attendees: 50,000. Free to public. Apply online via www.zapplication.org. Deadline: see website. Application fee: $25. Space fee: $395. Exhibition space: 10×10 and 10×20. For more information, artists should e-mail, call, or visit website. Festival located at Osceola St. in Stuart FL.

TIPS "You have to start somewhere. First, assess where you are, and what you'll need to get things off the ground. Next, make a plan of action. Outdoor street art shows are a great way to begin your career and lifetime as a working artist. You'll meet a lot of other artists who have been where you are now. Network with them!"

DOWNTOWN VENICE ART FESTIVAL

270 Central Blvd., Suite 107B, Jupiter FL 33458. (561)746-6615. Fax: (561)746-6528. E-mail: info@art-festival.com. Website: www.artfestival.com. Contact: Malinda Ratliff, communications manager. Estab. 1987. Fine art & craft fair held semiannually in early March & mid-November. Outdoors. Accepts photography, jewelry, mixed media, sculpture, wood, ceramic, glass, painting, digital, fiber, metal. Juried. Number exhibitors: 130-200. Number attendees: 50,000. Free to public. Apply online via www.zapplication. org. Deadline: see website. Application fee: $25. Space fee: $350-395. Exhibition space: 10×10 and 10×20. For more information, artists should e-mail, call, or visit website. Festival located at W. Venice Ave. in downtown Venice, FL.

TIPS "You have to start somewhere. First, assess where you are, and what you'll need to get things off the ground. Next, make a plan of action. Outdoor street art shows are a great way to begin your career and lifetime as a working artist. You'll meet a lot of other artists who have been where you are now. Network with them!"

DOYLESTOWN ARTS FESTIVAL

E-mail: info@doylestownalliance.org. Website: www. doylestownartsfestival.com. "This 2-day festival is the largest event of the year in the heart of beautiful Doylestown Borough in Bucks County, PA. This annual festival has grown to include more than 160 exhibitors and a food court. Diverse activities are available at numerous locations throughout the downtown area. Live music features solo acts as well as rock, pop, folk, big band, and music for kids. The festival is a free event for the community."

DRIFTLESS AREA ART FESTIVAL

E-mail: info@driftlessareaartfestival.com. Website: www.driftlessareaartfestival.com. The Driftless Area Art Festival celebrates the visual, performing, and culinary arts of the Driftless Area.

DUBUQUEFEST FINE ARTS FESTIVAL

DubuqueFest Arts Festival, c/o Paula Neuhaus, 8 Lindberg Terrace, Dubuque IA 52001. (563)564-5290. E-mail: paula@dubuquefest.org. Website: www. dubuquefest.org. Contact: Paula Neuhaus, art fair director. Estab. 1977. Fine arts & crafts fair held annually in May. Outdoors. Accepts handmade crafts and other mediums. Juried. Awards/prizes: 1st place, 2nd place, 3rd place. Exhibitors: 70. Number of attendees: varies. Admission: Free to public. Apply online.

ADDITIONAL INFORMATION Deadline for entry: see website. Application fee: $15. Space fee: $110. Exhibition space: 12×12. For more information, artists should e-mail, visit website, or call.

EAGLE RIVER WATERMELON DAYS CRAFT & GIFT FESTIVAL

705 Bugbee Ave., Wausau WI 54401. (715)675-6201. Fax: (715)675-7649. E-mail: mmccallin@charter.net. Website: www.macproductionllc.com. Contact: Mac & Bonnie McCallin. Fine arts & crafts fair held annually in July. Outdoors. Accepts handmade crafts

and other mediums. Juried. Exhibitors: see website. Number of attendees: varies. Admission: Free to public. Apply online.

ADDITIONAL INFORMATION Deadline for entry: see website. Application fee: see website. Space fee: varies. Exhibition space: 12×10. For more information, artists should e-mail, visit website or call.

EAST LANSING ART FESTIVAL

410 Abbot Rd., East Lansing MI 48823. (517)319-6804. E-mail: info@elartfest.com. Website: www.elartfest. com. Contact: Michelle Carlson, festival director. Estab. 1963. Fine arts & crafts fair held annually in May. Outdoors. Accepts handmade crafts and other mediums. Juried. Awards/prizes: over $5,500 in cash awards. Exhibitors: see website. Number of attendees: varies. Admission: Free to public. Apply online.

ADDITIONAL INFORMATION Deadline for entry: November. Application fee: $25. Space fee: $300 (single); $600 (double). Exhibition space: 10×10 (single); 10×20 (double). For more information, artists should e-mail, visit website, or call.

EASTON ART AFFAIR

(330)284-1082. Fax: (330)494-0578. E-mail: bhuff@ eastonartaffair.com. Website: www.eastonartaffair. com. Contact: Barb Huff. Estab. 1999. Fine arts & crafts fair held annually in June. Outdoors. Accepts handmade crafts, ceramics, digital art, drawing, glass, jewelry, metalwork, mixed media, painting, photography, printmaking & graphics, sculpture, wearable art, wood. Juried. Awards/prizes: Best of Show, Honorable Mention. Exhibitors: 105. Number of attendees: varies. Admission: Free to public. Apply via Zapplication.org.

ADDITIONAL INFORMATION Deadline for entry: March 1. Application fee: $25. Space fee: $300 (single); $600 (double). Exhibition space: 10×10 (single); 10×20 (double). For more information, artists should e-mail, visit website, or call.

ECHO PARK CRAFT FAIR

Website: www.echoparkcraftfair.com. "The EPCF is a biannual design event in Silver Lake featuring over 70 artists and designers. Beatrice Valenzuela and Rachel Craven founded the Echo Park Craft Fair (EPCF) in

2009. The pair visualized a space that would showcase and nurture the many talented artisans, designers, and craftspeople living in their inspired community on the east side of Los Angeles. Originally held in Valenzuela's backyard featuring just a handful of friends, The Echo Park Craft Fair has grown into a highly anticipated biannual arts event, attracting thousands of visitors from around Los Angeles...and beyond."

EDINA ART FAIR

(952)922-1524. Fax: (952)922-4413. Website: www.edinaartfair.com. Fine arts & crafts fair held annually in June. Outdoors. Accepts handmade crafts, ceramics, enamel, fiber, glass, jewelry, mixed media, photography, sculpture, wearable art, wood. Juried. Awards/prizes: Best of Show, Best Display, Awards of Excellence, Merit Awards. Number exhibitors: 300. Number attendees: 165,000. Free to public. Apply online.

ADDITIONAL INFORMATION Deadline for entry: February. Application fee: $35. Space fee: $425 (single); $850 (double). Exhibition space: 10×10 (single); 10×20 (double). For more information, artists should visit website, or call.

EDMOND QUILT FESTIVAL

(405)348-2233. E-mail: wonderland48@cox.net. Website: www.edmondquiltguild.us. Contact: Alice Kellog. Quilt show held annually in July. Indoors. Accepts handmade quilts. Entry only open to Edmond Quilt Guild members. Juried. Awards/prizes: Founder's Award, Best Hand Quilting, Best of Show, Judges' Choice, Viewers' Choice. Number exhibitors: see website. Number attendees: see website. Free to public. Apply online.

ADDITIONAL INFORMATION Deadline for entry: mid-July. Application fee: see website. Space fee: see website. Exhibition space: see website. For more information, artists should e-mail, visit website, or call.

ELK RIVER ARENA'S FALL CRAFT SHOW

1000 School St., Elk River MN 55330. (763)635 1145. Fax: (763)635-1144. E-mail: lestby@elkrivermn.gov. Website: www.elkriverarena.com. Contact: Laura Estby, office assistant. Estab. 1997. Annual fine arts & crafts show held mid-September. Indoors & outdoors. Accepts handmade crafts, paintings, ceramics, pho-

tography, woodwork. Juried. Exhibitors: 85+. Number of attendees: 1,500. Free to public.

ADDITIONAL INFORMATION Deadline for entry: until filled. Space fee: $53-78. Exhibition space: 90-126 sq. ft. For more information e-mail or see website.

TIPS "Be pleasant to customers; have unique items that are well crafted!"

ELK RIVER ARENA'S SPRING CRAFT SHOW

1000 School St., Elk River MN 55330. (763)635-1145. Fax: (763)635-1144. E-mail: lestby@elkrivermn.gov. Website: www.elkriverarena.com. Contact: Laura Estby, office assistant. Estab. 1990. Annual fine arts & crafts show held early May. Indoors. Accepts handmade crafts, paintings, ceramics, photography, upcycled items. Juried. Exhibitors: 85+. Number of attendees: 1,200. Free to public. Apply online at elkriverarena.com.

ADDITIONAL INFORMATION Deadline for entry: until filled. Space fee: $50-75. Exhibition space: 90-126 sq. ft. For more information e-mail or see website.

TIPS "Be pleasant to customers; have unique items that are well crafted!"

ESSEX FALL CRAFT SHOW

P.O. Box 8139, Essex VT 05451. (802)879-6837. E-mail: info@vtcrafts.com. Website: www.vtcrafts.com. Contact: Kathy Rose, owner. Estab. 1981. Arts & crafts show held annually in October. Indoors. Accepts fine art & handmade crafts. Exhibitors: 200. Number of attendees: 10,000. Admission: $8. Artists should apply via website.

ADDITIONAL INFORMATION Deadline for entry: see website. Application fee: none. Space fee: $525. Exhibition space: 10×10. For more information, artists should visit website.

ESSEX SPRING CRAFT SHOW

P.O. Box 8139, Essex VT 05451. (802)879-6837. E-mail: info@vtcrafts.com. Website: www.vtcrafts.com. Contact: Kathy Rose, owner. Estab. 1997. Arts & crafts show held annually in May. Indoors. Accepts fine art & handmade crafts. Juried. Exhibitors: 120. Number of attendees: 8,000. Admission: $7. Artists should apply via website.

ADDITIONAL INFORMATION Deadline for entry: see website. Application fee: none. Space fee: $350. Exhibition space: 10×10. For more information, artists should visit website.

EVANSTON ART & BIG FORK FESTIVAL

Amdur Productions, P.O. Box 550, Highland Park IL 60035. (847)926-4300. Fax: (847)926-4330. E-mail: info@amdurproductions.com. Website: www.amdur-productions.com. Art & craft show held annually in September. Outdoors. Accepts handmade crafts and other mediums. Juried. Awards/prizes: given at artist breakfast. Number exhibitors: 30. Number attendees: varies. Free to public. Apply online.

ADDITIONAL INFORMATION Deadline for entry: early May. Application fee: $25. Space fee: $430. Exhibition space: 10×10. For more information, artists should e-mail, call, or visit website.

EVANSTON ETHNIC ARTS FAIR

Evanston Cultural Arts Programs, Morton Civic Center, Parks, Recreation & Community Services, 2100 Ridge Ave., Room 1116, Evanston IL 60201. (847)448-8260. Fax: (847)448-8051. E-mail: pbattaglia@cityofevanston.org. Website: www.cityofevanston.org/festivals-concerts/ethnic-arts-festival. Contact: Patricia Battaglia. Estab. 1984. Fine arts & crafts fair held annually in July. Outdoors. Accepts handmade crafts and other media. Juried. Awards/prizes: see website. Number exhibitors: see website. Number attendees: varies. Free to public. Apply online.

ADDITIONAL INFORMATION Deadline for entry: see website. Application fee: see website. Space fee: see website. Exhibition space: see website. For more information, artists should email, visit website, or call.

FALL CRAFT FEST

Ozark Regional Promotions, 5557 Walden St., Lowell AR 72745. (479)756-6954. E-mail: karenlloyd@juno.com. Website: www.ozarkregionalartsandcrafts.com. Art & craft show held annually in October. Indoors. Accepts handmade crafts and other mediums. Juried. Number exhibitors: see website. Number attendees: varies. Free to public. Apply online.

ADDITIONAL INFORMATION Deadline for entry: mid-August. Application fee: none. Space fee: varies.

Exhibition space: varies. For more information, artists should e-mail, call, or visit website.

FALL FESTIVAL OF THE ARTS OAKBROOK CENTER

Amdur Productions, P.O. Box 550, Highland Park IL 60035. (847)926-4300. Fax: (847)926-4330. E-mail: info@amdurproductions.com. Website: www.amdurproductions.com. Estab. 1962. Fine arts & crafts fair held annually in September. Outdoors. Accepts handmade crafts, jewelry, ceramics, painting, photography, digital, printmaking, and more. Juried. Number exhibitors: see website. Number attendees: varies. Admission: Free to public. Apply online.

ADDITIONAL INFORMATION Deadline for entry: see website. Application fee: $25. Space fee: $460. Exhibition space: 10×10. For more information, artists should e-mail, call, or visit website.

FALL FESTIVAL ON PONCE

Olmstead Park, North Druid Hills, 1451 Ponce de Leon, Atlanta GA 30307. (404)873-1222. E-mail: info@affps.com. Website: festivalonponce.com. Contact: Lisa Windle, festival director. Estab. 2010. Arts & crafts show held annually mid-October. Outdoors. Accepts handmade crafts, painting, photography, sculpture, leather, metal, glass, jewelry. Juried by a panel. Awards/prizes: ribbons. Number of exhibitors: 125. Number of attendees: 45,000. Free to public. Apply online at www.zapplication.com.

ADDITIONAL INFORMATION Deadline for entry: August 21. Application fee: $25. Space fee: $275. Exhibition space: 10×10. For more information, e-mail or see website.

TIPS "Offer a variety of price ranges, have a professional setup and display materials, greet guests."

FAUST HERITAGE FESTIVAL

15185 Olive Blvd., St. Louis MO 63017. (314)615-8328. E-mail: lritchey@stlouisco.com. Website: www.stlouisco.com/parks. Contact: Lori Ritchey, museum educator. Historic arts & crafts festival held annually in September. Outdoors. Accepts historic arts & crafts, watercolor, jewelry, wood, floral, baskets, prints, drawing, mixed media, folk art. Must be approved by staff to attend festival. Number exhibitors: 20-30.

Number of attendees: 4,000. Admission: $5 adults; $2 children ages 4-12; 3 & under free. Apply by contacting festival coordinator.

ADDITIONAL INFORMATION Deadline for entry: August. Space fee: 15% of gross sales. Exhibition space: varies; setup must be historically accurate with no plastic tents. For more information, artists should e-mail.

FESTIVAL FETE

Festival Fete, P.O. Box 2552, Newport RI 02840. (401)207-8115. E-mail: pilar@festivalfete.com. Website: www.festivalfete.com. Fine arts & crafts fair held annually in July. Outdoors. Accepts handmade crafts, painting, sculpture, photography, drawing, fabric, crafts, ceramics, glass, and jewelry. Juried. Awards/prizes: see website. Number exhibitors: 150. Number attendees: varies. Free to public. Apply online.

ADDITIONAL INFORMATION Deadline for entry: see website. Application fee: see website. Space fee: $175. Exhibition space: 10×10. For more information, artists should email, visit website, or call.

◐ FESTIVAL FOR THE ENO

(919)620-9099 ext. 203. E-mail: crafts@enoriver.org. Website: www.enoriver.org/festival. "The Festival for the Eno is presented by the Eno River Association to celebrate and preserve the natural, cultural, and historic resources of the Eno River Valley. All participants must recognize that the Festival is a combined effort toward this specific goal. As one of its chief attractions, the Festival features the excellence and diversity of the region's arts and crafts. The Festival is held at West Point on the Eno, a Durham City Park on Roxboro Road, open to residents of the Carolinas, Virginia, Georgia, and Tennessee only, and all items must be the handiwork of the participant, who must be present." See website for more information.

FESTIVAL OF THE VINE

8 S. Third St., Geneva IL 60134. (630)232-6060. Fax: (630)232-6083. E-mail: chamberinfo@genevacham-ber.com. Website: www.genevachamber.com. Contact: Ellen Townsley, volunteer coordinator. Estab. 1981. Arts & crafts show held annually in mid-September. Outdoors. Accepts handmade crafts. Juried.

Exhibitors: 100. Number of attendees: 200,000. Free to public. Apply online.

ADDITIONAL INFORMATION Deadline for entry: June 1. Application fee: none. Space fee: $175. Exhibition space: 10×10. For more information, artists should send e-mail, visit website, or call.

FESTIVAL OF TREES CRAFT & GIFT SHOW

The Family Tree Center, 2520 Fifth Ave. S., Billings MT 59101-4342. (406)252-9799. Fax: (406)256-3014. Website: www.familytreecenterbillings.org. Estab. 1985. "Begun in 1985, the Festival of Trees has become synonymous with the holiday season in Billings. For many residents and visitors, the holidays would not be complete without at least one visit to view the trees or participate in the weekend activities. Each year, the Festival of Trees provides an opportunity for community members to help prevent child abuse and neglect in Yellowstone County and the surrounding area. Donating or buying a tree, sponsoring the event, or participating in one of the many weekend activities during the Festival helps raise money and awareness; both help The Family Tree Center. Over the course of this 4-day event, over 10,000 people pass through the doors to view the unique Holiday Trees and participate in the assortment of activities. All dollars raised at the Festival go where they are needed most—toward the many child abuse prevention programs in place at The Family Tree Center. Referrals are increasing, and the number of families that we serve continues to grow. Now more than ever, the Family Tree Center needs your support." See website for more details.

FIESTA ARTS FAIR

Southwest School of Art, 300 Augusta St., San Antonio TX 78205. (210)224-1848. Fax: (210)224-9337. Website: www.swschool.org/fiestaartsfair. Art & craft market/show held annually in April. Outdoors. Accepts handmade crafts, ceramics, paintings, jewelry, glass, photography, wearable art, and other mediums. Juried. Number exhibitors: 125. Number attendees: 12,000. Admission: $16 weekend pass; $10 daily adult pass; $5 daily children pass; children 5 & under free. Apply via Zapplication.org.

ADDITIONAL INFORMATION Deadline for entry: November. Application fee: none. Space fee: varies.

Exhibition space: varies. For more information, artists should call or visit website.

FINE ART FAIR

Foster Arts Center Building, 203 Harrison St., Peoria IL 61602. (309)637-2787. E-mail: events@peoriaartguild.org. Website: www.peoriaartguild.org. Contact: Special events coordinator. Estab. 1962. Fine arts & crafts fair held annually in September. Outdoors. Accepts handmade crafts, painting, sculpture, photography, drawing, fabric, crafts, ceramics, glass, and jewelry. Juried. Number exhibitors: 150. Number attendees: varies. Admission: $7 adults; children 12 & under free; Peoria Art Guild members free. Apply online.

ADDITIONAL INFORMATION Deadline for entry: see website. Application fee: see website. Space fee: see website. Exhibition space: see website. For more information, artists should email, visit website, or call.

FINE CRAFT SHOW

Memorial Art Gallery of the University of Rochester, 500 University Ave., Rochester NY 14607. (585)276-8900. Fax: (585)473-6266. E-mail: maginfo@mag.rochester.edu. Website: www.mag.rochester.edu/events/fine-craft-show/. Estab. 2000. Fine arts & crafts fair held annually in October. Indoors. Accepts handmade crafts, ceramics, glass, jewelry, metal, leather, wood, wearable art, and more. Juried. Number exhibitors: 40. Number attendees: varies. Admission: $12; $5 college students w/ID. Apply online.

ADDITIONAL INFORMATION Deadline for entry: see website. Application fee: see website. Space fee: see website. Exhibition space: see website. For more information, artists should email, visit website, or call.

FINE CRAFT SHOW AND SALE - MEMORIAL ART GALLERY

500 University Ave., Rochester NY 14607. (585)276-8910. E-mail: smcnamee@mag.rochester.edu. Website: www.magrochester.edu. Contact: Sharon McNamee, gallery council assistant. Estab. 2000. Fine craft show held annually late October/early November. Indoors. Accepts handmade crafts, glass, ceramics, leather, wearables, jewelry, wood, furniture, metal. Juried. Awards/prizes: Best in Show; Award of Excellence (2). Exhibitors: 40. Number of attendees: 2,000. Admission: $10-12. Apply online.

ADDITIONAL INFORMATION Deadline for entry: March 31. Application fee: $35. Space fee: $475. Exhibition space: 10×10. Average sales: $1,500-6,000. For more information, artists should e-mail or visit website.

TIPS "One of a kind or limited edition."

FIREFLY ART FAIR

Wauwatosa Historical Society, 7406 Hillcrest Drive, Wauwatosa WI 53213. (414)774-8672. E-mail: staff@wauwatosahistoricalsociety.org. Website: www.wauwatosahistoricalsociety.org. Estab. 1985. Fine arts & crafts fair held annually in August. Outdoors. Accepts handmade crafts, painting, sculpture, photography, ceramics, jewelry, fiber, printmaking, glass, paper, leather, wood. Juried. Number exhibitors: 150. Number attendees: varies. Free to public. Apply online.

ADDITIONAL INFORMATION Deadline for entry: March. Application fee: $15. Space fee: $140. Exhibition space: 10×10. For more information, artists should email, visit website, or call.

FIREFLY HANDMADE MARKET

Firefly Handmade Markets, P.O. Box 3195, Boulder CO 80307. E-mail: fireflyhandmade@gmail.com. Website: www.fireflyhandmade.com. Estab. 2010. Fine crafts fair held 3 times a year. Outdoors. Accepts handmade crafts. Juried. Number exhibitors: 100. Number attendees: 6,000. Free to public. Apply online.

ADDITIONAL INFORMATION Deadline for entry: May. Application fee: $25. Space fee: varies. Exhibition space: varies. For more information, artists should email or visit website.

FIRST FRIDAY & SATURDAY ON THE RIVER

404 E. Bay St., Savannah GA 31401. (912)234-0295. Fax: (912)234-4904. E-mail: info@riverstreetsavannah.com. Website: www.riverstreetsavannah.com. Contact: Scott Harris, artist relations manager. Arts & crafts show held annually first Friday & Saturday of each month March-December. Outdoors. Accepts handmade crafts. Juried. Exhibitors: 30-50. Number of attendees: 10,000. Free to public.

ADDITIONAL INFORMATION Deadline for entry: early January. Application fee: $15. Space fee: $150-300. Exhibition space: 10×10 (double booth space also available). For more information, artists should e-mail or visit website.

FLINT ART FAIR

(810)695-0604. E-mail: committee@flintartfair.org. Website: www.flintartfair.org. Fine arts & crafts fair held annually in June. Outdoors. Accepts handmade crafts and other mediums. Juried. Number exhibitors: see website. Number attendees: varies. Admission: $5 adults; $3 children 12 & under, seniors, and FOMA members. Apply online.

ADDITIONAL INFORMATION Deadline for entry: see website. Application fee: see website. Space fee: see website. Exhibition space: see website. For more information, artists should email, visit website, or call.

FOUNTAIN HILLS GREAT FAIR

P.O. Box 17598, Fountain Hills AZ 85269. E-mail: sharon@fountainhillschamber.com. Website: www.fountainhillschamber.com/the-great-fair.asp. Contact: Sharon Morgan. "This 3-day juried art fair features nearly 500 artists and artisans from across the United States and around the globe, and attracts 200,000+ visitors. Food booths, beer garden, and seating areas abound throughout the venue, with great breakfast, lunch, and rest stops situated at locations in the middle and at both ends of the festival area. Live musical entertainment." See website for more info.

FREDERICK FESTIVAL OF THE ARTS

11 West Patrick St., Suite 201, Frederick MD 21701. (301)662-4190. E-mail: kris.fair.ffota@gmail.com. Website: www.frederickartscouncil.org. Estab. 1993. Fine arts & crafts fair held annually in June. Outdoors. Accepts handmade crafts, jewelry, photography, painting, glass, wood, metal, drawing, digital, sculpture, fiber, and other forms of mixed media. Juried. Number exhibitors: 110. Number attendees: varies. Free to public. Apply online.

ADDITIONAL INFORMATION Deadline for entry: see website. Application fee: see website. Space fee: see website. Exhibition space: see website. For more information, artists should email, visit website, or call.

FREDERICKSBURG FALL HOME & CRAFTS FESTIVAL

Ballantine Management Group of Virginia, 2371 Carl D. Silver Parkway, Fredericksburg VA 22401. (540)548-5555, ext.108. Fax: (540)548-5577. E-mail: csilversmith@bmg1.com. Website: www.fredericksburgartsandcraftsfaire.com. Contact: Casey Silversmith. Estab. 2006. Handmade-only crafts fair held annually in October. Indoors. Accepts handmade arts & crafts only. Number exhibitors: see website. Number attendees: varies. Admission: $8 at door; $7 online & seniors 60+; children 12 & under free. Apply online.

ADDITIONAL INFORMATION Deadline for entry: see website. Application fee: see website. Space fee: varies. Exhibition space: varies. For more information, artists should email, visit website, or call.

FREDERICKSBURG HOLIDAY CRAFT SHOW

Ballantine Management Group of Virginia, 2371 Carl D. Silver Parkway, Fredericksburg VA 22401. (540)548-5555, ext. 108. Fax: (540)548-5577. E-mail: csilversmith@bmg1.com. Website: www.fredericksburgholidaycraftshow.com. Contact: Casey Silversmith. Estab. 2006. "Check your list and see who has been naughty or nice before you head over to the Holiday Craft Show. The Fredericksburg Holiday Craft Show is the largest Craft Show ever held at the Expo Center. Vendors will showcase one-of-a-kind handmade arts & crafts that will make wonderful gifts for your family, friends, and even your pets. Browse through aisles filled with holiday ornaments, knick-knacks and wreaths, jewelry, soaps and lotions, gourmet foods, glassware, artwork, organic dog treats, clothing, candles, and much more." See website for more information.

FREDERICKSBURG SPRING ARTS & CRAFTS FAIRE

Ballantine Management Group of Virginia, 2371 Carl D. Silver Parkway, Fredericksburg VA 22401. (540)548-5555, ext. 108. Fax: (540)548-5577. E-mail: csilversmith@bmg1.com. Website: www.fredericksburgartsandcraftsfaire.com. Contact: Casey Silversmith. Estab. 2007. Handmade arts & crafts fair held annually in March. Indoors. Accepts handmade crafts and other mediums. Number exhibitors: see website. Number attendees: varies. Admission: $8 at door; $7 online & seniors 60+; children 12 & under free. Apply online.

ADDITIONAL INFORMATION Deadline for entry: see website. Application fee: see website. Space fee: varies. Exhibition space: varies. For more information, artists should email, visit website, or call.

FRIENDS OF THE KENOSHA PUBLIC MUSEUMS ART FAIR

5500 First Ave., Kenosha WI 53140. (262)653-4140. E-mail: pgregorski@kenosha.org. Website: www.kenoshapublicmuseum.org. Contact: Peggy Gregorski, deputy director. Estab. 1964. Fine arts & crafts show held annually 3rd Sunday of July. Indoors & outdoors. Accepts handmade crafts. Juried. Awards/prizes: 5 awards totaling $2,000. Exhibitors: 125. Number of attendees: 7,000. Free to public. Apply online.

ADDITIONAL INFORMATION Deadline for entry: May 1. Application fee: none. Space fee: $125-200. Exhibition space: 10×10 (indoors); 15×15 (outdoors). For more information, artists should send e-mail or visit website.

FUNKY JUNK ROUNDUP

E-mail: montagefestivals@earthlink.net. Website: www.montagefestivals.com. One-day shopping extravaganza held in May. Indoors. Accepts handmade crafts, junktiques, artisan designs, antique & vintage, home decor & inspiration, and more. Exhibitors: varies. Number of attendees: varies. Admission: $3 adults; under 12 free. Apply via website.

ADDITIONAL INFORMATION Deadline for entry: see website. Application fee: see website. Space fee: $95 (10×10); $165 (10×20). Exhibition space: 10×10; 10×20. For more information send e-mail or visit website.

GAITHERSBURG-KENTLANDS DOWNTOWN ART FESTIVAL

270 Central Blvd., Suite 107B, Jupiter FL 33458. (561)746-6615. Fax: (561)746-6528. E-mail: info@artfestival.com. Website: www.artfestival.com. Contact: Malinda Ratliff, communications manager. Estab. 2015. Fine art & craft fair held annually in September. Outdoors. Accepts photography, jewelry, mixed media, sculpture, wood, ceramic, glass, painting, digital, fiber, metal. Juried. Number exhibitors:

see website. Number attendees: see website. Free to public. Apply online via zapplication.org. Deadline: see website. Application fee: $25. Space fee: $450. Exhibition space: 10×10 and 10×20. For more information, artists should e-mail, call, or visit website. Festival located at The Streets of Market and Main at Kentlands Downtown.

TIPS "You have to start somewhere. First, assess where you are, and what you'll need to get things off the ground. Next, make a plan of action. Outdoor street art shows are a great way to begin your career and lifetime as a working artist. You'll meet a lot of other artists who have been where you are now. Network with them!"

GARAGE SALE ART FAIR

E-mail: bonnie@garagesaleartfair.com. Website: www.garagesaleartfair.com. Fine arts & crafts fair held annually in February. Indoors. Accepts handmade crafts and other mediums. Juried. Number exhibitors: 125. Number attendees: 3,500. Free to public. Apply online.

ADDITIONAL INFORMATION Deadline for entry: see website. Application fee: see website. Space fee: varies. Exhibition space: varies. For more information, artists should e-mail or visit website.

GASLIGHT CRAFT FAIR

7010 E. Broadway Blvd., Tucson AZ 85710. (520)886-4116. Fax: (520)722-6232. E-mail: glt@qwestoffice.net. Contact: Teresa, bookkeeper. Estab. 2012. Art & craft show/seasonal/holiday show held every Saturday (weather permitting); Friday-Sunday in November & December. Outdoors. Accepts handmade crafts. Exhibitors: 30. Number of attendees: 300. Free to public. Apply online.

ADDITIONAL INFORMATION Deadline for entry: 1 week before event. Application fee: none. Space fee: $10/space per day; $30 in November & December. Exhibition space: 8×10 (under tent); 12×12 (in parking lot). For more information, artists should send e-mail, call, or visit Facebook page.

GASPARILLA FESTIVAL OF THE ARTS

P.O. Box 10591, Tampa FL 33679. (813)876-1747. E-mail: info@gasparillaarts.com. Website: www.gasparilla-arts.com. Estab. 1970. Fine arts & crafts fair held annually in March. Outdoors. Accepts handmade crafts, ceramic, digital, drawing, fiber, glass, jewelry, mixed media, painting, photography, printmaking, sculpture, watercolor, and wood. Juried. Awards/prizes: $74,500 in cash awards. Number exhibitors: 300. Number attendees: 250,000. Free to public. Apply online.

ADDITIONAL INFORMATION Deadline for entry: September. Application fee: $40. Space fee: $375. Exhibition space: 10×10. For more information, artists should e-mail, visit website, or call.

GATHERING AT THE GREAT DIVIDE

Mountain Art Festivals, P.O. Box 3578, Breckenridge CO 80424. (970)547-9326. E-mail: info@mountain-artfestivals.com. Website: www.mountainartfestivals.com. Estab. 1975. Fine arts & crafts fair held annually in August. Outdoors. Accepts handmade crafts, painting, sculpture, photography, drawing, fabric, crafts, ceramics, glass, and jewelry. Juried. Number exhibitors: see website. Number attendees: varies. Free to public. Apply online.

ADDITIONAL INFORMATION Deadline for entry: April. Application fee: $35. Space fee: $500. Exhibition space: 10×10. For more information, artists should email, visit website, or call.

GERMANTOWN FRIENDS SCHOOL JURIED CRAFT SHOW

31 W. Coulter St., Philadelphia PA 19144. (215)900-7734. E-mail: craftshow@gfsnet.org. Website: www.germantownfriends.org/parents/parents-association/craft-show/index.aspx. "This jewel of a show, located on the GFS campus, has been ranked among the top 10% of the nation's craft shows by the authoritative ArtFair SourceBook." See website for more information.

GLAM INDIE CRAFT SHOW

E-mail: glamcraftshow@gmail.com. Website: www.glamcraftshow.com. Fine arts & crafts fair held annually in December. Outdoors. Accepts handmade crafts, painting, sculpture, photography, drawing, fabric, crafts, ceramics, glass and jewelry. Juried. Number exhibitors: varies. Number attendees: var-

ies. Admission: $3 adults; children 10 & under free. Apply online.

ADDITIONAL INFORMATION Deadline for entry: September. Application fee: see website. Space fee: varies. Exhibition space: varies. For more information, artists should e-mail or visit website.

GLENCOE FESTIVAL OF ART

Amdur Productions, P.O. Box 550, Highland Park IL 60035. (847)926-4300. E-mail: info@amdurproductions.com. Website: www.amdurproductions.com. Fine arts & crafts fair held annually in August. Outdoors. Accepts handmade crafts, painting, sculpture, photography, drawing, fabric, crafts, ceramics, glass, and jewelry. Juried. Number exhibitors: 120. Number attendees: 35,000. Free to public. Apply online.

ADDITIONAL INFORMATION Deadline for entry: see website. Application fee: $25. Space fee: varies. Exhibition space: varies. For more information, artists should e-mail or visit website.

GLENVIEW OUTDOOR ART FAIR

Glenview Art League, P.O. Box 463, Glenview IL 60025-0463. (847)724-4007. E-mail: glenview-artleague@att.net. Website: www.glenviewartleague.org. Fine arts & crafts fair held annually in July. Outdoors. Accepts handmade crafts, paintings, sculpture, hand-pulled artist's prints (e.g., etchings), drawings, mixed media, ceramics, photography, and jewelry. Juried. Awards/prizes: Best of Show, Awards of Excellence, Merit Awards. Number exhibitors: see website. Number attendees: varies. Free to public. Apply online.

ADDITIONAL INFORMATION Deadline for entry: May. Application fee: $10. Space fee: varies. Exhibition space: 12×12. For more information, artists should e-mail, call, or visit website.

GLENWOOD AVE. ARTS FEST

E-mail: info@glenwoodave.org. Website: www.glenwoodave.org. "The Glenwood Avenue Arts Fest (GAAF) is a free, weekend-long event that features artists, open studios, and live entertainment on three outdoor stages. Experience art, theater, music, as well as food and drink, on the brick-laid streets of the Glenwood Avenue Arts District in Chicago's historic Rogers Park neighborhood." See website for more details.

GLOUCESTER COUNTY SPRING CRAFT & HOME SHOW

P.O. Box 925, Millville NJ 08332. (856)765-0118. Fax: (856)765-9050. E-mail: bkenterprisenj@aol.com. Website: www.gloucestercraftfair.com. Contact: Kathy Wright, organizer. Estab. 2010. Arts & crafts show held annually 1st Saturday in May. Indoors & outdoors. Accepts fine art & handmade crafts, home & garden, food. Awards/prizes: $100 for Best Spring Booth. Exhibitors: 150. Number of attendees: 2,500. Free to public. Artists should apply via website.

ADDITIONAL INFORMATION Deadline for entry: late September. Application fee: none. Space fee: $30 (one day). Exhibition space: 10×10. For more information, artists should e-mail, visit website, or call.

GOLD CANYON ARTS FESTIVAL

5301 S. Superstition Mountain Dr., Suite 104, #183, Gold Canyon AZ 85118. E-mail: info.gcartsfest@gmail.com. Website: www.gcartsfest.com. Fine arts & crafts fair held annually the 4th Saturday in January. Outdoors. Accepts handmade crafts and other mediums. Juried. Number exhibitors: 85. Number attendees: 6,000. Free to public. Apply online.

ADDITIONAL INFORMATION Deadline for entry: November. Application fee: none. Space fee: $60. Exhibition space: 10×10. For more information, artists should e-mail, call, or visit website.

GOLD COAST ART FAIR

Amdur Productions, P.O. Box 550, Highland Park IL 60035. (847)926-4300. E-mail: info@amdurproductions.com. Website: www.amdurproductions.com. Fine arts & crafts fair held annually in June. Outdoors. Accepts handmade crafts and other mediums. Juried. Awards: announced at festival. Number exhibitors: 300. Number attendees: 100,000. Free to public. Apply online.

ADDITIONAL INFORMATION Deadline for entry: see website. Application fee: $35. Space fee: $595. Exhibition space: see website. For more information, artists should e-mail, call, or visit website.

GOLDEN FINE ARTS FESTIVAL

Golden Fine Arts Festival, 1010 Washington Ave., Golden CO 80401. (303)279-3113. E-mail: info@goldencochamber.org. Website: www.goldenfineartsfestival.org. Fine arts & crafts fair held annually in August. Outdoors. Accepts handmade crafts, ceramics, fiber, glass, jewelry, mixed media, 2D, painting, photography, and sculpture. Juried. Number exhibitors: see website. Number attendees: 40,000. Free to public. Apply online.

ADDITIONAL INFORMATION Deadline for entry: April. Application fee: $25. Space fee: $350. Exhibition space: 10×10. For more information, artists should e-mail, call, or visit website.

GOT CRAFT

E-mail: info@gotcraft.com. Website: www.gotcraft.com. "Founded in 2007, Got Craft? is held twice a year in May and December featuring 75+ handmade designers, craft workshops, tasty treats, music, FREE swag bags, and an average attendance of 6,000 a year." See website for more info.

GRAND LAKE STREAM FOLK ART FESTIVAL

P.O. Box 465, Princeton ME 04668-0465. (207)796-8199. E-mail: grandlakestreamfolkartfestival@gmail.com. Contact: Cathy or Bill Shamel. Estab. 1994. Arts & crafts show held annually last full weekend in July. Outdoors. Accepts handmade crafts, canoe building. Juried. Exhibitors: 60. Number of attendees: 3,000. Admission: $8. Apply via e-mail or call.

ADDITIONAL INFORMATION Deadline for entry: none. Application fee: none. Space fee: $300 (10×10); $450 (10×15); $600 (10×20). Exhibition space: 10×10; 10×15; 10×20. For more information, artists should send e-mail or call.

TIPS "Upscale display and good lighting."

GREAT GULFCOAST ARTS FESTIVAL

Website: www.ggaf.org. "The Great Gulfcoast Arts Festival is a juried art show. Each year, we receive more than 600 applications for the festival. Each applicant is required to submit 3 images of their work and 1 image of their display area along with their application. Qualified jurors are shown each artist's images simultaneously and anonymously, and collectively choose more than 200 artists who will be invited to exhibit their work. Best of Show, Awards of Distinction, Awards of Excellence, Awards of Honor, and Awards of Merit winners from the previous year's festival are exempt from the jurying process." See website for more info.

GREAT LAKES ART FAIR

46100 Grand River Rd., Novi MI 48374. (248)348-5600, ext 208. Fax: (248)347-7720. E-mail: info@greatlakesartfair.com. Website: www.greatlakesartfair.com. Contact: Jackie McMahon, event director. Estab. 2009. Fine art show held annually in April. Indoors. Accepts handmade crafts, wood, ceramics, painting, 3D mixed media, photography. Juried. Awards/prizes: $900 in cash & prizes; free booth next show. Exhibitors: 200. Number of attendees: 10,000. Admission: $7. Apply online.

ADDITIONAL INFORMATION Deadline for entry: early February. Application fee: $30. Space fee: $400. Exhibition space: 10×12. For more information, artists should send e-mail, call, or visit website.

GREAT MIDWEST ART FEST

Amdur Productions, P.O. Box 550, Highland Park IL 60035. (847)926-4300. Fax: (847)926-4330. E-mail: info@amdurproductions.com. Website: www.amdurproductions.com. Estab. 2014. Art & craft show held annually in July. Outdoors. Accepts handmade crafts and other mediums. Juried. Number exhibitors: 50. Number attendees: varies. Free to public. Apply online.

ADDITIONAL INFORMATION Deadline for entry: early May. Application fee: $25. Space fee: $230. Exhibition space: 10×10. For more information, artists should e-mail, call, or visit website.

TIPS "Visit our website! We have many tips for how to succeed as an artist!"

GREEN VALLEY ART FESTIVAL

Alan Smith, 2050 W. State Route 89A, Lot 237, Cottonwood AZ 86326. (928)300-4711. E-mail: alan@runningbearproductions.net. Website: www.runningbearproductions.net. Fine art and craft show held three times a year. See website or e-mail for more info.

GREEN WITH INDIE

E-mail: stlouiscraftmafia@gmail.com. Website: www.greenwithindiecraftshow.com. Fine arts & crafts fair held annually in March. Indoors. Accepts handmade crafts and vintage items. Juried. Number exhibitors: 65. Number attendees: varies. Free to public. Apply online.

ADDITIONAL INFORMATION Deadline for entry: January. Application fee: none. Space fee: varies. Exhibition space: varies. For more information, artists should e-mail or visit website.

GUMTREE FESTIVAL

GumTree Festival, P.O. Box 786, Tupelo MS 38802. (662)844-2787. Website: www.gumtreefestival.com. "The Festival is highly respected, and brings an influx of 30,000 people to downtown Tupelo the actual weekend of the Festival. GumTree Festival showcases the artwork of around 100 artists from all over the South and beyond. GumTree Festival is an iconic institution for the fine arts." See website for more details.

HALIFAX ART FESTIVAL

P.O. Box 2038, Ormond Beach FL 32175-2038. (386)304-7247 or (407)701-1184. E-mail: patabernathy2012@hotmail.com. Website: www.halifaxartfestival.com. Estab. 1962. Fine arts & crafts fair held annually in November. Outdoors. Accepts handmade crafts, ceramics, fiber, glass, jewelry, mixed media, 2D, painting, photography, and sculpture. Juried. Awards/prizes: Best of Show, Judges' Choice, Awards of Excellence, Awards of Distinction, Awards of Honor, Awards of Merit, Student Art Awards, Purchase Award, Patron Purchase Award. Number exhibitors: 200. Number attendees: 45,000. Free to public. Apply online.

ADDITIONAL INFORMATION Deadline for entry: August. Application fee: $30. Space fee: $225 (competitive); $125 (noncompetitive). Exhibition space: see website. For more information, artists should e-mail, call, or visit website.

HAMPTON FALLS CRAFT FESTIVAL

Castleberry Fairs & Festivals, 38 Charles St., Rochester NH 03867. (603)332-2616. E-mail: info@castleberryfairs.com. Website: www.castleberryfairs.com.

Estab. 2008. Fine arts & crafts fair held annually in September. Outdoors. Accepts handmade crafts and other mediums. Juried. Number exhibitors: see website. Number attendees: varies. Free to public. Apply online.

ADDITIONAL INFORMATION Deadline for entry: see website. Application fee: see website. Space fee: $225. Exhibition space: 10×10. For more information, artists should e-mail, call, or visit website.

HANDMADE ARCADE

(412)654-3889. E-mail: info@handmadearcade.com. Website: www.handmadearcade.com; www.facebook.com/handmadearcade. "Handmade Arcade (HA), founded in 2004, is Pittsburgh's first and largest independent craft fair. HA brings young, innovative crafters and progressive do-it-yourself designers to the David L. Lawrence Convention Center to sell their handmade, locally produced, and offbeat wares at a bustling marketplace. A highly anticipated annual event, HA attracts more than 8,000 attendees in one day. Spaces are $150. HA provides craft artists working outside mainstream and fine arts sectors with a grassroots, high-visibility venue to sell wares, build community, network, and share their artistic practice." See website for more information.

TIPS "Carefully planning your display for the space and following our guidelines that we put forth online every year. Consider your pricing carefully. We are happy to help newer vendors with this challenge. In the past, we have had vendors overprice and not do well and conversely underprice and sell out too quickly."

⏣ HANDMADE BABY FAIR

Om Baby, 2201 Rear Market St., Camp Hill PA 17011. (717)761-4975. E-mail: holly@ombabycenter.com. Website: www.ombabycenter.com/Handmade_Baby. html. Fine craft fair featuring local, handmade, natural and sustainable baby products. "If you are seeking unique, handmade, local baby and children's items, then this is the event to attend! You'll find everything from bibs to diapers, clothing and nursery decor for your special little one!" See website for more details.

HANDMADE CITY SPRING FAIR

E-mail: handmadecityinfo@gmail.com. Website: www.handmade-city.com. Fine arts & crafts fair held annually in December. Indoors. Accepts handmade crafts and other mediums. Juried. Number exhibitors: see website. Number attendees: varies. Free to public. Apply online.

ADDITIONAL INFORMATION Deadline for entry: October. Application fee: none. Space fee: $40. Exhibition space: 6×10. For more information, artists should e-mail or visit website.

HANDMADE HARVEST

(613)461-6233. E-mail: hello@handmadeharvest.com. Website: www.handmadeharvest.com. "The Handmade Harvest Craft Show takes place in Almonte, Ontario, a quaint little tourist town about 30 minutes west of Ottawa. Founded in 2010, the show is organized by local Almonte business owner Emily Arbour." See website for details.

HANDMADE MARKET CHICAGO

Website: www.handmadechicago.com. "Handmade Market is a unique event to connect the makers of beautiful things to people who appreciate the unique and handmade." See website for details.

HANDMADE TOLEDO MAKER'S MART

Website: www.handmadetoledo.com. "45+ handmade vendors from all over the Midwest will showcase their wares for a 1-day pop-up shop. Grab some grub from local food trucks and bakeries, sip on some locally roasted coffee, enjoy the sounds of some of Toledo's talented buskers, shop handmade, and celebrate 419 Day with us! Handmade fun for the whole family! There will be kid-friendly activities, crafty make and takes, and much more!" See website for details.

HANDWEAVERS GUILD OF BOULDER ANNUAL SALE

Barbara Olson, 2111 Hermosa Dr., Boulder CO 80304. (303)444-1010. E-mail: frey.barb@gmail.com. Website: www.handweaversofboulder.org. Fine arts & crafts fair held annually in October. Outdoors. Accepts handmade crafts. Juried. Open to members only.

Awards/prizes: Jurors' Award, People's Choice Award. Number exhibitors: see website. Number attendees: varies. Free to public. Apply online.

ADDITIONAL INFORMATION Deadline for entry: October. Application fee: $15. Space fee: see website. Exhibition space: see website. For more information, artists should e-mail, call, or visit website.

HARVEST FESTIVAL ORIGINAL ART & CRAFT SHOW

2181 Greenwich St., San Francisco CA 94123. (415)447-3205. Fax: (415)346-4965. E-mail: harvest@weshows.com. Website: www.harvestfestival. com. Contact: Lori Walker. Estab. 1972. Arts & crafts show held annually September-December. Indoors. Accepts handmade crafts. Juried. Number of exhibitors: varies. Number of attendees: varies. Admission fee: $9 adults; $7 seniors; $4 youth; 12 & under free. Apply online.

ADDITIONAL INFORMATION Deadline for entry: until filled. Exhibition space: 10×10; 10×15; 10×20; 10×30. Space fee: varies by location and size; corners additional $125. For more information, e-mail or visit website.

TIPS "We look for quality and variety."

HEARTFEST: A FINE ART SHOW

Stookey Companies, P.O. Box 31083, Des Moines IA 50310. (515)278-6200. Fax: (515)276-7513. E-mail: suestookey@att.net. Website: www.stookeyshows. com. Fine art & fine crafts fair held annually in February on the weekend before Valentine's Day. Indoors. Accepts handmade artwork. Juried. Number exhibitors: see website. Number attendees: see website. Free to public. Apply online at Zapplication.org.

ADDITIONAL INFORMATION Deadline for entry: January. Application fee: $25. Space fee: $185. Exhibition space: varies. For more information, artists should e-mail, call, or visit website.

HIGHLAND PARK FESTIVAL OF FINE CRAFT

Amdur Productions, P.O. Box 550, Highland Park IL 60035. (847)926-4300. E-mail: info@amdurproductions.com. Website: www.amdurproductions. com. Fine arts & crafts fair held annually in June.

Outdoors. Accepts handmade crafts, ceramics, fiber, glass, jewelry, wood, and more. Juried. Number exhibitors: 130. Number attendees: varies. Free to public. Apply online.

ADDITIONAL INFORMATION Deadline for entry: April. Application fee: $35. Space fee: $455. Exhibition space: 10×10. For more information, artists should e-mail, call, or visit website.

HIGHWOOD LAST CALL ART FAIR

Amdur Productions, P.O. Box 550, Highland Park IL 60035. (847)926-4300. Fax: (847)926-4330. E-mail: info@amdurproductions.com. Website: www.amdurproductions.com. "The Highwood Last Call Art Fair features great art at great prices. The show gives the public the chance to buy end-of-the-season original art, leftover inventory, slightly damaged, bruised, and odd pieces at discounted prices. Artists decide how much to discount their work and can use festival stickers to mark work at 10% to 50% off." See website for more information.

HILTON HEAD ISLAND ART FESTIVAL WITH CRAFT MARKETPLACE

270 Central Blvd., Suite 107B, Jupiter FL 33458. (561)746-6615. Fax: (561)746-6528. E-mail: info@ artfestival.com. Website: www.artfestival.com. Contact: Malinda Ratliff, communications manager. Estab. 2009. Fine art & craft fair held annually in late May. Outdoors. Accepts photography, jewelry, mixed media, sculpture, wood, ceramic, glass, painting, digital, fiber, metal. Juried. Number exhibitors: 100. Number attendees: 60,000. Free to public. Apply online via www.zapplication.org. Deadline: see website. Application fee: $25. Space fee: $375. Exhibition space: 10×10 and 10×20. For more information, artists should e-mail, call, or visit website. Festival located at Shelter Cove Harbour and Marina on Hilton Head Island.

TIPS "You have to start somewhere. First, assess where you are, and what you'll need to get things off the ground. Next, make a plan of action. Outdoor street art shows are a great way to begin your career and lifetime as a working artist. You'll meet a lot of other artists who have been where you are now. Network with them!"

HISTORIC SHAW ART FAIR

(314)773-3935. E-mail: greg@gobdesign.com. Website: www.shawartfair.org. Contact: Greg Gobberdiel, coordinator. Fine arts & crafts fair held annually in October. Outdoors. Accepts handmade crafts, ceramics, fiber, glass, jewelry, mixed media, painting, photography, and sculpture. Juried. Number exhibitors: see website. Number attendees: varies. Free to public. Apply online.

ADDITIONAL INFORMATION Deadline for entry: April. Application fee: $25. Space fee: $280. Exhibition space: 10×10. For more information, artists should e-mail, call, or visit website.

HOBE SOUND FESTIVAL OF THE ARTS & CRAFT SHOW

270 Central Blvd., Suite 107B, Jupiter FL 33458. (561)746-6615. Fax: (561)746-6528. E-mail: info@artfestival.com. Website: www.artfestival.com. Contact: Malinda Ratliff, communications manager. Estab. 2006. Fine art & craft fair held annually in February. Outdoors. Accepts photography, jewelry, mixed media, sculpture, wood, ceramic, glass, painting, digital, fiber, metal. Juried. Number exhibitors: 130. Number attendees: 70,000. Free to public. Apply online via www.zapplication.org. Deadline: see website. Application fee: $25. Space fee: $395. Exhibition space: 10×10 and 10×20. For more information, artists should e-mail, call, or visit website. Show located at A1A/Dixie Highway where the street intersects with Bridge Road in Hobe Sound, FL.

TIPS "You have to start somewhere. First, assess where you are, and what you'll need to get things off the ground. Next, make a plan of action. Outdoor street art shows are a great way to begin your career and lifetime as a working artist. You'll meet a lot of other artists who have been where you are now. Network with them!"

HOLIDAY CRAFT & VENDOR SHOW

140 Oak St., Frankfort IL 60423. (815)469-9400. Fax: (815)469-9275. E-mail: cdebella@frankfortparks.org. Website: www.frankfortparks.org. Contact: Cali DeBella, special events coordinator. Estab. 1993. Arts & crafts/holiday show held annually in November. Indoors. Accepts handmade crafts. Exhibitors: 65. Number of attendees: 500-700. Free to public. Apply online.

ADDITIONAL INFORMATION Deadline for entry: early October. Application fee: $45. Space fee: $45. Exhibition space: 10×6. For more information e-mail or visit website.

HOLIDAY HANDMADE CAVALCADE

Website: www.handmadecavalcade.com. "The Handmade Cavalcade is a biannual craft fair in NYC, put together by the dedication and DIY drive of Etsy New York local New York metro area Etsy Sellers. Come out and shop the unique handmade gifts of your local Etsy Shops while snacking on locally made sweets and connecting with other small crafty businesses." See website for details.

HOLIDAY SIZZLE - POTOMAC FIBER ARTS GALLERY

Website: www.potomacfiberartsgallery.com. "Potomac Fiber Arts Gallery (Studio 18) announces the opening of the juried show 'Holiday Sizzle.' In this show, our artists excel in holiday spirit and sparkle. Whether for self or gifts, jewelry, sculpture, clothing, and wall pieces are some of the items that will be exhibited." See website for details.

HOMEWOOD FINE ARTS & CRAFTS FESTIVAL

Pacific Fine Arts Festivals, P.O. Box 280, Pine Grove CA 95665. (209)267-4394. Fax: (209)267-4395. E-mail: pfa@pacificfinearts.com. Website: www.pacificfinearts.com. This free event brings together an exciting group of more than 50 artists showcasing an assortment of collectible arts and crafts in a variety of media including paintings, ceramics, jewelry, woodwork, photography, and much more. See website for more information.

HONOLULU GLASS ART & BEAD FESTIVAL

Soft Flex Company, Attn: Sara Oehler/Scott Clark, P.O. Box 80, Sonoma CA 95476. (707)732-3513. Fax: (707)938-3097. E-mail: thomas@softflexcompany.com; sara@softflexcompany.com. Website: www.softflexcompany.com/WSWrapper.jsp?mypage=FestivalHI_Main.html. Beading event held semiannually in March & September. Indoors.

Accepts beads, gemstones, findings, collectible glass art & jewelry. Juried. Number exhibitors: see website. Number attendees: see website. Free to public. Apply online.

ADDITIONAL INFORMATION Deadline for entry: March. Application fee: see website. Space fee: varies. Exhibition space: varies. For more information, artists should e-mail, call, or visit website.

HOPI FESTIVAL OF ARTS & CULTURE

(928)774-5213. Website: www.musnaz.org/hp/hopi_fest.shtml. "A Fourth of July tradition since the 1930s, the Hopi Festival of Arts & Culture is the oldest Hopi show in the world. Attendees will enjoy two days of authentic food, artist demonstrations, musical performances, dancing, and a not-to-be missed children's area that will entertain the young at heart with take-home crafts related to Hopi culture." See website for more information.

HUDSON MOHAWK WEAVERS GUILD ANNUAL SHOW & SALE

Website: www.hmwg.org/showandsale.html. "For 4 days each November, the Guild takes over the historic Pruyn House and turns it into a showcase for the best of modern handweaving, from traditional to contemporary. Guild members work all year to produce a tremendous variety of handwoven items, from rugs and other home goods to clothing pieces such as scarves, shawls, and jackets. Holiday gifts such as cards and ornaments are also available. Each room in the Pruyn House is devoted to a particular class of items such as linens or scarves and staffed with an accomplished local weaver to assist and answer questions. Admission is free, and visitors can watch fashion shows featuring woven goods or take in demonstrations of handweaving and spinning." See website for more info.

HUNGRY MOTHER ARTS & CRAFTS FESTIVAL

Website: www.hungrymotherfestival.com. "Every summer the Hungry Mother State Park, in Marion, Virginia, opens its doors to visitors and artisans from all over the country. Three days of art, entertainment, food, and fun are guaranteed." See website for more information and to apply.

HYDE PARK SQUARE ART SHOW

Hyde Park Square Art Show, P.O. Box 8402, Cincinnati OH 45208. (513)353-2045. E-mail: hpartshow-info@aol.com. Website: www.hydeparksquare.org/hydeparkartshow.html. Fine arts & crafts fair held annually in August. Outdoors. Accepts handmade crafts, ceramics, fiber, glass, jewelry, mixed media, 2D, painting, photography, and sculpture. Juried. Awards/prizes: Best of Show, 1st Place, 2nd Place, 3rd Place, Honorable Mention. Number exhibitors: see website. Number attendees: see website. Free to public. Apply online.

ADDITIONAL INFORMATION Deadline for entry: March. Application fee: $35. Space fee: $125. Exhibition space: see website. For more information, artists should e-mail, call, or visit website.

IDAHO ARTISTRY IN WOOD SHOW

(208)466-4899. E-mail: marlies-schmitt@clearwire.net. Website: www.idahoartistryinwood.org. Contact: Marlies Schmitt, publicity chair. Estab. 2009. Fine arts & crafts show held annually last weekend of February. Indoors. Accepts handmade crafts, artwork made from wood or gourds. Awards/prizes: prize ribbons. Number exhibitors: 120 competitors; 7 vendors. Number of attendees: 1,000. Admission: $4; 12 & under free. Artists should apply online.

ADDITIONAL INFORMATION Deadline for entry: February 15 for advance registration; registration can de done at exhibit site on day before show opens. Application fee: $3 per piece in advance; $5 at the door. Space fee: $75. Exhibition space: 100 sq. ft. For more information artists should e-mail or visit website.

TIPS "This show is primarily a competition and exhibition. Although opportunities for sales are given, the focus is not on sales, so there are no guarantees, especially for high-price items."

IMAGES – A FESTIVAL OF THE ARTS

E-mail: images@imagesartfestival.org. Website: www.imagesartfestival.org. Fine arts & crafts fair held annually in January. Outdoors. Accepts handmade crafts, ceramics, fiber, glass, jewelry, mixed media, 2D, painting, photography, and sculpture. Juried. Awards/prizes: $100,000 in awards and prizes. Number exhibitors: 225. Number attendees: 45,000. Free to public. Apply online.

ADDITIONAL INFORMATION Deadline for entry: October. Application fee: $40. Space fee: $250. Exhibition space: 11×12. For more information, artists should e-mail, call, or visit website.

INDIE CRAFT BAZAAR

E-mail: indiecraftbazaar@gmail.com. Website: www.getupandcraft.com/Indie_Craft_Bazaar.html. "Indie Craft Bazaar is your local source for orginal art, handmade items, vintage, recycled, and vegan goods! 'These 'ain't your grandma's crafts!' ICB is a pop-up shop filled with all sorts of imaginative, impressive and, oftentimes quirky, handmade curiosities! Support our community, small business, and the arts by joining us at the next show! Admission is $5." See website for more info.

INDIE CRAFT EXPERIENCE

E-mail: craft@ice-atlanta.com. Website: www.ice-atlanta.com. "The Indie Craft Experience was founded in January 2005. With a vision to provide indie crafters an opportunity to sell and promote their creations in Atlanta, ICE quickly caught on as a favorite event for participants and attendees alike. ICE is a grassroots effort, organized by two Atlanta crafters—Christy Petterson and Shannon Mulkey. Inspired by indie craft markets in Chicago and Austin, the Indie Craft Experience was founded in order to provide Atlanta with a major indie craft event. In addition to craft markets, ICE also organizes a vintage market called Salvage and an annual Pop-Up Shop during the holiday season." See website for more info and to apply.

INDIE CRAFT PARADE

E-mail: info@indiecraftparade.com. Website: www.indiecraftparade.com. Contact: Elizabeth Ramos, executive director. Estab. 2010. Annual arts & crafts show held annually in Greenville, SC, in September 2 weekends after Labor Day. Indoors. Accepts handmade crafts, 2D/3D fine art, fiber art, paper goods, handmade wearables, and an etc. category (toys, home & garden, artisan food, supplies). Juried. Awards/prizes: small cash prize for best booth display. Exhibitors: 80. Number of attendees: 7,000. Admission: $2; children free. Apply via website.
ADDITIONAL INFORMATION Deadline for entry: June 25. Application fee: $20. Space fee: $95 & $125.

Exhibition space: 32 sq. ft.; 16 sq. ft. Average sales: $3,000. For more information e-mail or see website.
TIPS "To sell successfully, understand your market. Attendees at Indie Craft include a vast range from high school/college students to well-established families to retired adults. Have products that fit within a variety of price ranges; make a well-built display that prominently shows your products; be engaging with your potential customers."

INDIEMADE CRAFT MARKET

P.O. Box 3204, Allentown PA 18106. (610)703-8004. E-mail: ann@indiemadecraftmarket.com. Website: www.indiemadecraftmarket.com. Contact: Ann Biernat-Rucker, co-producer. Estab. 2007. Arts & craft show held annually the 1st Saturday in December. Indoors. Accepts handmade crafts. Juried. Exhibitors: see website. Number of attendees: see website. Admission: $3. Apply online.
ADDITIONAL INFORMATION Deadline for entry: April 1. Application fee: none. Space fee: $50. Exhibition space: 8 ft. table. For more information, artists should visit website.

INDIE SOUTH FAIR

660 N. Chase St., Athens GA 30601. E-mail: indiesouthfair@gmail.com. Website: www.indiesouthfair.com. Contact: Serra Ferguson, organizer. Estab. 2007. Arts & Crafts show held semiannually the 1st weekends of May & December. Outdoors. Accepts handmade crafts and all other mediums. Exhibitors: 100. Number of attendees: 3,000. Free to public. Apply via website.
ADDITIONAL INFORMATION Deadline for entry: March 2 for spring show; September 28 for holiday market. Application fee: $15. Space fee: $175 (10×10); $90 (6×4). Exhibition space: 10×10; 6×4. Average sales: $800-1,200. For more information send e-mail.
TIPS "Create beautiful and functional art, present it well, and have a friendly, outgoing demeanor."

ITASCA ART & WINE FESTIVAL

Village of Itasca, 550 W. Irving Park Rd., Itasca IL 60143-1795. (630)773-0835. Fax: (630)773-2505. Website: www.itasca.com. "Annual juried Fine Arts and Wine Festival, Benches on Parade, takes place in historic downtown Itasca, located in scenic Usher Park near the gateway to the newly created River Walk. There will be live music in the gazebo, a backdrop for meandering through the winding walkways of the park with wine tasting and painted iron benches (up for silent auction) on display throughout." See website or call for details.

JACKSON HOLE FALL ARTS FESTIVAL

Website: www.jacksonholechamber.com/fall_arts_festival. "The Jackson Hole Fall Arts Festival is widely recognized as one of the premier cultural events in the Rocky Mountain West. Thousands of art enthusiasts are drawn each year to experience the diverse artwork and breathtaking natural surroundings that make Jackson Hole a leading cultural center. Experience the world-class installments of contemporary, culinary, landscape, Native American, wildlife, and Western, arts. Visitors will appreciate the works of nationally and internationally acclaimed artists along with an exceptional array of art, music, cuisine, and wine. More than 50 events round out our 11-day festival." See website for more information.

JAMAICA PLAIN OPEN STUDIOS

JPAC, P.O. Box 300222, Jamaica Plain MA 02130. (617)855-5767. E-mail: coordinator@jpopenstudios.com. Website: www.jpopenstudios.com. "Jamaica Plain Open Studios, is the premiere annual arts event in one of Boston's most eclectic neighborhoods. JPOS is an opportunity to take a rare public peek at some private spaces. The free event showcases the artwork of over 200 artists at dozens of sites including artists' studios, the historic Eliot School, the Sam Adams brewery complex, the Arnold Arboretum, and more." See website for more information.

JEFFERSON QUILT SHOW
"QUILTS ON THE BAYOU"

120 E. Austin St., Jefferson TX 75657. (903)926-6695. E-mail: jqshow@yahoo.com. Website: www.jeffersonquiltshow.com. Contact: Edris McCrary. Estab. 2002. Quilt show held annually in Janury. Indoors. Accepts handmade crafts. Juried. Exhibitors: 150. Number of attendees: 1,200-1,500. Admission: $5 adults; $4 children. Apply online.

ADDITIONAL INFORMATION Deadline for entry: until full. Application fee: $5 per item. Space fee: varies. Exhibition space: varies. For more information send e-mail or visit website.

JINGLE FEST HANDMADE CRAFT FAIR

Website: www.eventcalifornia.com. "One of the largest handmade tabletop craft fair events in San Jose and in the San Francisco Bay Area. Jingle Fest Craft Fair is a curated handmade craft marketplace showcasing the best Bay Area talents in contemporary craft and artwork. Our show brings the best local artists and designers out of their studios and workshops and into the spotlight for a festive one-day celebration of everything handmade." See website for more information.

JUNO BEACH CRAFT FESTIVAL
ON THE OCEAN

270 Central Blvd., Suite 107B, Jupiter FL 33458. (561)746-6615. Fax: (561)746-6528. E-mail: info@artfestival.com. Website: www.artfestival.com. "Join us in Jupiter for another fantastic weekend craft festival. Shop handcrafted leather goods, paintings, photography, personalized products, glassworks, and much more, all made in the USA! A Palm Beach favorite, this craft festival is not to be missed! Stroll along the scenic A1A and shop handmade fine crafts that suit every budget, while visiting with some of the nation's best crafters. Get a jumpstart on holiday gifts at this fabulous free craft event." See website for more information.

KEEPSAKE COLLECTION
ART & CRAFT SHOWS

(989)681-4023 or (989)781-9165. E-mail: craftpeddler@nethawk.com; bonnmur9@aol.com. Website: www.keepsakecollectionshows.com. Contact: Leslie Needham or Bonnie Murin. "The Keepsake Collection endeavors to connect quality artists and craftspeople with interested buyers of unique and desirable workmanship. To ensure this goal categories are limited both in scope and number. You'll always find professional quality exhibitors and merchandise at our shows as all are juried. Advertising is extensive; including direct mail, postcards, flyers, radio advertising, newspaper ads, in-ground signs, billboards, etc." See website for more information.

KENTUCKY CRAFTED

Capital Plaza Tower, 500 Mero St., 21st Floor, Frankfort KY 40601-1987. (502)564-3757 or (888)833-2787. Fax: (502)564-2839. E-mail: Ed.Lawrence@ky.gov. Website: www.artscouncil.ky.gov/KentuckyArt/Event_Market.htm. Art & craft market/show held annually in March. Indoors. Accepts handmade crafts, ceramics, fiber, metal, and other mediums. Juried. Number exhibitors: 200. Number attendees: varies. Admission: $10, 1-day ticket; $15, 2-day ticket; children 15 & under free. Apply online.
ADDITIONAL INFORMATION Deadline for entry: see website. Application fee: see website. Space fee: varies. Exhibition space: varies. For more information, artists should e-mail, call, or visit website.

KEY BISCAYNE ART FESTIVAL

270 Central Blvd., Suite 107B, Jupiter FL 33458. (561)746-6615. Fax: (561)746-6528. E-mail: info@artfestival.com. Website: www.artfestival.com. Contact: Malinda Ratliff, communications manager. Estab. 1964. Fine art & craft fair held annually in March. Outdoors. Accepts photography, jewelry, mixed media, sculpture, wood, ceramic, glass, painting, digital, fiber, metal. Juried. Number exhibitors: 125. Number attendees: 50,000. Free to public. Apply online via www.zapplication.org. Deadline: see website. Application fee: $25. Space fee: $395. Exhibition space: 10×10 and 10×20. For more information, artists should e-mail, call, or visit website. Festival located at Village Green Park in Key Biscayne, FL.
TIPS "You have to start somewhere. First, assess where you are, and what you'll need to get things off the ground. Next, make a plan of action. Outdoor street art shows are a great way to begin your career and lifetime as a working artist. You'll meet a lot of other artists who have been where you are now. Network with them!"

KEY WEST CRAFT SHOW

KEY WEST CRAFT SHOW, 301 Front St., Key West FL 33040. (305)294-1243. E-mail: kwcraftshow@earthlink.net. Website: www.keywestartcenter.com/craft.html. Fine arts & crafts fair held annually in January. Outdoors. Accepts handmade crafts and other mediums. Juried. Number exhibitors: 100. Number attendees: 25,000. Free to public. Apply online.
ADDITIONAL INFORMATION Deadline for entry: September. Application fee: $25. Space fee: $225; $340. Exhibition space: 10×10; 10×15. For more information, artists should e-mail, call, or visit website.

KINGS BEACH FINE ARTS & CRAFTS ON THE SHORE

Pacific Fine Arts Festivals, P.O. Box 280, Pine Grove CA 95665. (209)267-4394. Fax: (209)267-4395. E-mail: pfa@pacificfinearts.com. Website: www.pacificfinearts.com. The annual Fine Arts and Crafts on the Shore at Kings Beach is one of Lake Tahoe's must-attend events, showcasing an outstanding array of creations that capture the imagination and inspire the heart. Set among the towering pine trees along the shores of Lake Tahoe at Kings Beach State Park, this free outdoor festival is sponsored by the North Tahoe Business Association and features original collectables including watercolor and oil paintings, glasswork, sculptures, photography, fine crafts, jewelry, and much more. See website for more information.

KIRK SCHOOL SPRING SHOWCASE OF ARTS & CRAFTS

NSSEO, 799 W. Kensington Rd., Mt. Prospect IL 60056. (847)463-8105. E-mail: showcase@nsseo.org. Website: www.nsseo.org. Fine arts & crafts fair held annually in March. Indoors. Accepts handmade crafts and other items. Juried. Number exhibitors: 90. Number attendees: 1,600. Free to public. Apply online.
ADDITIONAL INFORMATION Deadline for entry: March. Application fee: none. Space fee: $75. Exhibition space: 10×5. For more information, artists should e-mail, call, or visit website.

KPFA CRAFT FAIR

1929 MLK Jr. Way, Berkeley CA 94704. (510)848-6767, ext. 243. E-mail: events@kpfa.org. Website: www.kpfa.org/craftsfair/. Contact: Jan Etre, coordinator. Fine arts & crafts fair held annually in December. Indoors. Accepts handmade crafts, ceramics, fiber, glass, jewelry, mixed media, 2D, painting, photography, and sculpture. Juried. Number exhibitors: 200. Number attendees: see website. Admission: $10; disabled, 65+, and children under 17 free. Apply online.

ADDITIONAL INFORMATION Deadline for entry: see website. Application fee: $20. Space fee: varies. Exhibition space: 10×10. For more information, artists should e-mail, call, or visit website.

KRIS KRINGLE HOLIDAY CRAFT SHOW

Linda Williams, 14735 National Pike, Clear Springs MD 21722. (301)582-1233. Website: www.kriskringlecraftshow.com. Fine arts & crafts fair held annually in November. Indoors. Accepts handmade crafts and other mediums. Juried. Number exhibitors: see website. Number attendees: see website. Free to public. Apply online.

ADDITIONAL INFORMATION Deadline for entry: see website. Application fee: see website. Space fee: varies. Exhibition space: varies. For more information, artists should call or visit website.

LABOR DAY WEEKEND CRAFT FAIR AT THE BAY

38 Charles St., Rochester NH 03867. (603)332-2616. E-mail: info@castleberryfairs.com. Website: www.castleberryfairs.com. Fine arts & crafts fair held annually in August. Indoors & outdoors. Accepts handmade crafts and other items. Juried. Number exhibitors: see website. Number attendees: see website. Free to public. Apply online.

ADDITIONAL INFORMATION Deadline for entry: see website. Application fee: see website. Space fee: $350. Exhibition space: varies. For more information, artists should e-mail, call, or visit website.

LA JOLLA FESTIVAL OF THE ARTS

(619)744-0534. E-mail: info@ljfa.org. Website: www.ljfa.org. Contact: Kaylie Rolin. Estab. 1987. Annual fine art show held the 3rd weekend in June. Outdoors. Accepts handmade crafts, sculpture, glass, ceramics, paper, wood, paint, mix, fiber/textile, photography, jewelry. Juried. Awards/prizes: Best of Show in each category. Exhibitors: 195. Number of attendees: 7,000. Admission: $9-16. Apply via www.zapplication.org.

ADDITIONAL INFORMATION Deadline for entry: March 1. Application fee: $25. Space fee: $500-$800.

Exhibition space: 10×10, 10×20. For more information see website.

TIPS "Apply on Zaapplication as soon as registration opens in December of the previous year. Take full advantage of social networking and marketing tools to inform customers about the LJFA and how to obtain discount tickets to attend."

LAKE CABLE WOMAN'S CLUB CRAFT SHOW

5725 Fulton Dr. NW, Canton OH 44718. (330)323-3202. E-mail: lcwccraftshow@gmail.com. Contact: Connie Little, chairman. Estab. 1982. Craft show held semiannually the first Sunday in March & November. Indoors. Accepts handmade crafts. Juried. Number of exhibitors: 60. Number of attendees: 500-800. Free to public. Call or e-mail for application.

ADDITIONAL INFORMATION Deadline for entry: varies. Space fee: Starting at $30. Exhibition space: 8×5. For more information, call or e-mail.

TIPS "We look for quality and variety."

LAKEFRONT FESTIVAL OF ART

700 N. Art Museum Dr., Milwaukee WI 53202. (414)224-3853. E-mail: lfoa@mam.org. Website: www.mam.org/lfoa. Contact: Krista Renfrew, festival director. Estab. 1963. Fine art show held annually the 3rd week in June. Indoors & outdoors. Accepts printmaking, sculpture, wood, painting, jewelry, ceramics, digital, drawing/pastel, MM2, fiber-non, wearable fiber, glass, photography, metal, NM. Juried. Awards/prizes: Artist Awards (10), Honorable Mention (10), Sculpture Garden. Exhibitors: 176. Number of attendees: 25,000. Admission: $17 general; $10 members & advance; 12 & under free. Apply via Zapplication.org.

ADDITIONAL INFORMATION Deadline for entry: November 25. Application fee: $35. Space fee: $500; $600 corner. Exhibition space: 10×10. For more information send e-mail or visit website.

LAKELAND CRAFT FESTIVAL, THE

270 Central Blvd., Suite 107B, Jupiter FL 33458. (561)746-6615. Fax: (561)746-6528. E-mail: info@artfestival.com. Website: www.artfestival.com. Contact: Malinda Ratliff, communications manager. Estab. 2013. Fine art & craft fair held annually in late

March. Outdoors. Accepts photography, jewelry, mixed media, sculpture, wood, ceramic, glass, painting, digital, fiber, metal. Juried. Number exhibitors: 110. Number attendees: 18,000. Free to public. Apply online via www.zapplication.org or visit website for paper application. Deadline: see website. Application fee: $15. Space fee: $250. Exhibition space: 10×10 and 10×20. For more information, artists should e-mail, call, or visit website. Festival located at Lakeside Village in Lakeland, FL.

TIPS "You have to start somewhere. First, assess where you are, and what you'll need to get things off the ground. Next, make a plan of action. Outdoor street art shows are a great way to begin your career and lifetime as a working artist. You'll meet a lot of other artists who have been where you are now. Network with them!"

LAKE NORMAN FOLK ART FESTIVAL

Hickory Museum of Art, Attn: Lake Norman Folk Art Festival, 243 Third Ave. N.E., Hickory NC 28601. (828)327-8576. E-mail: blohr@hickorymuseumofart. org. Website: www.lakenormanfolkartfestival.com. Fine arts & crafts fair held annually in October. Outdoors. Accepts handmade crafts and other mediums. Juried. Number exhibitors: see website. Number attendees: see website. Free to public. Apply online.

ADDITIONAL INFORMATION Deadline for entry: July. Application fee: none. Space fee: $75. Exhibition space: see website. For more information, artists should e-mail, call, or visit website.

LAKESHORE ART FESTIVAL

380 W. Western, Suite 202, Muskegon MI 49440. (231)724-3176. Fax: (231)728-7281. E-mail: artfest@ muskegon.org. Website: www.lakeshoreartfestival. org. Contact: Carla Flanders, director. Estab. 2013. Fine arts & crafts show held annually the first Friday & Saturday in July. Outdoors. Accepts handmade crafts. Juried. Awards/prizes: First place/Best in Show, $1,000; 2nd place, $800; 3rd place, $600; Honorable Mention, $400; Committee's Choice, $200. Exhibitors: 300. Number of attendees: 50,000. Free to public. Apply via website or Zaaplication.

ADDITIONAL INFORMATION Deadline for entry: March. Application fee: $30. Space fee: $250 fine art/ craft; $180 craft, Children's Lane, Artisan Food Market. Exhibition space: 12×12. Average sales: $800-1,200. For more information send e-mail, call, or visit website.

TIPS "The Lakeshore Art Festival is seeking unique, quality, handcrafted products so be sure your items fall within these areas. Also, we strongly recommend that all images submitted are good quality of your best pieces so that we can accurately categorize your work."

LAKE ST LOUIS FARMERS AND ARTISTS MARKET

Lake St Louis Farmers and Artists Market, P.O. Box 91, Warrenton MO 63383-0091. (314)495-2531. E-mail: lakestlouisfarmersmarket@gmail.com. Website: www.themeadowsatlsl.com. Farmer & craft market held annually every Saturday, April-October. Outdoors. Accepts handmade crafts, jewelry, art, pottery, soap, candles, clothing, woodcrafts and other crafts. Exhibitors: varies. Number of attendees: varies. Free to public. Apply online.

ADDITIONAL INFORMATION Deadline for entry: see website. Application fee: none. Space fee: $325 (full season); $25 (daily vendor). Exhibition space: 10×10. For more information, artists should send e-mail, visit website, or call.

LAKE SUMTER ART & CRAFT FESTIVAL

270 Central Blvd., Suite 107B, Jupiter FL 33458. (561)746-6615. Fax: (561)746-6528. E-mail: info@ artfestival.com. Website: www.artfestival.com. Contact: Malinda Ratliff, communications manager. Estab. 2010. Fine art & craft fair held annually in mid-February. Outdoors. Accepts photography, jewelry, mixed media, sculpture, wood, ceramic, glass, painting, digital, fiber, metal. Juried. Number exhibitors: 205. Number attendees: 20,000. Free to public. Apply online via www.zapplication.org or visit website for paper application. Deadline: see website. Application fee: $15. Space fee: $265. Exhibition space: 10×10 and 10×20. For more information, artists should e-mail, call, or visit website. Festival located at Lake Sumter Landing in The Villages, FL.

TIPS "You have to start somewhere. First, assess where you are, and what you'll need to get things off the ground. Next, make a plan of action. Outdoor street art shows are a great way to begin your career and lifetime as a working artist. You'll meet a lot of other artists who have been where you are now. Network with them!"

LAKEVIEW EAST FESTIVAL OF THE ARTS

(773)348-8608. Website: www.lakeviewcastfestivalofthearts.com. "The Lakeview East Festival of the Arts showcases more than 150 juried artists featuring paintings, sculpture, photography, furniture, jewelry, and more. These original pieces are for sale in a wide range of prices. In addition to the art, the Festival has become a center of activity for the weekend with live demonstrations, entertainment stages, family activities, and a garden oasis. Lakeview East is a dynamic and diversified neighborhood community rich in culture, history, and the arts. The Lakeview East Chamber of Commerce works hand in hand with their local residents and business owners and is pleased to offer its neighbors and the Chicagoland area one of the premier fine art outdoor festivals." For more information, sponsorship and volunteer opportunities, please call (773)348-8608.

LAKEWOOD ARTS FESTIVAL

The Lakewood Arts Festival, P.O. Box 771288, Lakewood OH 44107. (216)529-6651. Website: www.lakewoodartsfest.org. Fine arts & crafts fair held annually in August. Outdoors. Accepts handmade crafts and other mediums. Juried. Number exhibitors: 164. Number attendees: 10,000. Free to public. Apply online.

ADDITIONAL INFORMATION Deadline for entry: March. Application fee: $10. Space fee: $100. Exhibition space: 10×10. For more information, artists should call or visit website.

LANSDOWNE ARTS FESTIVAL

E-mail: events@lansdownesfuture.org. Website: www.lansdowneartsfestival.com. "The Lansdowne Arts Festival is a weekend-long event featuring an array of creative and performing arts, including painting, crafts, sculpture, jewelry, live music, demonstrations, and children's events. Set in the historic suburb of Lansdowne, Pennsylvania, the festival has grown to include over 50 exhibiting artists and musical acts. All festival events will be held at the historic Twenti-

eth Century Club at 84 S. Lansdowne Avenue." See website for more information.

LAS OLAS ART FAIR

270 Central Blvd., Suite 107B, Jupiter FL 33458. (561)746-6615. Fax: (561)746-6528. E-mail: info@artfestival.com. Website: www.artfestival.com. Contact: Malinda Ratliff, communications manager. Estab. 1988. Fine art & craft fair held annually in January, March, and mid-October. Outdoors. Accepts photography, jewelry, mixed media, sculpture, wood, ceramic, glass, painting, digital, fiber, metal. Juried. Number exhibitors: 280/January, 260/March, 150/October. Number attendees: 100,000/January, 100,000/March, 70,000/October. Free to public. Apply online via www.zapplication.org. Deadline: see website. Application fee: $25. Space fee: $400/January, $400/March, $395/October. Exhibition space: 10×10 and 10×20. For more information, artists should e-mail, call, or visit website. Fair located on Las Olas Blvd. in Ft. Lauderdale, FL.

TIPS "You have to start somewhere. First, assess where you are, and what you'll need to get things off the ground. Next, make a plan of action. Outdoor street art shows are a great way to begin your career and lifetime as a working artist. You'll meet a lot of other artists who have been where you are now. Network with them!"

LATIMER HALL ARTS & CRAFT SHOW

103 Towne Lake Parkway, Woodstock GA 30188. (347)216-4691. E-mail: mainstreetcraftshow@yahoo.com. Website: www.mainstreetcraftshow.com. Contact: Deb Skroce, director. Estab. 2013. Monthly arts & crafts. Indoors & outdoors. Accepts handmade crafts, repurposed items. Exhibitors: 50. Number of attendees: 1,000. Free to public. Apply via e-mail or website.

ADDITIONAL INFORMATION Deadline for entry: see website or contact by e-mail. Space fee: $50 & $30. Exhibition space: 10×10, 10×9, 9×6. For more information e-mail or see website.

TIPS "Share the event page on Facebook."

LAUDERDALE BY THE SEA CRAFT FESTIVAL

270 Central Blvd., Suite 107B, Jupiter FL 33458. (561)746-6615. Fax: (561)746-6528. E-mail: info@Art-

Festival.com. Website: www.artfestival.com. "Come visit with more than 100 crafters exhibiting and selling their work in an outdoor gallery. From photography, paintings, sculpture, jewelry, and more showcased from local and traveling crafters, your visit to Lauderdale By the Sea is promised to be a feast for the senses. This spectacular weekend festival is not to be missed. Spanning along A1A and Commercial Blvd. the venue is right off the beach and is set up amongst the restaurants and retailers."

LEAGUE OF NH CRAFTSMEN ANNUAL FAIR

League of NH Craftsmen, 49 S. Main St., Suite 100, Concord NH 03301-5080. (603)224-3375. Fax: (603)225-8452. E-mail: twiltse@nhcrafts.org. Website: https://www.nhcrafts.org/craftsmens-fair-overview. php. Contact: Susie Lowe-Stockwell, executive director. "Starting the first Saturday in August and running for 9 days, the Annual Craftsmen's Fair showcases the work of some of the finest craftspeople in the country. The Fair is the place to explore how design and passion inspire our lives. See and shop for one-of-a-kind fine craft that is both beautiful and functional. Meet the makers and learn about their vision and passion for their craft." See website for more information.

LEESBURG FINE ART FESTIVAL

Paragon Fine Art Festivals, 8258 Midnight Pass Rd., Sarasota FL 34242. (941)487-8061. Fax: (941)346-0302. E-mail: admin@paragonartfest.com. Website: www.paragonartevents.com/lee. Contact: Bill Kinney. Fine arts & crafts fair held annually in September. Outdoors. Accepts handmade crafts, ceramics, fiber, glass, jewelry, mixed media, painting, photography, and sculpture. Juried. Number exhibitors: 115. Number attendees: varies. Free to public. Apply online.
ADDITIONAL INFORMATION Deadline for entry: July. Application fee: $30. Space fee: $395. Exhibition space: see website. For more information, artists should e-mail, call, or visit website.

LEVIS COMMONS FINE ART FAIR

The Guild of Artists & Artisans, 118 N. Fourth Ave., Ann Arbor MI 48104. (734)662-3382, ext. 101. E-mail: info@theguild.org; nicole@theguild.org. Website: www.theguild.org. Contact: Nicole McKay, artist relations director. Fine arts & crafts fair held annually in September. Outdoors. Accepts handmade crafts, jewelry, ceramics, painting, glass, photography, fiber, and more. Juried. Number exhibitors: 130. Number attendees: 35,000. Free to public. Apply online.
ADDITIONAL INFORMATION Deadline for entry: April. Application fee: $25 members; $30 nonmembers. Space fee: varies. Exhibition space: varies. For more information, artists should e-mail, call, or visit website.

LEWISTON ART FESTIVAL

P.O. Box 1, Lewiston NY 14092. (716)754-0166. Fax: (716)754-9166. E-mail: director@artcouncil.org. Website: www.artcouncil.org. Estab. 1966. Arts & crafts show held annually in August. Outdoors. Accepts handmade crafts, drawing, printmaking, computer-generated art, 2D/3D mixed media, photography, ceramics, fiber, glass, jewelry, sculpture, wood. Juried. Exhibitors: 175. Number of attendees: 35,000. Free to public. Apply online.
ADDITIONAL INFORMATION Deadline for entry: early May. Application fee: $15. Space fee: $175. Exhibition space: 10×10. For more information, artists should send e-mail or visit website.

LINCOLN ARTS FESTIVAL

E-mail: melissa@artscene.org. Website: www.artscene.org/lincoln-arts-festival. Fine arts & crafts fair held annually in September. Outdoors. Accepts handmade crafts, jewelry, ceramics, painting, glass, photography, fiber, and more. Juried. Awards/prizes: $6,000 in awards & prizes. Number exhibitors: see website. Number attendees: varies. Free to public. Apply online.
ADDITIONAL INFORMATION Deadline for entry: May. Application fee: $25. Space fee: $190 (10×10); $310 (10×20). Exhibition space: 10×10; 10×20. For more information, artists should e-mail or visit website.

LINCOLNSHIRE ART FESTIVAL

E-mail: info@amdurproductions.com. Website: www.amdurproductions.com. Fine arts & crafts fair held annually in August. Outdoors. Accepts handmade crafts, jewelry, ceramics, painting, glass, photography, fiber, and more. Juried. Awards/prizes: given at festival. Number exhibitors: 130. Number attendees: 30,000. Free to public. Apply online.

ADDITIONAL INFORMATION Deadline for entry: January. Application fee: $25. Space fee: $430. Exhibition space: 10×10. For more information, artists should e-mail or visit website.

LITTLE FALLS ARTS & CRAFTS FAIR

200 First St. NW, Little Falls MN 56345-1365. (320)632-5155. Fax: (320)632-2122. E-mail: artsandcrafts@littlefallsmnchamber.com. Website: www. littlefallsmnchamber.com. Contact: Stacy, registrar. Estab. 1972. Arts & crafts show held annually the first weekend after Labor Day in September. Outdoors. Accepts handmade crafts. Juried. Exhibitors: 600. Number of attendees: 125,000. Free to public. Apply online.

ADDITIONAL INFORMATION Deadline for entry: March 20. Application fee: $10. Space fee: $195. Exhibition space: 10×10. Average sales: $5,000. For more information send e-mail, call, or visit website.

TIPS "Have quality product that is reasonably priced!"

LONG GROVE ART FEST

Star Events, 1609 W. Belmont Ave., 2nd Floor, Chicago IL 60657. E-mail: info@starevents.com. Website: www.starevents.com/festivals/long-grove-art-fest. "More than 100 local artists will captivate festivalgoers with their inspiration and talent in various art forms including oil, acrylic, watercolor, jewelry, sculpture, photography, wood, fiber, glass, paper, metal, and mixed media, all in the relaxed setting of the streets of Long Grove. Artists will also be able to submit their 2D and 3D creations to the festival's annual art competition." See website for more information.

LONG ISLAND STREET FAIRS

(516)442-6000. Fax: (516)543-5170. E-mail: alan@nassaucountycraftshows.com. Website: www.longislandstreetfairs.com. Contact: Alan Finchley, owner. Estab. 2008. Art & craft shows, seasonal/holiday and street fairs held year-round on Long Island. Indoors & outdoors. Accepts handmade crafts and other mediums. Juried. Exhibitors: 100. Number of attendees: varies by event. Most events free to public. Apply online.

ADDITIONAL INFORMATION Deadline for entry: when events are sold out. Application fee: none. Space fee: $175. Exhibition space: 10×10. Average sales: $1,000. For more information, artists should send e-mail, call, send SASE, or visit website.

LONG'S PARK ART & CRAFT FESTIVAL

Long's Park Amphitheater Foundation, 630 Janet Ave., Suite A-111, Lancaster PA 17601-4541. (717)735-8883. Website: www.longspark.org/art-craft-festival. Fine arts & crafts fair held annually Labor Day weekend. Outdoors. Accepts handmade crafts, jewelry, ceramics, painting, glass, photography, fiber, and more. Juried. Number exhibitors: 200. Number attendees: varies. Admission: see website. Apply online.

ADDITIONAL INFORMATION Deadline for entry: February. Application fee: see website. Space fee: $510 (single); $645 (double). Exhibition space: 10×10 (single); 10×20 (double). For more information, artists should call or visit website.

LORING PARK ART FESTIVAL

E-mail: info@loringparkartfestival.com. Website: www.loringparkartfestival.com. "The Loring Park Art Festival is produced by Artists for Artists LLP, an organization of experienced artists. The juried festival is a 2-day event in Loring Park near downtown Minneapolis. The hours are Saturday, 10-6 and Sunday, 10-5. The Festival consists of 140 visual artists displaying their orginal work in 12×12 booths, strolling musicians, scheduled stage performances, children's activities, and food booths. The artwork presented will be from a variety of media including painting, photography, printmaking, handmade paper, wood, jewelry, clay, sculpture, fiber, mixed media, and glass. Within these categories will be a variety of styles from traditional to abstract in a variety of price ranges with the goal being 'something for everyone.'" See website for more information.

LOS ALTOS ROTARY FINE ART SHOW

Website: www.rotaryartshow.com. "Each year, the Los Altos Rotary Club presents Fine Art in the Park—one of the Bay Area's premier open-air art shows, featuring original, juried works by some 170 artists. Fine art pieces range from paintings and sculpture to ceramics, jewelry, and unique gifts. Entertainment, food, and beverages make this an ideal occasion for shopping and family fun. As you stroll through the lovely park viewing first-rate art, you'll take comfort knowing that your purchase goes to support a great cause. All proceeds of the Rotary Fine Art in the Park show go to support a wide range of community service agencies in the Bay Area, and support international development projects in places like Nepal, Mexico, Malaysia, and Afghanistan. Come for a day of fun and great art. There is free parking at Los Altos High School, with shuttles to the park." See website for more information.

LOUISVILLE FESTIVAL OF THE ARTS WITH CRAFT MARKETPLACE AT PADDOCK SHOPS

270 Central Blvd., Suite 107B, Jupiter FL 33458. (561)746-6615. Fax: (561)746-6528. E-mail: info@ artfestival.com. Website: www.artfestival.com. Contact: Malinda Ratliff, communications manager. Estab. 2008. Fine art & craft fair held annually in mid-June. Outdoors. Accepts photography, jewelry, mixed media, sculpture, wood, ceramic, glass, painting, digital, fiber, metal. Juried. Number exhibitors: 130. Number attendees: 50,000. Free to public. Apply online via www.zapplication.org. Deadline: see website. Application fee: $25. Space fee: $375. Exhibition space: 10×10 and 10×20. For more information, artists should e-mail, call, or visit website. Show located at Paddock Shops on Summit Plaza Dr. in Louisville, KY.
TIPS "You have to start somewhere. First, assess where you are, and what you'll need to get things off the ground. Next, make a plan of action. Outdoor street art shows are a great way to begin your career and lifetime as a working artist. You'll meet a lot of other artists who have been where you are now. Network with them!"

MADEIRA BEACH CRAFT FESTIVAL

270 Central Blvd., Suite 107B, Jupiter FL 33458. (561)746-6615. Fax: (561)746-6528. E-mail: info@Art-Festival.com. Website: www.artfestival.com. "Join us in Madeira Beach to browse and purchase a wide variety of ceramics, jewelry, stained glass, metalworks and much more. Our Green Market offers live flora, freshly popped kettle corn, gourmet spices, and sauc-

es. Come meet and visit with some of the nation's best crafters at this free, weekend event, where you're sure to find something for everyone on your gift list."

MADEIRA BEACH THANKSGIVING WEEKEND CRAFT FESTIVAL

270 Central Blvd., Suite 107B, Jupiter FL 33458. (561)746-6615. Fax: (561)746-6528. E-mail: info@ artfestival.com. Website: www.artfestival.com. Contact: Malinda Ratliff, communications manager. Estab. 2012. Fine art & craft fair held annually in November. Outdoors. Accepts photography, jewelry, mixed media, sculpture, wood, ceramic, glass, painting, digital, fiber, metal. Juried. Number exhibitors: 80. Number attendees: 13,000. Free to public. Apply online via www.zapplication.org or visit website for paper application. Deadline: see website. Application fee: $15. Space fee: $250. Exhibition space: 10×10 and 10×20. For more information, artists should e-mail, call, or visit website. Festival located at Madeira Way between Gulf Blvd. & 150th Ave.
TIPS "You have to start somewhere. First, assess where you are, and what you'll need to get things off the ground. Next, make a plan of action. Outdoor street art shows are a great way to begin your career and lifetime as a working artist. You'll meet a lot of other artists who have been where you are now. Network with them!"

MAGNOLIA BLOSSOM FESTIVAL

Magnolia/Columbia County Chamber of Commerce, P.O. Box 866, Magnolia AR 71754. (870)901-2216 or (870)693-5265. E-mail: jpate006@centurytel.net ; jpate002@centurytel.net. Website: www.blossomfestival.org. Craft show held annually in May. Outdoors. Accepts handmade crafts, ceramics, paintings, jewelry, glass, photography, wearable art, and other mediums. Juried. Number exhibitors: see website. Number attendees: varies. Free to public. Apply online.
ADDITIONAL INFORMATION Deadline for entry: late March. Application fee: none. Space fee: varies. Exhibition space: varies. For more information, artists should call, e-mail, or visit website.

MAINE CRAFTS GUILD ANNUAL DIRECTIONS SHOW

The Maine Crafts Guild, 369 Old Union Rd., Washington ME 04574. (207)557-3276. E-mail: mdi.show@mainecraftsguild.com. Website: www.mainecraftsguild.com/shows. "The Maine Craft Guild's Mount Desert Island Directions Show is often referred to as the most outstanding, most successful, and longest-running craft show in Maine. At the annual Show, 80 of Maine's finest craftspeople will fill the newly renovated gymnasium and cafeteria at the Mount Desert Island High School with their work, transforming the space into a gallery-like setting of carefully designed individual displays. Come and meet extraordinary artisans and purchase work of heirloom quality handmade here in Maine. Admission: $6 adults; children under 18 free."

MAINSAIL ARTS FESTIVAL

E-mail: artist@mainsailart.org. Website: www.mainsailart.org. Fine arts & crafts fair held annually in April. Outdoors. Accepts handmade crafts, ceramics, digital art, fibers, glass, graphics, jewelry, metal, mixed media, oil/acrylic, photography, sculpture, watercolor, and wood. Juried. Awards/prizes: $60,000 in cash awards. Number exhibitors: 270. Number attendees: 100,000. Free to public. Apply online.

ADDITIONAL INFORMATION Deadline for entry: December. Application fee: $35. Space fee: $275. Exhibition space: 10×10. For more information, artists should e-mail or visit website.

MAIN STREET FORT WORTH ARTS FESTIVAL

777 Taylor St., Suite 100, Fort Worth TX 76102. (817)336-2787. Fax: (817)335-3113. E-mail: festivalinfo@dfwi.org. Website: www.mainstreetartsfest.org. "Presented by Downtown Fort Worth Initiatives, Inc. ,MAIN ST. has a history of attracting tens of thousands of people annually during the 4-day visual arts, entertainment, and cultural event. MAIN ST. showcases a nationally recognized fine art and fine craft juried art fair, live concerts, performance artists, and street performers on the streets of downtown Fort Worth. We invite a total of 223 artists to the show (including 12 Emerging Artists), which includes approximately 26 award artists from the previous year's

event. We project our images at our jury using state-of-the-art projectors direct from the exact electronic files submitted by the artists." See website for more information.

MAIN STREET TO THE ROCKIES ART FESTIVAL

270 Central Blvd., Suite 107B, Jupiter FL 33458. (561)746-6615. Fax: (561)746-6528. E-mail: info@artfestival.com. Website: www.artfestival.com. Contact: Malinda Ratliff, communications manager. Estab. 2007. Fine art & craft fair held annually in mid-August. Outdoors. Accepts photography, jewelry, mixed media, sculpture, wood, ceramic, glass, painting, digital, fiber, metal. Juried. Number exhibitors: 100. Number attendees: 60,000. Free to public. Apply online via www.zapplication.org. Deadline: see website. Application fee: $35. Space fee: $475. Exhibition space: 10×10 and 10×20. For more information, artists should e-mail, call, or visit website. Festival located at Main St. in Downtown Frisco, CO.

TIPS "You have to start somewhere. First, assess where you are, and what you'll need to get things off the ground. Next, make a plan of action. Outdoor street art shows are a great way to begin your career and lifetime as a working artist. You'll meet a lot of other artists who have been where you are now. Network with them!"

MAKER FAIRE - BAY AREA

E-mail: makers@makerfaire.com. Website: www.makerfaire.com. "Part science fair, part county fair, and part something entirely new, Maker Faire is an all-ages gathering of tech enthusiasts, crafters, educators, tinkerers, hobbyists, engineers, science clubs, authors, artists, students, and commercial exhibitors. All of these 'makers' come to Maker Faire to show what they have made and to share what they have learned. The launch of Maker Faire in the Bay Area in 2006 demonstrated the popularity of making and interest among legions of aspiring makers to participate in hands-on activities and learn new skills at the event. A record 195,000 people attended the 2 flagship Maker Faires in the Bay Area and New York in 2013, with 44% of attendees first-timers at the Bay Area event, and 61% in New York. A family event, 50% attend the event with children. Maker Faire is primarily designed to be forward-looking, showcasing makers who are exploring new forms and new technologies. But it's not just for the novel in technical fields; Maker Faire features innovation and experimentation across the spectrum of science, engineering, art, performance, and craft." See website for more information.

MAKER FAIRE - NEW YORK

E-mail: makers@makerfaire.com. Website: www. makerfaire.com. "Part science fair, part county fair, and part something entirely new, Maker Faire is an all-ages gathering of tech enthusiasts, crafters, educators, tinkerers, hobbyists, engineers, science clubs, authors, artists, students, and commercial exhibitors. All of these 'makers' come to Maker Faire to show what they have made and to share what they have learned. The launch of Maker Faire in the Bay Area in 2006 demonstrated the popularity of making and interest among legions of aspiring makers to participate in hands-on activities and learn new skills at the event. A record 195,000 people attended the 2 flagship Maker Faires in the Bay Area and New York in 2013, with 44% of attendees first-timers at the Bay Area event, and 61% in New York. A family event, 50% attend the event with children. Maker Faire is primarily designed to be forward-looking, showcasing makers who are exploring new forms and new technologies. But it's not just for the novel in technical fields; Maker Faire features innovation and experimentation across the spectrum of science, engineering, art, performance, and craft." See website for more information.

MAMMOTH LAKES FINE ARTS & CRAFTS FESTIVAL

Pacific Fine Arts Festivals, P.O. Box 280, Pine Grove CA 95665. (209)267-4394. Fax: (209)267-4395. E-mail: pfa@pacificfinearts.com. Website: www.pacificfinearts.com. This free event, which runs from 10 a.m. to 5 p.m. each day, will give attendees the opportunity to meet with talented artists and artisans from throughout the western United States as they present their original works against the majestic background of the Sierra Nevada mountains. On display will be a wide variety of arts and crafts including photography, watercolor and oil paintings, ceramics, jewelry,

woodwork, and much more. See website for more information.

MANAYUNK ARTS FESTIVAL

4312 Main St., Philadelphia PA 19127. (215)482-9565. E-mail: info@manayunk.org. Website: www.manayunk.com. Contact: Caitlin Maloney, director of marketing & events. Estab. 1990. Arts & craft show held annually late June. Outdoors. Accepts handmade crafts, fiber, glass, ceramics, jewelry, mixed media, painting, photography, wood, sculpture. Juried. Awards/prizes: Best in each category; Best in Show. Exhibitors: 300. Number of attendees: 200,000. Free to public. Apply via Zapplication.org.

ADDITIONAL INFORMATION Deadline for entry: March 1. Application fee: $30. Space fee: $450. Exhibition space: 10×10. Average sales: $2,000-7,000. For more information send e-mail or call.

TIPS "Displaying your work in a professional manner and offering items at a variety of price points always benefits the artist."

MANDEVILLE CRAFT SHOW

812 Park Ave., Mandeville LA 70448. (985)373-2307. E-mail: dasistas@outlook.com. Website: www.mandevillecraftshow.com. Contact: Joy Frosch, manager. Estab. 2013. Biannual arts & crafts show held in early April & late September. Indoors & outdoors. Accepts handmade crafts. Juried. Exhibitors: 70. Number of attendees: 1,200. Admission: $2 adults; children 12 & under free. See website for application.

ADDITIONAL INFORMATION Deadline for entry: February 7. Space fee: varies. Exhibition space: 8×8, 8×16, 10×10, 10×20. Average sales: $3,700. For more information e-mail, call, or see website.

TIPS "Presentation is everything-look online for suggestions on setup and presentation."

MARCO ISLAND FESTIVAL OF THE ARTS

270 Central Blvd., Suite 107B, Jupiter FL 33458. (561)746-6615. Fax: (561)746-6528. E-mail: info@artfestival.com. Website: www.artfestival.com. Contact: Malinda Ratliff, communications manager. Estab. 2014. Fine art & craft fair held annually in mid-March. Outdoors. Accepts photography, jewelry, mixed media, sculpture, wood, ceramic, glass, paint-

ing, digital, fiber, metal. Juried. Number exhibitors: 175. Number attendees: 40,000. Free to public. Apply online via www.zapplication.org. Deadline: see website. Application fee: $25. Space fee: $415. Exhibition space: 10×10 and 10×20. For more information, artists should e-mail, call, or visit website. Festival located at Veteran's Park off N. Collier Blvd. in Marco Island, FL.

TIPS "You have to start somewhere. First, assess where you are, and what you'll need to get things off the ground. Next, make a plan of action. Outdoor street art shows are a great way to begin your career and lifetime as a working artist. You'll meet a lot of other artists who have been where you are now. Network with them!"

MARION ARTS FESTIVAL

Marion Arts Festival, 1225 Sixth Ave., Ste. 100, Marion IA 52302. Website: www.marionartsfestival.com. Fine arts & crafts fair held annually in May. Outdoors. Accepts handmade crafts, jewelry, ceramics, painting, photography, digital, printmaking, and more. Juried. Awards/prizes: Best of Show, IDEA Award. Number exhibitors: 50. Number attendees: 14,000. Free to public. Apply via Zapplication.org.

ADDITIONAL INFORMATION Deadline for entry: January. Application fee: $25. Space fee: $225. Exhibition space: 10×10. For more information, artists should visit website.

MARITIME MAGIC ARTS & CRAFTS SHOW

107 S. Harrison St., Ludington MI 49431. (231)845-2787. E-mail: artcraftshows@ludingtonartscenter.org. Website: www.ludingtonartscenter.org. Contact: Marion Riedl, show chair. Estab. 2012. Arts & crafts show held annually in June. Indoors. Accepts handmade crafts and fine art. Exhibitors: 30. Number of attendees: 500. Admission: $1; children 12 & under and LACA members free. Apply by calling or sending e-mail.

ADDITIONAL INFORMATION Deadline for entry: April 1. Application fee: none. Space fee: varies. Exhibition space: varies. For more information send e-mail or visit website.

TIPS "Remember, this is an arts/crafts show; items selling for a reasonable price are more successful."

MARKET ON THE GREEN ARTS & CRAFTS FAIR

(203)333-0506. E-mail: crdraw9@aol.com. Outdoor show featuring 70 quality artisans, food vendors, bake booth, flowers, and raffle booth. Held annually in May. Call or e-mail for more information.

MARSHFIELD ART FAIR

New Visions Gallery, 1000 N. Oak Ave., Marshfield WI 54449. (715)387-5562. E-mail: newvisions.gallery@frontier.com. Website: www.marshfieldartfair.weebly.com. "Share a Marshfield tradition with family and friends at this FREE community celebration of the arts, held each year on Mother's Day. Marshfield Art Fair offers a wide variety of fine art and craft by more than 100 Midwestern artists. Musicians and performers entertain throughout the day. Hands-On-Art activities are available for kids." See website for more information.

MCGREGOR SPRING ARTS & CRAFTS FESTIVAL

McGregor-Marquette Chamber of Commerce, P.O. Box 105, McGregor IA 52157. (800)896-0910 or (563)873-2186. E-mail: mcgregormarquettechamber@gmail.com. Website: www.mcgreg-marq.org. Fine arts & crafts fair held annually in May & October. Indoors & outdoors. Accepts handmade crafts, jewelry, ceramics, painting, photography, digital, printmaking, and more. Number exhibitors: see website. Number attendees: varies. Free to public. Apply via online.

ADDITIONAL INFORMATION Deadline for entry: see website. Application fee: none. Space fee: $75 outdoor; $100 indoor. Exhibition space: 10×10. For more information, artists should e-mail, call, or visit website.

MENDOTA SWEET CORN FESTIVAL CRAFTERS MARKET PLACE & FLEA MARKET

Mendota Area Chamber of Commerce, P.O. Box 620, Mendota IL 61342. (815)539-6507. Fax: (815)539-6025. E-mail: rfriedlein@mendotachamber.com. Website: www.sweetcornfestival.com. Contact: Roberta Friedlein, administrative assistant. Estab. 1979. Arts & crafts show held annually in August. Outdoors. Accepts handmade crafts, fine art, antiques, flea market items. Exhibitors: 200. Number of attendees: 55,000. Free to public. Apply by calling or sending e-mail.

ADDITIONAL INFORMATION Deadline for entry: until full. Application fee: none. Space fee: $70. Exhibition space: 10×10. For more information send e-mail, call, or visit website.

MESA ARTS FESTIVAL

Mesa Arts Center, One E. Main St., Mesa AZ 85201. (480)644-6627. Fax: (480)644-6503. E-mail: shawn.lawson@mesaartscenter.com. Website: www.mesaartscenter.com. Fine arts & crafts fair held annually in December. Outdoors. Accepts handmade crafts, jewelry, ceramics, painting, photography, digital, printmaking, and more. Number exhibitors: see website. Number attendees: varies. Free to public. Apply online.

ADDITIONAL INFORMATION Deadline for entry: see website. Application fee: $25. Space fee: $250. Exhibition space: 10×10. For more information, artists should e-mail, call, or visit website.

MESA MACFEST

E-mail: info@macfestmesa.com. Website: www.macfestmesa.com. "The Mission of Mesa Arts and Crafts Festival (MACFest) is to provide an environment that encourages the economic and artistic growth of emerging and established artists and crafters while revitalizing downtown Mesa and building a sense of community. MACFest is a free event featuring unique artist creations, music, and fun for the whole family." See website for more information.

MESQUITE QUILT SHOW

Rutherford Recreation Center, 900 Rutherford Dr., P.O. Box 850137, Mesquite TX 75185-0137. (972)523-7672. Website: www.mesquitequiltguildinc.com. Juried quilt show. See website for more information.

THE MIAMI PROJECT

Art Market Productions, 109 S. Fifth St., Suite 407, Brooklyn NY 11249. (212)518-6912. Fax: (212)518-7142. E-mail: info@art-mrkt.com. Website: www.miami-project.com. "Miami Project is a contemporary and modern art fair that takes place during Miami's art fair week. Working with a focused selection of galleries from around the globe, Miami Project presents a diverse selection of work by today's leading artists. What sets Miami Project apart is its unique venue which is constructed for the most optimal viewing experience for both dealers and collectors alike." See website for more information.

MICHIGAN FIRST SUMMER IN THE VILLAGE

City of Lathrup Village, 27400 Southfield Road, Lathrup Village MI 48076. (248)557-2600 ext. 224. E-mail: recreation@lathrupvillage.org. Website: www.summerinthevillage.com. Estab. 2003. Arts & crafts show held annually in June. Outdoors. Accepts handmade crafts, ceramics, fiber, glass, jewelry, metal, mixed media, painting, photography, printmaking, sculpture, wood. Juried. Exhibitors: varies. Number of attendees: varies. Free to public. Apply online.

ADDITIONAL INFORMATION Deadline for entry: see website. Application fee: $20. Space fee: $85. Exhibition space: 10×10. For more information, artists should send e-mail, visit website, or call.

MIDSUMMER ARTS FAIRE

P.O. Box 24, Quincy IL 62306. (217)779-2285. Fax: (217)222-8698. E-mail: info@artsfaire.org. Website: www.artsfaire.org. Contact: Kris Eyler, coordinator. Fine art show held annually in June. Outdoors. Accepts photography, paintings, pottery, jewelry. Juried. Awards/prizes: various totaling $5,000. Exhibitors: 60. Number of attendees: 7,000. Free to public. Apply via Zapplication.org.

ADDITIONAL INFORMATION Deadline for entry: February 28. Application fee: $20. Space fee: $100. Exhibition space: 10×10. Average sales: $2,500. For more information, artists should e-mail, call, see Facebook page, or visit website.

TIPS "Variety of price points with several options at a lower price point as well."

MIDWEST FIBER & FOLK ART FAIR

Midwest Fiber & Folk Art Fair, P.O. Box 754, Crystal Lake IL 60039-0754. (815)276-2537. E-mail: carol@artaffairs.org. Website: www.fiberandfolk.com. "The Midwest Fiber & Folk Art Fair annually on the 1st weekend of August. Come on out for shopping in the

Marketplace, featuring both supplies and finished goods (wearable art), take a workshop, watch the demonstrations, listen to the music, pet an alpaca, or enjoy the food." See website for more information.

MILLENIUM ART FESTIVAL

Amdur Productions, P.O. Box 550, Highland Park IL, 60035. (847)926-4300. E-mail: info@amdurproductions.com. Website: www.amdurproductions.com. Fine arts & crafts fair held annually in May. Outdoors. Accepts handmade crafts and other mediums. Juried. Exhibitors: 110. Number of attendees: varies. Admission: Free to public. Apply online.
ADDITIONAL INFORMATION Deadline for entry: see website. Application fee: see website. Space fee: $495. Exhibition space: see website. For more information, artists should e-mail, visit website, or call.

MILL VALLEY FALL ARTS FESTIVAL

MVFAF, P.O. Box 300, Mill Valley CA 94942. (415)381-8090. E-mail: mvfafartists@gmail.com. Website: www.mvfaf.org. "The Mill Valley Fall Arts Festival has been recognized as a fine art and craft show of high-quality original artwork for over 55 years. The Festival draws well-educated buyers from nearby affluent neighborhoods of Marin County and the greater San Francisco Bay Area. The event provides an exceptional opportunity for the sale of unique, creative, and high-end work." Artists interested in participating must apply via Zapplication.org. Applications open mid-January and close mid-April. See website for more information.

MILWAUKEE AVENUE ARTS FESTIVAL

E-mail: info@iamlogansquare.com. Website: www.milwaukeeavenueartsfestival.org. A celebration of the art, music, and culture of Logan Square. See website for more information.

MILWAUKEE DOMES ART FESTIVAL

Website: www.milwaukeedomesartfestival.com. Fine arts & crafts fair held annually in August. Indoors & outdoors. Accepts handmade crafts, jewelry, ceramics, painting, photography, digital, printmaking, and more. Juried. Awards/prizes: $10,500 in awards and prizes. Number exhibitors: see website. Number attendees: varies. Free to public. Apply online.
ADDITIONAL INFORMATION Deadline for entry: see website. Application fee: $35. Space fee: $250 outdoor; $450 indoor. Exhibition space: 10×10. For more information visit website.

MINNE-FAIRE: A MAKER AND DIY EXPOSITION

E-mail: fair@tcmaker.org. Website: www.tcmaker.org. "This 2-day event will be returning to its roots. Admission will be free, though we'll happily accept donations to keep it running. We'll be showing off our expanded space and capabilities and celebrating all things Maker— that is after all what this is all about. If you're interested in participating, feel free to email us at fair@tcmaker.org." See website for more information.

MINNESOTA WOMEN'S ART FESTIVAL

E-mail: nlsiegal@aol.com. Website: www.womensartfestival.com. "The mission of the Women's Art Festival is to provide a welcoming place for women artists to show and sell their creations and to provide a fun and festive atmosphere for guests to shop, gather, and enjoy community. Supporting local women artists of all experience levels, from first-time exhibitors to experienced professionals, we are a nonjuried show with the expectation that all goods are of excellent quality, made and sold by local women. We do not accept dealers or importers and define local as any woman who wants to travel to Minneapolis for a day of fun, camaraderie, community, and creativity. Now held at the Colin Powell Youth Leadership Center, 2924 4th Ave. S, in Minneapolis, the event has grown to include over 130 women artists working in a large variety of media. There is live music by women performers throughout the day and a women-owned coffee shop providing food, beverages, and treats. Artists and guests alike comment on the quality of the artistic work, the fun and comfortable atmosphere, the caliber of the music and the wonderful addition of good food, good coffee, and the chance to see good friends." See website for more information.

MISSION FEDERAL ARTWALK

2210 Columbia St., San Diego CA 92101. (619)615-1090. Fax: (619)615-1099. E-mail: info@artwalksandiego.org. Website: www.artwalksandiego.org. Fine arts & crafts fair held annually in April. Outdoors. Accepts handmade crafts, jewelry, ceramics, painting, photography, digital, printmaking, and more. Juried. Number exhibitors: 350. Number attendees: 90,000. Free to public. Apply online.

ADDITIONAL INFORMATION Deadline for entry: January. Application fee: none. Space fee: varies. Exhibition space: varies. For more information, artists should e-mail, call, or visit website.

MOLLIE MCGEE'S HOLIDAY MARKET

Mollie McGee's Market, P.O. Box 6324, Longmont CO 80501. (303)772-0649. E-mail: mollie@molliemcgee.com. Website: www.molliemcgee.com. Fine arts & crafts fair held annually in October & November. Outdoors. Accepts handmade crafts and other mediums. Juried. Number exhibitors: see website. Number attendees: varies. Free to public. Apply online.

ADDITIONAL INFORMATION Deadline for entry: see website. Application fee: none. Space fee: varies. Exhibition space: varies. For more information, artists should e-mail, call, or visit website.

MONTE SANO ART FESTIVAL

706 Randolph Ave., Huntsville AL 35801. (256)653-3654. E-mail: curtisbenzle@gmail.com. Website: www.montesanoartfestival.com. Contact: Curtis Benzle, director. Estab. 1998. Annual arts & crafts show held in September. Outdoors. Accepts handmade crafts, painting, sculpture, photography, prints. Juried. Exhibitors: 130. Number of attendees: 4,000. Admission: $7. Apply via website.

ADDITIONAL INFORMATION Deadline for entry: May 1. Application fee: $15. Space fee: $125. Exhibition space: 100 sq. ft. Average sales: $2,000. For more information see website.

TIPS "Apply with a quality booth slide."

MONUMENT SQUARE ART FESTIVAL

Monument Square Art Festival, c/o The Racine Arts Council, 316 Sixth St., Racine WI 53403. E-mail: jeff@theelementsgallery.com. Website: www.monumentsquareartfest.com. Fine arts & crafts fair held annually in May. Outdoors. Accepts handmade crafts and other mediums. Juried. Number exhibitors: see website. Number attendees: varies. Free to public. Apply online.

ADDITIONAL INFORMATION Deadline for entry: April. Application fee: none. Space fee: varies. Exhibition space: varies. For more information, artists should e-mail or visit website.

MORNING GLORY FINE CRAFT FAIR

(262)894-0038. E-mail: bethhoffman@wi.rr.com. Website: www.wdcc.org. Contact: Beth Hoffman. Fine craft fair held annually in August. Outdoors (on the grounds of the Marcus; enter at Red Arrow Park). Accepts fine crafts. Juried. Awards/prizes: $3,000 in cash and prizes. Number exhibitors: 135. Number attendees: 7,000. Free to public. Apply via Zapplication.org.

ADDITIONAL INFORMATION Deadline for entry: March. Application fee: $35. Space fee: $300-650. Exhibition space: 10×10; limited number of double booths available. For more information, artists should e-mail, call, or visit website.

MOUNT DORA ARTS FESTIVAL

Mount Dora Center for the Arts, 138 East Fifth Ave., Mount Dora FL 32757. (352)383-0880. Fax: (352)383-7753. Website: www.mountdoracenterforthearts.org/arts-festival. "A juried fine arts festival, for art lovers, casual festival-goers, and families, nothing compares to the Mount Dora Arts Festival. In addition to the endless rows of fine art, including oil paintings, watercolors, acrylics, clay, sculpture, and photography, the festival features local and regional musical entertainment at a main stage in Donnelly Park." See website for more information.

MOUNT MARY STARVING ARTIST SHOW

Website: www.mtmary.edu/alumnae/events/starving-artists-show.html. Contact: Alumnae & Parent Engagement Office. "Always the Sunday after Labor Day! This annual outdoor art show features local and national artists that work in all mediums and sell original artwork for $100 or less." See website for more information.

MULLICA HILL ARTS AND CRAFTS FESTIVAL

50 S. Main St., Mullica Hill NJ 08062. (856)418-1135. E-mail: mullicahillartcenter@gmail.com. Website: www.mullicahillartcenter.com. Contact: Lynne Perez or Chelsea Hagerty. Estab. 2011. Fine arts & crafts show held annually in May. Outdoors. Accepts handmade crafts and original art. Exhibitors: 100. Number of attendees: 3,000. Free to public. Apply online.

ADDITIONAL INFORMATION Deadline for entry: early April. Application fee: $30. Space fee: $30. Exhibition space: 15×15. For more information e-mail.

TIPS "Register early and stay for the day."

MYSTIC OUTDOOR ART FESTIVAL

E-mail: Cherielin@MysticChamber.org. Website: www.mysticchamber.org/?sec=sec&s=44. "The annual Mystic Outdoor Art Festival has evolved in many ways from its humble beginnings. In 1957, Milton Baline and several other local business owners and art lovers proposed that Mystic pattern a festival after the famous Washington Square Festival in New York. That first show featured 105 artists and 500 paintings. Between 4,000 and 6,000 visitors came to admire and purchase art. Today the Mystic Outdoor Art Festival stretches over 2 miles and is the oldest of its kind in the Northeast. The Mystic Outdoor Art Festival has grown to over 250 artists who come from all corners of the United States and bring more than 100,000 works of art." See website for more information.

NAMPA FESTIVAL OF ARTS

131 Constitution Way, Nampa ID 83686. (208)468-5858. Fax: (208)465-2282. E-mail: rec@cityofnampa.us. Website: www.nampaparksandrecreation.org. Contact: Wendy Davis, program director. Estab. 1986. Fine art & craft show held annually mid-August. Outdoors. Accepts handmade crafts, fine art, photography, metal, anything handmade. Juried. Awards/prizes: cash. Exhibitors: 180. Number of attendees: 15,000. Free to public. See website for application.

ADDITIONAL INFORMATION Deadline for entry: July 10. Space fee: $40-90. Exhibition space: 10×10, 15×15, 20×20. For more information send e-mail, call, or visit website.

TIPS "Price things reasonably and have products displayed attractively."

NAPERVILLE WOMAN'S CLUB ART FAIR

(630)209-1246. E-mail: naperartfair@comcast.net. Website: www.napervillewomansclub.org. Contact: Roxanne Lang. "Over 100 local and national artists will be displaying original artwork in clay, fiber, glass, jewelry, mixed media, metal, painting, photography, sculpture, and wood. Ribbons and cash prizes are awarded to winning artists by local judges and NWC. The Naperville Woman's Club Art Fair is the longest continuously running art fair in Illinois. Activities at this event include entertainment, a silent auction, artist demonstrations, the Empty Bowl Fundraiser to benefit local food pantries, and the Petite Picassos children's activities tent. This is the largest fundraiser of the year for the Naperville Woman's Club. Proceeds from the event help fund a local art scholarship and local charities. Admission and parking are free. For more information please e-mail us at: naperartfair@comcast.net."

NAPLES NATIONAL ART FESTIVAL

Website: www.naplesart.org. "The annual Naples National Art Festival is consistently voted among the top 10 art festivals in the country by *Sunshine Artist* Magazine, and the local community continues to count the Naples National Art Festival among its premiere, must-see events. This festival features the talents of more than 260 artists from around the country and awards $5,000 in cash to top artists. The festival draws crowds in excess of 22,000. Don't miss it!" See website for more information.

NATIVE AMERICAN FINE ART FESTIVAL

E-mail: tkramer@litchfield-park.org. Website: www.litchfield-park.org. Contact: Tricia Kramer. "The Native American Arts Festival highlights the finest southwest Native American artists including traditional and contemporary Native American jewelry, pottery, basketry, weaving, katsinas, painting, and beadwork. The event includes a variety of Native American art, entertainment, and learning opportunities. Admission fee is $5 per person, $3 students with I.D., children 12 and under admitted free. For more information call 623-935-9040."

NEACA'S FALL CRAFT SHOW

NEACA Fall Show, Attn: Annie Hannah, 2100 My-thewood Dr., Huntsville AL 35803. (256)859-0511; (256)883-4028. Website: www.neaca.org. Craft show held annually in September. Indoors. Accepts hand-made crafts, ceramics, paintings, jewelry, glass, pho-tography, wearable art, and other mediums. Juried. Number exhibitors: 150. Number attendees: 25,000. Free to public. Apply online.

ADDITIONAL INFORMATION Deadline for entry: August. Application fee: none. Space fee: $225. Ex-hibition space: 10×12. For more information, artists should call, e-mail, or visit website.

NEPTUNE ART AND CRAFT SHOW

E-mail: christie@virginiamoca.org. Website: www. virginiamoca.org/outdoor-art-shows/neptune-arts-craft-show. "The Neptune Festival Art & Craft Show is part of a citywide festival at the Virginia Beach oceanfront. The Art & Craft Show portion is produced by The Virginia Museum of Contemporary Art and showcases 250 artists and crafters." See website for more information.

NEW ENGLAND HOLIDAY
CRAFT SPECTACULAR

38 Charles St., Rochester NH 03867. (603)332-2616. E-mail: info@castleberryfairs.com. Website: www.cas-tleberryfairs.com. Fine arts & crafts fair held annually in December. Indoors. Accepts handmade crafts, jew-elry, ceramics, painting, photography, digital, print-making, and more. Juried. Number exhibitors: see website. Number attendees: varies. Admission: $7 adults; children 12 & under free. Apply online.

ADDITIONAL INFORMATION Deadline for entry: see website. Application fee: see website. Space fee: varies. Exhibition space: varies. For more informa-tion, artists should e-mail, call, or visit website.

NEWTON ARTS FESTIVAL

Piper Promotions, 4 Old Green Rd., Sandy Hook CT 06482. (203)512-9100. E-mail: staceyolszewski@ya-hoo.com. Website: www.newtownartsfestival.com. Contact: Stacey Olszewski. Fine arts & crafts fair held annually in September. Outdoors. Accepts handmade crafts, jewelry, ceramics, painting, photography, digi-

tal, printmaking, and more. Juried. Number exhibi-tors: see website. Number attendees: varies. Admis-sion: $5; children 12 & under free. Apply online.

ADDITIONAL INFORMATION Deadline for en-try: August. Application fee: none. Space fee: $105 (booth); $225 (festival tent). Exhibition space: 10×10. For more information, artists should e-mail, call, or visit website.

NIANTIC OUTDOOR ART & CRAFT SHOW

Niantic Outdoor Art & Craft Show, P.O. Box 227, Niantic CT 06357. (860)739-9128. E-mail: artshow-woody@yahoo.com. Website: www.nianticartsand-craftshow.com. Contact: Craig Woody. Fine art & craft show held annually in July. Outdoors. Accepts handmade crafts, ceramics, fiber, glass, graphics, jew-elry, leather, metal, mixed media, painting, photog-raphy, printmaking, sculpture, woodworking. Juried. Number exhibitors: 142. Number attendees: varies. Free to public. Apply online.

ADDITIONAL INFORMATION Deadline for entry: March. Application fee: $20. Space fee: varies. Exhi-bition space: varies. For more information, artists should e-mail, call, or visit website.

NORTH CHARLESTON ARTS FESTIVAL

P.O. Box 190016, North Charleston SC 29419-9016. (843)740-5854. E-mail: culturalarts@northcharles-ton.org. Website: www.northcharlestonartsfest.com. Fine arts & crafts fair held annually in May. Outdoors. Accepts handmade crafts, jewelry, ceramics, painting, photography, digital, printmaking and more. Juried. Number exhibitors: see website. Number attendees: 30,000. Admission: see website. Apply online.

ADDITIONAL INFORMATION Deadline for entry: January. Application fee: see website. Space fee: see website. Exhibition space: see website. For more in-formation, artists should e-mail, call or visit website.

NORTHERN ILLINOIS ART SHOW

Website: www.kval.us. Held annually in June in Syc-amore, Illinois, on the DeKalb County Courthouse Lawn, the Northern Illinois Art Show features the work of 70 artists from across the Midwest. For more information go to www.kval.us or call Tamara Shriver at (815)758-2606.

TIPS "All work must be original and handcrafted by the artist. No buy/sell or imports. The artist must be present during the show."

NORTHERN VIRGINA FINE ARTS FESTIVAL

(703)471-9242. E-mail: info@restonarts.org. Website: www.northernvirginiafineartsfestival.org. Fine arts & crafts fair held annually in May. Outdoors. Accepts handmade crafts, jewelry, ceramics, painting, photography, digital, printmaking, and more. Juried. Number exhibitors: 200. Number attendees: varies. Admission: $5; children 18 & under free. Apply online.

ADDITIONAL INFORMATION Deadline for entry: see website. Application fee: see website. Space fee: see website. Exhibition space: see website. For more information, artists should e-mail, call, or visit website.

NORTH IOWA EVENT CENTER'S SPRING EXTRAVAGANZA

(641)529-3003. E-mail: craftsunited@gmail.com. Contact: Jennifer Martin. Annual indoor craft show at the North Iowa Events Center in Mason City, Iowa. Hourly door prizes given away. Admission is free; will donation to the North Iowa Humane Society. Hand crafted items, hand baked goods, and home based businesses allowed. Email or call for more information.

NORTH SHORE FESTIVAL OF ART

Amdur Productions, P.O. Box 550, Highland Park IL 60035. (847)926-4300. E-mail: info@amdurproductions.com. Website: www.amdurproductions.com. Fine arts & crafts fair held annually in July. Outdoors. Accepts handmade crafts, jewelry, ceramics, painting, photography, digital, printmaking, and more. Juried. Number exhibitors: 100. Number attendees: 84,000. Free to public. Apply online.

ADDITIONAL INFORMATION Deadline for entry: see website. Application fee: $25. Space fee: $445. Exhibition space: 10×10. For more information, artists should e-mail, call, or visit website.

NORWALK ART FESTIVAL

(518)852-6478. E-mail: suebg.art@gmail.com. Website: www.norwalkfestival.org; gordonfinearts.org. Estab. 2012. Arts & crafts show held annually in June. Outdoors. Accepts handmade crafts and fine art. Juried. Awards/prizes: cash & ribbons. Exhibitors: 150. Number of attendees: 7,000-10,000. Free to public. Apply online.

ADDITIONAL INFORMATION Deadline for entry: April 1. Application fee: $25. Space fee: $350. Exhibition space: 10×12. For more information visit website, send e-mail, or call.

TIPS "Display your best works."

NORWAY ARTS FESTIVAL

Irina Kahn, Western Maine Art Group, P.O. Box 122, Norway ME 04268. (207)890-3649. E-mail: kahnig@yahoo.com. Website: www.norwayartsfestival.org. "Norway Arts Festival is a 4-day event held in Norway, Maine. The Festival starts on Thursday evening with a focus feature and continues Friday evening with music. Saturday is the Art Show and myriad events and performances that are held along Norway's historic Main Street. All events are free and open to all ages." See website for more information.

NOT YO MAMA'S CRAFT FAIR

E-mail: notyomamajc@gmail.com. Website: www.notyomamasaffairs.com. "Not Yo Mama's Craft Fair is an exclusive and unique event where the best and brightest creatives from the Jersey City metro area can hock their DIY wares to the coolest cats in Chill Town." See website for more information.

NOT YOUR GRANDMA'S CRAFT FAIR

E-mail: dizzycupcake@gmail.com. Website: www.nygcf.org. Contact: Jessie or Heather. "Not Your Grandma's Craft Fair spawned from the need to fill a gap in the local artsy craft market. After attending many local craft fairs, Dizzy Cupcakes realized they just didn't quite fit in. They wanted somewhere to not only sell their wares but also a place to see artists like them, a little estranged from the potholder/doily crowd. The Dizzy Cupcakes created Not Your Grandma's Craft Fair to be a showcase of the area's best artists and crafters, attracting crowds who might not make it to the average church basement bazaar." See website or e-mail for more information.

NUTS ABOUT ART

E-mail: nps@grics.net. Website: www.thenextpicture-show.com/pdf/NAA2014.pdf. Fine Art Show Sponsored by The Next Picture Show at John Dixon Park. Free Admission. See website for more information.

OCONOMOWOC FESTIVAL OF THE ARTS

Oconomowoc Festival of the Arts, P.O. Box 651, Oconomowoc WI 53066. Website: www.oconomowocarts.org. Estab. 1970. Fine arts & crafts fair held annually in August. Outdoors. Accepts handmade crafts, jewelry, ceramics, painting, photography, digital, printmaking, and more. Juried. Awards/prizes: $3,500 in awards & prizes. Number exhibitors: 140. Number attendees: varies. Admission: Free to public. Apply online.

ADDITIONAL INFORMATION Deadline for entry: March. Application fee: $40. Space fee: $250. Exhibition space: 10×10. For more information, artists should visit website.

ODD DUCK BAZAAR

P.O. Box 813045, Hollywood FL 33081. E-mail: info@oddduckbazaar.com. Website: www.oddduckbazaar.com. Contact: Shelley Mitchell, co-producer. Estab. 2010. Arts & crafts show (specializes in "odd" or unusual) held annually in late March or early April. Indoors. Accepts handmade crafts, vintage, antique. Juried. Exhibitors: 65. Number of attendees: 3,000. Admission: $5. Apply online.

ADDITIONAL INFORMATION Deadline for entry: see website. Application fee: $3. Space fee: $75-100. Exhibition space: 36-72 sq. ft. For more information, artists should send e-mail, visit website, or see social media.

TIPS "We are looking for outside of the norm, so feel free to experiment."

OHIO MART

Stan Hywet Hall and Gardens, 714 N. Portage Path, Akron OH 44303. (330)836-5533; (888)836-5533. E-mail: info@stanhywet.org. Website: www.stanhywet.

org. Estab. 1966. Fine arts & crafts fair held annually in October. Outdoors. Accepts handmade crafts, jewelry, ceramics, painting, photography, digital, printmaking, and more. Juried. Number exhibitors: see website. Number attendees: varies. Admission: $9 adults; $2 youth. Apply online.

ADDITIONAL INFORMATION Deadline for entry: see website. Application fee: see website. Space fee: see website. Exhibition space: see website. For more information, artists should call, e-mail, or visit website.

OKLAHOMA CITY FESTIVAL OF THE ARTS

Arts Council of Oklahoma City, 400 W. California, Oklahoma City OK 73102. (405)270-4848. Fax: (405)270-4888. E-mail: info@artscouncilokc.com. Website: www.artscouncilokc.com. Estab. 1967. Fine arts & crafts fair held annually in April. Outdoors. Accepts handmade crafts, jewelry, ceramics, painting, photography, digital, printmaking, and more. Juried. Number exhibitors: 144. Number attendees: varies. Free to public. Apply online.

ADDITIONAL INFORMATION Deadline for entry: see website. Application fee: see website. Space fee: see website. Exhibition space: see website. For more information, artists should call, e-mail, or visit website.

OLD CAPITOL ART FAIR

Springfield Old Capitol Art Fair, P.O. Box 5701, Springfield IL 62705. (405)270-4848. Fax: (405)270-4888. E-mail: artistinfo@yahoo.com. Website: www.socaf.org. Contact: Kate Baima. Estab. 1961. Fine arts & crafts fair held annually in May. Outdoors. Accepts handmade crafts, jewelry, ceramics, painting, photography, digital, printmaking, and more. Juried. Awards/prizes: 1st Place, 2nd Place, 3rd Place, Awards of Merit. Number exhibitors: see website. Number attendees: varies. Free to public. Apply online.

ADDITIONAL INFORMATION Deadline for entry: November. Application fee: $35. Space fee: $300 (single); $550 (double). Exhibition space: 10×10 (single); 10×20 (double). For more information, artists should call, e-mail, or visit website.

OLD FASHIONED CHRISTMAS- REDMOND

Central Oregon Shows, P.O. Box 1555, Sisters OR 97759. (541)420-0279. E-mail: centraloregonshows@

gmail.com. Website: www.centraloregonshows.com. "The theme is an old-fashioned atmosphere, with dimmed lighting to set the buying mood for the variety of arts, crafts, antiques, and entertainment. There will be a candy-land maze leading to Santa, 3 resting stations with flat-screen televisions playing classic holiday movies, and a festive entrance lined with Christmas trees, garland, Chanukah, and Kwanzaa displays. Free parking for customers and exhibitors. The entrance fee is $4.00 with a canned food for a local charity." See website for more information.

OLD FASHIONED CHRISTMAS- SALEM

Central Oregon Shows, P.O. Box 1555, Sisters OR 97759. (541)420-0279. E-mail: centraloregonshows@gmail.com. Website: www.centraloregonshows.com. "The theme is an old-fashioned atmosphere, with dimmed lighting to set the buying mood for the variety of arts, crafts, antiques, and entertainment. There will be a candy-land maze leading to Santa, 3 resting stations with flat-screen televisions playing classic holiday movies, and a festive entrance lined with Christmas trees, garland, Chanukah, and Kwanzaa displays. Free parking for customers and exhibitors. The entrance fee is $4.00 with a canned food for a local charity." See website for more information.

OLD FOURTH WARD PARK ARTS FESTIVAL

592 N. Angier Ave. NE, Atlanta GA 30308. (404)873-1222. E-mail: info@affps.com, Website: oldfourthwardparkartsfestival.com. Contact: Lisa Windle, festival director. Estab. 2013. Arts & crafts show held annually late June. Outdoors. Accepts handmade crafts, painting, photography, sculpture, leather, metal, glass, jewelry. Juried by a panel. Awards/prizes: ribbons. Number of exhibitors: 130. Number of attendees: 25,000. Free to public. Apply online at www.zapplication.com.

ADDITIONAL INFORMATION Deadline for entry: late April. Application fee: $25. Space fee: $225. Exhibition space: 10×10. For more information, send e-mail or see website.

TIPS "Offer a variety of price ranges, have a professional setup and display materials, greet guests."

OLD SAYBROOK ARTS & CRAFTS SHOW

Website: www.oldsaybrookchamber.com/pages/Arts-CraftsFestival/. "From acrylics to photography, jewelry and oil painting, wood sculptures and glass creations, the 51st annual juried show will feature fine art and handmade crafts sure to please a wide array of tastes and interests. Admission and ample parking are free." See website for more information and to apply.

OLD TOWN ART FESTIVAL

Old Town San Diego Chamber of Commerce, P.O. Box 82686, San Diego CA 92138 (619)233-5008. Fax: (619)233-0898. E-mail: rob-vslmedia@cox.net; otsd@aol.com. Website: www.oldtownartfestival.com. Fine arts & crafts fair held annually in September. Outdoors. Accepts handmade crafts, jewelry, ceramics, painting, photography, digital, printmaking, and more. Juried. Number exhibitors: see website. Number attendees: 15,000. Free to public. Apply online.

ADDITIONAL INFORMATION Deadline for entry: September 1. Application fee: $25. Space fee: varies. Exhibition space: varies. For more information, artists should call, e-mail, or visit website.

OMAHA SUMMER ARTS FESTIVAL

Vic Gutman & Associates, P.O. Box 31036, Omaha NE 68131. (402)345-5401. Fax: (402)342-4114. E-mail: ebalazs@vgagroup.com. Website: www.summerarts.org. Estab. 1975. Fine arts & crafts fair held annually in June. Outdoors. Accepts handmade crafts, jewelry, ceramics, painting, photography, digital, printmaking, and more. Juried. Number exhibitors: 135. Number attendees: varies. Free to public. Apply online.

ADDITIONAL INFORMATION Deadline for entry: see website. Application fee: see website. Space fee: varies. Exhibition space: varies. For more information, artists should call, e-mail, or visit website.

◯ONE OF A KIND
CRAFT SHOW (ONTARIO)

One of a Kind Show & Sale, 10 Alcorn Ave., Suite 100, Toronto, Ontario M4V 3A9 Canada. (416)960-5399. Fax: (416)923-5624. E-mail: jill@oneofakindshow.com. Website: www.oneofakindshow.com. Contact: Jill Benson. Estab. 1975. Fine arts & crafts fair held annually 3 times a year. Outdoors. Accepts handmade

crafts, jewelry, ceramics, painting, photography, digital, printmaking, and more. Juried. Number exhibitors: varies per show. Number attendees: varies per show. Free to public. Apply online.
ADDITIONAL INFORMATION Deadline for entry: see website. Application fee: see website. Space fee: varies. Exhibition space: varies. For more information, artists should call, e-mail, or visit website.

ORANGE BEACH FESTIVAL OF ART

Orange Beach Arts Festival, 26389 Canal Road, Orange Beach AL 36561. (251)981-2787. Fax: (251)981-6981. E-mail: helpdesk@orangebeachartcenter.com. Website: www.orangebeachartsfestival.com. Fine art & craft show held annually in March. Outdoors. Accepts handmade crafts, ceramics, paintings, jewelry, glass, photography, wearable art, and other mediums. Juried. Number exhibitors: 90. Number attendees: varies. Free to public. Apply online.
ADDITIONAL INFORMATION Deadline for entry: See website. Application fee: see website. Space fee: varies. Exhibition space: varies. For more information, artists should call, e-mail, or visit website.

❤THE ORIGINAL VINTAGE & HANDMADE FAIR

E-mail: info@cowboysandcustard.com. Website: www.vintageandhandmade.co.uk. "This popular event is always a joy to attend with 40 stalls brimming with scrumptious vintage goodies & divine handmade lovelies. Showcasing some of the best vintage dealers, artists, and creative designer-makers from the South-West & beyond, it is a day not to be missed. With everything from vintage china & glass, toys & games, books & ephemera, fabrics & haberdashery, homewares, handmade hats, quilts, notebooks, cards, purses, bags, and so much more, you will find much to inspire & delight you!" See website for more information.

OUTDOOR ART FESTIVAL OF THE BRUCE MUSEUM

(518)852-6478. E-mail: sue@brucemuseum.org. Website: www.brucemuseum.org. Estab. 1979. Arts & crafts show held annually in October. Outdoors. Accepts handmade crafts and fine art. Juried. Awards/prizes: cash & ribbons. Exhibitors: 90. Number of attendees: 7,000-10,000. Admission: $8; free for members. Apply online.
ADDITIONAL INFORMATION Deadline for entry: December 1. Application fee: $25. Space fee: $360. Exhibition space: 10×12. For more information visit website, send e-mail, or call.

OUTDOOR CRAFTS FESTIVAL OF THE BRUCE MUSEUM

(518)852-6478. E-mail: sue@brucemuseum.org. Website: www.brucemuseum.org. Estab. 1985. Arts & crafts show held annually in May. Outdoors. Accepts handmade crafts and fine art. Juried. Awards/prizes: cash & ribbons. Exhibitors: 85. Number of attendees: 7,000-10,000. Admission: $8; free for members. Apply online.
ADDITIONAL INFORMATION Deadline for entry: December 1. Application fee: $25. Space fee: $360. Exhibition space: 10×12. For more information visit website, send e-mail, or call.

PACIFIC CITY ART ON THE BEACH

Central Oregon Shows, P.O. Box 1555, Sisters OR 97759. (541)420-0279. E-mail: centraloregonshows@gmail.com. Website: www.centraloregonshows.com. "This event features a variety of arts, crafts, antiques, food, and entertainment with a special fundraiser benefiting a local charity." See website for more information.

PACIFIC INTERNATIONAL QUILT FESTIVAL

Mancuso Show Management, P.O. Box 667, New Hope PA 18938. (215)862-5828. Fax: (215)862-9753. E-mail: mancuso@quiltfest.com. Website: www.quiltfest.com. "This well-recognized and largest quilt show on the West Coast, known to quilters as P.I.Q.F., is held at the Santa Clara Convention Center in the greater San Francisco Bay Area. Not only does this incredible event feature astounding works of quilt art, it also offers a wide array of workshops and lectures presented by world-renowned instructors. A 300-booth Merchants Mall can be found with the best in fabrics, notions, machines, wearable art, and everything for the quilter, artist, and home sewer." See website for more information.

PA GUILD OF CRAFTSMEN FINE CRAFT FAIRS

Center of American Craft, 335 N. Queen St., Lancaster PA 17603. (717)431-8706. E-mail: nick@pacrafts.org. Website: www.pacrafts.org/fine-craft-fairs. Contact: Nick Mohler. Fine arts & crafts fair held 5 times a year. Outdoors. Accepts handmade crafts, jewelry, ceramics, painting, photography, digital, printmaking, and more. Juried. Number exhibitors: varies per show. Number attendees: varies per show. Free to public. Apply online.

ADDITIONAL INFORMATION Deadline for entry: January. Application fee: $25. Space fee: varies. Exhibition space: 10×10. For more information, artists should call, e-mail, or visit website.

PALM BEACH FINE CRAFT SHOW

Crafts America, LLC, P.O. Box 603, Green Farms CT 06838. (203)254-0486. Fax: (203)254-9672. E-mail: info@craftsamericashows.com. Website: www.craftsamericashows.com. Fine crafts fair held annually in February. Indoors. Accepts handmade crafts, basketry, ceramics, fiber, furniture, glass, jewelry, leather, metal, mixed media, paper, wood. Juried. Number exhibitors: 125. Number attendees: varies. Admission: $15 general; $14 senior citizens; children 12 & under free. Apply online.

ADDITIONAL INFORMATION Deadline for entry: October. Application fee: $45. Space fee: varies. Exhibition space: varies. For more information, artists should e-mail, call or visit website.

PALMER PARK ART FAIR

Integrity Shows, P.O. Box 1070, Ann Arbor MI 48106. E-mail: info@integrityshows.com. Website: www.palmerparkartfair.com/. Contact: Mark Loeb. Estab. 2014. Fine arts & crafts show held annually in May. Outdoors. Accepts photography and all fine art and craft mediums. Juried by 3 independent jurors. Awards/prizes: purchase and merit awards. Number of exhibitors: 80. Public attendance: 7,000. Free to the public. Apply online.

ADDITIONAL INFORMATION Deadline for entry: see website. Application fee: $25. Booth fee: $295. Electricity limited; fee: $100. For more information, visit website.

PALM SPRINGS ARTS FESTIVAL

Palm Springs Arts Festival, 78206 Varner Rd., Ste D-114, Palm Desert CA 92211-4136. Website: www.palmspringsartsfestival. "In the birthplace of Western Chic, Palm Springs Arts Festivals is pleased to present 175 of the finest traditional and contemporary artists from throughout the West, Southwest, and the World to dazzle your eyes." See website for more information.

PALM SPRINGS DESERT ART FESTIVAL

West Coast Artists, P.O. Box 750, Acton CA 93510. (818)813-4478. E-mail: info@westcoastartists.com. Website: www.westcoastartists.com. Fine arts & crafts fair held several times a year. Outdoors. Accepts handmade crafts and other mediums. Juried. Number exhibitors: varies. Number attendees: varies. Free to public. Apply online.

ADDITIONAL INFORMATION Deadline for entry: varies. Application fee: see website. Space fee: varies. Exhibition space: varies. For more information, artists should e-mail, call, or visit website.

PALM SPRINGS FINE ART FAIR

HEG — Hamptons Expo Group, 223 Hampton Rd., Southampton NY 11968. (631)283-5505. Fax: (631)702-2141. E-mail: info@hegshows.com. Website: www.palmspringsfineartfair.com. Fine art fair held annually in February. Indoors. Accepts fine art from galleries. Juried. Number exhibitors: 60. Number attendees: 12,000. Admission: see website. Apply online.

ADDITIONAL INFORMATION Deadline for entry: see website. Application fee: none. Space fee: varies. Exhibition space: varies. For more information, artists should e-mail, call, or visit website.

PALO ALTO FESTIVAL OF THE ARTS

MLA Productions, 1384 Weston Rd., Scotts Valley CA 95066. (831)438-4751. E-mail: marylou@mla-productions.com. Website: www.mlaproductions.com/PaloAlto/index.html. "This high-quality, community-friendly event is sponsored by the Palo Alto Chamber of Commerce and the City of Palo Alto. In the past it has attracted over 150,000 people every year from throughout California and the West Coast. The festival takes place on tree-lined University Avenue in beautiful downtown Palo Alto, a vital economic area 35 miles south of San Francisco." See website for more details.

PARK CITY KIMBALL ARTS FESTIVAL

638 Park Ave., P.O. Box 1478, Park City UT 84060. (435)649-8882. Fax: (435)649-8889. E-mail: artsfest@kimballartcenter.org. Website: www.kimballartcenter.org. Estab. 1970. Fine art show held annually 1st weekend in August. Outdoors. Accepts ceramics, drawing, fiber, glass, jewelry, metalwork, mixed media, painting, photography, printmaking, sculpture, wood. Juried. Awards/prizes: Best in Show. Exhibitors: 210. Number of attendees: 55,000. Admission: see website. Apply online.

ADDITIONAL INFORMATION Deadline for entry: March 1. Application fee: $50. Space fee: $550-1,500. Exhibition space: 100 sq.ft-200 sq. ft. For more information, artists should visit website.

PARK POINT ART FAIR

(218)428-1916. E-mail: coordinator@parkpointartfair.org. Website: www.parkpointartfair.org. Contact: Carla Tamburro, art fair coordinator. Estab. 1970. Fine arts & crafts fair held annually in June. Outdoors. Accepts handmade crafts, jewelry, ceramics, painting, photography, digital, printmaking, and more. Juried. Awards/prizes: $1,300 in awards. Number exhibitors: 120. Number attendees: 10,000. Free to public. Apply online.

ADDITIONAL INFORMATION Deadline for entry: March. Application fee: $15. Space fee: $185. Exhibition space: 10×10. For more information, artists should e-mail, call, or visit website.

PATCHWORK SHOW

E-mail: hello@patchworkshow.com. Website: www.patchworkshow.com. Fine handmade fair held bi-annually in Spring & Fall in 4 locations. Outdoors. Accepts handmade crafts and other mediums. Juried. Number exhibitors: see website. Number attendees: varies. Free to public. Apply online.

ADDITIONAL INFORMATION Deadline for entry: see website. Application fee: $10. Space fee: varies. Exhibition space: varies. For more information, artists should e-mail or visit website.

PEACHTREE HILLS FESTIVAL OF THE ARTS

285 Peachtree Hills Rd. NE, Atlanta GA 30305. (404)873-1222. E-mail: lisa@affps.com. Website: www.peachtreehillsfestival.com. Contact: Lisa Windle, festival director. Estab. 2011. Arts & crafts show held annually late May/early June. Outdoors. Accepts handmade crafts, painting, photography, sculpture, leather, metal, glass, jewelry. Juried by a panel. Awards/prizes: ribbons. Number of exhibitors: 125. Number of attendees: 25,000. Free to public. Apply online at www.zapplication.com.

ADDITIONAL INFORMATION Deadline for entry: April 11. Application fee: $25. Space fee: $225. Exhibition space: 10×10. For more information, see website.

PEMBROKE ARTS FESTIVAL

Website: www.pembrokeartsfestival.org. Fine Arts & Crafts Fair held annually in August. See website for more information.

PENROD ARTS FAIR

The Penrod Society, P.O. Box 40817, Indianapolis IN 46240. E-mail: artists@penrod.org. Website: www.penrod.org. Fine handmade fair held annually in September. Outdoors. Accepts handmade crafts and other mediums. Juried. Awards/prizes: Best in Show. Number exhibitors: 350. Number attendees: varies. Admission: see website. Apply via Zapplication.org.

ADDITIONAL INFORMATION Deadline for entry: April. Application fee: see website. Space fee: varies. Exhibition space: varies. For more information, artists should e-mail or visit website.

PENTWATER FINE ARTS & CRAFT FAIR

Pentwater Jr. Women's Club, P.O. Box 357, Pentwater MI 49449. E-mail: pentwaterjuniorwomensclub@yahoo.com. Website: www.pentwaterjuniorwomensclub.com. "Always the 2nd Saturday in July, the fair is held on the beautiful Village Green located in downtown Pentwater, Michigan, during the height of the summer resort season. The fair is held regardless of the weather, and space is limited for this juried show." Artists can apply via www.zapplication.org. See website for more information.

PETERS VALLEY FINE CRAFTS FAIR

Sussex County Fair Grounds, 37 Plains Rd., Augusta NJ 07822. (973)948-5200. Fax: (973)948-0011. E-mail: craftfair@petersvalley.org. Website: www.petersvalley.org. Contact: Craft fair director. Estab. 1970. Fine craft show held annually the last full weekend in September that doesn't conflict with a holiday. Indoors. Accepts handmade crafts. Juried. Awards/prizes: free booth space next year. Exhibitors: 150. Number of attendees: 7,000. Admission: $9/day; $12/2-day; group rates also available. Apply via Zapplication.org.

ADDITIONAL INFORMATION Deadline for entry: see website. Application fee: $35. Space fee: $415+. Exhibition space: 10×10. For more information, artists should send e-mail, call, or visit website.

PHILADELPHIA MUSEUM OF ART CONTEMPORARY CRAFT SHOW

P.O. Box 7646, Philadelphia PA 19101-7646. (215)684-7930. E-mail: twcpma@philamuseum.org. Website: www.pmacraftshow.org. Estab. 1977. Fine craft show (specializes in "odd" or unusual) held annually 2nd weekend in November. Indoors. Accepts handmade crafts, clay, glass, wood, fiber, metal. Juried. Exhibitors: 195. Number of attendees: 18,000. Admission: $15. Apply online.

ADDITIONAL INFORMATION Deadline for entry: April 1. Application fee: $50. Space fee: $1,200+. Exhibition space: see website. For more information, artists should visit website.

PICCOLO SPOLETO FINE CRAFTS SHOW

Fine Craft Shows Charleston, P.O. Box 22152, Charleston SC 29413-2152. (843)364-0421. E-mail: piccolo@finecraftshowscharleston.com. Website: www.finecraftshowscharleston.com. Fine handmade fair held annually in May. Outdoors. Accepts handmade crafts and other mediums. Juried. Awards/prizes: $5-6,000 in cash awards. Number exhibitors: 95. Number attendees: 9,000. Admission: $3 adults; children 18 & under free. Apply via Zapplication.org.

ADDITIONAL INFORMATION Deadline for entry: February. Application fee: $30. Space fee: $250. Exhibition space: 10×10. For more information, artists should e-mail, call, or visit website.

PICNIC MUSIC & ARTS FESTIVAL

E-mail: picnicportland@gmail.com. Website: www.picnicportland.com. Estab. 2008. Indie craft fair & music festival held twice a year in August & December. Outdoors (August); Indoors (December). Accepts handmade crafts and other mediums. Juried. Number exhibitors: 100. Number attendees: varies. Free to public. Apply online.

ADDITIONAL INFORMATION Deadline for entry: mid-May. Application fee: $10. Space fee: $125. Exhibition space: 10×10 (August show); 8×4 (December show). For more information, artists should e-mail or visit website.

PIEDMONT PARK ARTS FESTIVAL

1701 Piedmont Ave., Atlanta GA 30306. (404)873-1222. E-mail: lisa@affps.com. Website: www.piedmontparkartsfestival.com. Contact: Lisa Windle, festival director. Estab. 2011. Arts & crafts show held annually in mid-August. Outdoors. Accepts handmade crafts, painting, photography, sculpture, leather, metal, glass, jewelry. Juried by a panel. Awards/prizes: ribbons. Number of exhibitors: 250. Number of attendees: 60,000. Free to public. Apply online at www.zapplication.com.

ADDITIONAL INFORMATION Deadline for entry: June 6. Application fee: $25. Space fee: $275. Exhibition space: 10×10. For more information artists should visit website.

PITTSBURGH ART, CRAFT & LIFESTYLE SHOW

Huff's Promotions, Inc., 4275 Fulton Rd. NW, Akron OH 44718. (330)493-4130. Fax: (330)493-7607. E-mail: shows@huffspromo.com. Website: www.huffspromo.com. Art & Craft show held several times a year. Indoors. Accepts handmade crafts and other mediums. Juried. Number exhibitors: see website. Number attendees: varies. Free to public. Apply online.

ADDITIONAL INFORMATION Deadline for entry: varies. Application fee: see website. Space fee: varies. Exhibition space: see website. For more information, artists should e-mail, call, or visit website.

PLAZA ART FAIR

Plaza Art Fair, c/o Melissa Anderson, Highwoods Properties, 4706 Broadway, Suite 260, Kansas City MO 64112. (816)753-0100. Fax: (816)753-4625. E-mail: countryclubplaza@highwoods.com. Website: www.countryclubplaza.com. Estab. 1931. Art & craft show held annually in September. Outdoors. Accepts handmade crafts and other mediums. Juried. Awards/prizes: $10,000 in cash awards. Number exhibitors: 240. Number attendees: 300,000. Free to public. Apply via Zapplication.org.

ADDITIONAL INFORMATION Deadline for entry: May. Application fee: $35. Space fee: $425. Exhibition space: 12×12. For more information, artists should e-mail, call, or visit website.

PORT CLINTON ART FESTIVAL

Amdur Productions, P.O. Box 550, Highland Park IL 60035. (847)926-4300. Fax: (847)926-4330. E-mail: info@amdurproductions.com. Website: www.amdurproductions.com. Art & craft show held annually in August. Outdoors. Accepts handmade crafts and other mediums. Juried. Awards/prizes: bestowed at artist breakfast. Number exhibitors: 260. Number attendees: 250,000. Free to public. Apply online.

ADDITIONAL INFORMATION Deadline for entry: early January. Application fee: $50. Space fee: $765. Exhibition space: 10×10. For more information, artists should e-mail, call, or visit website.

POWDERHORN ART FAIR

Powderhorn Art Fair c/o PPNA, 821 E. 35th St., Minneapolis MN 55407. (612)767-3515. E-mail: dixie@powderhornartfair.org. Website: www.powderhornartfair.com. Contact: Dixie Treichel. Estab. 1991. Art & craft show held annually in August. Outdoors. Accepts handmade crafts and other mediums. Juried. Awards/prizes: Best in Show, 2nd Place, 3rd Place, Merit Award, Spirit of Powderhorn. Number exhibitors: 184. Number attendees: 20,000. Free to public. Apply via Zapplication.org.

ADDITIONAL INFORMATION Deadline for entry: early March. Application fee: $35. Space fee: $240. Exhibition space: 11×11. For more information, artists should e-mail, call, or visit website.

PRAIRIE VILLAGE ART FAIR

Website: www.prairievillageshops.com. Annual art fair held in May. See website for more information.

PROMENADE OF ART

Amdur Productions, P.O. Box 550, Highland Park IL 60035. (847)926-4300. Fax: (847)926-4330. E-mail: info@amdurproductions.com. Website: www.amdurproductions.com. Art & craft show held annually in June. Outdoors. Accepts handmade crafts and other mediums. Juried. Awards/prizes: given at festival. Number exhibitors: 125. Number attendees: 35,000. Free to public. Apply online.

ADDITIONAL INFORMATION Deadline for entry: early January. Application fee: $25. Space fee: $460. Exhibition space: 10×10. For more information, artists should e-mail, call, or visit website.

PUNTA GORDA SULLIVAN STREET CRAFT FESTIVAL

270 Central Blvd., Suite 107B, Jupiter FL 33458. (561)746-6615. Fax: (561)746-6528. E-mail: info@ArtFestival.com. Website: www.artfestival.com. "Since it's inception, the Punta Gorda Craft Fair continues to grow and highlight the talents of many unique crafters, providing the area with one of its most enjoyable summer traditions. Come meet and visit with some of the nation's best crafters while enjoying the charming streets of Punta Gorda."

QUILT & FIBER ARTS SHOW

P.O. Box 3481, Pahrump NV 89041. (775)751-6776. E-mail: pahrumppacinfo@gmail.com. Website: www.pvpac.org. "This 3-day event offers a chance to see gorgeous quilts of all sizes, as well as needlework, wearable art, and other fiber arts. The show also offers demonstrations, a bed turning, door prizes, vendors, a silent auction, quilt appraiser, theme challenge, featured quilter, food counter, and a pick-a-prize raffle. And each year an Opportunity Quilt with a custom quilt display rack is raffled off to one lucky winner on the last day." See website for more information.

QUILT, CRAFT & SEWING FESTIVAL

Website: www.quiltcraftsew.com/phoenix.html. "At the Quilt, Craft & Sewing Festival you will find a wide variety of Sewing, Quilting, Needle-Art, and Craft supply exhibits from many quality companies." See website for more information.

REDMOND STREET FESTIVAL

Central Oregon Shows, P.O. Box 1555, Sisters OR 97759. (541)420-0279. E-mail: centraloregonshows@gmail.com. Website: www.centraloregonshows.com. This event caters to a variety of arts, crafts, antiques, food, and entertainment with a small section for a limited amount of commercial booths. The booths will run down the center of street leaving room on the sidewalks for storefronts to have sidewalk sales. See website for more information.

RED RIVER QUILTERS
ANNUAL QUILT SHOW

Website: www.redriverquilters.com. Judged quilt show held annually in October. See website for more information.

THE RENEGADE CRAFT FAIR - AUSTIN

Renegade Craft Fair, 1910 S. Halsted St., Suite #2, Chicago IL 60608. E-mail: rachel@renegadecraft.com. Website: www.renegadecraft.com. "Renegade Craft Fair is the world's premier network of events serving the DIY craft community. RCF was the first event of its kind when it was founded in 2003, and we are still the largest and most far-reaching with 14 annual events in Chicago, IL; New York, NY; San Francisco, CA; Los Angeles, CA; Austin, TX; Portland, OR; London, UK. On average, our events are attended by over 250,000 people annually, and hundreds of craft-based businesses have been launched successfully out of the fairs." See website for more information and specific details about each city and how to apply.

THE RENEGADE CRAFT FAIR - BROOKLYN

Renegade Craft Fair, 1910 S. Halsted St., Suite #2, Chicago IL 60608. E-mail: rachel@renegadecraft.com. Website: www.renegadecraft.com. "Renegade Craft Fair is the world's premier network of events serv-

ing the DIY craft community. RCF was the first event of its kind when it was founded in 2003, and we are still the largest and most far-reaching with 14 annual events in Chicago, IL; New York, NY; San Francisco, CA; Los Angeles, CA; Austin, TX; Portland, OR; London, UK. On average, our events are attended by over 250,000 people annually, and hundreds of craft-based businesses have been launched successfully out of the fairs." See website for more information and specific details about each city and how to apply.

THE RENEGADE CRAFT FAIR - CHICAGO

Renegade Craft Fair, 1910 S. Halsted St., Suite #2, Chicago IL 60608. E-mail: rachel@renegadecraft.com. Website: www.renegadecraft.com. "Renegade Craft Fair is the world's premier network of events serving the DIY craft community. RCF was the first event of its kind when it was founded in 2003, and we are still the largest and most far-reaching with 14 annual events in Chicago, IL; New York, NY; San Francisco, CA; Los Angeles, CA; Austin, TX; Portland, OR; London, UK. On average, our events are attended by over 250,000 people annually, and hundreds of craft-based businesses have been launched successfully out of the fairs." See website for more information and specific details about each city and how to apply.

THE RENEGADE CRAFT FAIR - LONDON

Renegade Craft Fair, 1910 S. Halsted St., Suite #2, Chicago IL 60608. E-mail: rachel@renegadecraft.com. Website: www.renegadecraft.com. "Renegade Craft Fair is the world's premier network of events serving the DIY craft community. RCF was the first event of its kind when it was founded in 2003, and we are still the largest and most far-reaching with 14 annual events in Chicago, IL; New York, NY; San Francisco, CA; Los Angeles, CA, Austin, TX; Portland, OR; London, UK. On average, our events are attended by over 250,000 people annually, and hundreds of craft-based businesses have been launched successfully out of the fairs." See website for more information and specific details about each city and how to apply.

THE RENEGADE CRAFT FAIR - LOS ANGELES

Renegade Craft Fair, 1910 S. Halsted St., Suite #2, Chicago IL 60608. E-mail: rachel@renegadecraft.com. Website: www.renegadecraft.com. "Renegade Craft Fair is the world's premier network of events serving the DIY craft community. RCF was the first event of its kind when it was founded in 2003, and we are still the largest and most far-reaching with 14 annual events in Chicago, IL; New York, NY; San Francisco, CA; Los Angeles, CA; Austin, TX; Portland, OR; London, UK. On average, our events are attended by over 250,000 people annually, and hundreds of craft-based businesses have been launched successfully out of the fairs." See website for more information and specific details about each city and how to apply.

THE RENEGADE CRAFT FAIR - SAN FRANCISCO

Renegade Craft Fair, 1910 S. Halsted St., Suite #2, Chicago IL 60608. E-mail: rachel@renegadecraft.com. Website: www.renegadecraft.com. "Renegade Craft Fair is the world's premier network of events serving the DIY craft community. RCF was the first event of its kind when it was founded in 2003, and we are still the largest and most far-reaching with 14 annual events in Chicago, IL; New York, NY; San Francisco, CA; Los Angeles, CA; Austin, TX; Portland, OR; London, UK. On average, our events are attended by over 250,000 people annually, and hundreds of craft-based businesses have been launched successfully out of the fairs." See website for more information and specific details about each city and how to apply.

RIDGELAND FINE ARTS FESTIVAL

(253)344-1058. E-mail: bobmcfarland2@hotmail. com. Website: www.ridgelandartsfest.com. Fine art & craft show held annually in April. Outdoors. Accepts handmade crafts and other mediums. Juried. Awards/prizes: $7,500 in awards. Number exhibitors: 80. Number attendees: varies. Free to public. Apply via Zapplication.org.

ADDITIONAL INFORMATION Deadline for entry: November. Application fee: see website. Space fee: varies. Exhibition space: varies. For more information, artists should e-mail, call, or visit website.

RISING SUN FESTIVAL OF FINE ARTS & CRAFTS

E-mail: andrea@enjoyrisingsun.com. Website: www.enjoyrisingsun.com. Fine arts & craft show held annually in September. Outdoors. Accepts handmade crafts and other mediums. Juried. Awards/prizes: $8,000 in awards. Number exhibitors: see website. Number attendees: varies. Free to public. Apply via Zapplication.org.

ADDITIONAL INFORMATION Deadline for entry: July. Application fee: $15. Space fee: $100 (single); $200 (double). Exhibition space: 10×10 (single); 10×20 (double). For more information, artists should e-mail or visit website.

RIVERWALK FINE ART FAIR

Naperville Art League, 508 N. Center St., Naperville IL 60563. (630)355-2530. Fax: (630)355-3071. E-mail: naperartleague@aol.com. Website: www.napervilleartleague.com. Estab. 1984. Fine art & fine craft show held annually the 3rd weekend in September. Outdoors. Accepts handmade crafts and other mediums. Juried. Awards/prizes: Best of Show, 1st Place, Honorable Mentions, Purchase Awards. Number exhibitors: 130. Number attendees: 76,000. Free to public. Apply via Zapplication.org.

ADDITIONAL INFORMATION Deadline for entry: March 30. Application fee: $35. Space fee: $400. Exhibition space: 10×12. For more information, artists should e-mail, call, or visit website.

TIPS "No reproductions; artists sell well to an affluent and appreciative crowd."

ROCK 'N ROLL CRAFT SHOW

(314)649-7727. E-mail: info@rocknrollcraftshow.com. Website: www.rocknrollcraftshow.com. "Rock N Roll Craft Show is St. Louis's original alternative art, craft, and music event! RRCS showcases unique items handcrafted from new and recycled materials by talented artisans, as well as locally and nationally acclaimed bands!" See website for more information.

ROCKPORT ART FESTIVAL

Rockport Center for the Arts, 902 Navigation Circle, Rockport TX 78382. (361)729-5519. E-mail: info@rockportartcenter.com. Website: www.rockportartcenter.com. "Over 120 artists, live music & food, and A/C party tent, kids' activities, and more just steps away from Aransas Bay and Rockport Beach Park!" See website for more information.

ROTARY KEY BISCAYNE ART FESTIVAL

270 Central Blvd, Suite 107B, Jupiter FL 33458. (561)746-6615. Fax: (561)746-6528. E-mail: info@artfestival.com. Website: www.artfestival.com. Estab. 1963. "The annual Key Biscayne Art Fair benefits our partner and coproducer, the Rotary Club of Key Biscayne. Held in Key Biscayne, an affluent island community in Miami-Dade County, just south of downtown Miami, the annual Key Biscayne Art Festival is one not to be missed! In fact, visitors plan their springtime vacations to South Florida around this terrific outdoor festival that brings together longtime favorites and the newest names in the contemporary art scene. Life-size sculptures, spectacular paintings, one-of-a-kind jewels, photography, ceramics, and much more make for one fabulous weekend." See website for more information.

ROUND THE FOUNTAIN ART FAIR

Round The Fountain Art, P.O. Box 1134, Lafayette IN 47902. (765)491-6298. Website: www.roundthefountain.org. Estab. 1973. Art & craft show held annually in May. Outdoors. Accepts handmade crafts and other mediums. Juried. Awards/prizes: Best of Show, 2nd Place, 3rd Place, Merit Awards, Aldo Award. Number exhibitors: 100. Number attendees: varies. Free to public. Apply via Zapplication.org.

ADDITIONAL INFORMATION Deadline for entry: early April. Application fee: $35. Space fee: $150 (single); $300 (double). Exhibition space: 10×10 (single); 10×20 (double). For more information, artists should call or visit website.

ROYAL OAK CLAY, GLASS AND METAL SHOW

Integrity Shows, P.O. Box 1070, Ann Arbor MI 48106. E-mail: info@integrityshows.com. Website: http://integrityshows.wix.com/royal-oak-cgm. Contact: Mark Loeb. Estab. 1994. Art show featuring works made of clay, glass or metal only held annually in June. Outdoors. Accepts clay, glass, and metal only. We encour-

age demonstrations. Juried by 3 independent jurors. Awards/prizes: purchase and merit awards. Number of exhibitors: 120. Public attendance: 35,000. Free to the public. Apply online.

ADDITIONAL INFORMATION Deadline for entry: see website. Application fee: $25. Booth fee: $295. Electricity limited; fee: $100. For more information, visit website.

RUBBER STAMP & PAPER ARTS FESTIVALS

(541)574-8000. E-mail: info@heirloompro.com. Website: www.heirloompro.com. Estab. 1993. "Retail Consumer Events featuring Art Stamps, Cardmaking, Scrapbooking, and Paper Arts. You will find art stamps, paper, cardstock and envelopes, inks and pads, die-cuts, brass stencils, glitter, embossing powder, tools, pencils, pens and markers, embellishments, and more. Classes, workshops, Design & Treasure, make 'n' takes, demonstrations. Learn, become inspired, and shop." See website for more information.

SACRAMENTO ARTS FESTIVAL

American Art Festivals, Inc., P.O. Box 3037, Atascadero CA 93423. (805)461-6700. E-mail: americanartfestivals@yahoo.com. Website: www.sacartsfest.com. Art & craft show held annually in November. Outdoors. Accepts handmade crafts and other mediums. Juried. Number exhibitors: see website. Number attendees: 10,000. Free to public. Apply via Zapplication.org.

ADDITIONAL INFORMATION Deadline for entry: April. Application fee: $10. Space fee: varies. Exhibition space: varies. For more information, artists should e-mail, call, or visit website.

SALEM ART FAIR & FESTIVAL

Salem Art Association, 600 Mission St. SE, Salem OR 97302. (503)581-2228. Fax: (503)371-3342. Website: www.salemart.org. "SAA is the proud organization behind the nationally ranked Salem Art Fair & Festival which is both our largest annual fundraiser and the largest festival of its kind in Oregon. Each year, the SAF&F attracts approximately 35,000 visitors from all over the nation and is committed to upholding the importance of fine arts and crafts by providing access to a range of artistic mediums appealing to both art appreciators and art collectors alike. With a variety of different activities and offerings, the art fair is an experience the whole family can enjoy." See website for more information.

SALEM ARTS FESTIVAL

(978)744-0004, ext.15. E-mail: kylie@salemmain-streets.org. Website: www.salemartsfestival.com. Contact: Kylie Sullivan. "The Salem Arts Festival promotes the arts in downtown Salem through a collaborative festival for residents and visitors providing opportunities to highlight the existing artist community and encourage general community participation in the arts. The festival regularly draws over 4,000 visitors. The festival is looking for art and performance for the sophisticated art patron as well as for the art novice including interactive events for children. It will engage participants of diverse backgrounds and ages by reaching out to current art patrons, local students, and the community at large." See website for more information.

SALT FORK ARTS & CRAFTS FESTIVAL

P.O. Box 250, Cambridge OH 43725. (740)439-9379. E-mail: director@saltforkfestival.org. Website: www.saltforkfestival.org. "The Salt Fork Arts & Crafts Festival (SFACF) is a juried festival that showcases high quality art in a variety of mediums, painting, pottery, ceramics, fiber art, metalwork, jewelry, acrylics, mixed media, photography, and more. Between 90 and 100 artists come from all over the US, for this 3-day event. In addition, the festival heralds Heritage of the Arts. This program offers a look at Early American and Appalachian arts and crafts, many of which are demonstrated by craftsmen practicing arts such as basket weaving, flint knapping, spindling, flute making, quilting, blacksmithing, and more. Area students are given the opportunity to display their work, visitors are entertained throughout the weekend by a variety of talented performing artists, concessionaires offer satisfying foods, and there are crafts for kids and adults." See website for more information.

SALT LAKE'S FAMILY CHRISTMAS GIFT SHOW

South Towne Exposition Center, 9575 S. State St., Sandy UT 84070. (800)521-7469. Fax: (425)889-8165. E-mail: saltlake@showcaseevents.org. Website: www.showcaseevents.org. Contact: Kristine Vannoy, show manager. Estab. 1999. Seasonal holiday show held annually in November. Indoors. Accepts handmade crafts, art, photography, pottery, glass, jewelry, clothing, fiber. Juried. Exhibitors: 400. Number of attendees: 25,000. Admission: $11.50 (for all 3 days); 13 & under free. Apply via website or call or e-mail for application.

ADDITIONAL INFORMATION Deadline for entry: October 31. Space fee: see website. Exhibition space: 10×10. For more information send e-mail, call, send SASE, or visit website.

TIPS "Competitive pricing, attractive booth display, quality product, something unique for sale, friendly & outgoing personality."

SANDY SPRINGS ARTSAPALOOZA

6100 Lake Forrest Dr. NE, Sandy Springs GA 30328. (404)873-1222. E-mail: lisa@affps.com. Website: www.sandyspringsartsapalooza.com. Contact: Lisa Windle, festival director. Estab. 2011. Arts & crafts show held annually mid-April. Outdoors. Accepts handmade crafts, painting, photography, sculpture, leather, metal, glass, jewelry. Juried by a panel. Awards/prizes: ribbons. Number of exhibitors: 150. Number of attendees: 25,000. Free to public. Apply online at www.zapplication.com.

ADDITIONAL INFORMATION Deadline for entry: February 14. Application fee: $25. Space fee: $200. Exhibition space: 10×10. For more information, see website.

SANDY SPRINGS FESTIVAL & ARTISTS MARKET

6075 Sandy Springs Circle, Sandy Springs GA 30328. (404)873-1222. E-mail: lisa@affps.com. Website: www.sandyspringsfestival.com. Contact: Lisa Windle, festival director. Estab. 1986. Arts & crafts show held annually late June. Outdoors. Accepts handmade crafts, painting, photography, sculpture, leather, metal, glass, jewelry. Juried by a panel. Awards/prizes: ribbons. Number of exhibitors: 120. Number of attendees: 40,000. Free to public. Apply online at www.zap-plication.com.

ADDITIONAL INFORMATION Deadline for entry: July 25. Application fee: $25. Space fee: $250. Exhibition space: 10×10. For more information, see website.

SAN FRANCISCO BAZAAR

1559B Sloat Blvd. #198, San Francisco CA 94132. (415)684-8447. E-mail: sf_info@sanfranciscobazaar.org. Website: www.sanfranciscobazaar.org. Contact: Jamie Chan, director. Estab. 2007. Handmade, independent DIY art & design festival held annually 5 times a year (see website for dates). Indoors & outdoors. Accepts handmade crafts, locally and domestically designed goods. Juried. Exhibitors: 150. Number of attendees: 10,000. Free to public. Apply online at www.sanfranciscobazaar.org/apply.

TIPS "Each year San Francisco Bazaar curates hundreds of carefully juried artists and designers. Shoppers can expect to find the crème de la crème of indie goods: handbags, pottery, letterpress stationery, silk-screened t-shirts, baby clothes, zines, posters, body products, and more! Please make sure you have a comprehensive website, e-commerce shop, or photo album at the time of application so that we may best understand your products offered and your artistic mission."

SAN FRANCISCO FINE CRAFT SHOW

American Craft Council Shows, 155 Water St., 4th Floor, Unit 5, Brooklyn NY 11201. (800)836-3470. Fax: (612)355-2330. E-mail: shows@craftcouncil.org. Website: www.craftcouncil.org. Art & craft show held annually in August. Indoors. Accepts handmade crafts, ceramics, fiber, metal, and other mediums. Juried. Awards/prizes: Awards of Excellence. Number exhibitors: 225. Number attendees: varies. Free to public. Apply online.

ADDITIONAL INFORMATION Deadline for entry: August. Application fee: $30 + $10 handling/processing fee for each set of images. Space fee: varies. Exhibition space: varies. For more information, artists should e-mail, call, or visit website.

SAN MARCO ART FESTIVAL

270 Central Blvd., Suite 107B, Jupiter FL 33458. (561)746-6615. Fax: (561)746-6528. E-mail: info@Art-Festival.com. Website: www.artfestival.com. "Browse and purchase original handmade works including: glass, photography, painting, mixed media, fiber, jewelry, and much more. Artists will be onhand all weekend to share their inspirations for each uniquely crafted piece. No matter what you're looking for, you'll be sure to find it among the numerous artisans participating in this greatly anticipated, juried, community art fair."

SANTA CRUZ COUNTY HERITAGE FOUNDATION HOLIDAY CRAFT & GIFT FAIR

Freedom Post Office, P.O. Box 1806, Freedom CA 95019. (831)612-9118. E-mail: heritageholidayfair@gmail.com. Website: www.sccfheritage.org/heritage-holiday-craft-fair. "This festive event full of holiday cheer includes crafts, folk art, antiques, collectibles, gift foods, delicious refreshments at the food courts, and free parking. The 25-foot Christmas tree will light up your child's eyes! The Agricultural History Project will host a County Christmas. Children under 5 are free." See website for more information.

SANTA FE COLLEGE SPRING ARTS FESTIVAL

3000 NW 83rd St., Gainesville FL 32606. (352)395-5355. Fax: (352)336-2715. E-mail: kathryn.lehman@sfcollege.edu. Website: www.springartsfestival.com. Contact: Kathryn Lehman, cultural program coordinator. Estab. 1969. Fine art show held annually in March or April. Outdoors. Accepts painting, photography, fabrics, glass, watercolor, wood, 2D/3D mixed media, grapics, sculpture. Juried. Awards/prizes: $20,000 cash awards; ribbons. Exhibitors: 190. Number of attendees: 110,000. Free to public. Apply via Zapplication.org.

ADDITIONAL INFORMATION Deadline for entry: December. Application fee: see website. Space fee: see website. Exhibition space: 12×12. For more information, artists should e-mail, call, or visit website.

TIPS "Original, medium prices."

SARASOTA CRAFT FAIR

270 Central Blvd., Suite 107B, Jupiter FL 33458. (561)746-6615. Fax: (561)746-6528. E-mail: info@art-festival.com. Website: www.artfestival.com. Contact:

Malinda Ratliff, communications manager. "Behold contemporary crafts from more than 100 of the nation's most talented artisans. A variety of jewelry, pottery, ceramics, photography, painting, clothing, and much more—all handmade in America—will be on display, ranging from $15-3,000. An expansive Green Market with plants, orchids, exotic flora, handmade soaps, gourmet spices, and freshly popped kettle corn further complements the weekend, blending nature with nurture." See website for more information.

SARATOGA ARTS CELEBRATION

(518)852-6478. E-mail: suebg.art@gmail.com. Website: www.saratogaartscelebration.org; gordonfinearts.org. Estab. 2008. Arts & crafts show held annually in August. Outdoors. Accepts handmade crafts and fine art. Juried. Awards/prizes: cash & ribbons. Exhibitors: 100. Number of attendees: 7,000-10,000. Free to public. Apply online.

ADDITIONAL INFORMATION Deadline for entry: April 1. Application fee: $25. Space fee: $350-450. Exhibition space: 10×12. For more information visit website, send e-mail, or call.

SAULT SAINTE MARIE ART, CRAFT & FAMILY FUN FAIR

Sault Arts Crafts and Family Fun Fair, c/o EUP Community Dispute Resolution Center, P.O. Box 550, Sault Sainte Marie MI 49783. (906)253-9840. Fax: (888)664-6402. E-mail: coordinator@saultcraftfair.org. Website: www.saultcraftfair.org. "This event is held annually on the last Friday of June. Please join us on the lawn of Historic City Hall, overlooking the east end of the Sault Locks and the St. Mary's River." See website for more information.

SAWDUST ART FESTIVAL

935 Laguna Canyon Rd., Laguna Beach CA 92651. (949)494-3030. E-mail: info@sawdustartfestival.org. Website: www.sawdustartfestival.org. Contact: Tom Klingenmeier, general manager. Estab. 1967. Annual arts & crafts show held annually June-August (see website for dates; also has winter shows). Outdoors. Accepts handmade crafts, all art mediums. Awards/prizes: peer awards. Exhibitors: 210 (summer); 175 (winter). Number of attendees: 300,000 (summer);

20,000 (winter). Admission: $8.50, adults; $7, seniors; $4 children ages 6-12; children 5 & under free. Application release date varies (see website).

ADDITIONAL INFORMATION Deadline for entry: varies (see website). Application fee: $30 per show. Space fee: $1,250+ (summer). Exhibition space: 10×8. For more information, call, e-mail, or see website.

TIPS "Be here on the grounds exhibiting your artwork."

SCOTTSDALE CELEBRATION OF FINE ARTS

Celebration of Fine Art, 7900 E. Greenway Rd., Suite 101, Scottsdale AZ 85260-1714. (480)443-7695. Fax: (480)596-8179. E-mail: info@celebrateart.com. Website: www.celebrateart.com. "The Celebration of Fine Art™ is a juried show. We jury not only for quality but variety. This helps insure that direct competition is minimized and that you will have the best opportunity for success. All styles of art in all mediums are welcome. In addition to painting and sculpture we also have fine crafts such as furniture, jewelry, ceramics, basketry, and weaving. Only work created by the artist and handmade work is accepted. We do not allow manufactured goods of any kind. Artists who have previously been selected for the show will be juried in the 2 months following the current exhibit. Additional details, prices, and other information are contained in the artist application packet." See website for more information.

SCRAPBOOK EXPO

Scrapbook EXPO, 1353 Walker Ln., Corona CA 92879. (951)734-4307. Fax: (951)848-0711. E-mail: exhibitors@scrapbookexpo.com. Website: www.scrapbookexpo.com. "Scrapbook Expo combines Scrapbooking, Paper Crafting, and Stamping and offers YOU the crafter the most amazing crafting experience you'll ever find." See website for dates and more information.

SEASONS OF THE HEART CRAFT, DECOR & GIFT FAIRE

P.O. Box 191, Ramona CA 92064. (760)445-1330. E-mail: seasonsoftheheart@cox.net. Website: seasonsoftheheartcraftfaire.com. Contact: Linda or Ron Mulick, owners/promoters. Estab. 1988. Arts & crafts show, seasonal/holiday show held annually in November. Indoors. Accepts handmade crafts, collectibles, gourmet foods. Exhibitors: 100. Number of attendees: 6,000. Free to public. Apply online.

ADDITIONAL INFORMATION Deadline for entry: October 1. Application fee: none. Space fee: $225 + 15% of sales. Exhibition space: 10×10. Average sales: $2,000. For more information, artists should send e-mail, visit website, or call.

TIPS "Do quality work and price your items reasonably."

SEATTLE HANDMADE

Website: www.seattlehandmade.com. "Enjoy the official beginning of the Holiday gift-shopping season and find the perfect gifts for the loved ones on your list at the Seattle Handmade Holiday Show (formerly etsyRAIN Handmade Holiday Show). Celebrating many fabulous years of supporting the handmade community of Seattle and the greater Pacific NW." See website for more details.

SEATTLE'S HOLIDAY DIY FAIR

The Vera Project, Attn: DIY Holiday Fair, 305 Harrison St., Seattle WA 98109. E-mail: fundraising@ theveraproject.org. Website: www.theveraproject. org. "This extravaganza features several independent NW record and cassette labels, musicians, silk-screened show posters, vintage record dealers, local artists, craft-makers, and designers selling their wares throughout Vera's venue. This is the perfect opportunity to find a one of a kind gift just in time for the holidays. Interactive entertainments will take place throughout the day, including the Surrealist Songwriting Project and live silk-screening lessons, and the event will also include Hollow Earth DJs spinning on-site, a bake sale, and a raffle for rare posters, records, and more!" See website for more information.

SEATTLE WEAVERS GUILD
ANNUAL SHOW & SALE

Seattle Weavers' Guild, 1245 Tenth Ave. E., Seattle WA 98102. E-mail: sale@seattleweaversguild.com. Website: www.seattleweaversguild.com/sale.asp. "The annual sale showcases one-of-a-kind handcrafted items, including towels, rugs, blankets, tapestries, exquisite jewelry, accessories for pets, children's items, handmade cards, household goods, hats, bags, wall art,

jackets, scarves, wraps, sculptural basketry, liturgical weaving, hand spun and/or hand-dyed yarns along with weaving and spinning tools. There will also be demonstrations of spinning, weaving, and other fiber crafts during the sale. Proceeds from the sale are used to fund the guild's volunteer outreach program and to bring talented practicing artists to Seattle Weavers' Guild to educate both its members and the public. Parking and entrance to the sale are free." Open to members only. See website for more information.

SELDAN HANDMADE FAIR

(757)664-6880. "Selden HandMade Fair showcases the work of contemporary indie-craft artists. Crafters and do-it-yourselfers will offer original handmade goods in a wide variety of media. Enjoy live artist demonstrations and a variety of musical performances. FREE and open to the public!" See website for more information.

SELL-A-RAMA

Tyson Wells Sell-A-Rama, P.O. Box 60, Quartzsite AZ 85346. (928)927-6364. E-mail: tysonwells@tds. net. Website: www.tysonwells.com. Arts & craft show held annually in January. Outdoors & indoors. Accepts handmade crafts, ceramics, paintings, jewelry, glass, photography, wearable art, and other mediums. Juried. Number exhibitors: see website. Number attendees: varies. Free to public. Apply online.

ADDITIONAL INFORMATION Deadline for entry: see website for dates. Application fee: none. Space fee: varies. Exhibition space: varies. For more information, artists should call, e-mail, or visit website.

SFUSD ARTS FESTIVAL

(415)695-2441. Fax: (415)695-2496. E-mail: sfusdaf2014@gmail.com. Website: sfusdartsfestival.org. "The San Francisco Unified School District proudly presents the SFUSD Arts Festival; a celebration of student creativity in visual, literary, media, and performing arts. This unique San Francisco event, (formerly *Young at Art*), has been a point of destination for families, teachers, artists, and community members from San Francisco and beyond. The promise of equity and access in arts education for all students K-12 during the curricular day, made real by the SFUSD's ground-breaking Arts Education Master Plan, finds its point of destination in this festival, where all who attend may see for themselves the inspiration and creativity inherent in all of our youngest San Franciscans!" See website for more information.

SHADYSIDE ART & CRAFT FESTIVAL

270 Central Blvd., Suite 107B, Jupiter FL 33458. (561)746-6615. Fax: (561)746-6528. E-mail: info@artfestival.com. Website: www.artfestival.com. Contact: Malinda Ratliff, communications manager. Estab. 1996. Fine art & craft fair held annually in late May. Outdoors. Accepts photography, jewelry, mixed media, sculpture, wood, ceramic, glass, painting, digital, fiber, metal. Juried. Number exhibitors: 125. Number attendees: 60,000. Free to public. Apply online via www.zapplication.org. Deadline: see website. Application fee: $25. Space fee: $395. Exhibition space: 10×10 and 10×20. For more information, artists should e-mail, call, or visit website. Festival located at Walnut St. in Shadyside (Pittsburgh, PA).

TIPS "You have to start somewhere. First, assess where you are, and what you'll need to get things off the ground. Next, make a plan of action. Outdoor street art shows are a great way to begin your career and lifetime as a working artist. You'll meet a lot of other artists who have been where you are now. Network with them!"

SHADYSIDE...THE ART FESTIVAL ON WALNUT STREET

270 Central Blvd., Suite 107B, Jupiter FL 33458. (561)746-6615. Fax: (561)746-6528. E-mail: info@artfestival.com. Website: www.artfestival.com. Contact: Malinda Ratliff, communications manager. Estab. 1996. Fine art & craft fair held annually in late August. Outdoors. Accepts photography, jewelry, mixed media, sculpture, wood, ceramic, glass, painting, digital, fiber, metal. Juried. Number exhibitors: 125. Number attendees: 100,000. Free to public. Apply online via zapplication.org. Deadline: see website. Application fee: $25. Space fee: $450. Exhibition space: 10×10 and 10×20. For more information, artists should e-mail, call, or visit website. Festival located at Walnut St. in Shadyside (Pittsburgh, PA).

TIPS "You have to start somewhere. First, assess where you are, and what you'll need to get things off the

ground. Next, make a plan of action. Outdoor street art shows are a great way to begin your career and lifetime as a working artist. You'll meet a lot of other artists who have been where you are now. Network with them!"

SHIPSHEWANA QUILT FESTIVAL

P.O. Box 245, Shipshewana IN 46565. (260)768-4887. E-mail: info@shipshewanaquiltfest.com. Website: www.shipshewanaquiltfest.com. Contact: Nancy Troyer, show organizer. Estab. 2009. Quilt & vendor show held annually late June. Indoors. Accepts handmade crafts and other mediums. Juried. Awards/prizes: cash. Exhibitors: 20. Number of attendees: 4,000. Admission: $8/day; $12/week. Apply online.

ADDITIONAL INFORMATION Deadline for entry: see website. Application fee: none. Space fee: varies. Exhibition space: varies. Average sales: $5,000-10,000. For more information, artists should send e-mail, call, or visit website.

TIPS "Booth presentation and uniqueness of product a must."

SIESTA FIESTA

270 Central Blvd., Suite 107B, Jupiter FL 33458. (561)746-6615. Fax: (561)746-6528. E-mail: info@artfestival.com. Website: www.artfestival.com. Contact: Malinda Ratliff, communications manager. Estab. 1978. Fine art & craft fair held annually in April. Outdoors. Accepts photography, jewelry, mixed media, sculpture, wood, ceramic, glass, painting, digital, fiber, metal. Juried. Number exhibitors: 85. Number attendees: 40,000. Free to public. Apply online via www.zapplication.org. Deadline: see website. Application fee: $25. Space fee: $350. Exhibition space: 10×10 and 10×20. For more information, artists should e-mail, call, or visit website. Festival located at Ocean Blvd. in Siesta Key Village.

TIPS "You have to start somewhere. First, assess where you are, and what you'll need to get things off the ground. Next, make a plan of action. Outdoor street art shows are a great way to begin your career and lifetime as a working artist. You'll meet a lot of other artists who have been where you are now. Network with them!"

SIESTA KEY CRAFT FESTIVAL

270 Central Blvd., Suite 107B, Jupiter FL 33458. (561)746-6615. Fax: (561)746-6528. E-mail: info@ artfestival.com. Website: www.artfestival.com. "Join us at the annual Siesta Key Craft Festival and take in the sand and the sea along Ocean Boulevard and Beach Road as you discover wonderful creations from more than 100 crafters exhibiting and selling their work in an outdoor gallery. From photography, paintings, sculpture, jewelry, and more showcased from local and traveling crafters, your visit to Siesta Key is promised to be a feast for the senses. This spectacular weekend festival is not to be missed." See website for more information.

SISTERS ANTIQUES IN THE PARK

Central Oregon Shows, P.O. Box 1555, Sisters OR 97759. (541)420-0279. E-mail: centraloregonshows@ gmail.com. Website: www.centraloregonshows.com. This event features antiques, collectibles, some crafts, food, and entertainment. This event runs the same time as the Sisters Chamber of Commerce annual Classic Car Show. This is a Friday and Saturday event. See website for more information.

SISTERS ART IN THE PARK

Central Oregon Shows, P.O. Box 1555, Sisters OR 97759. (541)420-0279. E-mail: centraloregonshows@ gmail.com. Website: www.centraloregonshows.com. This annual event features a variety of arts, crafts, food, entertainment, and a special fundraiser benefiting the Make-A-Wish Foundation of Oregon. This event runs the same time as the Sisters Rodeo and is located in the Sisters Creekside Park (Highway 20 & Jefferson Street).

SISTERS ARTIST MARKETPLACE

Central Oregon Shows, P.O. Box 1555, Sisters OR 97759. (541)420-0279. E-mail: centraloregonshows@gmail.com. Website: www.centraloregonshows.com. There will be a variety of arts, crafts, food, and entertainment. This event is on a Friday and Saturday only and requires a city business license for each vendor (see online application). See website for more information.

SISTERS ARTS & CRAFTS FESTIVAL

Central Oregon Shows, P.O. Box 1555, Sisters OR 97759. (541)420-0279. E-mail: centraloregonshows@ gmail.com. Website: www.centraloregonshows.com. It is an annual event that features a variety of arts, crafts, food, and entertainment with a special fundraiser benefiting the Make-A-Wish Foundation of Oregon. See website for more information.

SISTERS FALL STREET FESTIVAL

Central Oregon Shows, P.O. Box 1555, Sisters OR 97759. (541)420-0279. E-mail: centraloregonshows@ gmail.com. Website: www.centraloregonshows.com. This annual event features a variety of arts, crafts, food, and entertainment with a special fundraiser benefiting the Sisters High School Visual Arts Department. See website for more information.

SISTERS OUTDOOR QUILT SHOW

220 S. Ash St. #4, Sisters OR 97759. (541)549-0989. E-mail: info@soqs.org. Website: www.sistersoutdoorquiltshow.org. Contact: Jeanette Pilak, executive director. Estab. 1975. Quilt show held in July. Outdoors. Accepts handmade & machine-made quilts. Juried. Exhibitors: 600. Number of attendees: 12,000. Free to public. Apply online.

ADDITIONAL INFORMATION Deadline for entry: June 1 (or when filled). Application fee: $10. Space fee: none. Exhibition space: quilts are hung. For more information visit website.

TIPS "Watch the video on the home page of our website, then read the submission information on the registration page."

SISTERS WILD WEST SHOW

Central Oregon Shows, P.O. Box 1555, Sisters OR 97759. (541)420-0279. E-mail: centraloregonshows@ gmail.com. Website: www.centraloregonshows.com. There will be a variety of arts, crafts, antiques, and food. Entertainment will be 6 western skits with a western front town and demonstrations. See website for more information.

SLIDELL NEWCOMERS SELL-A-BRATION ARTS & CRAFTS SHOW

P.O. Box 2681, Slidell LA 70459. (985)641-2021. E-mail: ncsellabration@aol.com. Website: www.sell-a-brationcraftshow.webs.com. Contact: Linda Tate, show chair. Estab. 1982. Arts & crafts show held annually in October. Indoors. Accepts handmade crafts, original artwork, original photography. Number of exhibitors: 70-80. Number of attendees: 2,200-2,300. Free to public. Apply online.

ADDITIONAL INFORMATION Deadline for entry: October 5. Space fee: Starting at $100. Exhibition space: 10×10; 10×15; 10×20. For more information, see website.

SMITHSONIAN CRAFT SHOW

MRC 037 P.O. Box 37012, SIB Room T472, Washington, D.C. 20013-7012. (202)633-5069. E-mail: joneshl@smithsonian.si.edu. Website: www.smithsoniancraftshow.org. Contact: Hannah Jones, administrative assistant. Estab. 1983. Art & craft show held annually in April. Indoors. Accepts handmade crafts, basketry, ceramics, decorative fiber, furniture, glass, jewelry, leather, metal, mixed media, paper, wearable art, and wood. Juried. Awards/prizes: Gold Award, Silver Award, Bronze Award, Excellence Awards, Exhibitor's Choice Awards. Number exhibitors: 125. Number attendees: 8,000. Admission: see website for rates. Apply online.

ADDITIONAL INFORMATION Deadline for entry: September. Application fee: $50. Space fee: varies. Exhibition space: varies. For more information, artists should e-mail or visit website.

SMOKY HILL RIVER FESTIVAL FINE ART SHOW

(785)309-5770. E-mail: sahc@salina.org. Website: www.riverfestival.com. Fine art & craft show held annually in June. Outdoors. Accepts handmade crafts, ceramics, jewelry, fiber, mixed media, painting, drawing/pastels, glass, metal, wood, graphics/printmaking, digital, paper, sculpture, and photography. Juried. Awards/prizes: Jurors' Merit Awards, Purchase Awards. Number exhibitors: 90. Number attendees: 60,000. Admission: $10 in advance; $15 at gate; children 11 & under free. Apply via Zapplication.org.

ADDITIONAL INFORMATION Deadline for entry: February. Application fee: $30. Space fee: $275. Exhibition space: 10×10. For more information, artists should e-mail or visit website.

SMOKY HILL RIVER FESTIVAL FOUR RIVERS CRAFT SHOW

(785)309-5770. E-mail: sahc@salina.org. Website: www.riverfestival.com. Fine art & craft show held annually in June. Outdoors. Accepts handmade crafts, ceramics, folk art, leather, paper, clothing, glass, metal, herbal/soaps, basketry, wood, mixed media, jewelry, fiber, and more. Juried. Awards/prizes: Jurors' Merit Awards. Number exhibitors: 50. Number attendees: 60,000. Admission: $10 in advance; $15 at gate; children 11 & under free. Apply via Zapplication.org.

ADDITIONAL INFORMATION Deadline for entry: February. Application fee: $30. Space fee: $325. Exhibition space: 10×10. For more information, artists should e-mail or visit website.

SNAKE ALLEY ART FAIR

Website: www.snakealley.com/artfair.html. Art fair held annually on Father's Day. Features 104 selected artists from throughout the Midwest. See website for more information.

SOFA

(800)563-7632. Fax: (773)326-0660. Website: www.sofaexpo.com. The annual Exposition of Sculpture Objects & Functional Art + Design Fair (SOFA) is a gallery-presented, international art exposition dedicated to bridging the worlds of design, decorative, and fine art. Works by emerging and established artists and designers are available for sale by premier galleries and dealers. See website for more information.

SONORAN FESTIVAL OF FINE ART

(623)734-6526; (623)386-2269. E-mail: cvermillion12@cox.net; info@sonoranartsleague.com. Website: www.vermillionpromotions.com. Contact: Candy Vermillion. "The prestigious Sonoron Arts Festival is one of the largest open-air fine art venues in the Southwest featuring more than 125 local and nationally acclaimed artists. Sponsored each year by the Sonoran Arts League, the Festival is a juried show open to artists from around the country. With more than 400 members, the Arts League is a vital contributor to the cultural life in the Foothills, and a focal point for artists and art patrons." See website for more information.

SOUTH JERSEY PUMPKIN SHOW

P.O. Box 925, Millville NJ 08332. (856)765-0118. Fax: (856)765-9050. E-mail: sjpumpkinshow@aol.com. Website: www.sjpumpkinshow.com. Contact: Kathy Wright, organizer. Estab. 2003. Arts & crafts show held annually 2nd weekend in October. Indoors & outdoors. Accepts fine art & handmade crafts, wood, metal, pottery, glass, quilts. Awards/prizes: $100 for Fall Booth. Exhibitors: 175. Number of attendees: 10,500. Admission: $5/car (good all 3 days). Artists should apply via website.

ADDITIONAL INFORMATION Deadline for entry: late September. Application fee: none. Space fee: $40 (one day); $100 (weekend). Exhibition space: 10×10. For more information, artists should e-mail, visit website, or call.

SOUTHWEST ARTS FESTIVAL

81800 Avenue 51, Indio CA 92201. (760)347-0676. Fax: (760)347-6069. E-mail: swaf@indiochamber.org. Website: www.indiochamber.org. Contact: Joshua R. Bonner, president/CEO. Estab. 1986. Fine art show held annually in January. Outdoors. Accepts handmade crafts, clay, drawing, glass, jewelry, metalworks, and some art that does not fit into listed categories. Juried. Awards/prizes: Best of Show. Exhibitors: 250. Number of attendees: 10,000-15,000. Admission: $8; $12 2-day pass; 16 & under free. Apply online.

ADDITIONAL INFORMATION Deadline for entry: see website. Application fee: Earlybird, $45; regular, $55 (fee is nonrefundable). Space fee: $250 + 15% of all sales. Exhibition space: 12×12. For more information visit website.

SPACE COAST ART FESTIVAL

Space Coast Art Festival, P.O. Box 320135, Cocoa Beach FL 32932. (321)784-3322. Fax: (866)815-3322. E-mail: info@spacecoastartfestival.com. Website: www.

spacecoastartfestival.com. Art & craft show held annually in November. Outdoors. Accepts handmade crafts and other mediums. Juried. Awards/prizes: up to $50,000 in awards. Number exhibitors: 250. Number attendees: varies. Admission: see website. Apply online.

ADDITIONAL INFORMATION Deadline for entry: early July. Application fee: $40. Space fee: $300. Exhibition space: 12×12. For more information, artists should e-mail, call, or visit website.

SPANISH SPRINGS ART & CRAFT FESTIVAL

270 Central Blvd., Suite 107B, Jupiter FL 33458. (561)746-6615. Fax: (561)746-6528. E-mail: info@artfestival.com. Website: www.artfestival.com. Contact: Malinda Ratliff, communications manager. Estab. 1997. Fine art & craft fair, held annually in January & November. Outdoors. Accepts photography, jewelry, mixed media, sculpture, wood, ceramic, glass, painting, digital, fiber, metal. Juried. Number exhibitors: 210. Number attendees: 20,000. Free to public. Apply online via www.zapplication.org or visit website for paper application. Deadline: see website. Application fee: $15. Space fee: $265. Exhibition space: 10×10 and 10×20. For more information, artists should e-mail, call, or visit website. Festival located at Spanish Springs, The Villages, FL.

TIPS "You have to start somewhere. First, assess where you are, and what you'll need to get things off the ground. Next, make a plan of action. Outdoor street art shows are a great way to begin your career and lifetime as a working artist. You'll meet a lot of other artists who have been where you are now. Network with them!"

SPANKER CREEK FARM ARTS & CRAFTS FAIR

Spanker Creek Farm Arts & Craft Fair, P.O. Box 5644, Bella Vista AR 72714. (479)685-5655. E-mail: info@spankercreekfarm.com. Website: www.spankercreekfarm.com. Arts & craft show held biannually in the spring & fall. Outdoors & indoors. Accepts handmade crafts, ceramics, paintings, jewelry, glass, photography, wearable art, and other mediums. Juried. Number exhibitors: see website. Number attendees: varies. Free to public. Apply online.

ADDITIONAL INFORMATION Deadline for entry: see website for dates. Application fee: none. Space fee: varies. Exhibition space: varies. For more information, artists should call, e-mail, or visit website.

SPRING CRAFT & VENDOR SHOW

140 Oak St., Frankfort IL 60423. (815)469-9400. Fax: (815)469-9275. E-mail: cdebella@frankfortparks.org. Website: www.frankfortparks.org. Contact: Cali De-Bella, special events coordinator. Estab. 1999. Arts & crafts show held annually in March. Indoors. Accepts handmade crafts. Exhibitors: 65. Number of attendees: 500-700. Free to public. Apply online.

ADDITIONAL INFORMATION Deadline for entry: early October. Application fee: $45. Space fee: $45. Exhibition space: 10×6. For more information e-mail or visit website.

TIPS "Keep prices reasonable."

SPRING CRAFT FEST

Ozark Regional Promotions, 5557 Walden St., Lowell AR 72745. (479)756-6954. E-mail: karenlloyd@juno. com. Website: www.ozarkregionalartsandcrafts.com. Art & craft show held annually in May. Indoors. Accepts handmade crafts and other mediums. Juried. Number exhibitors: see website. Number attendees: varies. Free to public. Apply online.

ADDITIONAL INFORMATION Deadline for entry: March. Application fee: none. Space fee: varies. Exhibition space: varies. For more information, artists should e-mail, call, or visit website.

SPRING FESTIVAL: AN ARTS & CRAFTS AFFAIR

Huffman Productions, Inc., P.O. Box 655, Antioch IL 60002. (402)331-2889. E-mail: hpifestivals@cox.net. Website: www.hpifestivals.com. Fine arts & crafts fair held annually 3 times a year in the Spring. Indoors. Accepts handmade crafts and other mediums. Juried. Number exhibitors: see website. Number of attendees: varies per show. Admission: varies per show. Apply online.

ADDITIONAL INFORMATION Deadline for entry: see website. Application fee: none. Space fee: see website. Exhibition space: 10×10. For more information, artists should send e-mail, visit website, or call.

SPRING FESTIVAL OF THE ARTS OAKBROOK CENTER

Amdur Productions, P.O. Box 550, Highland Park IL 60035. (847)926-4300. Fax: (847)926-4330. E-mail: info@amdurproductions.com. Website: www.amdurproductions.com. Art & craft show held annually in May. Outdoors. Accepts handmade crafts and other mediums. Juried. Number exhibitors: see website. Number attendees: varies. Free to public. Apply online.

ADDITIONAL INFORMATION Deadline for entry: early April. Application fee: $25. Space fee: $460. Exhibition space: 10×10. For more information, artists should e-mail, call, or visit website.

SPRING FESTIVAL ON PONCE

Olmstead Park, North Druid Hills, 1451 Ponce de Leon, Atlanta GA 30307. (404)873-1222. E-mail: Lisa@affps.com. Website: festivalonponce.com. Contact: Lisa Windle, festival director. Estab. 2011. Arts & crafts show held annually early April. Outdoors. Accepts handmade crafts, painting, photography, sculpture, leather, metal, glass, jewelry. Juried by a panel. Awards/prizes: ribbons. Number of exhibitors: 125. Number of attendees: 40,000. Free to public. Apply online at www.zapplication.com.

ADDITIONAL INFORMATION Deadline for entry: February 7. Application fee: $25. Space fee: $250. Exhibition space: 10×10. For more information, see website.

SPRING GREEN ARTS & CRAFTS FAIR

Spring Green Arts & Crafts Fair Committee, P.O. Box 96, Spring Green WI 53588. E-mail: springgreenartfair@gmail.com. Website: www.springgreenartfair. com. Fine arts & crafts fair held annually June. Indoors. Accepts handmade crafts, glass, wood, painting, fiber, graphics, pottery, sculpture, jewelry, photography. Juried. Awards/prizes: Best of Show, Award of Excellence. Number exhibitors: see website. Number of attendees: varies per show. Admission: varies per show. Apply online.

ADDITIONAL INFORMATION Deadline for entry: mid-February. Application fee: $10-20. Space fee: $150. Exhibition space: 10×10. For more information, artists should send e-mail or visit website.

SPRINGTIME IN OHIO

P.O. Box 586, Findlay OH 45839-0586. (419)436-1457. Fax: (419)435-5035. E-mail: hello@cloudshows.biz. Website: www.cloudshows.biz. Estab. 1988. Arts & crafts show held annually in May. Indoors & outdoors. Accepts handmade crafts and other items. Exhibitors: 280. Admission: $5; children 12 & under free. Apply online.

ADDITIONAL INFORMATION Deadline for entry: see website. Application fee: see website. Space fee: see website. Exhibition space: see website. For more information, artists should send e-mail, visit website.

SQUARE TOMATOES CRAFT FAIR

Sally Parker, P.O. Box 4471, Davis CA 95617. (530)758-4903. E-mail: squaretcrafts@gmail.com. Website: www.squaretomatoescrafts.com. Contact: Sally Parker. Fine arts & crafts fair held annually July. Outdoors. Accepts handmade crafts and other mediums. Juried. Number exhibitors: see website. Number of attendees: varies. Free to public. Apply online.

ADDITIONAL INFORMATION Deadline for entry: see website. Application fee: none. Space fee: $25. Exhibition space: 10×10. For more information, artists should send e-mail, call, or visit website.

STAMFORD ART FESTIVAL

(518)852-6478. E-mail: suebg.art@gmail.com. Website: www.stamfordartfestival.org; gordonfinearts.org. Estab. 2015. Arts & crafts show held annually in July. Outdoors. Accepts handmade crafts and fine art. Juried. Awards/prizes: cash & ribbons. Exhibitors: 150. Number of attendees: 3,000-7,000. Free to public. Apply online.

ADDITIONAL INFORMATION Deadline for entry: April 1. Application fee: $25. Space fee: $350. Exhibition space: 10×12. For more information visit website, send e-mail, or call.

ST. ARMANDS CIRCLE CRAFT FESTIVAL

270 Central Blvd., Suite 107B, Jupiter FL 33458. (561)746-6615. Fax: (561)746-6528. E-mail: info@artfestival.com. Website: www.artfestival.com. Contact: Malinda Ratliff, communications manager. Estab. 2004. Fine art & craft fair held biannually in January & November. Outdoors. Accepts photography, jewelry, mixed media, sculpture, wood, ceramic, glass, painting, digital, fiber, metal. Juried. Number exhibitors: 180-210. Number attendees: 80,000-100,000. Free to public. Apply online via www.zapplication.org. Deadline: see website. Application fee: $25. Space fee: $415-435. Exhibition space: 10×10 and 10×20. For more information, artists should e-mail, call, or visit website. Fair held in St. Armands Circle in Sarasota, FL.

TIPS "You have to start somewhere. First, assess where you are, and what you'll need to get things off the ground. Next, make a plan of action. Outdoor street art shows are a great way to begin your career and lifetime as a working artist. You'll meet a lot of other artists who have been where you are now. Network with them!"

ST. CLAIR ART FAIR

Alice W. Moore Center for the Arts, 201 N. Riverside Ave. (in Riverview Plaza), Saint Clair MI 48079. (810)329-9576. Fax: (810)329-9464. Website: www.stclairart.org. The annual St. Clair Art Fair is one of the oldest art fairs in eastern Michigan. This juried Art Fair is traditionally the last full weekend in June, Saturday and Sunday. See website for more information.

STITCHES IN BLOOM QUILT SHOW AT THE OREGON GARDEN

879 W. Main St., Silverton OR 97381. (503)874-8100. E-mail: info@oregongarden.org. Website: www.oregongarden.org. Contact: Mary Ridderbusch, events coordinator. Estab. 2005. Arts & crafts/quilt show held annually in late January. Indoors. Accepts handmade crafts and quilts. Awards/prizes: People's Choice; Challenge Quilt. Exhibitors: 20. Number of attendees: 2,300. Admission: $11. Apply online at www.oregongarden.org/events/quiltshow.

ADDITIONAL INFORMATION Deadline for entry: January 9. Application fee: $10. Space fee: $150-260. Exhibition space: 9,000 sq. ft. For more information e-mail or see website.

STITCH ROCK

E-mail: info@rockthestitch.com. Website: www.rockthestitch.com. "Stitch Rock is South Florida's largest annual indie craft fair & bazaar bringing back old-school crafting techniques with new-school flair! Wth over 80 vendors the show is full of uncommon handmade goods like DIY fashion, funky home deco items, adorable plushies, natural bath & body goodies, vintage finds, hot rod paintings, pinup photography, & much more!" See website for more information.

ST. JOHN MEDICAL CENTER FESTIVAL OF THE ARTS

(440)808-9201. E-mail: ardis.radak@csauh.com. Website: www.sjws.net/festival_of_arts.aspx. Contact: Ardis Radak. Art & craft show held annually in July. Outdoors. Accepts handmade crafts, ceramics, glass, fiber, glass, graphics, jewelry, leather, metal, mixed media, painting, photography, printmaking, sculpture, woodworking. Juried. Awards/prizes: Best of Show, 1st Place, 2nd Place, Honorable Mention. Number exhibitors: 200. Number attendees: 15,000. Free to public. Apply via Zapplication.org.

ADDITIONAL INFORMATION Deadline for entry: May. Application fee: $15. Space fee: $300 (single); $600 (double). Exhibition space: 10×10 (single); 10×20 (double). For more information, artists should e-mail, call, or visit website.

ST. JOHN'S CHRISTMAS CRAFT SHOW

(207)725-5507. E-mail: craftshow@sjcsbme.org. Website: www.sjcsbme.org; Facebook.com/sjcscraftshow. Contact: Amy Pelletier, show director. Estab. 1973. Arts & crafts/holiday show held in December. Indoors. Accepts handmade crafts, art, photography, packaged artisan foods. Juried. Exhibitors: 30. Number of attendees: 400-600. Free to public. Apply by phone or e-mail.

ADDITIONAL INFORMATION Deadline for entry: July 1. Application fee: none. Space fee: varies. Exhibition space: varies. For more information e-mail, call, or visit website.

TIPS "Local artisans should submit completed application with clear focused photos by deadline for best chance of acceptance. Incomplete apps will be rejected. This is a school fundraiser and is less than 2 weeks before Christmas."

ST. MARY'S SAUERKRAUT FESTIVAL CRAFT FAIR

301 W. Tielky St., Bear Creek WI 54929. (715)460-5202. Fax: (715)823-6010. E-mail: songofbernadette@

gmail.com. Website: http://srmparishes.org. Contact: Jennifer Wood, chair. Estab. 2010. Arts & crafts show held annually the 1st week of August. Outdoors. Accepts handmade crafts, party plans, unique gifts, antiques. Exhibitors: 30. Number of attendees: 200. Free to public. Apply via website.

ADDITIONAL INFORMATION Deadline for entry: see website. Space fee: $25. Exhibition space: 10×10. For more information send e-mail.

TIPS "The festival is a family event with carnival games, car show, parade, and dinner. It is located in a high-traffic area. Keep displays simple and bright to attract attention."

STONE MOUNTAIN OKTOBERFEST & ARTIST MARKET

6655 James B. Rivers Dr., Stone Mountain GA 30083. (404)873-1222. E-mail: lisa@affps.com. Website: www.stonemountainvillage.com/oktoberfest0809.html. Contact: Lisa Windle, festival director. Estab. 2011. Arts & crafts show held annually mid-October. Outdoors. Accepts handmade crafts, painting, photography, sculpture, leather, metal, glass, jewelry. Juried by a panel. Awards/prizes: ribbons. Number of exhibitors: 150. Number of attendees: 7,500. Free to public. Apply online at www.zapplication.com.

ADDITIONAL INFORMATION Deadline for entry: August 22. Application fee: $25. Space fee: $150. Exhibition space: 10×10. For more information, see website.

ST. PAUL FINE CRAFT SHOW

American Craft Council Shows, 155 Water St., 4th Floor, Unit 5, Brooklyn NY 11201. (800)836-3470. Fax: (612)355-2330. E-mail: shows@craftcouncil.org. Website: www.craftcouncil.org. Art & craft show held annually in April. Indoors. Accepts handmade crafts, ceramics, fiber, metal, and other mediums. Juried. Awards/prizes: Awards of Excellence. Number exhibitors: 240. Number attendees: varies. Free to public. Apply online.

ADDITIONAL INFORMATION Deadline for entry: August. Application fee: $30 + $10 handling/processing fee for each set of images. Space fee: varies. Exhibition space: varies. For more information, artists should e-mail, call, or visit website.

ST. PETE BEACH COREY AREA CRAFT FESTIVAL

270 Central Blvd., Suite 107B, Jupiter FL 33458. (561)746-6615. Fax: (561)746-6528. E-mail: info@Art-Festival.com. Website: www.artfestival.com. "Corey Avenue in St. Pete Beach comes alive with the nation's best crafters displaying their handmade pottery, jewelry, paintings, and so much more! This open-air craft festival also includes a Green Market featuring exotic live plants, handmade soaps, savory dips, and gourmet sauces. Join us for a fun, free event in the heart of St. Pete Beach."

SUGARLOAF CRAFT FESTIVALS

Sugarloaf Mountain Works, Inc., 19807 Executive Park Circle, Germantown MD 20874. (301)990-1400; (800)210-9900. Fax: (301)253-9620. E-mail: sugarloafinfo@sugarloaffest.com. Website: www.sugarloafcrafts.com. "For over 30 years, the nation's most talented artisans have personally sold their contemporary crafts and fine art at Sugarloaf Craft Festivals. You will find Sugarloaf Craft Festivals in five great locations in the Mid-Atlantic area. Sugarloaf art fairs and craft festivals are among the nation's best and largest shows of their kind. Each show features a variety of work by the most talented craft designers and fine artists. From blown glass and sculpture to fine art and designer clothing, you'll find the handcrafted creations you're looking for at Sugarloaf!" See website for more information.

SUGAR PLUM BAZAAR

E-mail: sugarplumbazaar@yahoo.com. Website: www.sugarplumbazaar.com. Handmade and vintage event. Juried. Apply online. See website for more details.

SUGARPLUM MARKETPLACE

E-mail: sugarplum1market@yahoo.com. Website: www.jltheshoals.org/sugarplummarketplace.htm. "This 3-day marketplace includes an array of children's events, and shopping opportunities. Shoppers from across the Southeast will enjoy more than 90 merchants from throughout the United States offering unique gifts and holiday trends in a festive, family-friendly atmosphere. The Sugarplum Marketplace serves as a major fundraiser for the Junior League of the Shoals. Funds raised support the League's ongoing efforts to improve the Shoals community through the effective action and leadership of trained volunteers." See website for more information.

SUMMER ON SOUTHPORT

Amdur Productions, P.O. Box 550, Highland Park IL 60035. (847)926-4300. Fax: (847)926-4330. E-mail: info@amdurproductions.com. Website: www.amdurproductions.com. Art & craft show held annually in July. Outdoors. Accepts handmade crafts and other mediums. Juried. Number exhibitors: 100. Number attendees: varies. Admission: $5 donation to Southport Neighbors Association. Apply online.

ADDITIONAL INFORMATION Deadline for entry: early January. Application fee: $25. Space fee: $335. Exhibition space: 10×10. For more information, artists should e-mail, call, or visit website.

SUMMIT ART FESTIVAL

Website: www.summitartfest.org. Fine arts & crafts fair held annually October. Outdoors. Accepts handmade crafts, jewelry, ceramics, painting, glass, photography, fiber, and more. Juried. Awards/prizes: Best of Show, 2nd place, 3rd place, Mayor's Award, Jurors' Merit Award. Number exhibitors: see website. Number attendees: varies. Free to public. Apply online.

ADDITIONAL INFORMATION Deadline for entry: July. Application fee: $25. Space fee: $255. Exhibition space: 10×10. For more information, artists should visit website.

SUNCOAST ARTS FESTIVAL

E-mail: info@suncoastartsfest.com. Website: www.suncoastartsfest.com. "The Suncoast Arts Fest (SAF) has brought together quality fine artists and craftspeople with area art lovers who are motivated to buy. The event takes place in the heart of the Tampa Bay area, convenient to major interstates. SAF is a family-oriented cultural event. Artwork exhibited must be appropriate for viewers of all ages. The SAF committee has the sole exclusive and final authority to determine if any work is not acceptable for display." See website for more information.

SUN VALLEY CENTER ARTS & CRAFTS FESTIVAL

P.O. Box 656, Sun Valley ID 83353. (208)726-9491. Fax: (208)726-2344. E-mail: festival@sunvalleycenter. org. Website: www.sunvalleycenter.org. Contact: Sarah Kolash, festival director. Estab. 1968. Annual fine art & craft show held 2nd weekend in August. Outdoors. Accepts handmade crafts, ceramics, drawing, fiber, glass, jewelry, metalwork, mixed media, painting, photography, printmaking, sculpture, woodwork. Juried. Exhibitors: 130. Number of attendees: 12,000. Free to public. Apply via www.zapplication.org.

ADDITIONAL INFORMATION Deadline for entry: February 28. Application fee: $35. Space fee: $450 & $900. Exhibition space: 10×10 & 10×20. Average sales: $3,700. For more information e-mail or see website.

SWEET PEA, A FESTIVAL OF THE ARTS

424 E. Main St., Ste. 203B, Bozeman MT 59715. (406)586-4003. Fax: (406)586-5523. E-mail: admin@ sweetpeafestival.com. E-mail: spartscrafts@sweetpeafestival.org. Website: www.sweetpeafestival.org. Contact: Arts & crafts chair. Estab. 1978. Arts & crafts show held annually in August. Outdoors. Accepts handmade crafts and other mediums. Juried. Exhibitors: 110. Number of attendees: 14,000. Admission: $10/day; $15, 3-day pass. Apply via Zapplication.org.

ADDITIONAL INFORMATION Deadline for entry: early April. Application fee: $40. Space fee: $345 (10×10); $495 (10×20). Exhibition space: 10×10; 10×20. For more information send e-mail, call, or visit website.

TACOMA HOLIDAY FOOD & GIFT FESTIVAL

Tacoma Dome, 2727 E. D St., Tacoma WA 98421. (800)521-7469. Fax: (425)889-8165. E-mail: tacoma@ showcaseevents.org. Website: www.showcaseevents. org. Contact: Susie O'Brien Borer, show manager. Estab. 1982. Seasonal holiday show held annually in October. Indoors. Accepts handmade crafts, art, photography, pottery, glass, jewelry, clothing, fiber, seasonal food. Juried. Exhibitors: 500. Number of attendees: 40,000. Admission: $14.50 (for all 5 days)- a $1 off coupon online at holidaygiftshows.com; 12 & under free. Apply via website or call or e-mail for application.

ADDITIONAL INFORMATION Deadline for entry: until full. Space fee: see website. Exhibition space:

6×10, 10×10. For more information send e-mail, call, send SASE, or visit website.

TIPS "Competitive pricing, attractive booth display, quality product, something unique for sale, friendly & outgoing personality."

TAHOE ARTS PROJECT ART FAIR

(530)542-3632. E-mail: tahoearts@aol.com. Website: www.tahoeartsproject.org. "Tahoe Arts Project Art Festival is an art show nestled in a pine forest in the heart of South Lake Tahoe. Festival admission and parking will be free for artists." See website for more information.

TAHOE CITY FINE ARTS & CRAFTS FESTIVAL

Pacific Fine Arts Festivals, P.O. Box 280, Pine Grove CA 95665. (209)267-4394. Fax: (209)267-4395. E-mail: pfa@pacificfinearts.com. Website: www.pacificfinearts.com. The annual Tahoe City Fine Arts and Crafts Festival will give visitors a special opportunity to meet with more than 45 artisans and craftspeople showcasing a wide variety of arts and crafts including photography, oil paintings, ceramic vessels, jewelry, and much more. See website for more information.

TALBOT STREET ART FAIR

Talbot Street Art Fair, P.O. Box 489, Danville IN 46122. (317)745-6479. E-mail: talbotstreetartfair@ hotmail.com. Website: www.talbotstreet.org. "With over 270 artists from across the nation, this juried art fair continues to be ranked as one of the finest fairs in the country. Talbot Street Art Fair is located between 16th & 20th / Delaware & Pennsylvania - Indianapolis in the historic Herron-Morton Neighborhood. This is a family-friendly event with plenty to see and do for everyone." See website for more information.

⬆ TAOS FALL ARTS FESTIVAL

P.O. Box 675, Taos NM 87571. (575)758-4648. E-mail: tfafvolunteer@gmail.com. Website: www.taosfallarts. com. Contact: Patsy S. Wright. Estab. 1974. "This festival is the oldest art festival in Taos, premiering in 1974 and only showcasing artists who reside in Taos County. It includes 3 major art shows: the curated exhibit titled 'Distinguished Achievement Award Series', a juried exhibit titled Taos Select, and the Taos Open, as its name implies, an exhibit open to all artists working in Taos County. The festival represents over 250 Taos County artists working in a variety of mediums. Each year a limited-edition poster is printed to commemorate the arts festival. The proceeds from the shows will benefit art programs for Taos County children." See website for more information.

TAHOE ARTS PROJECT ART FAIR

(530)542-3632. E-mail: tahoearts@aol.com. Website: www.tahoeartsproject.org. "Tahoe Arts Project Art Festival is an art show nestled in a pine forest in the heart of South Lake Tahoe. Festival admission and parking will be free for artists." See website for more information.

THIRD WARD ART FESTIVAL

Amdur Productions, P.O. Box 550, Highland Park IL 60035. (847)926-4300. Fax: (847)926-4330. E-mail: info@amdurproductions.com. Website: www.amdurproductions.com. Art & craft show held annually in August. Outdoors. Accepts handmade crafts and other mediums. Juried. Awards/prizes: given at festival. Number exhibitors: 135. Number attendees: 30,000. Free to public. Apply online.

ADDITIONAL INFORMATION Deadline for entry: early January. Application fee: $25. Space fee: $450. Exhibition space: 10×10. For more information, artists should e-mail, call, or visit website.

THOUSAND OAKS ART FESTIVAL

Thousand Oaks Arts Festival, c/o City of Thousand Oaks, Cultural Affairs Department, 2100 E. Thousand Oaks Blvd., Thousand Oaks CA 91362. (805)498-6591. E-mail: richardswilliams@roadrunner.com. Website: www.toartsfestival.com. "2-Day Festival with more than 60 visual art exhibitors. Continuous live performances, children's hands-on artistic and interactive art exhibits, and over 12,000 visitors. FREE admission and parking. Smoke-Free Premises. Wine Tasting at THE LAKES." See website for more information.

THREE RIVERS ART FESTIVAL

P.O. Box 633, Covington LA 70434. (985)327-9797. E-mail: info@threeriversartfestival.com. Website: www.threeriversartfestival.com. "With 200 artists from more than 20 states. A juried show of original works. Tent after colorful tent ranged along the streets of historic downtown Covington, Louisiana. Arts and fine crafts demonstrations. Music. Food. Three Rivers Run. And lots of activities just for kids. It's the Covington Three Rivers Art Festival. Where the fun starts with art and goes on for 2 wonderful days." See website for more information.

TILLAMOOK ART ON THE GREEN

Central Oregon Shows, P.O. Box 1555, Sisters OR 97759. (541)420-0279. E-mail: centraloregonshows@gmail.com. Website: www.centraloregonshows.com. "This event features a variety of arts, crafts, antiques, food, and entertainment with a special fundraiser benefiting a local charity." See website for more information.

TALUCA LAKE FINE ARTS FESTIVAL

West Coast Artists, P.O. Box 750, Acton CA 93510. (818)813-4478. Fax: (661)526-4575. E-mail: info@westcoastartists.com. Website: www.westcoastartists.com. "Open to all media of original fine art and fine crafts. All work will be juried. Categories will be limited. No commercial, manufactured, imported, mass-produced or purchased for resale items will be accepted. No clothing. No representatives," See website for more information.

TORRIANO CRAFT & HANDMADE FAIR

E-mail: torrianoparents@gmail.com. Website: www.facebook.com/TorrianoCraftMarket/info. "biannual pop-up market selling affordable and original creations. Have-a-go craft demos, portraits, and face painting for children." See website for more information.

TRENTON AVE ARTS FESTIVAL

E-mail: info@trentonaveartsfest.org. Website: www.trentonaveartsfest.org. "Free and open to the public, the Trenton Avenue Arts Festival celebrates East

Kensington's incredible mix of local artists, musicians, and eateries. Organized by the dedicated volunteers of the East Kensington Neighbors Association and featuring over 200 local arts and food vendors, TAAF attracts 10k+ attendees to raise funds for neighborhood projects and revitalization. The festival is held on Trenton Avenue, a wide cobblestone street that has been part of Kensington's rich creative history for over a hundred years. By hosting the Trenton Avenue Arts Festival, EKNA continues that tradition." See website for more information.

TRUMBULL ARTS FESTIVAL

(203)452-5065. Fax: (203)452-3853. E-mail: arts@trumbull-ct.gov. Website: www.trumbull-ct.gov. Contact: Emily Areson, arts coordinator. Estab. 1978. Arts & crafts show held annually in September. Outdoors. Accepts handmade crafts and fine art. Juried. Awards/prizes: cash & ribbons. Exhibitors: 75. Number of attendees: 3,500. Free to public. Apply by calling or sending e-mail.

ADDITIONAL INFORMATION Deadline for entry: early April. Application fee: none. Space fee: varies. Exhibition space: 10×10. For more information send e-mail, SASE, or call.

TIPS "Display your best works."

UC SPRING ART FAIR

32 Campus Dr., UC Room 232, Missoula MT 59812-0012. (406)243-5622. E-mail: ucartfair.student@mso.umt.edu. Website: www.umt.edu/uc/Arts-Entertainment/uc-art-fairs. Contact: Brianna McLean, art fair coordinator. Estab. 1970s. Arts & crafts show held 3 times/year in April (spring show), September, and December. Indoors. Accepts handmade crafts, photography, jewelry, prints, painting, pottery. Juried. Exhibitors: 60. Number of attendees: 20,000. Free to public. Apply online.

ADDITIONAL INFORMATION Deadline for entry: March 20. Application fee: $10. Space fee: varies. Exhibition space: varies. For more information visit website, send e-mail, or call.

TIPS "Have an original product, have reasonable prices for college students (as that is obviously the major demographic on a college campus), be friendly and inviting to customers, and have an attractive display for product."

⊙ UNIQUE LA

Website: www.stateofunique.com. "UNIQUE LA was created by community leader and designer Sonja Rasula as a way to bring local-made design and art to the masses while helping to grow and support the US economy and small businesses. Currently 20,000+ attendees come to discover independent designers/artists and buy local (an estimated $1.5 million is spent at each 2-day show). The largest independent design show in the country, attendees get the rare chance to meet and shop directly from hundreds of hand-selected designers and artists in one space. All of the products at the show are made right here in the USA. UNIQUE makes it easy for shoppers to support the local economy, discover great design and deals, join in community, and have a blast with DJs/free drinks/free craft projects and workshops and more." See website for more information.

⊙ UNPLAZA ART FAIR

E-mail: PeaceWorksKC@gmail.com. Website: www.peaceworkskc.org/unplaza.html. Art fair. Annual fundraiser for Peace Works Kansas City. See website for more information and to apply.

UPPER ARLINGTON LABOR DAY ARTS FESTIVAL

(614)583-5000. Website: www.uaoh.net/egov/docs/1389217117601.htm. Fine art & craft show held annually in September. Outdoors. Accepts handmade crafts, ceramics, fiber, glass, graphics, jewelry, leather, metal, mixed media, painting, photography, printmaking, sculpture, woodworking. Juried. Awards/prizes: $1,350 in awards. Number exhibitors: 200. Number attendees: 25,000. Free to public. Apply via Zapplication.org.

ADDITIONAL INFORMATION Deadline for entry: February. Application fee: see website. Space fee: varies. Exhibition space: varies. For more information, artists should call or visit website.

URBAN CRAFT UPRISING

(206)728-8008. E-mail: kristen@urbancraftuprising.com. Website: www.urbancraftuprising.com. Contact: Kristen Rask, president. "Urban Craft Uprising is Seattle's largest indie craft show! At UCU, now in its 8th year, fans can choose from a wide variety of hand-crafted goods, including clothing of all types, jewelry, gifts, bags, wallets, buttons, accessories, aprons, children's goods, toys, housewares, paper goods, candles, kits, art, food, and much, much more. Each show is carefully curated and juried to ensure the best mix of crafts and arts, along with quality and originality. This biannual show showcases over 100 vendors excelling in the world of craft, art, and design." See website for more information.

UTAH ARTS FESTIVAL
230 S. 500 W. #120, Salt Lake City UT 84101. (801)322-2428. E-mail: lisa@uaf.org. Website: www.uaf.org. "The annual Festival takes place the 4th weekend of June each summer and is held downtown in Salt Lake City at Library and Washington Squares. A full-time staff of 4 and 1 part-time person work year-round to produce the Festival. In addition, we engage seasonal coordinators to help plan and implement artistic programs each year. A technical staff, stage and production crews, along with more than 1,000 volunteers round out the personnel needed to produce the annual event. The Utah Arts Festival is the largest outdoor multi-disciplinary arts event in Utah with attendance hovering over 80,000 each summer. Having garnered numerous awards internationally, nationally, and locally, the event remains one of the premiere events that kicks off the summer in Utah each June." See website for more information.

VAGABOND INDIE CRAFT FAIR
E-mail: info@urbanbazaarsf.com. Website: www.urbanbazaarsf.com. "This event, which includes more than 20 talented local artists and craftspeople selling their work over 2 days (different vendors each day!), takes place in the back garden of Urban Bazaar. The merchandise offered at Vagabond will include all manner of gifts, with a focus on jewelry, accessories, and affordable artwork." See website for more information.

VERMONT MAPLE FESTIVAL
E-mail: info@vtmaplefestival.org. Website: www.vtmaplefestival.org. "Glittery jewelry, taste-tempting specialty foods, classy clothing, assorted artwork,

wooden things, fine photographs, and so much more! Now enlarged to more than 60 vendors, the show offers both traditional and the latest in craft innovations, AS WELL AS the fine specialty foods for which Vermont is famous! It's one of the first LARGE craft shows of the year, and it's ADMISSION FREE - a show that folks who delight in creativity have on their 'don't miss' list." See website for more information.

VICTORIAN CHRISTMAS IN LANDMARK PARK
Arts and Crafts Landmark Park, P.O. Box 6362, Dothan AL 36302. (334)794-3452. Website: www.landmarkpark.com/events.html#current. "Warm up to some holiday hospitality during an afternoon centered on the pleasures of Christmas past. Visitors are invited to sample turn-of-the-century desserts and sip hot chocolate or mulled cider while children try their hand at making traditional Christmas decorations. A circuit-riding preacher will arrive on horseback to deliver a Christmas message at the church. Arts and crafts, holiday music, wagon rides, and more. Free admission, visitors are encouraged to bring a non-perishable food item for donation to the Wiregrass Area United Way Food Bank." See website for more information.

VILLAGES CRAFT FESTIVAL AT COLONY PLAZA
270 Central Blvd., Suite 107B, Jupiter FL 33458. (561)746-6615. Fax: (561)746-6520. E-mail: info@ArtFestival.com. Website: www.artfestival.com. "There's something for everyone at this craft festival, featuring arts and crafts all created in the USA. Handmade one-of-a-kind jewelry pieces you will not find anywhere else, personalized wall hangings, art for your pets, ceramics, functional and decorative, and much, much more. An expansive Green Market lends plants, exotic flora, and homemade soaps. Come find that unique gift and we will see you there!"

THE VILLAGES CRAFT FESTIVAL AT LA PLAZA GRANDE
270 Central Blvd., Suite 107B, Jupiter FL 33458. (561)746-6615. Fax: (561)746-6528. E-mail: info@ArtFestival.com. Website: www.artfestival.com/Festi-

vals/The_Villages_Craft_Festival_La_Plaza_Grande. ASPX. Arts & crafts show held annually in January. Outdoors. Accepts handmade crafts and other items. Juried. Exhibitors: see website. Number of attendees: varies. Admission: see website. Apply online.

ADDITIONAL INFORMATION Deadline for entry: see website. Application fee: see website. Space fee: see website. Exhibition space: see website. For more information, artists should send e-mail, visit website, or call.

VINTAGE DAYS CRAFTS FAIRE

(559)278-2741. E-mail: vintagecraftsfaire@gmail.com. Website: www.fresnostate.edu/studentaffairs/studentinvolvement/traditions/vintagedays/crafts.html. The Vintage Days Crafts Faire is a marketplace for over 100 exhibitors specializing in handmade items including jewelry, children's toys, home decor, and more. To ensure high quality and innovative items, all applications are juried. See website for more information.

VIRGINIA BEACH DOWNTOWN ART FAIR

270 Central Blvd., Suite 107B, Jupiter FL 33458. (561)746-6615. Fax: (561)746-6528. E-mail: info@ artfestival.com. Website: www.artfestival.com. Contact: Malinda Ratliff, communications manager. Estab. 2015. Fine art & craft fair held annually in April. Outdoors. Accepts photography, jewelry, mixed media, sculpture, wood, ceramic, glass, painting, digital, fiber, metal. Juried. Number exhibitors: 80. Number attendees: see website. Free to public. Apply online via www. zapplication.org. Deadline: see website. Application fee: $25. Space fee: $395. Exhibition space: 10×10 and 10×20. For more information, artists should e-mail, call, or visit website. Festival located Main St. between Central Park Ave. and Constitution Dr.

TIPS "You have to start somewhere. First, assess where you are, and what you'll need to get things off the ground. Next, make a plan of action. Outdoor street art shows are a great way to begin your career and lifetime as a working artist. You'll meet a lot of other artists who have been where you are now. Network with them!"

VIRTU ART FESTIVAL

(401)596-7761. Fax: (401)596-2190. E-mail: lkonicki@ westerlychamber.org. Website: www.westerlychamber.org. Contact: Lisa Konicki, executive director. Estab. 1996. Arts & crafts show held annually in May. Outdoors. Accepts original fine art & handmade crafts, oils, acrylics, prints, wood, watercolor, pottery, glass, jewelry, sculpture. Juried. Exhibitors: 150. Number of attendees: 20,000. Free to public. Artists should apply via website.

ADDITIONAL INFORMATION Deadline for entry: February 20. Application fee: none. Space fee: $200. Exhibition space: 12×12. For more information, artists should e-mail.

WALK IN THE WOODS ART FAIR

Hawthorn Hollow, 880 Green Bay Rd., Kenosha WI 53144. (334)794-3452. E-mail: hawthornhollow@ wi.rr.com. Website: www.hawthornhollow.org/ events/art-fair. "The Walk in the Woods Art Fair has grown to be one of the more popular and well respected in southeastern Wisconsin, where over 60 artists display their creations along the wooded trails and gardens of Hawthorn Hollow. Fine art ranging from jewelry to acrylic and watercolor paintings, from photography to wood sculpting, glass and garden art will all be available for purchase. We also feature live entertainment throughout the day, face painting, food/ beverages for sale, and a Silent Auction. A $5 donation per vehicle is requested. Come and enjoy a beautiful day combining fine art with music and nature." See website for more information.

WALNUT CREEK SIDEWALK FINE ARTS & CRAFTS FESTIVAL

Pacific Fine Arts Festivals, P.O. Box 280, Pine Grove CA 95665. (209)267-4394. Fax: (209)267-4395. E-mail: pfa@pacificfinearts.com. Website: www.pacificfinearts.com. The annual Fine Arts and Crafts Festival is free to the public and will feature more than 150 professional artists traveling from throughout California and the Western United States to showcase original paintings, sculpture, photography, jewelry, clothing, and other fine works. See website for more information.

WASHINGTON CRAFT SHOW

Crafts America, LLC, P.O. Box 603, Green Farms CT 06838. (203)254-0486. Fax: (203)254-9672. E-mail: info@craftsamericashows.com. Website: www.craftsamericashows.com/WASH_main.htm. Fine crafts fair held annually in October. Indoors. Accepts handmade crafts, basketry, ceramics, fiber, furniture, glass, jewelry, leather, metal, mixed media, paper, wood. Juried. Awards/prizes: cash awards. Number exhibitors: see website. Number attendees: varies. Admission: $15 general; $14 seniors; children 12 & under free. Apply online.

ADDITIONAL INFORMATION Application deadline: mid-October. Application fee: $45. Space fee: varies. Exhibition space: varies. For more information, artists should email, call, or visit website.

WATERFRONT INVITATIONAL ART FAIR

Saugatuck Douglas Art Club, Box 176, Saugatuck MI 49453-0176. (334)794-3452. E-mail: artclub@saugatuckdouglasartclub.org. Website: www.saugatuckdouglasartclub.org. Juried art & craft fair. See website for more information.

WASAU FESTIVAL OF ARTS

P.O. Box 1763, Wausau WI 54402. (715)842-1676. E-mail: info@wausaufoa.org. Website: www.wausaufoa.org. Since its inception in 1965, this outdoor celebration of the arts has become an annual event in the heart of Wausau's historic downtown and an integral part of Wausau's Artrageous weekend. Patrons can enjoy and purchase artwork in a variety of styles and price ranges from over 120 juried, professional artists from all over the United States. See website for more information.

◎ WEDGWOOD ART FESTIVAL

Wedgwood Art Festival, P.O. Box 15246, Seattle WA 98115. E-mail: wafestival@gmail.com. Website: www.wedgwoodfestival.com. "The Wedgwood Art Festival is a 2-day event supporting and celebrating arts for the community of Wedgwood, Seattle. Most participating artists reside in Seattle and the Puget Sound area. A few guest Northwest artists who live outside the Puget Sound area are also included to add variety to the show." See website for more information.

WELLS STREET ART FESTIVAL

E-mail: rrobinson@chicagoevents.com. Website: www.chicagoevents.com. "One of the city's largest and most acclaimed fine arts happenings, it's held in the heart of Chicago's historic Old Town neighborhood. The annual art extravaganza features the works of more than 250 juried artists with the eclectic mix running the gamut from paintings, sculptures, and glasswork to photography, ceramics, woodwork, and much more. It also features the tasty cuisine of Old Town restaurants, the always-hoppin' music stage, and a silent auction." See website for more information.

WEST SHORE ART FAIR

107 S. Harrison St., Ludington MI 49431. (231)845-2787. E-mail: wsaf@ludingtonartscenter.org. Website: www.ludingtonartscenter.org. Contact: Christine Plummer, WSAF coordinator. Estab. 1968. Fine art fair held annually in July. Outdoors. Accepts photography, clay, drawing, jewelry, leather, mixed media, wood, glass, painting, printmaking, fiber, metal. Juried. Awards/prizes: 1st Place; 2nd Place; 3rd Place; Sponsor Purchase. Number exhibitors: 115. Number attendees: 10,000. Free to public. Apply online via www.zapplication.org. Deadline: late November. Application fee: $25. Space fee: $125 (single); $250 (double). Exhibition space: 10×10 and 12×12. For more information, artists should e-mail, call, or visit website. Festival located at Ludington City Park.

WICKFORD ART FESTIVAL

Wickford Art Association, 36 Beach St., North Kingstown RI 02852. (401)294-6840. E-mail: festivaldirector@wickfordart.org. Website: www.wickfordart.org. Contact: Judy Salvadore, director. Estab. 1962. Fine art show held annually in July. Outdoors. Accepts fine art, painting, jewelry, drawing, photography. Juried. Exhibitors: 250. Number of attendees: 50,000. Free to public. Apply online.

ADDITIONAL INFORMATION Deadline for entry: April 1. Application fee: $35. Space fee: $200 (members); $240 (nonmembers). Exhibition space: 10×10. For more information visit website, send e-mail, or call.

TIPS "Fine artists only should apply—no functional art accepted. Rhode Island does not collect sales tax on fine art. Festival is outdoors, rain or shine so be prepared for New England weather which could be hot & humid, rainy, or gorgeous! Festival has a long history in coastal Wickford Village and is a summer highlight in Southern New England."

WILLOUGHBY ARTSFEST

WWLCC ArtsFest, 28 Public Square, Willoughby OH 44094. (440)942-1632. E-mail: info@wwlcchamber.com. Website: www.wwlcchamber.com. "Historical Downtown Willoughby, in the hub of Lake County, is located 20 miles east of Cleveland and easily accessible from both Interstate 2 and 90. Featuring over 125 artists, entertainment, and food, this show welcomes over 10,000 people. Willoughby ArtsFest—you won't want to miss it!" See website for more information.

☺ WINNIPEG FOLK FESTIVAL HAND-MADE VILLAGE

Winnipeg Folk Festival, 203-211 Bannatyne Avenue, Winnipeg, Manitoba R3B 3P2 Canada. (204)231-0096; (866)301-3823. Fax: (204)231-0076. E-mail: info@winnipegfolkfestival.ca. Website: www.winnipegfolkfestival.ca. "The Hand-Made Village celebrates the long-standing history that folk art shares with folk music festivals. Our village features the handmade work of up to 50 artisans from across Canada." See website for more information.

WINTER PARK SIDEWALK ART FESTIVAL

Winter Park Sidewalk Art Festival, P.O. Box 597, Winter Park FL 32790-0597. (407)644-7207. E-mail: wpsaf@yahoo.com. Website: www.wpsaf.org. "The Winter Park Sidewalk Art Festival is one of the nation's oldest, largest, and most prestigious juried outdoor art festivals, consistently rated among the top shows by *Sunshine Artist* and *American Style* magazines. Each year more than 350,000 visitors enjoy the show." See website for more information.

WOODLANDS WATERWAY ARTS FESTIVAL

The Woodlands Waterway Arts Festival, P.O. Box 8184, The Woodlands TX 77387. E-mail: info@woodlandsartsfestival.com. Website: www.woodlandsartsfestival.com. "The Woodlands Waterway Arts Festival (WWAF) weekend event is a celebration of visual, culinary and performing arts. The Festival gives patrons the rare and special opportunity to meet and talk with artists from around the country, sample great food, watch the Art of Food demos, enjoy live music, and entertain their families at our interactive 'ARTOPOLY' area. Adult tickets are $12.00, a Weekend pass is $15.00, and children 12 and under are admitted free. Cash ONLY at all gates and food vendors." See website for more information.

WOODSSTOCK MUSIC & ARTS FESTIVAL

(954)748-8370. Website: http://www.woodstockartsfest.com. Fine art & craft show held annually. Outdoors. Accepts handmade crafts, ceramics, drawing, fiber, glass, jewelry, leather, metal, mixed media, painting, photography, sculpture, wood. Juried. Awards/prizes: Best of Show, Honorable Mention. Number exhibitors: see website. Number attendees: varies. Admission: $25 general; $45 VIP. Apply via Zapplication.org.

ADDITIONAL INFORMATION Deadline for entry: June. Application fee: $20. Space fee: $100 (single); $150 (double). Exhibition space: 10×10 (single); 10×20 (double). For more information, artists should visit website.

YELLOW DAISY FESTIVAL

E-mail: ydf@stonemountainpark.com. Website: www.stonemountainpark.com/events/Yellow-Daisy-Festival.aspx. More than 400 artists and crafters from 38 states and 2 countries display their works for your appreciation and purchase. Daily live entertainment, Children's Corner activities, and crafter demonstrations throughout the event as well as fabulous festival foods. Yellow Daisy Festival is free with paid parking admission. Vehicle entry to the park is $15 for a 1-day permit or $40 for an annual permit. See website for more information.

ONLINE MARKETPLACES

///

Most crafters are aware of Etsy, but there are other online marketplaces that provide support for craft artisans. Whether you choose to diversify your online presence by selling across multiple platforms, or choose to focus on one or two sites, you need to be aware of the ever-changing landscape of online sales. Visit their website and take a look around. Do they offer a functionality that would be helpful to your online sales? Do you recognize anyone who is selling on that site? What is the competition? How do images appear? What is the site's financial take of your sales, or do they charge a flat fee per listing? Consider all of your options and do your research to make sure you are maximizing your online opportunities. Also, be sure to read the interview with Carter Seibels Singh of WomanShopsWorld for her approach to a successful Etsy business.

The listings here are only the tip of the iceberg. More and more online venues sprout up everyday. As a crafter and business person, get to know the venues in advance. If you can, order from a vendor to gain a firsthand understanding of the user's experience. Try to talk with someone who has a shop on the site—or sites—you're interested in.

KEY TO SYMBOLS & ABBREVIATIONS

⚜	Canadian market
🜨	market located outside of the U.S. and Canada
⌂	market prefers to work with local artists/ designers
b&w	black & white (photo or illustration)
SASE	self-addressed, stamped envelope
SAE	self-addressed envelope
IRC	International Reply Coupon, for use when mailing to countries other than your own

COMPLAINT PROCEDURE

If you feel you have not been treated fairly by a company listed in *Crafter's Market*, we advise you to take the following steps:

- First, try to contact the company. Sometimes one e-mail or letter can quickly clear up the matter.
- Document all your correspondence with the company. If you write to us with a complaint, provide the details of your submission, the date of your first contact with the company, and the nature of your subsequent correspondence.
- We will enter your complaint into our files.
- The number and severity of complaints will be considered in our decision whether to delete the listing from the next edition.
- We reserve the right to not list any company for any reason.

ARTFIRE

E-mail: service@artfire.com. Website: www.artfire.com. Geared towards handmade items. Provides shopping cart feature. Products sold: handmade items, vintage, supplies, PDF downloads, patterns/books. Setup costs: $12.95/month. Accepted payment methods: Visa, MasterCard, American Express, PayPal, Bill Me Later, ProPay, Amazon Payments. Sales disputes: dedicated customer service team to resolve disputes and answer queries. Provided to sellers: community forums/chats, additional free marketing opportunities, groups.

ARTFUL HOME

E-mail: artists@artfulhome.com. Website: www.artfulhome.com. Geared towards handmade items & other merchandise. Provides shopping cart feature. Products sold: handmade, craft, art, vintage. Provided to sellers: community forums/chats, additional free marketing opportunities, groups.

ARTULIS

E-mail: help@artulis.com. Website: www.artulis.com. Artulis is an online marketplace for artists, makers, and craftspeople to showcase their work and find new buyers for their talents. We provide an online shop as well as a range of tools to help keep track of sales and messages from buyers.

BONANZA

109 W. Denny Way, #312, Seattle WA 98119. E-mail: support@bonanza.com. Website: www.bonanza.com. Products sold: handmade items, vintage, supplies, art, crafts, accessories, apparel. Setup costs: free. Accepted payment methods: see website. Sales disputes: dedicated customer service team to resolve disputes and answer queries. Provided to sellers: community forums/chats.

CAFEPRESS

Website: www.cafepress.com. "CafePress is where the world's creative minds join forces to provide an unparalleled marketplace. We give you the power to create custom products and personalized gifts on a variety of high-quality items such as t-shirts, hoodies, posters, bumper stickers, and mugs. CafePress also allows you to set up online shops where you can design and sell your own unique merchandise. Our design tools make it easy to add photos, text, images, and even create cool designs or logos from scratch. As if it couldn't get any better, you can even find content from major entertainment partners such as The Hunger Games, Big Bang Theory and Star Trek as well as products dedicated to hobbies, birthdays, the military and more. At CafePress we print each item as it's ordered and many products ship within 24 hours."

CORIANDR

Mookle Studios Limited, 12 Parklands Close, Chandlers Ford, Eastleigh Hants SO53 2EQ, United Kingdom. E-mail: support@coriandr.com. Website: www.coriandr.com. Geared towards handmade items. Setup costs: see website. Accepted payment methods: credit card, PayPal. Provided to sellers: community forums/chats, groups.

CRAFT IS ART

Las Vegas NV Website: www.craftisart.com. Estab. 2009. Geared towards handmade items. Provides shopping cart feature. Setup costs: free option; premium option $79.99/yr. Accepted payment methods: Visa, MasterCard, American Express, PayPal, Amazon Payments, Google Checkout. Provided to sellers: community forums/chats, Facebook integration, customizable store, coupons, business cards, postcards.

CRAFTSY

999 18th St., Suite 240, Denver CO 80202. Website: www.craftsy.com. Estab. 2010. "Craftsy provides education and tools to help you bring your creativity to life. Our hundreds of classes in quilting, sewing, knitting, cake decorating, art, photography, cooking, and many more categories, bring the world's best instructors to you. Learn at your pace with easy-to-follow HD video lessons you can access on your computer and mobile device anytime, anywhere, forever. Craftsy's Supplies Shop is carefully curated to bring you the best brands at incredible values, ensuring you always have exactly what you need for your next project. Find your new favorite fabric collections, designer yarns, art supplies, books, class materi-

als, and more. Find your next project in Craftsy's Pattern Marketplace, featuring thousands of beautiful patterns from the world's best independent designers. All proceeds go directly to supporting passionate designers, and you can instantly download high-quality patterns for chic shawls, adorable baby booties, couture dresses, scalloped lace hats, and so much more!"

DAWANDA

Windscheidstr 18, Berlin 10627, Germany. (44)20 3608 1414. E-mail: english@dawanda.com. Website: en.dawanda.com. Estab. 2006. Geared towards handmade items. Provides shopping cart feature. Products sold: handmade items, vintage, supplies, PDF downloads, patterns/books. Setup costs: free; 5% commission on successful sales. Handling and tax should be included by seller in item price; shipping is added automatically at checkout. Accepted payment methods: Visa, MasterCard, American Express, PayPal, checking account, Wirecard, voucher, cash on collection. Sales disputes: dedicated customer service team to resolve disputes and answer queries within 24 hours. Standard listings: 4 photos & 5,000 characters. Other listing features: detailed product description, size/dimensions/weight, materials utilized, production method, customization options, keywords. Site statistics: 250,000 designers, 4 million products, 3.8 million members, over 200 million page impressions a month, 18 million page visits per month, strong social media presence. Provided to sellers: community forums/chats, additional free marketing opportunities, groups.

TIPS "As an international community, we would recommend sellers translate their listings into a selection of our 7 languages available. In addition, we would recommend uploading high-quality photos with your product on a light, neutral background-Dawanda is a very visual community. Don't forget to tell the story behind your products too! Dawanda is the online marketplace for unique and handmade products and gives creatives and designers the opportunity to offer their one-of-a-kind and limited-edition products for sale. Dawanda centers around the idea of 'social commerce,' allowing customers to interact with designers, comment on favorite products, and pass on recommendations. Our lively and passionate community allows buyers and sellers to interact and personalize the shopping experience-going against the grain of mass-produced products. Dawanda is an international community available in 7 languages and offers a space for designers and creatives to develop their business, talents, and success, in turn allowing them to make a living from doing what they love."

ELECTRONIC COTTAGE

Website: www.electroniccottage.com. Estab. 2010. "This arts portal is first and foremost a direct connection between those individuals who enjoy purchasing originally created handmade art & craftwork, and those professionals who enjoy creating that work. The extent of this connection is only made possible through the use of computers and the World Wide Web, exactly as Joseph Deken predicted decades ago. At EC Gallery, there is no need to join a club, become a member, make up a username, remember a password, leave us your e-mail, or jump through any other hoops. All we ask is that you sit back and enjoy your visits to the studio websites of the immensely talented people from around the world who exhibit via this online gallery. At EC Gallery you can connect directly to make purchases from the distinct websites of over 2,000 contemporary and traditional artists & craftspeople. Each cyberstudio is a truly unique experience, so explore and have fun ... you will find much amazing work throughout our community of talented professionals."

ETSY

Website: www.etsy.com. Geared towards handmade items. Shopping cart checkout feature. Products sold: handmade items, vintage, craft supplies. Setup costs: 20¢ to list an item; 3.5% fee on sale price. Listing features: user profiles, photos, shop banner.

FARMMADE

3300 NW 185th #129, Portland OR 97229. Contact: Rex Long, CEO. Estab. 2010. Geared towards handmade items and other merchandise. Provides shopping cart feature. Products sold: handmade items, vintage, supplies, patterns/books. Setup costs: none; also has free trial period. Ongoing fees: after trial period, monthly subscription fee of $5. Per listing fee: none; allow unlimited listings per seller. Transaction fee: 5% per sale. Shipping/handling & tax: added automatically. Accepted payment methods: Visa, MasterCard, American Express, PayPal. Sales disputes: sellers are required to set up their own shop policies for returns, etc. In the event there is a dispute, the seller is responsible for resolving it with the understanding that all transactions are subject to be reviewed by their customers. Standard listings: photos & words. Other listing features: each seller has the ability to tell their personal farm story and to connect their shop to supported social media platforms including personal blogs. Site statistics: startup company with a newsletter, blog and social media presence with followers reaching into the thousands. Provided to sellers: additional free marketing opportunities.

TIPS "A seller's farm story is essential to selling their product. A buyer will connect with a farmer if they can visualize who that farmer is, where they live, and how they created their product. This connection is the key to creating a customer for life. A farmers reputation for being hardworking, fair, and honest are well-known traits. We qualify our sellers to be involved in agriculture and/or livestock on some scale; whether that is in their backyard or 100 acres of rural farmland, our handmade artists strongly identify with a farmer's way of life. Being self-sufficient and using sustainable practices creates this web of interconnectedness that you can't replicate anywhere else. This is reflected in the quality of their products."

☉ FOLKSY

Harland Works, 72 John Street, Sheffield S2 4QU, United Kingdom. Website: www.folksy.com. Geared towards handmade items. Setup costs: see website. Folksy currently only supports sellers who are living and working in the UK.

GLC CRAFT MALL

(604)946-8041. E-mail: info@glcmall.com. Website: www.glccraftmall.com. Geared towards handmade items. Setup costs: see website. Provides shopping cart checkout feature. Shipping & handling handled by individual shops. Payments accepted: credit cards, PayPal.

GOODSMITHS

218½ Fifth St., West Des Moines IA 50265. Website: www.goodsmiths.com. Geared towards handmade items. Setup costs: see website. Provides shopping cart checkout feature. Payments accepted: MasterCard, Visa, PayPal.

HANDMADE ARTISTS' SHOP

Website: www.handmadeartists.com. Geared towards handmade items. Setup costs: must have a subscription to the Handmade Artists' Shop ($5/month; $50/year). Provides shopping cart checkout feature. Payments accepted: MasterCard, Visa, Discover, American Express, PayPal. Provided to sellers: items added to Google Product Search and The Find, search engine optimization (SEO), internal PM system, coupons, forums, community.

HANDMADE CATALOG

(800)851-0183. E-mail: pam@handmadecatalog.com. Website: www.handmadecatalog.com. Estab. 2002. Geared towards handmade items. Setup costs: see website. Provides shopping cart checkout feature. Provided to sellers: website maintenance, marketing, feature in weekly e-mail newsletter, no contracts & cancel anytime.

ICRAFT

Website: www.icraftgifts.com. Geared towards handmade items. Setup costs: $25 + monthly subscription fee. Provides shopping cart checkout feature. Provided to sellers: search engine optimization (SEO), Facebook & Twitter integration, free Seller's Bootcamp, free blogging software, iCraft community.

I MADE IT! MARKETPLACE

P.O. Box 9613, Pittsburgh PA 15226. (412)254-4464. Website: www.imadeitmarket.com. Contact: Carrie Nardini, director. Estab. 2007. Geared towards handmade items. Products sold: handmade items. Setup costs: currently none for online sales. Ongoing fees: see website. Provided to sellers: community forums/chats, additional paid marketing opportunities, additional free marketing opportunities, seminars, social events, workshops.

TIPS "We have built a reputation for fun, unique, high-quality handmade wares including a wide variety of work that is ideal for anyone on a shopper's list."

MADE IT MYSELF

P.O. Box 888, Fresno CA 93714. E-mail: support@madeitmyself.com. Website: www.madeitmyself.com. Geared towards handmade items. Setup costs: none; 3% fee for every item sold.

MAIN STREET REVOLUTION

Website: www.overstock.com/Main-Street-Revolution/39/store.html. "Main Street Revolution is Overstock.com showing its commitment to small businesses across the United States. By giving local shopkeepers a broader audience, we're supporting the American Dream."

MELA ARTISANS

Website: www.melaartisans.com. "Mela Artisans is a luxury lifestyle brand that combines traditional handcrafting techniques with the freshness and functionality of contemporary design. Our distinctive and original collections fuse modern designs with enduring techniques passed down through generations in artisan communities."

MISI

27 Old Gloucester Street, London WC1N 3AX, England. E-mail: admin@misi.co.uk. Website: www.misi.co.uk. Estab. 2008. Geared towards handmade items. Setup costs: none; 3% fee for every item sold. Provided to sellers: crafter's blog, free domain, 12-month listing, forum.

NOT MASS PRODUCED

Orchard Cottage, Station Road, Longstanton, Cambridge, Cambridgeshire CB24 3DS, England. 01954 261066. E-mail: enquiries@notmassproduced.com. Website: www.notmassproduced.com. Estab. 2008. Geared towards handmade items. All artisans are vetted. "Designers are from the UK and no further than Europe."

REDBUBBLE

650 Castro St., Suite 120-275, Mountain View CA 94041. Website: www.redbubble.com. "Redbubble is a free marketplace that helps thousands of artists reach new audiences and sell their work more easily. RB gives you access to a wide range of high-quality products, just waiting for your designs to make them more amazing. We coordinate everything from printing and shipping through to ongoing customer service, giving you more time to focus on creating great art and design (and occasionally watching cat videos on the Internet)."

SHOP HANDMADE

11901 137th Ave. Ct. KPN, Gig Harbor WA 98329-6617. E-mail: Service@ShopHandmade.com. Website: www.shophandmade.com. Geared towards handmade items. Setup fee: none. Payments accepted: PayPal.

SILK FAIR

Website: www.silkfair.com. Geared towards handmade items and other merchandise. Setup fee: see website.

SPOONFLOWER

2810 Meridian Parkway, Suite 176, Durham NC 27713. (919)886-7885. Website: www.spoonflower.com. Geared towards handmade items. Products sold: fabric, wallpaper, decals, and gift wrap. Setup fee: see website. "At Spoonflower we make it possible for individuals to design, print, and sell their own fabric, wallpaper, decals, and gift wrap. It was founded in May 2008 by two Internet geeks who had crafty wives but who knew nothing about textiles. The company came about because Stephen's wife, Kim, persuaded him that being able to print her own fabric for curtains was a really cool idea. She wasn't alone. The Spoonflower community now numbers over a million individuals who use their own fabric to make curtains, quilts, clothes, bags, furniture, dolls, pillows, framed artwork, costumes, banners, and much, much more. The Spoonflower marketplace offers the largest collection of independent fabric designers in the world."

STORENVY

Website: www.storenvy.com. Geared towards hand-made items. Setup costs: none. Payments accepted: all major credit cards, PayPal. Provided to sellers: customizable options, Facebook integration, visitor stats, mobile & tablet-friendly sites, custom domain option, inventory, & order tracking.

SUPERMARKET

E-mail: thisisawesome@supermarkethq.com. Website: www.supermarkethq.com. Geared towards hand-made items. "Supermarket is a curated collection of awesome designed products."

TOPHATTER

292 Lambert Ave., Palo Alto CA 94306. Website: www.tophatter.com. "Tophatter is a virtual auction house. It also happens to be the world's most entertaining live marketplace. Tophatter conducts live online auctions every day where buyers and sellers can interact, chat, and transact in a wide variety of categories. Tophatter is based in Palo Alto, CA, and backed by leading venture capital firms."

ZIBBET

Website: www.zibbet.com. Geared towards handmade items. Products sold: handmade goods, fine art, vintage, craft supplies. Setup costs: see website. Provided to sellers: search engine optimization (SEO), Etsy importer, business cards, and more.

BOOK PUBLISHERS

///

Seeing your name on the cover of a book is both a dream and a goal for many professional crafters. This section of listings is dedicated to book publishers that publish craft books of some kind. Keep in mind that a large publisher may have many different imprints, or trade names, under which books for a more specific demographic are published. For example, F+W Media, Inc., publishes mixed-media craft books under the North Light imprint and quilting books under the Fons & Porter imprint. Where appropriate, we have included different imprints in order to specify the type of craft that imprint publishes.

Before sending off queries to book publishers, make sure you have a strong idea with industry research to back it up. Just like you, publishers are trying to generate a profit, so make sure your idea is well thought out and is unique but relevant. Most successful book proposals will be accompanied by photos of potential projects. However, until they are specifically requested by an editor, never send physical materials to a publisher; it is possible you will never see those samples again. Instead, take some simple but beautiful photos of your samples for inclusion in your proposal.

Each publisher is different in the way they accept submissions and draft proposals, so read the instructions for each publisher's information to understand their process. Also, do further research on any company in which you are interested in submitting a proposal. Visit the company's website, look at books they have published and where those books are sold. Do you respect the authors they have worked with previously? Do you like the content they produce? What is the reputation of the company or of their books? Do you like the photography and design? Although each book is different, keep in mind that similarities amongst a publisher's entire line of books will likely impact yours as well. Read Diane Gilleland's article, "Crafting a Book," for insights into the why's and why not's of book writing.

Before signing a contract, identify your goals for writing a book and make sure that your contract is meeting those expectations. Where will your book be sold? What kind of marketing and promotional assistance will the publisher give you? Will you receive an advance and royalty on book sales, or will you receive one flat fee for the book, regardless of sales? Is it important for you to have a say in the photography or not? Don't sign a contract before making sure that your goals are in line with your publisher and specified in the contract.

Writing a book is a lot of hard work, but sharing your craft with the world through a published book will provide you with a strong foothold in the professional craft world. Good luck with your book proposal!

4TH LEVEL INDIE

E-mail: 4thlevelindie@gmail.com. Website: www.4thlevelindie.com. Estab. 2012. Types of books published: alternative craft & hobby. A small book publishing company based in San Francisco, CA. Currently publishes 1-2 titles/year.

ADAMS MEDIA

Division of F+W Media, Inc., 57 Littlefield St., Avon MA 02322. (508)427-7100. Fax: (800)872-5628. E-mail: adamsmediasubmissions@fwmedia.com. Website: www.adamsmedia.com. Contact: Acquisitions editor. Estab. 1980. Publishes hardcover originals, trade paperback, e-book originals, and reprints. Adams Media publishes commercial nonfiction, including self-help, women's issues, pop psychology, relationships, business, careers, pets, parenting, New Age, gift books, cookbooks, how-to, reference, and humor. Does not return unsolicited materials. Publishes more than 250 titles/year.

RECENT TITLE(S) *Oh Boy, You're Having a Girl*, by Brian A. Klems; *Graphic the Valley*, by Peter Hoffmeister.

AMERICAN QUILTER'S SOCIETY

5801 Kentucky Dam Rd., Paducah KY 42003. (270)898-7903. Fax: (270)898-1173. E-mail: editor@aqsquilt.com. Website: www.americanquilter.com. Contact: Elaine Brelsford, executive book editor (primarily how-to and patterns, but other quilting books sometimes published, including quilt-related fiction). Estab. 1984. Publishes trade paperbacks. "American Quilter's Society publishes how-to and pattern books for quilters (beginners through intermediate skill level). We are not the publisher for non-quilters writing about quilts. We now publish quilt-related craft cozy romance and mystery titles, series only. Humor is good. Graphic depictions and curse words are bad." Publishes 20-24 titles/year.

RECENT TITLE(S) *Liberated Quiltmaking II*, by Gwen Marston; *T-Shirt Quilts Made Easy*, by Martha Deleonardis; *Decorate Your Shoes*, by Annemart Berendse.

ANDREWS MCMEEL PUBLISHING

100 Front Street, Riverside NJ 08075. (816)581-8921 or (800) 851-8923. Fax: (816)932-6781 or (816) 581-7486.

E-mail: tlynch@amuniversal.com; marketing@amuniversal.com. Website: www.andrewsmcmeel.com. Contact: Tim Lynch, executive art director. Estab. 1972.

TIPS "We want designers who can read a manuscript and design a concept for the best possible cover. Communicate well and be flexible with design." Designer portfolio review once a year in New York City.

ANNESS PUBLISHING LTD./SOUTHWATER

Anness Publishing Ltd - Book Trade Services, 108 Great Russell Street, London WC1B 3NA, United Kingdom. 0116 275 9060. Fax: 0116 275 9090. E-mail: info@anness.com. Website: www.annesspublishing. com. Estab. 1999.

ANNIE'S PUBLISHING

Website: www.annies-publishing.com. Estab. 1985. "Annie's is the media division of DRG. Its products—including magazines, books, kits and supplies, online classes, and TV programming—are targeted to home and family interests, including crafts, nostalgia, and home décor."

AXIS PUBLISHING

Huntsville AL. Website: www.axis-publishing.webs. com. Estab. 2008. "Our mission is to empower authors across the globe, through cutting-edge and innovative writings, recordings, techniques, and technologies."

BLACK DOG & LEVENTHAL PUBLISHERS

1290 Avenue of the Americas, New York NY 10104. (212)364-1100. E-mail: info@blackdogandleventhal. com. Website: www.blackdogandleventhal.com. "Black Dog & Leventhal books represent hours of reading and visual pleasure for book lovers of all types. We publish strikingly original books of light reference, humor, cooking, sports, music, film and entertainment, mysteries, history and biography, and much, much more. Many of them are in unusual formats and many are rich with color and imagery. Some are just for curling up with, some sharpen your mind, some teach valuable skills, while others are just pure pleasure."

C&T PUBLISHING

1651 Challenge Dr., Concord CA 94520. (925)677-0377. Fax: (925)677-0373. E-mail: ctinfo@ctpub.com. Website: www.ctpub.com. Contact: Roxane Cerda, acquisitions manager. Estab. 1983. Types of books published: sewing, quilting, mixed-media art. Publishes trade paperback originals, CD ROMs, DVDs, art materials, totes, journals, umbrellas, notecards. Specialty: quilting books. Titles can be found at JoAnn Fabric, Michaels and Hobby Lobby. Publishes 50+ titles/year. Available online.

HOW TO CONTACT Accepts unsolicited proposals and manuscripts; guidelines available on website at www.ctpub.com/client_pages/submissions.cfm. Keeps information on file. Samples not filed are returned. Considers simultaneous submissions.

NEEDS Buys all rights. Finds authors through submissions. Works with never-before-published authors frequently. Looks for original concept, popular concept, on-trend concept, large following on social media, existing fan base. Average book has 60-144 pages. Average craft/DIY book contains 6-20+ projects/patterns. Provides print-ready illustrations in-house. Provides photography.

TERMS Books undergo technical edit prior to publication. Payment based on royalty/advance and royalty only.

RECENT TITLE(S) *Me and My Sewing Adventure*; *All-in-One Quilter's Reference Tool*, 2nd Ed.; *The Modern Applique Workbook*; *Foolproof Crazy Quilting*.

TIPS "Provide a lot of visuals with your proposal. Try to really show me what you envision for your book and what makes your work special. Sell your author bio and your audience. I want to know how you reach your audience and how strong the number of followers you enjoy. Tell me what makes you the right person to write the book you are proposing. The biggest gimmie an author can offer is to be able to summarize in one sentence what makes their book stand out from the crowd. If a book's topic and uniqueness cannot be explained in a sentence (long sentences are okay), the resulting book will be hard to sell."

CHRONICLE BOOKS

680 Second St., San Francisco CA 94107. E-mail: submissions@chroniclebooks.com. Website: www.chroniclebooks.com "We publish an exciting range of books, stationery, kits, calendars, and novelty formats. Our list includes children's books and interactive formats; young adult books; cookbooks; fine art, design, and photography; pop culture; craft, fashion, beauty, and home decor; relationships, mind-body-spirit; innovative formats such as interactive journals, kits, decks, and stationery; and much, much more."Publishes 90 titles/year. Book catalog for 9×12 SAE and 8 first-class stamps.

HOW TO CONTACT Submit via mail only. Children's submissions only. Submit proposal (guidelines online) and allow up to 3 months for editors to review. Do not include SASE since our staff will not return materials.

TERMS Generally pays authors in royalties based on retail price, "though we do occasionally work on a flat fee basis." Advance varies. Illustrators paid royalty based on retail price or flat fee.

DAVID & CHARLES

Website: www.fwcommunity.com/uk. Publishes craft books.

DK PUBLISHING

Penguin Random House, 80 Strand, London WC2R 0RL, United Kingdom. Website: www.dk.com. "DK publishes photographically illustrated nonfiction for children of all ages." *DK Publishing does not accept unagented mss or proposals.*

DORLING KINDERSLEY (DK PUBLISHING)

345 Hudson St., 4th Floor, New York NY 10014. E-mail: ecustomerservice@randomhouse.com.. Website: www.dk.com/us. "DK produces content for consumers in over 87 countries and 62 languages, with offices in Delhi, London, Melbourne, Munich, New York, and Toronto. DK's aim is to inform, enrich, and entertain readers of all ages and everything DK publishes, whether print or digital, embodies the unique DK design approach. DK brings unrivaled clarity to a wide range of topics with a unique combination of words and pictures, put together to spectacular effect. We have a reputation for innovation in design for both print and digital products."

DOVER PUBLICATIONS, INC.

31 E. Second St., Mineola NY 11501. (516)294-7000. Fax: (516)873-1401. E-mail: hr@doverpublications. com. Website: www.doverpublications.com. Estab. 1941. Publishes trade paperback originals and reprints. Publishes 660 titles/year. Book catalog online. **HOW TO CONTACT** Query with SASE.

TERMS Makes outright purchase.

✪ FIREFLY BOOKS

50 Staples Ave., Unit 1, Richmond Hill, Ontario L4B 0A7 Canada. (416)499-8412. E-mail: service@firefly-books.com. E-mail: valerie@fireflybooks.com. Website: www.fireflybooks.com. Estab. 1974. Publishes high-quality nonfiction.

HOW TO CONTACT Prefers images in digital format, but will accept 35mm transparencies.

NEEDS "We're looking for book-length ideas, *not* stock. We pay a royalty on books sold, plus advance."

TERMS Send query letter with résumé of credits. Does not keep samples on file; include SAE/IRC for return of material. Simultaneous submissions OK. Payment negotiated with contract. Credit line given.

WALTER FOSTER PUBLISHING, INC.

3 Wrigley, Suite A, Irvine CA 92618. (800)426-0099. Fax: (949)380-7575. E-mail: info@walterfoster.com. Website: www.walterfoster.com. Contact: Submissions. Estab. 1922. Publishes trade paperback originals. "Walter Foster publishes instructional how-to/craft instruction as well as licensed products."

FOX CHAPEL PUBLISHING

1970 Broad St., East Petersburg PA 17520. (800)457-9112. Fax: (717)560-4702. E-mail: acquisitions@fox-chapelpublishing.com. Website: www.foxchapelpub-lishing.com. Contact: Peg Couch, acquisitions editor. Publishes hardcover and trade paperback originals and trade paperback reprints. Fox Chapel publishes craft, lifestyle, and woodworking titles for professionals and hobbyists.Publishes 50-90 titles/year.

RECENT TITLE(S) *Totally Awesome Rubber Band Jewelry; Beauty of Zentangle; Zenspirations.*

TIPS "We're looking for knowledgeable artists, craftspeople, and woodworkers, all experts in their fields, to write books of lasting value."

GUILD OF MASTER CRAFTSMAN PUBLICATIONS

166 High Street, Lewes East Sussex BN7 1XU, United Kingdom. 44 01273 477374. E-mail: helen.chrystie@thegmcgroup.com. Website: www.thegmcgroup.com. Types of books published: photography, woodworking, DIY, gardening, cookery, art, puzzles, all manner of craft subjects from knitting and sewing to jewelery making, doll houses, upholstery, paper crafts, and more. "Publishes and distributes over 3,000 books and magazines which are both valued by professional craftsmen/women and enjoyed by keen amateurs." Available online.

INTERWEAVE PRESS

201 E. Fourth St., Loveland CO 80537. (970)669-7672. Fax: (970)667-8317. E-mail: kbogert@interweave.com. Website: www.interweave.com. Contact: Kerry Bogert, acquisitions editor. Estab. 1975. Publishes hardcover and trade paperback originals. Interweave Press publishes instructive titles relating to the fiber arts and beadwork topics. Publishes 40-45 titles/year. Book catalog and guidelines online.

HOW TO CONTACT Submit outline, sample chapters. Accepts simultaneous submissions if informed of non-exclusivity.

NEEDS Subjects limited to fiber arts (spinning, knitting, dyeing, weaving, sewing/stiching, art quilting, mixed media/collage) and jewelry making (beadwork, stringing, wireworking, metalsmithing).

RECENT TITLE(S) *Beastly Crochet*, by Brenda K.B. Anderson; *Jewelry Maker's Field Guide*, by Helen Driggs.

TIPS "We are looking for very clear, informally written, technically correct manuscripts, generally of a how-to nature, in our specific fiber and beadwork fields only. Our audience includes a variety of creative self-starters who appreciate inspiration and clear instruction. They are often well educated and skillful in many areas."

KALMBACH PUBLISHING CO.

21027 Crossroads Circle, P.O. Box 1612, Waukesha WI 53187. (262)796-8776. Fax: (262)798-6468. Website: www.kalmbach.com. Estab. 1934. Publishes paperback originals and reprints. Publishes 40-50 titles/year.

NEEDS 10-20% require freelance illustration; 10-20% require freelance design. Book catalog free upon request. Approached by 25 freelancers/year. Prefers freelancers with experience in the hobby field. Uses freelance artists mainly for book layout/design and line art illustrations. Freelancers should have the most recent versions of Adobe InDesign, Photoshop, and Illustrator. Projects by assignment only.

TERMS Send query letter with résumé, tearsheets, and photocopies. No phone calls please. Samples are filed and will not be returned. Art director will contact artist for portfolio review. Finds artists through word of mouth, submissions. Assigns 10-12 freelance design jobs/year. Pays by the project. Assigns 3-5 freelance illustration jobs/year. Pays by the project.

TIPS "Our how-to books are highly visual in their presentation. Any author who wants to publish with us must be able to furnish good photographs and rough drawings before we'll consider his or her book."

KANSAS CITY STAR QUILTS

The Kansas City Star, 1729 Grand Blvd., Kansas City MO 64108. E-mail: info@kansascitystarquilts.com. Website: www.kansascitystarquilts.com. Types of books published: quilt books.

KNOPF

Imprint of Random House, 1745 Broadway, New York NY 10019. Fax: (212)940-7390. Website: knopfdoubleday.com/imprint/knopf. Contact: The editors. Estab. 1915. Publishes hardcover and paperback originals. Publishes 200 titles/year.

KRAUSE PUBLICATIONS

A Division of F+W Media, Inc., 700 E. State St., Iola WI 54990. (715)445-2214. Fax: (715)445-4087. Website: www.krausebooks.com. Contact: Paul Kennedy (antiques and collectibles, music, sports, militaria, humor, numismatics); Corrina Peterson (firearms); Chris Berens (outdoors); Brian Earnest (automotive). Publishes hardcover and trade paperback originals. "We are the world's largest hobby and collectibles publisher." Publishes 80 titles/year. Book catalog for free or on website.

HOW TO CONTACT Submit proposal package, including outline, TOC, a sample chapter, and letter explaining your project's unique contributions. Reviews

artwork/photos. Accepts only digital photography. Send sample photos.

RECENT TITLE(S) *Antique Trader Antiques & Collectibles 2015*; *The Ultimate Guide to Vintage Star Wars Action Figues*, by Mark Bellomo; *Standard Catalog of Firearms*, by Jerry Lee; *Collecting Rocks, Gems & Minerals*, by Patti Polk.

TIPS Audience consists of serious hobbyists. "Your work should provide a unique contribution to the special interest."

LANDAUER PUBLISHING

3100 101st St., Suite A, Urbandale IA 50322. (800)557-2144 or (515)287-2144. Fax: (515)276-5102. E-mail: info@landauercorp.com. E-mail: jeramy@landauercorp.com; books@landauercorp.com. Website: www.landauerpub.com. Contact: Jeramy Landauer. Estab. 1991.

HOW TO CONTACT In preparing a book proposal for review/discussion, please include the following: 1. Author Profile and The Book Concept: a brief paragraph about the author followed by the concept, namely, the vision for the book, the intended audience and why the book is needed/different from what is currently available. Please include tentative specs for the book: projects (how many/range), special features (e. g., an essay promoting/romancing the history/concept/author, unique teaching section, video, location photography, special needs such as full-size patterns). Also, please include author website. 2. A Table of Contents: the TOC gives the preliminary project list and shows project variety/balance. 3. Sample projects showing the quality of your work (at least 1 or 2 completed projects must accompany the proposal along with photo samples or print-outs of your work.) 4. A sample of how-to instructions, diagrams, and illustrations (can be rough or finished). 5. Author expectations from the publisher re: guarantees, royalty rates, etc. 6. Timing.

NEEDS "Landauer strives to publish books that are more than project books. We require quality. We look for clear concepts. Books often include a technique section or other features enabling us to enhance the book and expand the audience. Most importantly, we prefer to publish works that will sell for many seasons and lend themselves to add-on product and new editions."

TERMS Authors are expected to take an active role in promoting their books such as attending and introducing their book at Quilt Market, engaging in teaching, maintaining a website/blog, creating a promotional project pattern for social media and/or magazines.

LARK CRAFTS

166 Avenue of the Americas, 17th Floor, New York NY 10036. (212)532-7160. E-mail: info@larkbooks. com. E-mail: jewelryteam@larkcrafts.com; needleartsteam@larkcrafts.com; craftyourlifeteam@larkcrafts. com. Website: www.larkcrafts.com. Estab. 1979.

HOW TO CONTACT Send query letter via e-mail or mail (with information, your skills and qualifications in the subject area of your submission), résumé, and images of your work or a link to your website. Include SASE if you would like materials returned to you. Submissions should be sent to the attention of the category editor, e.g., the material on a ceramics book should be addressed to the Ceramics Editor; a craft book proposal should be addressed to the Craft Acquisitions Editor; and so on.

TERMS "Please note that, due to the volume of mail received, we cannot guarantee the return of unsolicited material. Please do not send original art or irreplaceable work of any kind; while we will make every effort to return your submissions, we are not responsible for any loss or damage."

LAURENCE KING PUBLISHING LTD.

361–373 City Rd., London EC1V 1LR, United Kingdom. 44 (0)20 7841 6900. Fax: 44 (0)20 7841 6910. E-mail: commissioning@laurenceking.com. Website: www.laurenceking.com.

HOW TO CONTACT See website for details.

LEISURE ARTS

104 Champs Blvd., Suite 100, Maumelle AR 72113. E-mail: submissions@leisurearts.com. Website: www. leisurearts.com. Estab. 1971. Leisure Arts is a leading publisher of lifestyle and instructional craft publications. In addition to printed publications, the Leisure Arts product line also includes e-books, digital downloads, and DVDs.

HOW TO CONTACT Submit an e-mail letter with a PDF file or JPEG attachments to: submissions@leisurearts.com. Please do not send the actual designs or instructions unless asked to do so.

MACMILLAN

175 Fifth Avenue, New York NY 10010. (646)307-5151. Website: www.us.macmillan.com. Publishes hardcover, trade paperback, and paperback books.

MARTINGALE PUBLISHING

19021 120th Ave. NE, Suite 102, Bothell WA 98011. (800)426-3126 or (425)483-3313. Fax: (425)486-7596. E-mail: creitan@martingale-pub.com. Website: www. shopmartingale.com. Contact: Cathy Reitan, editorial author liaison. Estab. 1976. Types of books published: quilting, sewing, knitting, and crochet. Publishes books and e-books.

HOW TO CONTACT Please e-mail your submission to Cathy Reitan, Editorial Author Liaison, at creitan@ martingale-pub.com.

TERMS "Manuscript proposals are reviewed on a monthly basis. Editorial, marketing, and production personnel are involved in the review. The final decision will be based on your proposal, your work sample, your completed Author Questionnaire, and our feasibility analysis. The feasibility analysis investigates such basics as our cost of producing the book and our ability to market your work successfully and competitively. Part of this process may also include a customer survey to test the concept. If your proposal is approved for publication, you will receive a call from one of the editors regarding a publishing contract. We pay quarterly royalty based on net sales of your book, as spelled out in the publishing contract that you will be asked to sign. As a service to you, Martingale applies for the copyright on your book in your name. After you have signed your contract, you will receive detailed guidelines for preparing your manuscript. You are responsible for sending the completed manuscript and projects for photography to us at your own expense by the due date specified in the contract. From then on, Martingale pays all expenses for book production, shipping, and handling. These expenses include editing, design, layout, illustration, and photography."

MEREDITH BOOKS

1716 Locust St., Des Moines IA 50309-3023. (515)284-3000. Website: www.meredith.com. Types of books published: food, home, family. "Meredith Books feature more than 300 titles focusing on food, home, and family."

NEW HOLLAND PUBLISHERS

The Chandlery, Unit 009, 50 Westminster Bridge Rd., London SE1 7QY, United Kingdom. 44(0) 207 953 75 65. Fax: 44(0) 207 953 76 05. E-mail: enquiries@nhpub.co.uk. Website: www.newhollandpublishers.com. "New Holland is a publishing house dedicated to the highest editorial and design standards."

NORTH LIGHT BOOKS

F+W Media, a Content + eCommerce Company, 10151 Carver Rd., Suite 200, Blue Ash OH 45242. Fax: (513)891-7153. E-mail: mona.clough@fwcommunity.com. Website: www.fwcommunity.com; www.artistsnetwork.com; www.createmixedmedia.com. Contact: Mona Clough, content director art and mixed media. Publishes hardcover and trade paperback how-to books. "North Light Books publishes art books, including watercolor, drawing, mixed media, acrylic that emphasize illustrated how-to art instruction. Currently emphasizing drawing including traditional, zen, doodle, and creativity and inspiration." Publishes 50 titles/year. Visit www.northlightshop.com. Does not return submissions.

HOW TO CONTACT Send query letter with photographs, digital images. Accepts e-mail submissions. Samples are not filed and are returned. Responds only if interested. Company will contact artist for portfolio review if interested.

NEEDS Buys all rights. Finds freelancers through art competitions, art exhibits, submissions, Internet, and word of mouth.

NORTHRIDGE PUBLISHING

Website: www.northridgepublishing.com. "At Northridge Publishing we share the passion of creating with our readers as we provide inspiration, support, and resources to crafters everywhere. Reader layouts, cards, and projects are featured throughout our publications as we provide a forum for readers to share the latest and best ideas."

PAGE STREET PUBLISHING

27 Congress St., Suite 103, Salem MA 01970. (978)594-8295. E-mail: info@pagestreetpublishing.com. Website: www.pagestreetpublishing.com. Publishes paperback originals. Publishes 20+ titles/year.

PENGUIN/PERIGEE TRADE

Website: www.penguin.com/meet/publishers/perigee.

HOW TO CONTACT "Due to the high volume of manuscripts received, most Penguin Group (USA) imprints do not normally accept unsolicited manuscripts. Neither the corporation nor its imprints assume responsibility for any unsolicited manuscripts which we may receive. As such, it is recommended that sole original copies of any manuscript not be submitted, as the corporation is not responsible for the return of any manuscript (whether sent electronically or by mail), nor do we guarantee a response. Further, in receiving a submission, we do not assume any duty not to publish a book based on a similar idea, concept, or story."

POTTER CRAFT/RANDOM HOUSE

1745 Broadway, New York NY 10019. Website: www.crownpublishing.com/imprint/potter-craft. Estab. 2006. Types of books published: knitting, crochet, sewing, papercrafts, jewelry making

HOW TO CONTACT Random House LLC does not accept unsolicited submissions, proposals, manuscripts, or submission queries via e-mail at this time.

PRACTICAL PUBLISHING INTERNATIONAL

0844 561 1202. E-mail: customerservice@practical-publishing.co.uk. Website: www.practicalpublishing.co.uk. "Practical holds market-leading positions within several craft sectors internationally. It has comprehensive global distribution of its key brands and distributes over 3 million magazines and books a year. It is also the UK's only specialist publisher to produce and directly distribute titles specifically for the independent craft retail channel."

QUARTO PUBLISHING GROUP USA

400 First Ave., N., Suite 400, Minneapolis MN 55401. E-mail: e-info@quartous.com. Website: www.quartoknows.com. Types of books published: general craft, art, design, sewing, crochet, knitting, quilting, papercraft, scrapbooking, mixed-media art. Publishes hardcover originals, trade paperback originals, trade paperback reprints. Titles can be found at Amazon, Barnes & Noble, craft chains, independents and internationally. Publishes 100 titles/year. Catalog available online or free on request.

HOW TO CONTACT Accepts unsolicited proposals and manuscripts; guidelines available on website. Does not keep information on file. If not filed, returned by SASE. Responds only if interested. Considers simultaneous submissions and previously published work.

NEEDS Rights purchased vary according to project. Will negotiate with those unwilling to sell rights. Finds authors through agents/reps, submissions, word of mouth, magazines, Internet. Works with never-before-published authors frequently. Looks for original concept, popular concept, on-trend concept, large following on social media, existing fan base. Average book has 128-160 pages. Average craft/DIY book contains 20-52 projects/patterns. Author provides print-ready illustrations when possible.

TERMS Some books undergo technical edits. Typical time frame from contract to manuscript due date is 4-6 months. Payment based on project. First-time authors typically paid $5,000-6,000.

RECENT TITLE(S) *One Zentangle a Day* by Beckah Krahula; *3D Art Lab for Kids* by Susan Schwake; *20 Ways to Draw a Cat* by Julia Kuo.

TIPS "Do your research. Be familiar with the other competitive books on your topic. Think about how your book is better and different."

QUIRK BOOKS

215 Church Street, Philadelphia PA 19106. (215)627-3581. Fax: (215)627-5220. E-mail: tiffany@quirkbooks.com. Website: www.quirkbooks.com. Contact: Tiffany Hill. Estab. 2002. Types of books published: unconventional, cookbooks, craft books, children's books, and nonfiction. Publishes books and e-books. Publishes 25 titles/year. Catalog available online.

HOW TO CONTACT "E-mail a query letter to one of our editors. The query letter should be a short description of your project. Try to limit your letter to a single page. If you have sample chapters, go ahead and include them. You can also mail materials directly to our office. If you would like a reply, please include a self-addressed stamped envelope. If you want your materials returned, please include adequate postage."

RODALE BOOKS

400 S. Tenth St., Emmaus PA 18098. (610)967-5171. Fax: (610)967-8961. Website: www.rodaleinc.com. Estab. 1932. "Rodale Books publishes adult trade titles in categories such health & fitness, cooking, spirituality, and pet care."

RUNNING PRESS BOOK PUBLISHERS

2300 Chestnut St., Suite 200, Philadelphia PA 19103. (215)567-5080. Fax: (215)568-2919. E-mail: frances.soopingchow@perseusbooks.com; perseus.promos@perseusbooks.com. Website: www.runningpress.com. Contact: Frances Soo Ping Chow, design director. Estab. 1972. Publishes hardcover originals, trade paperback originals. Subjects include adult and children's fiction and nonfiction; cooking; crafts, lifestyle, kits; miniature editions used for text illustrations, promotional materials, book covers, dust jackets.

HOW TO CONTACT Prefers images in digital format. Send via CD/DVD, via FTP/e-mail as TIFF, EPS files at 300 dpi.

NEEDS Buys a few hundred freelance photos/year and lots of stock images. Photos for gift books; photos of wine, food, lifestyle, hobbies, and sports. Model/property release preferred. Photo captions preferred; include exact locations, names of pertinent items or buildings, names and dates for antiques or special items of interest.

TERMS Send URL and provide contact info. Do not send original art or anything that needs to be returned. Responds only if interested. Simultaneous submissions and previously published work OK. Pays $500-1000 for color cover; $100-250 for inside. Pays 45 days after receipt of invoice. Credits listed on separate copyright or credit pages. Buys one-time rights.

RECENT TITLE(S) Examples of recently published titles: *Skinny Bitch, Eat What You Love, The Ultimate Book of Gangster Movies, Fenway Park, The Speedy Sneaky Chef, Les Petits Macarons, New York Fash-*

ion Week, I Love Lucy: A Celebration of All Things Lucy, Upcycling.

TIPS Submission guidelines available online.

RYLAND PETERS & SMALL

341 E. 116th St, New York NY 10029. (646)613-8682 or (646)613-8684 or (646)613-8685. Fax: (646)613-8683. E-mail: enquiries@rps.co.uk. Website: www.rylandpeters.com.

HOW TO CONTACT See website for details.

SEARCH PRESS USA

1338 Ross Street, Petaluma CA 94954-1117. (800)289-9276 or (707)762-3362. Fax: (707)762-0335. E-mail: info@searchpressusa.com. Website: www.searchpressusa.com. Types of books published: art, craft. "We have 30+ years experience in publishing art and craft instruction books exclusively."

SIMON & SCHUSTER

1230 Avenue of the Americas, New York NY 10020. (212)698-7000. Website: www.simonandschuster.com. *Accepts agented submissions only.*

HOW TO CONTACT Send query letter with tearsheets. Accepts disk submissions. Samples are filed and are not returned. Responds only if interested. Portfolios may be dropped off every Monday and Wednesday and should include tearsheets.

NEEDS Works with 50 freelance illustrators and 5 designers/year. Prefers freelancers with experience working with models and taking direction well. Uses freelancers for hand lettering, jacket/cover illustration and design, and book design. 100% of design and 75% of illustration demand knowledge of Illustrator and Photoshop. Works on assignment only.

TERMS Buys all rights. Originals are returned at job's completion.

SKYHORSE PUBLISHING

307 W. 36th St., 11th Floor, New York NY 10018. (212)643-6816. Fax: (212)643-6819. E-mail: klim@skyhorsepublishing.com. Website: www.skyhorsepublishing.com. Contact: Kim Lim, assistant to publisher. Estab. 2006. Types of books published: general craft, sewing, crochet, knitting, papercraft, wood-

working, interior decorating, household crafts, holiday crafts. Publishes hardcover originals, trade paperback originals, trade paperback reprints. Specialty: nonfiction. Titles can be found at Barnes & Noble, Amazon, Michaels. Publishes 10+ titles/year. Catalog available online.

HOW TO CONTACT Accepts unsolicited proposals and manuscripts; guidelines available on website. Does not keep information on file. If not filed, returned by SASE when specifically requested. Responds only if interested. Considers simultaneous submissions and previously published work.

NEEDS Negotiates rights. Finds authors through submissions, word of mouth, internet. Frequently works with never-before-published authors. Looks for original concept, popluar concept, on-trend concept, large following on social media, existing fan base. Average book has 96-200 pages. Average craft/DIY book contains 45-100 projects/patterns. Author provides print-ready illustrations if book will be illustrated. Author provides photography.

TERMS Typical time frame from contract to manuscript due date is 6 months, but can vary. Payment based on royalty/advance. First-time authors typically paid $1,000-10,000.

RECENT TITLE(S) *Loom Magic*; *To Knit or Not to Knit*; *Rustic Garden Projects*; *Vintage Crafts*; *Warm Mittens and Socks*; *Fun with Yarn and Fabric*; *Swedish Christmas Crafts*.

TIPS "Please be sure to read submission guidelines and be courteous. Should you not receive a response from us, we often appreciate receiving one follow-up e-mail. We wish every craft author will submit full proposal, a summary, author bio, projected TOC, comp titles, sample projects, and sample photography."

STC CRAFT

Imprint of Abrams, 115 W. 18th St., New York NY 10011. E-mail: stccraft@abramsbooks.com. Website: www.abramsbooks.com. Contact: STC Craft Editorial. Publishes a vibrant collection of exciting and visually stunning craft books specializing in knitting, sewing, quilting, felting, and other popular craft genres.

STC CRAFT/MELANIE FALICK BOOKS

115 W. 18th St., New York NY 10011. (212)206-7715. Fax: (212)519-1210. E-mail: stccraft@abramsbooks.

com. Website: www.abramsbooks.com. Estab. 1949. Types of books published: art, photography, cooking, interior design, craft, fashion, sports, pop culture, as well as children's books and general interest. Publishes high-quality art and illustrated books. Titles can be found at Amazon.com, Barnes & Noble, Books-A-Million, IndieBound, Indigo.

HOW TO CONTACT Accepts unsolicited proposals and manuscripts for STC Craft. No submission will be returned without a SASE. Please submit via email to stccraft@abramsbooks.com or mail your submission along with a SASE.

STOREY PUBLISHING

210 MASS MoCA Way, North Adams MA 01247. (800)793-9396. Fax: (413)346-2196. E-mail: feedback@storey.com. Website: www.storey.com. Contact: Deborah Balmuth, editorial director (building and mind/body/spirit). Estab. 1983. Publishes hardcover and trade paperback originals and reprints. "The mission of Storey Publishing is to serve our customers by publishing practical information that encourages personal independence in harmony with the environment. We seek to do this in a positive atmosphere that promotes editorial quality, team spirit, and profitability. The books we select to carry out this mission include titles on gardening, small-scale farming, building, cooking, home brewing, crafts, part-time business, home improvement, woodworking, animals, nature, natural living, personal care, and country living. We are always pleased to review new proposals, which we try to process expeditiously. We offer both work-for-hire and standard royalty contracts." Publishes 40 titles/year. Book catalog available free.

HOW TO CONTACT Reviews artwork/photos.

TATE PUBLISHING

127 East Trade Center Terrace, Mustang OK 73064. (888)361-9473 or (405)376-4900. Fax: (405)376-4401. Website: www.tatepublishing.com. "Tate Publishing & Enterprises, LLC, is a Christian-based, family-owned, mainline publishing organization with a mission to discover unknown authors. We combine unknown authors' undiscovered potential with Tate Publishing's unique approach to publishing and provide them with the highest-quality books and the most inclusive benefits package available."

HOW TO CONTACT "If you have a manuscript you would like us to consider for publication and marketed on nationwide television, please fill out the form on our website. If you choose to submit by postal mail or electronically, those manuscripts will not be returned and will be deleted or destroyed if not accepted for publication. Please retain at least one copy of your manuscript when submitting a hard copy or electronic version for our consideration and review."

THAMES & HUDSON

500 Fifth Ave., New York NY 10110. (212)354-3763. Fax: (212)398-1252. E-mail: bookinfo@thames. wwnorton.com. Website: www.thamesandhudsonusa.com. Estab. 1949.

HOW TO CONTACT "To submit a proposal by e-mail, please paste the text of your query letter and/or proposal into the body of the e-mail message. Please keep your proposal under 6 pages, and do not send attachments. Please note that we cannot accept complete manuscripts via e-mail. We cannot open packages that are unsolicited or do not have a return address."

TRAFALGAR SQUARE BOOKS

388 Howe Hill Rd., P.O. Box 257, North Pomfret VT 05053. (802)457-1911. Website: www.horseandriderbooks.com. Contact: Martha Cook, managing director; Rebecca Didier, senior editor. Estab. 1985. Publishes hardcover and trade paperback originals. "We publish high-quality instructional books for horsemen and horsewomen, always with the horse's welfare in mind." Publishes 12 titles/year. Catalog free on request and by e-mail.

RECENT TITLE(S) *The Art of Liberty Training for Horses*, by Jonathan Field; *When Two Spines Align: Dressage Dynamics*, by Beth Baumert.

TIPS "Our audience is comprised of horse lovers and riders interested in pursuing their passion and/or sport while doing what is best for horses."

TUTTLE PUBLISHING

364 Innovation Dr., North Clarendon VT 05759. (802)773-8930. Fax: (802)773-6993. E-mail: submissions@tuttlepublishing.com. Website: www.tuttlepublishing.com. Estab. 1832. Publishes hardcover

and trade paperback originals and reprints. Tuttle is America's leading publisher of books on Japan and Asia. "Familiarize yourself with our catalog and/or similar books we publish. Send complete book proposal with cover letter, table of contents, 1-2 sample chapters, target audience description, SASE. No e-mail submissions." Publishes 125 titles/year.

HOW TO CONTACT Query with SASE.

NEEDS "Familiarize yourself with our catalog and/or similar books we publish. Send complete book proposal with cover letter, table of contents, 1-2 sample chapters, target audience description, SASE. No e-mail submissions."

TERMS Pays 5-10% royalty on net or retail price, depending on format and kind of book.

ULYSSES PRESS

Ulysses Press Main Office, P.O. Box 3440, Berkeley CA 94703. (510)601-8301. Fax: (510)601-8307. E-mail: ulysses@ulyssespress.com. Website: www.ulyssespress.com. Catalog available online.

HOW TO CONTACT "We review unsolicited manuscripts on an ongoing basis." See website for submission guidelines. Please do not send e-mail submissions, attachments, or disks. Do not send original artwork, photographs, or manuscripts of which you do not retain a copy.

NEEDS "When it comes to finding new books, we are especially interested in titles that fill demonstrated niches in the trade book market. We seek books that take a specific and unique focus, a focus that can differentiate a book and make it stand out in a crowd."

USBORNE PUBLISHING

83-85 Saffron Hill, London En EC1N 8RT, United Kingdom. (44)207430-2800. Fax: (44)207430-1562. E-mail: mail@usborne.co.uk. Website: www.usborne.com. "Usborne Publishing is a multiple-award-winning, worldwide children's publishing company publishing almost every type of children's book for every age from baby to young adult."

HOW TO CONTACT Works with 100 illustrators per year. Illustrations only: Query with samples. Samples not returned; samples filed.

TERMS Pays authors royalty.

TIPS "Do not send any original work and, sorry, but we cannot guarantee a reply."

WILEY PUBLISHING (WILEY CRAFT)

John Wiley & Sons, Inc., Global Education, 111 River St., Hoboken NJ 07030-5774. Website: www.wiley.com.

WORKMAN PUBLISHING CO.

225 Varick St., New York NY 10014. E-mail: submissions@workman.com. Website: www.workman.com. Estab. 1967. Publishes hardcover and trade paperback originals, as well as calendars. "We are a trade paperback house specializing in a wide range of popular nonfiction. We publish no adult fiction and very little children's fiction. We also publish a full range of full-color wall and Page-A-Day calendars." Publishes 40 titles/year.

HOW TO CONTACT Query with SASE first for guidelines.

TIPS "We prefer electronic submissions."

MAGAZINES

A big part of building your craft business and boosting sales is name recognition. In an ever-growing sea of crafty celebrities, getting your name out there is critical to establishing yourself in the market as a resource, an expert, and a professional. Building name recognition requires constant work, especially in the beginning. Consistent social media, blogging, and representation at popular shows are important to making sure you are recognized in the industry, and magazines are a great way to reach your target demographic all at once. The listings in this section are geared toward craft magazines across the subgenres.

Do your research. Peruse the listings in this book, visit your local bookstore, and search online to find the magazines that will be the best fit for your work, and that reach your target demographic. For example, all quilt magazines are not geared toward the same audience; some are specifically targeting art quilters, while others cater to traditional or modern quilters. Be sure that you spend your precious time only submitting to those magazines that are a likely fit for your work and that will help grow your audience.

Be sure to follow directions when submitting content to magazines. Editors are busy people with tight deadlines and failure to follow submission instructions might immediately disqualify your awesome project. Also, be patient after submitting. While it may feel like a lifetime to you, there are a million reasons why you may not hear back immediately from the editor. Don't get disheartened and don't give up!

Also, think creatively when it comes to magazine submissions. Is there a certain magazine that serves a demographic you'd like to reach but currently don't? Is there a way to tailor a project for them that still represents you while meeting the needs of their audience? Or maybe you are an expert at crochet joining techniques; instead of submitting a project idea, pitch an idea for an article—or, better yet, a series of articles—on different crochet joining methods.

As with book publishing, make sure that your goals and needs are in line with those of the magazine. If your primary goal is to build your audience, driving more people to your website or blog, or increasing your social media following, make sure that the magazine is willing to include your name, website, and social media information before signing an agreement.

Remember that magazines need a lot of quality content to fill the pages. If you have great ideas to share with the craft world, persistence pays off. Stick with it, keep generating quality content, and you're certain to find success in magazine publishing.

KEY TO SYMBOLS & ABBREVIATIONS

	Canadian market
	market located outside of the U.S. and Canada
	market prefers to work with local artists/ designers
b&w	black & white (photo or illustration)
SASE	self-addressed, stamped envelope
SAE	self-addressed envelope
IRC	International Reply Coupon, for use when mailing to countries other than your own

HELPFUL RESOURCES

- A great source for new magazine leads is in the business section of your local library. Ask the librarian to point out the business and consumer editions of the *Standard Rate and Data Service* (*SRDS*) and *Bacon's Media Directory*. These huge directories list thousands of magazines and will give you an idea of the magnitude of magazines published today. Another good source is a yearly directory called *Samir Husni's Guide to New Magazines*, also available in the business section of the public library and online at www.mrmagazine.com. *Folio* magazine provides information about new magazine launches and redesigns.

- Each year the Society of Publication Designers sponsors a juried competition, the winners of which are featured in a prestigious exhibition. For information about the annual competition, contact the Society of Publication Designers at (212) 223-3332 or visit their website at www.spd.org.

- Networking with fellow artists and art directors will help you find additional success strategies. The Graphic Artists Guild (www.gag.org), The American Institute of Graphic Artists (www.aiga.org), your city's Art Directors Club (www.adcglobal.org) or branch of the Society of Illustrators (www.societyillustrators.org) hold lectures and networking functions. Attend one event sponsored by each organization in your city to find a group you are comfortable with, then join and become an active member.

ALTERED COUTURE

Altered Couture, 22992 Mill Creek Dr., Laguna Hills CA 92653. E-mail: alteredcouture@stampington.com. Website: www.stampington.com/altered-couture. *Altered Couture* is a 160-page publication dedicated to altered and embellished clothing and accessories. It is filled with gorgeous photographs of altered jackets, t-shirts, sweaters, jeans, skirts, and more, accompanied by easy-to-understand techniques and endless inspiration.

HOW TO CONTACT "We prefer submissions of original art. If original art is not available, our next preference is high-resolution digital images (300 dpi at 8½ × 10). If hi-res digital images are not available, we will very rarely consider professional-quality transparencies or color slides. Color-copy submissions are not accepted. All artwork must be identified with the artist's name, address, e-mail, and phone number clearly printed on a label attached to each sample. Inscribe your name and address somewhere on each piece of art. If you desire acknowledgment of artwork receipt, please include a self-addressed stamped postcard. If the artwork is three-dimensional, please attach your identification with a removable string, or pack the sample in a plastic bag with your identification. If you have a unique artistic technique you'd like to share with others, please send samples of your artwork accompanied by a query letter outlining your article idea to the respective managing editor at: Altered Couture, 22992 Mill Creek Drive, Laguna Hills, CA 92653. Managing editors also welcome brief e-mail inquiries."

NEEDS "Managing editors seek first-rate projects and encourage artists who have not published articles before to submit ideas, as editorial assistance will be provided."

TERMS Competitive editorial compensation is provided for all published articles. "We may hold your sample for an extended period of time—9–12 months is common. Due to the large volume of artwork we receive, *Altered Couture* will return only those submissions accompanied by sufficient postage in the form of cash, check, or money order made out to Stampington & Company. We cannot offer delivery confirmation; however, we are happy to put insurance on the submission. If you wish to have your artwork insured for the return journey, please include sufficient funds and indicate your preference in a postcard or letter enclosed with your submission. Please do not attach postage to packaging, and do not send loose postage stamps. Contributors from outside the US, please send cash, check, or money order in US funds to Stampington & Company. For questions regarding your artwork, please send inquiries to artmanagement@stampington.com."

AMERICAN CRAFT

American Craft Council, 1224 Marshall St. NE, Suite 200, Minneapolis MN 55413. (612)206-3115. E-mail: mmoses@craftcouncil.org. E-mail: query@craftcouncil.org. Website: www.americancraftmag.org. Contact: Monica Moses, editor in chief. Estab. 1943. Circ. 40,000.

HOW TO CONTACT Guidelines online.

TIPS "Keep pitches short and sweet, a paragraph or 2 at most. Please include visuals with any pitches."

AMERICAN PATCHWORK & QUILTING

E-mail: apq@meredith.com. Website: www.allpeoplequilt.com/magazines-more/american-patchwork-and-quilting. *American Patchwork & Quilting* magazine, part of the Better Homes and Gardens family, is the leading quilting magazine in the country.

AMERICAN QUILTER MAGAZINE

American Quilter's Society, 5801 Kentucky Dam Rd., Paducah KY 42003. E-mail: micheleduffy@aqsquilt.com; ginnyharris@aqsquilt.com. Website: www.americanquilter.com. Contact: Michele Duffy, editor in chief; Ginny Harris, editorial assistant. American Quilter Magazine is published six times per year and is the official publication of the American Quilter's Society.

HOW TO CONTACT Quilting-related article ideas or queries may be submitted via e-mail to Editor in Chief Michele Duffy at micheleduffy@aqsquilt.com. Manuscripts may be submitted on a CD in .doc or .docx format with a hard copy printout accompanying the disk or via e-mail with "submission" in the subject field to Editorial Assistant Ginny Harris at ginnyharris@aqsquilt.com. Articles may range from 500 to 1,000 words and have accompanying images. "Furthermore, the inclusion of high-quality photos increases the chance of article acceptance; several images of each quilt or project allow the committee to see your submission at its best."

APRONOLOGY

Apronology, 22992 Mill Creek Dr., Laguna Hills CA 92653. E-mail: apronology@stampington.com. Website: www.stampington.com/apronology. This new publication flirts with the many uses and looks of the apron.

HOW TO CONTACT "We prefer submissions of original art. If original art is not available, our next preference is high-resolution digital images (300 dpi at 8½ × 10). If hi-res digital images are not available, we will very rarely consider professional-quality transparencies or color slides. Color-copy submissions are not accepted. All artwork must be identified with the artist's name, address, e-mail, and phone number clearly printed on a label attached to each sample. Inscribe your name and address somewhere on each piece of art. If you desire acknowledgment of artwork receipt, please include a self-addressed stamped postcard. If the artwork is three-dimensional, please attach your identification with a removable string, or pack the sample in a plastic bag with your identification. If you have a unique artistic technique you'd like to share with others, please send samples of your artwork accompanied by a query letter outlining your article idea to the respective managing editor at: Apronology, 22992 Mill Creek Drive, Laguna Hills, CA 92653. Managing editors also welcome brief e-mail inquiries."

NEEDS "Managing editors seek first-rate projects and encourage artists who have not published articles before to submit ideas, as editorial assistance will be provided."

TERMS Competitive editorial compensation is provided for all published articles. "We may hold your sample for an extended period of time—9–12 months is common. Due to the large volume of artwork we receive, *Apronology* will return only those submissions accompanied by sufficient postage in the form of cash, check, or money order made out to Stampington & Company. We cannot offer delivery confirmation; however, we are happy to put insurance on the submission. If you wish to have your artwork insured for the return journey, please include sufficient funds and indicate your preference in a postcard or letter enclosed with your submission. Please do not attach postage to packaging, and do not send loose postage stamps. Contributors from outside the US, please send cash, check, or money order in US funds to Stampington & Company. For questions regarding your artwork, please send inquiries to artmanagement@stampington.com."

ART DOLL QUARTERLY

Art Doll Quarterly, 22992 Mill Creek Dr., Laguna Hills CA 92653. E-mail: artdollquarterly@stampington.com. Website: www.stampington.com/art-doll-quarterly. "This full-color, 128-page publication is dedicated to art dolls and sculptural figures made from cloth, polymer clay, Creative Paperclay®, wire armatures, mixed media, and much more. In each issue, you will find original doll patterns, creative challenges, doll-artist profiles, convention listings and reviews, book & video reviews, and a 35-page gallery of art dolls made by our readers."

HOW TO CONTACT "We prefer submissions of original art. If original art is not available, our next preference is high-resolution digital images (300 dpi at 8½ × 10). If hi-res digital images are not available, we will very rarely consider professional-quality transparencies or color slides. Color-copy submissions are not accepted. All artwork must be identified with the artist's name, address, e-mail, and phone number clearly printed on a label attached to each sample. Inscribe your name and address somewhere on each piece of art. If you desire acknowledgment of artwork receipt, please include a self-addressed stamped postcard. If the artwork is three-dimensional, please attach your identification with a removable string, or pack the sample in a plastic bag with your identification. If you have a unique artistic technique you'd like to share with others, please send samples of your artwork accompanied by a query letter outlining your article idea to the respective managing editor at: Art Doll Quarterly, 22992 Mill Creek Drive, Laguna Hills, CA 92653. Managing editors also welcome brief e-mail inquiries."

NEEDS "Managing editors seek first-rate projects and encourage artists who have not published articles before to submit ideas, as editorial assistance will be provided."

TERMS Competitive editorial compensation is provided for all published articles. "We may hold your sample for an extended period of time—9–12 months is common. Due to the large volume of artwork we receive, *Art Doll Quarterly* will return only those submissions accompanied by sufficient postage in the form of cash, check, or money order made out to Stampington & Company. We cannot offer delivery confirmation; however, we are happy to put insurance on the submission. If you wish to have your artwork insured for the return journey, please include sufficient funds and indicate your preference in a postcard or letter enclosed with your submission. Please do not attach postage to packaging, and do not send loose postage stamps. Contributors from outside the US, please send cash, check, or money order in US funds to Stampington & Company. For questions regarding your artwork, please send inquiries to artmanagement@stampington.com."

ARTFUL BLOGGING

Artful Blogging, 22992 Mill Creek Dr., Laguna Hills CA 92653. E-mail: artfulblogging@stampington.com. Website: www.stampington.com/artfulblogging. "Allow yourself to be inspired as you flip through the pages of *Artful Blogging*. Join along with the growing community of artful bloggers as they continue to share their mesmerizing stories and captivating photographs."

HOW TO CONTACT "We prefer submissions of original art. If original art is not available, our next preference is high-resolution digital images (300 dpi at 8½ × 10). If hi-res digital images are not available, we will very rarely consider professional-quality transparencies or color slides. Color-copy submissions are not accepted. All artwork must be identified with the artist's name, address, e-mail and phone number clearly printed on a label attached to each sample. Inscribe your name and address somewhere on each piece of art. If you desire acknowledgment of artwork receipt, please include a self-addressed stamped postcard. If the artwork is three-dimensional, please attach your identification with a removable string, or pack the sample in a plastic bag with your identification. If you have a unique artistic technique you'd like to share with others, please send samples of your artwork accompanied by a query letter outlining your article idea to the respective managing editor at: Artful Blogging, 22992 Mill Creek Drive, Laguna Hills, CA 92653. Managing editors also welcome brief e-mail inquiries."

NEEDS "Managing editors seek first-rate projects and encourage artists who have not published articles before to submit ideas, as editorial assistance will be provided."

TERMS Competitive editorial compensation is provided for all published articles. "We may hold your sample for an extended period of time—9–12 months is common. Due to the large volume of artwork we receive, *Artful Blogging* will return only those submissions accompanied by sufficient postage in the form of cash, check, or money order made out to Stampington & Company. We cannot offer delivery confirmation; however, we are happy to put insurance on the submission. If you wish to have your artwork insured for the return journey, please include sufficient funds and indicate your preference in a postcard or letter enclosed with your submission. Please do not attach postage to packaging, and do not send loose postage stamps. Contributors from outside the US, please send cash, check, or money order in US funds to Stampington & Company. For questions regarding your artwork, please send inquiries to artmanagement@stampington.com."

ARTISTS' CAFÉ MAGAZINE

E-mail: submissions@stampington.com. Website: www.stampington.com/artists-cafe. The publishers of *Somerset Studio* invite you to explore the finest moments from over a decade in print with *Artists' Café*. This decadent, 144-page magazine is jam-packed with the best paper-crafting and mixed-media projects, as collected from past issues of *Somerset Studio*, *Somerset Apprentice*, *Sew Somerset*, *Art Journaling*, and *Somerset Workshop*. Relive favorite articles, discover techniques you may have missed, or get reacquainted with an admired artist.

ART JEWELRY MAGAZINE

E-mail: editor@artjewelrymag.com. Website: www.art.jewelrymakingmagazines.com. *Art Jewelry*'s mission is to teach the beginning jewelry maker, broaden the skills of those at the intermediate level, challenge the advanced artisan — and inspire them all.

ART JOURNALING

Art Journaling, 22992 Mill Creek Dr., Laguna Hills CA 92653. E-mail: artjournaling@stampington.com. Website: www.stampington.com/art-journaling. "In every quarterly issue of *Art Journaling*, artists open their journals and share creative techniques for capturing their emotions. From stamping and collage art to painting and sketching, each journal is filled with innovative techniques that you'll want to try in your own art journal. Detailed photos and commentary will help you discover your journaling style, with hints and tricks for creating a stand-out page."

HOW TO CONTACT "We prefer submissions of original art. If original art is not available, our next preference is high resolution digital images (300 dpi at 8½ × 10). If hi-res digital images are not available, we will very rarely consider professional-quality transparencies or color slides. Color-copy submissions are not accepted. All artwork must be identified with the artist's name, address, e-mail, and phone number clearly printed on a label attached to each sample. Inscribe your name and address somewhere on each piece of art. If you desire acknowledgment of artwork receipt, please include a self-addressed stamped postcard. If the artwork is three-dimensional, please attach your identification with a removable string, or pack the sample in a plastic bag with your identification. If you have a unique artistic technique you'd like to share with others, please send samples of your artwork accompanied by a query letter outlining your article idea to the respective managing editor at: Art Journaling, 22992 Mill Creek Drive, Laguna Hills, CA 92653. Managing editors also welcome brief e-mail inquiries."

NEEDS "Managing editors seek first-rate projects and encourage artists who have not published articles before to submit ideas, as editorial assistance will be provided."

TERMS Competitive editorial compensation is provided for all published articles. "We may hold your sample for an extended period of time—9–12 months is common. Due to the large volume of artwork we receive, *Art Journaling* will return only those submissions accompanied by sufficient postage in the form of cash, check, or money order made out to Stampington & Company. We cannot offer delivery confirmation; however, we are happy to put insurance on the submission. If you wish to have your artwork insured for the return journey, please include sufficient funds and indicate your preference in a postcard or letter enclosed with your submission. Please do not attach postage to packaging, and do not send loose postage stamps. Contributors from outside the US, please send cash, check, or money order in US funds to Stampington & Company. For

questions regarding your artwork, please send inquiries to artmanagement@stampington.com."

ART QUILTING STUDIO

Art Quilting Studio, 22992 Mill Creek Dr., Laguna Hills CA 92653. E-mail: artquiltingstudio@stampington.com. Website: www.stampington.com/art-quilting-studio. "*Art Quilting Studio* magazine provides a playful and informative forum where quilt enthusiasts from all walks of life can cross-pollinate to share techniques, ideas, and inspiration."

HOW TO CONTACT "We prefer submissions of original art. If original art is not available, our next preference is high-resolution digital images (300 dpi at 8½ × 10). If hi-res digital images are not available, we will very rarely consider professional-quality transparencies or color slides. Color-copy submissions are not accepted. All artwork must be identified with the artist's name, address, e-mail, and phone number clearly printed on a label attached to each sample. Inscribe your name and address somewhere on each piece of art. If you desire acknowledgment of artwork receipt, please include a self-addressed stamped postcard. If the artwork is three-dimensional, please attach your identification with a removable string, or pack the sample in a plastic bag with your identification. If you have a unique artistic technique you'd like to share with others, please send samples of your artwork accompanied by a query letter outlining your article idea to the respective managing editor at: Art Quilting Studio, 22992 Mill Creek Drive, Laguna Hills, CA 92653. Managing editors also welcome brief e-mail inquiries."

NEEDS "Managing editors seek first-rate projects and encourage artists who have not published articles before to submit ideas, as editorial assistance will be provided."

TERMS Competitive editorial compensation is provided for all published articles. "We may hold your sample for an extended period of time—9–12 months is common. Due to the large volume of artwork we receive, *Art Quilting* will return only those submissions accompanied by sufficient postage in the form of cash, check, or money order made out to Stampington & Company. We cannot offer delivery confirmation; however, we are happy to put insurance on the submission. If you wish to have your artwork insured for the return journey, please include sufficient funds and indicate your preference in a postcard or letter enclosed with your submission. Please do not attach postage to packaging, and do not send loose postage stamps. Contributors from outside the US, please send cash, check, or money order in US funds to Stampington & Company. For questions regarding your artwork, please send inquiries to artmanagement@stampington.com."

BEAD & BUTTON

E-mail: editor@beadandbutton.com. Website: www. bnb.jewelrymakingmagazines.com. *Bead&Button* is a bimonthly magazine devoted to techniques, projects, and designs of beaded jewelry and accessories.

● BEAD

E-mail: usoffice@ashdown.co.uk. Website: www. beadmagazine.co.uk. "Created by bead lovers, for bead lovers, each issue of *Bead* is packed full of beautiful beadwork, wirework, and stringing projects. Plus stylish and quality lampwork, metal clay, and polymer clay designs, and much more!"

● BEADS & BEYOND

Traplet Publications Ltd., Traplet House, Pendragon Close Malvern WR14 1GA, United Kingdom. Website: www.beadsandbeyondmagazine.com. A monthly, design-led craft magazine featuring jewelery-making projects, new techniques, stunning photography and inspiration, interviews, reviews, best buys, competitions, and prizes.

BEAD STYLE

Bead Style, 21027 Crossroads Circle, P.O. Box 1612, Waukesha WI 53187-1612. Website: www.bds.jewelrymakingmagazines.com. *Bead Style*, the world's leading magazine for beaders. In every issue, *Bead Style* will deliver dozens of projects that show you how to make fast, fashionable, and fun jewelry that is uniquely you."

BEADWORK

Interweave Press, 201 E. Fourth St., Loveland CO 80537. E-mail: beadworksubmissions@interweave. com. Website: www.beadingdaily.com. "*Beadwork* is a bimonthly magazine devoted to everything about beads and beadwork. Our pages are filled with projects for all levels of beaders, with a focus on the learning needs of those who seek to master beadweaving stitches. We pride ourselves on our easy-to-follow instructions and technical illustrations as well as our informative and entertaining features."

HOW TO CONTACT Guidelines available on website. Query by e-mail or mail. If submitting a project idea, include high-resolution photo of project and contact info. If querying for a feature, submit proposal and contact info.

TERMS Acquires first rights and subsequent non-exclusive rights for use in print, electronic, or other Interweave publications and promotions.

BELLE ARMOIRE

Belle Armoire, 22992 Mill Creek Dr., Laguna Hills CA 92653. E-mail: bellearmoire@stampington.com. Website: www.stampington.com/belle-armoire. "*Belle Armoire* marries fabric arts with rubber stamping and embellishments, showcasing one-of-a-kind, handmade fashions and wearable-art projects. Whether you're an art stamper, embroidery artist, custom jewelry designer, fabric painter, or knitting and crocheting enthusiast, *Belle Armoire* provides the opportunity and inspiration to create fashions that are uniquely you."

HOW TO CONTACT "We prefer submissions of original art. If original art is not available, our next preference is high-resolution digital images (300 dpi at 8½ × 10). If hi-res digital images are not available, we will very rarely consider professional-quality transparencies or color slides. Color-copy submissions are not accepted. All artwork must be identified with the artist's name, address, e-mail, and phone number clearly printed on a label *attached to each sample*. Inscribe your name and address somewhere on each piece of art. If you desire acknowledgment of artwork receipt, please include a self-addressed stamped postcard. If the artwork is three-dimensional, please attach your identification with a removable string, or pack the sample in a plastic bag with your identification. If you have a unique artistic technique you'd like to share with others, please send samples of your artwork accompanied by a query letter outlining your article idea to the respective managing editor at: Belle Armoire, 22992 Mill Creek Drive, Laguna Hills, CA

92653. Managing editors also welcome brief e-mail inquiries."

NEEDS "Managing editors seek first-rate projects and encourage artists who have not published articles before to submit ideas, as editorial assistance will be provided."

TERMS Competitive editorial compensation is provided for all published articles. "We may hold your sample for an extended period of time—9–12 months is common. Due to the large volume of artwork we receive, *Belle Armoire* will return only those submissions accompanied by sufficient postage in the form of cash, check, or money order made out to Stampington & Company. We cannot offer delivery confirmation; however, we are happy to put insurance on the submission. If you wish to have your artwork insured for the return journey, please include sufficient funds and indicate your preference in a postcard or letter enclosed with your submission. Please do not attach postage to packaging, and do not send loose postage stamps. Contributors from outside the US, please send cash, check, or money order in US funds to Stampington & Company. For questions regarding your artwork, please send inquiries to artmanagement@stampington.com."

BELLE ARMOIRE JEWELRY

Belle Armoire Jewelry, 22992 Mill Creek Dr., Laguna Hills CA 92653. E-mail: bellearmoirejewelry@stampington.com. Website: www.stampington.com/belle-armoire-jewelry. "*Belle Armoire Jewelry* magazine is overflowing with exciting projects, such as necklaces, bracelets, earrings, and brooches. You'll be inspired by all of the projects, tips, and techniques you will find. Whether your passion is stringing or making polymer clay beads, incorporating found or natural objects, you'll enjoy the artisan-made creations inside *Belle Armoire Jewelry*."

HOW TO CONTACT "We prefer submissions of original art. If original art is not available, our next preference is high-resolution digital images (300 dpi at 8½ × 10). If hi-res digital images are not available, we will very rarely consider professional-quality transparencies or color slides. Color-copy submissions are *not* accepted. All artwork must be identified with the artist's name, address, e-mail, and phone number clearly printed on a label *attached to each sample*. Inscribe your name and address somewhere on each piece of art. If you desire acknowledgment of artwork receipt, please include a self-addressed stamped postcard. If the artwork is three-dimensional, please attach your identification with a removable string, or pack the sample in a plastic bag with your identification. If you have a unique artistic technique you'd like to share with others, please send samples of your artwork accompanied by a query letter outlining your article idea to the respective managing editor at: Belle Armoire Jewelry, 22992 Mill Creek Drive, Laguna Hills, CA 92653. Managing editors also welcome brief e-mail inquiries."

NEEDS "Managing editors seek first-rate projects and encourage artists who have not published articles before to submit ideas, as editorial assistance will be provided."

TERMS Competitive editorial compensation is provided for all published articles. "We may hold your sample for an extended period of time—9–12 months is common. Due to the large volume of artwork we receive, *Belle Armoire Jewelry* will return only those submissions accompanied by sufficient postage in the form of cash, check, or money order made out to Stampington & Company. We cannot offer delivery confirmation; however, we are happy to put insurance on the submission. If you wish to have your artwork insured for the return journey, please include sufficient funds and indicate your preference in a postcard or letter enclosed with your submission. Please do not attach postage to packaging, and do not send loose postage stamps. Contributors from outside the US, please send cash, check, or money order in US funds to Stampington & Company. For questions regarding your artwork, please send inquiries to artmanagement@stampington.com."

BETTER HOMES & GARDENS

Website: www.bhg.com. *Better Homes and Gardens* is the vibrant, down-to-earth guide for the woman who is passionate about her home and garden and the life she creates there.

● BRITISH PATCHWORK & QUILTING

Traplet Publications Ltd., Traplet House, Pendragon Close Malvern WR14 1GA, United Kingdom. E-mail: joanna.kent@traplet.com. Website: www.pandqmagazine.com. Contact: Joanna Kent, editor. *British Patchwork and Quilting* magazine is a monthly publication written by quilters, for quilters, with projects and features specifically to do with patchwork, quilting, applique, and textiles.

CARDMAKER

E-mail: submissions@cardmakermagazine.com. Website: www.cardmakermagazine.com. *CardMaker* is the leading print-and-digital publication for card-making enthusiasts on the market. Published bimonthly.

HOW TO CONTACT "We prefer to receive submissions via e-mail. Please send a completed submittal form, including an image of your project, along with your complete contact information, to Submissions@CardMakerMagazine.com. Your e-mail subject line should include the publication title and issue and project name—for example: CardMaker Winter 2014, Warm Holiday Wishes. Please keep the attached file size under 2MG. Please send one project submission per e-mail."

NEEDS Original, attractive designs and patterns for card projects that will appeal to readers of all skill levels. Technique-based projects and articles that include, but are not limited to: rubber stamping, paper folding, interactive card construction, quilling, die cutting, paper piecing, dry and heat embossing, paper cutting, handmade paper, etc. Your ideas for issue themes, new techniques, and project types to feature are welcome.

TERMS "When your project and instructions are approved, we will send an agreement with our payment offer and a business reply envelope. You should complete it with your signature and date, and return the original to us in the postage-paid envelope—the photocopy we send is for your records. If this is the first time we've worked with you or if it has been a while since we've accepted a project, you will also receive a W-9 (or a W-8 if you live outside the United States) which must be completed and returned before payments can be issued. You will be issued a check for payment within 45 days of the date we received your signed contract. We will keep your project until the magazine issue is published. Your project will be returned to you after publication. All manuscripts, diagrams, etc., remain our property. Since we purchase all rights to designs, you should

not sell that design—or one very similar to it—to another publication. If you have questions as to what constitutes an original design, please contact us."

CARD MAKING & PAPERCRAFT

Website: www.cardmakingandpapercraft.com. *Cardmaking & Papercraft* is published 13 times a year by Immediate Media.

CLOTH PAPER SCISSORS

E-mail: submissions@clothpaperscissors.com. Website: www.clothpaperscissors.com. Published 6 times a year, *Cloth Paper Scissors* covers all types of fiber arts and collage work, including mixed media, assemblage, art dolls, visual art journals, rubber stamping, stamp carving, printmaking, creative embroidery, and book arts. Geared for the beginning artist/crafter as well as the advanced, *Cloth Paper Scissors* has a playful, positive tone, encouraging both the beginning and seasoned artist to try new techniques and share their work and expertise with a greater audience.

HOW TO CONTACT Please send the following to submissions@clothpaperscissors.com: 2-3 photos and/or sketches of the project(s) you'd like to write about; a short outline of the project, including a materials list; a 100-word bio; and your full address and contact information, including blog, website, and social media information. Please put I HEART PAPER in the subject line.

NEEDS Beautiful, decorative, and/or practical projects that showcase paper.

COMPLETE CARDMAKING

Website: www.papercraftmagazines.com/the-magazines/complete-cardmaking. *Complete Cardmaking* is the UK's first and only magazine dedicated to digital crafts, helping you make beautiful cards with your PC. This bimonthly magazine is the ideal accompaniment for the avid digital crafter, providing a free CD-ROM with every issue.

COUNTRY SAMPLER

707 Kautz Rd., St. Charles IL 60174. (630)377-8000. Fax: (630)377-8194. E-mail: editors@countrysampler.com. Website: www.countrysampler.com. "*Country*

Sampler is a must-have, all-in-one resource for any country decorator. Our unbeatable combination of country-lifestyle articles and a complete catalog of decorating products provides all the tips and tools you need to make your house a country home."

CRAFTS

E-mail: crafts@craftscouncil.org.uk. Website: www.craftsmagazine.org.uk. Published 6 times a year and covering all disciplines, this is the perfect magazine for makers, collectors, and lovers of craft.

CRAFTS BEAUTIFUL

Aceville Publications. E-mail: sarah.crosland@aceville.co.uk. Website: www.crafts-beautiful.com. Contact: Sarah Crosland, editor. "Britain's best-selling craft magazine. Card making, papercraft, stitching, baking, and knits—we love it all!"

CRAFTSELLER

E-mail: yourletters@craft-seller.com. Website: www.craft-seller.com. "An exciting magazine packed with projects, inspiration, and advice for anyone who loves crafting and wants to make and sell their handmade crafts."

CRAFT STAMPER

Traplet Publications Ltd., Traplet House, Pendragon Close Malvern WR14 1GA, UK. E-mail: alix.merriman@traplet.com. Website: www.craftstamper.com. Contact: Alix Merriman, editor. The UK's best magazine for rubber-stamping enthusiasts.

CREATE WITH ME

Create With Me, 22992 Mill Creek Dr., Laguna Hills CA 92653. E-mail: createwithme@stampington.com. Website: www.stampington.com/create-with-me. "The articles cover a complete spectrum from fabric and wearable art to paint, papier-mâché, card making, and bedroom dècor—and there is something for every age group."

HOW TO CONTACT "We prefer submissions of original art. If original art is not available, our next preference is high-resolution digital images (300 dpi at $8^{1}/2 \times 10$). If hi-res digital images are not available, we will very rarely consider professional-quality transparencies or color slides. Color-copy submissions are *not* accepted. All artwork must be identified with the artist's name, address, e-mail, and phone number clearly printed on a label *attached to each sample*. Inscribe your name and address somewhere on each piece of art. If you desire acknowledgment of artwork receipt, please include a self-addressed stamped postcard. If the artwork is three-dimensional, please attach your identification with a removable string, or pack the sample in a plastic bag with your identification. If you have a unique artistic technique you'd like to share with others, please send samples of your artwork accompanied by a query letter outlining your article idea to the respective managing editor at: Create With Me, 22992 Mill Creek Drive, Laguna Hills, CA 92653. Managing editors also welcome brief e-mail inquiries."

NEEDS "Managing editors seek first-rate projects and encourage artists who have not published articles before to submit ideas, as editorial assistance will be provided."

TERMS Competitive editorial compensation is provided for all published articles. "We may hold your sample for an extended period of time—9–12 months is common. Due to the large volume of artwork we receive, *Create With Me* will return only those submissions accompanied by sufficient postage in the form of cash, check, or money order made out to Stampington & Company. We can not offer delivery confirmation; however, we are happy to put insurance on the submission. If you wish to have your artwork insured for the return journey, please include sufficient funds and indicate your preference in a postcard or letter enclosed with your submission. Please do not attach postage to packaging, and do not send loose postage stamps. Contributors from outside the US, please send cash, check, or money order in US funds to Stampington & Company. For questions regarding your artwork, please send inquiries to artmanagement@stampington.com."

CREATING KEEPSAKES

E-mail: editorial@creatingkeepsakes.com. Website: www.creatingkeepsakes.com. Estab. 1996. "*Creating Keepsakes* magazine is the leading magazine for inspiration and techniques for scrapbookers."

CREATIVE CARDMAKING

Website: www.creativemagazines.com. Each issue of *Creative Cardmaking* includes a FREE cardmaking kit and is packed full of fantastic ideas for using your craft stash as well as all of the latest products from your favorite craft companies.

CREATIVE KNITTING

E-mail: editor@creativeknittingmagazine.com. Website: www.creativeknittingmagazine.com. "*Creative Knitting* features clear instructions for classic and current trends in knitting design."

CREATIVE MACHINE EMBROIDERY

E-mail: info@cmemag.com. Website: www.cmemag.com. *Creative Machine Embroidery* is a bimonthly magazine devoted to all things embroidery.

CREATIVE STAMPING

Website: www.creativemagazines.com. "*Creative Stamping* is an amazing magazine devoted to the wonderful world of stamping."

CROCHET!

E-mail: editor@crochetmagazine.com. Website: www.crochetmagazine.com. Contact: Ellen Gormley, editor. *Crochet!* is a full-color, 100-page full-size magazine published quarterly.

CROCHET TODAY!

E-mail: feedback@crochettoday.com. Website: www.crochettoday.com. "*Crochet Today* features fresh and modern crochet patterns, including gorgeous fashions, beautiful home decor, and sweet baby gifts. We focus on enriching the crocheter's skill set with step-by-step tutorials on the latest crochet stitch trends."

CROCHET WORLD

E-mail: editor@crochet-world.com. Website: www.crochet-world.com. Contact: Carol Alexander, editor. *Crochet World* magazine is published bimonthly. This 68-page magazine offers techniques and patterns with complete directions for all types of crochet.

HOW TO CONTACT Begin each submission with a sentence or two about why you designed it. Include all contact information with your query, including name, address, phone number, and e-mail address. If you want your projects returned, they must be accompanied by correct return postage, either check or money order ONLY. Project review: Reviews are held approximately every 8 weeks. Check the Editorial Calendar for dates. Many of these projects are seasonal.

TERMS "If we accept your design(s), we will contact you within 2 weeks after the review date. We may choose to hold on to a project that might fit in another issue. All others will be returned as soon as possible."

CROSS-STITCH & NEEDLEWORK

E-mail: jfranchuk@c-sn.com. Website: www.c-sn.com. "From beginner to advanced, there's something for every stitcher in *Cross-Stitch & Needlework* magazine. Each issue is packed with captivating designs, engaging feature articles and designer profiles, large full-color charts, fantastic finishing ideas, and easy-to-follow instructions for cross-stitch, needlepoint, embroidery, Hardanger, and more." Published bimonthly.

HOW TO CONTACT "We are always open to design submissions. Please send photos of stitched models or copies of the charted designs via e-mail, or mail to Design Submissions, Bayview Publishing, PO Box 157, Plover, WI 54467."

TERMS "All designs must be your original creations, and may not have been previously published or sold. Please, do not send actual stitched models before contacting us first."

CROSS STITCH CARD SHOP

Website: www.cross-stitching.com/magazines/cross-stitch-card-shop.

CROSS STITCH COLLECTION

E-mail: csc@futurenet.com. Website: www.crossstitch-collection.com. "*Cross Stitch Collection* offers the most beautiful cross-stitch projects from the best designers, with high-value, top-quality charts."

CROSS STITCH CRAZY

Website: www.cross-stitching.com/magazines/cross-stitch-crazy.

CROSS STITCH FAVOURITES

Website: www.cross-stitching.com/magazines/cross-stitch-favourites.

CROSS STITCH GOLD

Website: www.cross-stitching.com/magazines/cross-stitch-gold.

DESIGNER KNITTING

E-mail: helen.chrystie@thegmcgroup.com. Website: www.thegmcgroup.com. "*Designer Knitting* (previously *Vogue Knitting*) offers undeniable style. For fascinating features, seasonable fashion, yarn news, and book reviews, this magazine is all you need and more."

EMBELLISH MAGAZINE

Website: www.artwearpublications.com.au/subscriptions/embellish-magazine.html. "*Embellish* magazine aims to fuse fashion, fantasy, and art into everyday items, gifts, and homewares. You will find in each issue a mix of techniques and articles as well as ideas and inspirational stories. Expect to see a range of projects including dye processes; fabric manipulation; knit and/or crochet embellished finishes; couture techniques; hand embellishing; machine embellishing; prints; custom designs; repurposed textiles and projects related to textile applications that incorporate fabric, yarn, felt, and/or fiber."

ENJOY CROSS STITCH

Website: www.cross-stitching.com/magazines/enjoy-cross-stitch.

FELT MAGAZINE

Website: www.artwearpublications.com.au/subscriptions/felt-magazine.html. Felt Magazine aims to inspire a new generation of fibre enthusiasts with comprehensive projects, articles, and an inspirational gallery. It includes a mix of easy, intermediate, and technical projects to suit a wide range of skill levels.

FLAIR MAGAZINE

E-mail: liz@flairmagazine.co.uk. Website: www.flair-magazine.co.uk. *Flair Machine Embroidery Magazine* for embroidery machine enthusiasts, full of projects, info, free embroidery designs, and much more. Published quarterly in the United Kingdom.

GENERATION Q MAGAZINE

6102 Ash St., Simi Valley CA 93063. E-mail: melissa@generationqmagazine.com. Website: www.generationqmagazine.com. Contact: Melissa Thompson Maher. Estab. 2011. Bimonthly consumer magazine. *Generation Q* magazine is a lifestyle publication reflecting the interests and obsessions of the modern and contemporary quilter and sewist.Circ. 10,000. Sample available for $5.

HOW TO CONTACT Information available for SAE and on website. Accepts unsolicited submissions. Approached by 30 project/pattern designers/year. Works with almost all freelancers. Has featured projects/patterns by Sara Lawson, Victoria Findlay Wolfe, Brigitte Heitland, Julie Herman, Heather Jones. Preferred subjects: sewing, quilting. Submission format: DOC files. Include sketch, photo, or other rendition with size info. Submit print-ready step-by-step/assembly diagrams. Model and property release preferred. Once agree to publish project, submit via e-mail as JPEG at 300 dpi. Only accepts DOC files for instructions and JPEGs or PDFs for illustrations.

TERMS Send e-mail with project concepts. Does not keep samples on file; samples are not returned. Responds in 2 months. Pays $200 minimum for project/pattern design and industry-related articles. Credit line given. Pays on publication. Buys rights for 6 months. Finds freelancers by submissions, word of mouth, online. Undergoes technical edit before publication.

TIPS "Our audience is a niche within the quilting/sewing world. We want projects that reflect modern and contemporary styles. We don't like working with single-fabric collection projects and we love newcomers!"

GOOD OLD DAYS

E-mail: editor@goodolddaysmagazine.com. Website: www.goodolddaysmagazine.com. *Good Old Days* magazine tells the real stories of the people who lived and grew up in "the good old days" (about 1935–1960). Sample available for $2.

HOW TO CONTACT "Manuscripts should be typed (preferably double-spaced) with the author's name, address, and phone number in the upper left-hand corner. Our preferred word length is 600–1,000 words. Please submit one manuscript at a time and enclose a SASE (self addressed stamped envelope) if you want your material acknowledged and/or returned. If your story is not accepted and you have enclosed a SASE, you will receive it back after the review process has taken place—generally about 6 months. Send your submissions to: Good Old Days Submissions, 306 E. Parr Rd., Berne, IN 46711. If you do not enclose an SASE, you will hear from us only if we offer you a contract for your story. We do accept submissions via email (Editor@GoodOldDaysMagazine.com) or fax (260-589-8093), but treat them the same as mailed unsolicited manuscripts without a SASE."

GREEN CRAFT

Green Craft Magazine, 22992 Mill Creek Dr., Laguna Hills CA 92653. E-mail: greencraft@stampington. com. Website: www.stampington.com/greencraft-magazine. "*GreenCraft Magazine* provides ideas for upcycling trash to treasures by showcasing projects where waste is repurposed into ecologically chic creations. To support sustainable production, the entire publication is printed on 100% recycled paper."

HOW TO CONTACT "We prefer submissions of original art. If original art is not available, our next preference is high resolution digital images (300 dpi at 8½ × 10). If hi-res digital images are not available, we will very rarely consider professional-quality transparencies or color slides. Color-copy submissions are *not* accepted. All artwork must be identified with the artist's name, address, e-mail, and phone number clearly printed on a label *attached to each sample*. Inscribe your name and address somewhere on each piece of art. If you desire acknowledgment of artwork receipt, please include a self-addressed stamped postcard. If the artwork is three-dimensional, please attach your identification with a removable string, or pack the sample in a plastic bag with your identification. If you

have a unique artistic technique you'd like to share with others, please send samples of your artwork accompanied by a query letter outlining your article idea to the respective managing editor at: Green Craft Magazine, 22992 Mill Creek Drive, Laguna Hills, CA 92653. Managing editors also welcome brief e-mail inquiries."

NEEDS "Managing editors seek first-rate projects and encourage artists who have not published articles before to submit ideas, as editorial assistance will be provided."

TERMS Competitive editorial compensation is provided for all published articles. "We may hold your sample for an extended period of time—9–12 months is common. Due to the large volume of artwork we receive, *Green Craft Magazine* will return only those submissions accompanied by sufficient postage in the form of cash, check, or money order made out to Stampington & Company. We cannot offer delivery confirmation; however, we are happy to put insurance on the submission. If you wish to have your artwork insured for the return journey, please include sufficient funds and indicate your preference in a postcard or letter enclosed with your submission. Please do not attach postage to packaging, and do not send loose postage stamps. Contributors from outside the US, please send cash, check, or money order in US funds to Stampington & Company. For questions regarding your artwork, please send inquiries to artmanagement@stampington.com."

HANDWOVEN

Interweave Press, 24520 Melott Rd., Hillsboro OR 97123. E-mail: aosterhaug@interweave.com. Website: www.weavingtoday.com. Contact: Anita Osterhaug. "The main goal of *Handwoven* articles is to inspire our readers to weave. Articles and projects should be accessible to weavers of all skill levels, even when the material is technical. The best way to prepare an article for *Handwoven* is to study the format and style of articles in recent issues."

HOW TO CONTACT Guidelines available on website.

HAUTE HANDBAGS

Haute Handbags, 22992 Mill Creek Dr., Laguna Hills CA 92653. E-mail: hautehandbags@stampington.

com. Website: www.stampington.com/haute-hand-bags. "How do you carry it? That's the question *Somerset Studio* & *Belle Armoire* would like to help answer through our exciting special publication titled *Haute Handbags*. Whether we use purses, clutches, totes, portfolios, sacks, bags, or attachés, there are many styles made with an astounding array of materials emerging from all corners of the creative world—all vying to be made and enjoyed!"

HOW TO CONTACT "We prefer submissions of original art. If original art is not available, our next preference is high-resolution digital images (300 dpi at 8½ × 10). If hi-res digital images are not available, we will very rarely consider professional-quality transparencies or color slides. Color-copy submissions are *not* accepted. All artwork must be identified with the artist's name, address, e-mail, and phone number clearly printed on a label *attached to each sample*. Inscribe your name and address somewhere on each piece of art. If you desire acknowledgment of artwork receipt, please include a self-addressed stamped postcard. If the artwork is three-dimensional, please attach your identification with a removable string, or pack the sample in a plastic bag with your identification. If you have a unique artistic technique you'd like to share with others, please send samples of your artwork accompanied by a query letter outlining your article idea to the respective managing editor at: Haute Handbags, 22992 Mill Creek Drive, Laguna Hills, CA 92653. Managing editors also welcome brief e-mail inquiries."

NEEDS "Managing editors seek first-rate projects and encourage artists who have not published articles before to submit ideas, as editorial assistance will be provided."

TERMS Competitive editorial compensation is provided for all published articles. "We may hold your sample for an extended period of time—9–12 months is common. Due to the large volume of artwork we receive, *Haute Hangbags* will return only those submissions accompanied by sufficient postage in the form of cash, check, or money order made out to Stampington & Company. We cannot offer delivery confirmation; however, we are happy to put insurance on the submission. If you wish to have your artwork insured for the return journey, please include sufficient funds and indicate your preference in a postcard or letter enclosed with your submission. Please do not attach postage to packaging, and

do not send loose postage stamps. Contributors from outside the US, please send cash, check, or money order in US funds to Stampington & Company. For questions regarding your artwork, please send inquiries to artmanagement@stampington.com."

HOLIDAYS & CELEBRATIONS
Holidays and Celebrations, 22992 Mill Creek Dr., Laguna Hills CA 92653. E-mail: holidaysandcelebrations@stampington.com. Website: www.stampington.com/somerset-holidays-and-celebrations. Learn how to create a lasting impression on special occasions like birthdays, Halloween, Christmas, Mother's Day, Valentine's Day, and more in each annual issue of *Somerset Holidays & Celebrations* — an endless source of handcrafted inspiration.

HOW TO CONTACT "We prefer submissions of original art. If original art is not available, our next preference is high-resolution digital images (300 dpi at 8½ × 10). If hi-res digital images are not available, we will very rarely consider professional-quality transparencies or color slides. Color-copy submissions are not accepted. All artwork must be identified with the artist's name, address, e-mail, and phone number clearly printed on a label attached to each sample. Inscribe your name and address somewhere on each piece of art. If you desire acknowledgment of artwork receipt, please include a self-addressed stamped postcard. If the artwork is three-dimensional, please attach your identification with a removable string, or pack the sample in a plastic bag with your identification. If you have a unique artistic technique you'd like to share with others, please send samples of your artwork accompanied by a query letter outlining your article idea to the respective managing editor at: Holidays and Celebrations, 22992 Mill Creek Drive, Laguna Hills, CA 92653. Managing editors also welcome brief e-mail inquiries."

NEEDS "Managing editors seek first-rate projects and encourage artists who have not published articles before to submit ideas, as editorial assistance will be provided."

TERMS Competitive editorial compensation is provided for all published articles. "We may hold your sample for an extended period of time—9–12 months is common. Due to the large volume of artwork we receive, *Holidays & Celebrations* will return only those submissions accompanied by sufficient postage in the form of cash, check, or money order made out to Stampington & Company. We cannot offer delivery confirmation; however, we are happy to put insurance on the submission. If you wish to have your artwork insured for the return journey, please include sufficient funds and indicate your preference in a postcard or letter enclosed with your submission. Please do not attach postage to packaging, and do not send loose postage stamps. Contributors from outside the US, please send cash, check, or money order in US funds to Stampington & Company. For questions regarding your artwork, please send inquiries to artmanagement@stampington.com."

HOMESTYLE SEWING

Website: www.cross-stitching.com/magazines/homestyle-sewing.

INTERWEAVE CROCHET

Interweave Press, 4868 Innovation Dr., Fort Collins CO 80525. E-mail: rachel.koon@fwmedia.com; crochet@interweave.com (general e-mail address). Website: www.crochetme.com. "*Interweave Crochet* is a quarterly publication of Interweave for all those who love to crochet. In each issue we present beautifully finished projects, accompanied by clear step-by-step instructions, as well as stories and articles of interest to crocheters. The projects range from quick but intriguing projects that can be accomplished in a weekend to complex patterns that may take months to complete. Engaging and informative feature articles come from around the country and around the world. Fashion sensibility and striking examples of craft technique are important to us."

HOW TO CONTACT Guidelines available on website.

INTERWEAVE KNITS

Interweave Press, 201 E. Fourth St., Loveland CO 80537. Website: www.knittingdaily.com. *Interweave Knits* is a quarterly publication of Interweave Press for all those who love to knit. In each issue we present beautifully finished projects, accompanied by clear step-by-step instruction, and stories and articles of interest to knitters. The projects range from quick but intriguing items that can be accomplished in a weekend, to complex patterns that may take months to complete. Feature articles (personally arresting but information rich) come from around the country and around the world. Fashion sensibility and striking examples of craft technique are important to us. *Interweave Knits* is published quarterly.

HOW TO CONTACT Guidelines available on website.

TIPS "Remember that your submission is a representation of who you are and how you work—if you send us a thoughtful, neat, and well-organized submission, we are likely to be intrigued."

JEWELRY AFFAIRE

Jewelry Affaire, 22992 Mill Creek Dr., Laguna Hills CA 92653. E-mail: jewelryaffaire@stampington.com. Website: www.stampington.com/jewelry-affaire. "*Jewelry Affaire* celebrates the beauty that can be found in easy-to-make jewelry. These pieces are not only feasts for the eyes, but they can easily dress up and adorn any outfit and its wearer. This jewelry is precious in its own right."

HOW TO CONTACT "We prefer submissions of original art. If original art is not available, our next preference is high-resolution digital images (300 dpi at 8½ × 10). If hi-res digital images are not available, we will very rarely consider professional-quality transparencies or color slides. Color-copy submissions are not accepted. All artwork must be identified with the artist's name, address, e-mail, and phone number clearly printed on a label attached to each sample. Inscribe your name and address somewhere on each piece of art. If you desire acknowledgment of artwork receipt, please include a self-addressed stamped postcard. If the artwork is three-dimensional, please attach your identification with a removable string, or pack the sample in a plastic bag with your identification. If you have a unique artistic technique you'd like to share with others, please send samples of your artwork accompanied by a query letter outlining your article idea to the respective managing editor at: Jewelry Affaire, 22992 Mill Creek Drive, Laguna Hills, CA 92653. Managing editors also welcome brief e-mail inquiries."

NEEDS "Managing editors seek first-rate projects and encourage artists who have not published articles before to submit ideas, as editorial assistance will be provided."

TERMS Competitive editorial compensation is provided for all published articles. "We may hold your sample for an extended period of time—9–12 months is common. Due to the large volume of artwork we receive, *Jewelry Affaire* will return only those submissions accompanied by sufficient postage in the form of cash, check, or money order made out to Stampington & Company. We cannot offer delivery confirmation; however, we are happy to put insurance on the submission. If you wish to have your artwork insured for the return journey, please include sufficient funds and indicate your preference in a postcard or letter enclosed with your submission. Please do not attach postage to packaging, and do not send loose postage stamps. Contributors from outside the US, please send cash, check, or money order in US funds to Stampington & Company. For questions regarding your artwork, please send inquiries to artmanagement@stampington.com."

JEWELRY STRINGING

E-mail: stringingsubmissions@interweave.com. Website: www.beadingdaily.com/blogs/stringing/default. aspx. *Jewelry Stringing* magazine is published quarterly. Each issue of *Jewelry Stringing* includes more than 70 fabulous necklaces, bracelets, and earrings, accompanied by clear step-by-step instructions and beautiful photography. The projects range from quick and easy to more complex, but all are made using basic stringing, wireworking, and knotting techniques. **HOW TO CONTACT** Please send the following to submissions@clothpaperscissors.com: 2-3 photos and/or sketches of the project(s) you'd like to write about; a short outline of the project, including a materials list; a 100-word bio; and your full address and contact information, including blog, website, and social-media information. Please put I HEART PAPER in the subject line.
NEEDS Beautiful, decorative, and/or practical projects that showcase paper.

JUST CROSSSTITCH

E-mail: editor@just-crossstitch.com. Website: www. just-crossstitch.com. Estab. 1983. *Just CrossStitch* is the first magazine devoted exclusively to counted cross-stitch and the only cross-stitch title written for the intermediate to advanced-level hobbyist.

KNIT NOW MAGAZINE

Practical Publishing, Suite G2, St. Christopher House, 217 Wellington Rd. S., Stockport United Kingdom SK2 6NG. Website: www.knitnowmag.co.uk. Estab. 2012. Four weekly (13 issues/year) consumer magazine. "*Knit Now Magazine* is the UK's best knitting magazine, focused on quick, simple, stylish knits. We are particularly committed to British wool, supporting independent designers, and publishing new and interesting knits every issue." Circ. 25,000 (per issue). Sample available by request.
HOW TO CONTACT Request via e-mail. Accepts unsolicited submissions. Approached by 300 project/pattern designers/year. Buys 130 project/pattern designs/year from freelancers. Preferred subjects: knitting, crochet. Submission format: PDF. Include swatch, sketch, and brief description.
TERMS Send PDF submission in response to a focused call for submission. Responds in 2 weeks. Pays $100 minimum, $320 maximum for project/pattern design. Credit line given. Pays on publication. Buys first rights. Finds freelancers through submissions, word of mouth. Undergoes technical edit before publication.
TIPS "See our blog post that offers advice for designers who want to work for us at www.knitnowmag.co.uk/item/193-submission-tips-for-designers. Be sure to include a clear swatch and sketch with submission."

KNITSCENE

E-mail: amy.palmer@fwcommunity.com. Website: www.knitscene.com. "In each issue, we feature up-and-coming designers, popular yarns, fun and concise tutorials, and fresh photography that invites the reader into a yarn-filled daydream. The projects are simple but intriguing, stylish but wearable, and designed for knitters of all ages and sizes."

☻ KNIT SIMPLE

E-mail: helen.chrystie@thegmcgroup.com. Website: www.thegmcgroup.com. "*Knit Simple* with easy-to-use and well-organised instructions, this magazine offers exactly what it says in the title. Whatever your skill level, here is a great resource for casual creations and simple, easy-to-wear knits that accommodate all shapes and sizes."

THE KNITTER

E-mail: theknitter@futurenet.com. Website: www.thek-nitter.co.uk. *The Knitter* is the magazine for knitters seeking a creative challenge. Published 13 times a year.

KNITTER'S MAGAZINE

Knitter's Magazine Submissions, 1320 S. Minnesota Ave., Floor 2, Sioux Falls SD 57105. E-mail: managingeditor@xrx-inc.com. Website: www.knittinguniverse.com/K113. A quarterly publication featuring popular designers and the latest knitwear fashions, techniques, and supplies.

HOW TO CONTACT All submissions should include a swatch, sketch, or picture of the project, and description of the design and techniques it will use. A short biography is helpful.

KNITTING

E-mail: helen.chrystie@thegmcgroup.com. Website: www.thegmcgroup.com. "*Knitting* is the UK's original and best magazine devoted to this popular craft. Bridging the divide between fashion and hand knitting, each issue offers at least 25 new and contemporary patterns including knits for women, men, children, and the home."

KNIT TODAY

Website: www.knit-today.co.uk. "*Knit Today* magazine is for everyone who enjoys knitting. Whether you've just started knitting or an experienced knitter, you'll find lots to read and at least 20 great patterns in every single issue. All our patterns are brand-new so you won't have seen them anywhere else before. We pride ourselves on having the most accurate, easy-to-follow pattern instructions so you can enjoy knitting to the very last stitch!" Published 13 times a year.

LAPIDARY JOURNAL JEWELRY ARTIST

E-mail: ljeditorial@interweave.com. Website: www.jewelrymakingdaily.com/blogs/jewelryartistmagazine/default.aspx.

LET'S GET CRAFTING

Website: www.letsgetcrafting.com. "*LGC Knitting & Crochet* contains everything you need to get started right away! Perfect for both beginners and experienced crafters, each issue comes with a high-value yarn pack, plus knitting needles and a crochet hook. We'll guide you step-by-step through gorgeous projects from some of the UK's leading designers, plus we have all the latest news and gossip from the UK crafting community as well as shopping guides and informative features."

LET'S KNIT

21-23 Phoenix Court, Hawkind Rd., Colchester Essex CO2 8JY, United Kingdom. E-mail: sarah.neal@aceville.co.uk. Website: www.letsknit.co.uk. Contact: Sarah Neal, editor. Estab. 2007. "*Let's Knit* is the UK's best knitting magazine! Every issue is packed with patterns for knitters of all ages and skill levels, with a fun and fashionable flavor that's perfect for today's knitter. It has all the practical help, informative features, and shopping info you could possibly want, along with a fantastic high-value free gift with every issue."

LOVE CRAFTING

Website: www.cross-stitching.com/magazines/lovecrafting. "*Love Crafting* is a brand-new magazine full of inspiration for crafters of all abilities. Inside our sewing special you will find over 50 amazing makes with easy-to-follow instructions and templates, plus our top budget buys!"

LOVE CROCHET

Website: www.immediate.co.uk/brands/love-crochet/. "*Love Crochet* is a quarterly magazine filled with over 30 beautiful crochet projects for clothes, accessories, and the home. As well as an inspiring mix of on-trend makes, you'll find all the latest crochet news plus designer interviews, blogs, courses, and kits. This is the perfect magazine for those who enjoy crochet or want to learn this exciting craft."

LOVE KNITTING FOR BABY

Website: www.immediate.co.uk/brands/love-knitting-for-baby. "*Love Knitting for Baby* is a bimonthly must-knit collection of beautiful clothes and accessories for babies and toddlers. Each issue includes over 25 knitting patterns, plus best buys, expert advice, baby yarn reviews, and interviews with top designers."

LOVE OF QUILTING

P.O. Box 171, Winterset NJ 50273. (515)462-1020. Fax: (515)462-5856. Website: www.fonsandporter.com. Contact: Diane Tomlinson, associate editor. Estab. 1996. Bimonthly consumer magazine. Also publishes special interest issues (*Easy Quilts*, *Quilting Quickly*, *Scrap & Patriotic Quilts*) quarterly and biannually. Focus is quilting projects. Circ. 350,000. Sample available by request.

HOW TO CONTACT Information available online Accepts unsolicited submissions. Approached by 200 project/pattern designers/year. Buys 400 projects/pattern designs/year from freelancers. Has featured projects/patterns by Liz Porter, Marianne Fons, Nancy Mahoney. Preferred subjects: quilting. Submission format: PDF, JPEG, and Illustrator files. Include detailed descriptions including measurements and fabric.

TERMS Send e-mail. Does not keep samples on file; samples not returned. Responds in 1 month. Pay varies by project. Pays on acceptance. Buys all rights (for contracted period of time). Finds freelancers through submissions, word of mouth, magazines, online. Edits as required.

TIPS "We are looking for traditional, easy, and precut quilt ideas in all skill levels. Have good artwork and descriptions."

LOVE PATCHWORK & QUILTING

Website: www.lovepatchworkandquilting.com. "*Love Patchwork & Quilting* is a dedicated modern quilting magazine from the makers of *Mollie Makes* and *Simply Crochet*. We publish 13 times a year, featuring projects, techniques, interviews, news, and reviews from the world of modern quilting. Every issue also comes with a FREE gift!"

MACHINE KNITTING MONTHLY

Website: www.machineknittingmonthly.net. *Machine Knitting Monthly* magazine is packed with great new pattern ideas, features on different stitches, letters, club news, reviews on related books and products, and much more.

MACHINE QUILTING UNLIMITED

Machine Quilting Unlimited Magazine, P.O. Box 918, Fort Lupton CO 80621. E-mail: submissions@ mqumag.com. Website: www.machinequilting. mqumag.com. "*Machine Quilting Unlimited* magazine is for the machine-quilting enthusiast. We cover techniques and fundamentals, whether using a domestic sewing machine, a small-frame system, a midarm machine, or a longarm machine. There will also be design inspiration, profiles of your favorite quilting stars, reviews of products, books, and DVDs, ideas for setting up your studio or workroom, help for beginners, and a calendar of quilt shows and events."

MAKE & SELL JEWELLERY MAGAZINE

1 Phoenix Court, Hawkins Rd., Colchester Essex CO2 8JY, United Kingdom. E-mail: melissa@aceville.com. Website: www.makeselljewellery.com. Contact: Melissa Hyland. "*Make & Sell Jewellery* magazine is the UK's glossiest and most glamorous dedicated jewelery making magazine, aimed at hobbyists and those wanting to sell their creations alike. Each issue features a regular Make & Sell section packed with advice and tips from experts to start your business and boost sales, plus exclusive, copyright-free projects. Beginners and those making for themselves aren't forgotten with step-by-step guides to create designer-style jewelery, from simple bead stringing and wirework to more advanced techniques such as polymer and precious metal clay and resin. Whether making jewelery as a hobby or small business, *Make & Sell Jewellery* provides all the know-how needed to create accessories that are both original and on-trend. With beautiful and clear photography including jewelery showcased on models so you can see how to wear the designs too, it stands out from other jewelery magazines. And with a bounty of shopping pages to help you with your purchases it really is the only jewelery magazine you need, whether a beginner or pro!"

MAKE

E-mail: editor@makezine.com. Website: www.makezine.com. Bimonthly magazine for DIY enthusiasts.

MAKING

E-mail: helen.chrystie@thegmcgroup.com. Website: www.thegmcgroup.com. "*Making* is the UK's first contemporary craft magazine, bringing its readers 25 bespoke projects every month. Filled with inspiration, beautiful projects, and stunning photography, Making is essential reading for the discerning crafter. Covering a wide range of techniques and disciplines, clear how-to's, and style advice along with regular features and shopping pages, *Making* is the perfect combination of craft and lifestyle for a creative audience."

MAKING JEWELLERY

E-mail: helen.chrystie@thegmcgroup.com. Website: www.thegmcgroup.com. "*Making Jewellery* is the UK's first and best-selling jewelery magazine. Each month we feature more than 45 projects to make stylish, fashionable, and professional-looking jewelery. There are step-by step projects for ever skill level using a variety of techniques from simple stringing to metal clays, polymer, shrink plastic, wirework, silversmithing, resin, lampworking, and more. *Making Jewellery* offers an innovative approach to jewelery making with instruction on basic techniques and insight into the creative minds of leading makers."

MARTHA STEWART LIVING

E-mail: living@marthastewart.com. Website: www.marthastewart.com. Monthly magazine for gardening, entertaining, renovating, cooking, collecting, and creating.

MCCALL'S QUICK QUILTS

E-mail: mcq@creativecraftsgroup.com. Website: www.mccallsquilting.com. Bimonthly consumer publication, nationally distributed, and written for quilters of all skill levels.

MCCALL'S QUILTING

E-mail: mcq@creativecraftsgroup.com. Website: www.mccallsquilting.com. Bimonthly consumer publication, nationally distributed, and written for quilters of all skill levels.

MINGLE

Mingle, 22992 Mill Creek Dr., Laguna Hills CA 92653. E-mail: mingle@stampington.com. Website: www.stampington.com/mingle. "*Mingle*, along with the uplifting stories behind uniquely creative get-togethers —from small and intimate "girls' nights in" to larger scale art retreats. Discover creative ways for bringing friends and loved ones together—is complete with entertaining tips, one-of-a-kind invitations and party favor ideas, recipes, artful décor, creative inspiration, and an all around good time! Make your next get-together "the talk of the town" with ideas from the pages of this photography-rich and engrossing magazine."

HOW TO CONTACT "We prefer submissions of original art. If original art is not available, our next preference is high resolution digital images (300 dpi at 8-1/2 x 10"). If hi-res digital images are not available, we will very rarely consider professional-quality transparencies or color slides. Color-copy submissions are not accepted. All artwork must be identified with the artist's name, address, e-mail, and phone number clearly printed on a label attached to each sample. Inscribe your name and address somewhere on each piece of art. If you desire acknowledgment of artwork receipt, please include a self-addressed stamped postcard. If the artwork is three-dimensional, please attach your identification with a removable string, or pack the sample in a plastic bag with your identification. If you have a unique artistic technique you'd like to share with others, please send samples of your artwork accompanied by a query letter outlining your article idea to the respective managing editor at: Mingle, 22992 Mill Creek Drive, Laguna Hills, CA 92653. Managing editors also welcome brief e-mail inquiries."

NEEDS "Managing editors seek first-rate projects and encourage artists who have not published articles before to submit ideas, as editorial assistance will be provided."

TERMS Competitive editorial compensation is provided for all published articles. "We may hold your sample for an extended period of time—9–12 months is common. Due to the large volume of artwork we receive, *Mingle* will return only those submissions accompanied by sufficient postage in the form of cash, check, or money order made out to Stampington & Company. We cannot offer delivery confirmation; however, we are happy to put insurance on the submission. If you wish to have your artwork insured for the return journey, please include sufficient funds and indicate your preference in a postcard or letter enclosed with your submission. Please do not attach postage to packaging, and do not send loose postage stamps. Contributors from outside the US, please send cash, check, or money order in US funds to Stampington & Company. For questions regarding your artwork, please send inquiries to artmanagement@stampington.com."

MODERN QUILTS UNLIMITED

Meander Publishing, Inc., P.O. Box 918, Fort Lupton CO 80621. E-mail: editor@mqumag.com. Website: www.modernquilts.mqumag.com. "*Modern Quilts Unlimited* is published quarterly and offers quilt, accessory and home-decoration patterns by exciting new designers, interviews with the innovators in this field, machine-quilting tips, and quilts and projects made by those who find that this new genre of quilting fits their needs and lifestyles."

MOLLIE MAKES

Website: www.molliemakes.com. *Mollie Makes* brings you the best of craft online, a look inside the homes of the world's most creative crafters, tutorials on inspiring makes, roundups of the most covetable stash, and tours of the crafty capitals of the world.

NEW STITCHES

E-mail: janice@ccpuk.co.uk. Website: www.newstitches.co.uk. Published monthly, *New Stitches* features designs for your favorite embroidery techniques such as Cross-stitch, Hardanger, Blackwork, and much more.

ONLINE QUILT MAGAZINE

P.O. Box 57, Buxton NSW 2571, Australia. (61)2-4683-2912. E-mail: jody@onlinequiltmagazine.com. Website: www.onlinequiltmagazine.com. Contact: Jody Anderson, editor. Estab. 2010. Monthly online publication. "We publish a monthly online quilting magazine that has a large readership around the world. Our readers range from beginners to more experienced quilters, and as such we like to offer a variety of articles, 'how to's,' and patterns so there is something to appeal to everyone. There is a smaller free version

each month and a super cheap twice-as-big paid issue as well." Circ. 20,000+. available by request.

HOW TO CONTACT Request via e-mail. Accepts unsolicited submissions. Exchanges free publicity and ad space for project/pattern designs. Has featured projects/patterns by Pat Durbin, Jenny Bowker, Kathy McNeil, Frieda Anderson, Toby Lischko, Elaine Quehl. Preferred subjects: quilting. Submission format: DOC and JPEG files. E-mail with general idea before submitting materials/content. Responsible for submitting print-ready photos and step-by-step/assembly diagrams for completed project. Photo captions only required if needed to make photo clear. Accepts images in digital format only via e-mail as JPEG file.

TERMS Send e-mail with project concepts. Responds in 7 days. Offers free publicity and ad space in exchange for designs/articles. Credit line given. Finds freelancers through word of mouth, online. Edits as required.

TIPS "We welcome everyone! We're always looking for new projects and quilting articles, and whilst we can't pay money for your submissions, we do offer great advertising promotion to our large reader base in exchange. It's a great way of attracting traffic to your site! Please just get in touch with me!"

PAPERCRAFTER MAGAZINE

E-mail: ella.johnston@aceville.co.uk. Website: www.papercraftermagazine.co.uk. Contact: Ella Johnston, editor. "PaperCrafter is a must-buy mag for makers who adore all things paper, offering everything you need to create cards and papercraft projects in one package. It comes with beautiful kits and paper books that are designed by a different illustrator every issue, giving projects a fresh new look and providing inspiration with every purchase."

PAPERCRAFT ESSENTIALS

Website: www.papercraftmagazines.com/the-magazines/papercraft-essentials. "*Papercraft Essentials* is packed with fun cards you can make in an evening! With the emphasis on cute and traditional styles, the magazine combines quick makes for beginners with more in-depth projects for intermediate and advanced crafters."

PAPERCRAFT INSPIRATIONS

E-mail: papercraft@futurenet.com. Website: www.papercraftinspirationsmagazine.co.uk. "Britain's best-selling card-making magazine-filled with help, advice, oodles of ideas, and techniques for card makers of all levels of experience!"

PAPER CRAFTS MAGAZINE

E-mail: editor@papercraftsmag.com. Website: www.papercraftsmag.com. *Paper Crafts & Scrapbooking* is an enthusiast-based magazine with worldwide circulation.

PIECEWORK

E-mail: piecework@interweave.com. Website: http://www.interweave.com/needle/. People with a passion for traditional knitting, embellished clothing, and beautiful lacework—all made by hand—are *PieceWork* magazine's core audience. *PieceWork* is a bimonthly magazine, explores the personal stories of traditional makers and what they made, and investigates how specific objects were crafted and the stories behind them. In-depth how-to techniques and step-by-step projects make the traditions come alive for today's knitters, embroiderers, lacemakers, and crocheters. Prefers digital submissions with images. Pays upon publication.

PIECEWORK MAGAZINE

Interweave/F+W Media, 4868 Innovation Dr., Fort Collins CO 80537. (800) 272-2193, Fax: (970)669-6117. E-mail: piecework@interweave.com. Website: www.interweave.com. Estab. 1993. *PieceWork* celebrates the rich tradition of needlework and the history of the people behind it. Stories and projects on embroidery, cross-stitch, knitting, crocheting, and quilting, along with other textile arts, are featured in each issue. Circ. 30,000. Writer's guidelines available at pieceworkmagazine.com.

TIPS Submit a well-researched article on a historical aspect of needlework complete with information on visuals and suggestion for accompanying project.

POPULAR PATCHWORK

E-mail: bridget.kenningham@myhobbystore.com. Website: www.popularpatchwork.com. Contact: Bridget Kenningham. "Bringing traditional and con-temporary patchwork & quilting to the fabricaholics of the United Kingdom."

POPULAR WOODWORKING MAGAZINE

F+W, A Content + Ecommerce Company, 8469 Blue Ash Rd., Suite 100, Cincinnati OH 45236. (513)531-2690, ext. 11348. E-mail: mike.wallace@fwcommunity.com. Website: www.popularwoodworking.com. Contact: Michael Wallace. Estab. 1981. "*Popular Woodworking Magazine* invites woodworkers of all skill levels into a community of professionals who share their hard-won shop experience through in-depth projects and technique articles, which help readers hone their existing skills and develop new ones for both hand and power tools. Related stories increase the readers' understanding and enjoyment of their craft. Any project submitted must be aesthetically pleasing, of sound construction, and offer a challenge to readers. On the average, we use 5 freelance features per issue. Our primary needs are 'how-to' articles on woodworking. Our secondary need is for articles that will inspire discussion concerning woodworking. Tone of articles should be conversational and informal but knowledgeable, as if the writer is speaking directly to the reader. Our readers are the woodworking hobbyist and small woodshop owner. Writers should have an extensive knowledge of woodworking and excellent woodworking techniques and skills." Circ. 150,000. Sample copy: $5.99 plus 9×12 SAE with 6 first-class stamps, or online.

HOW TO CONTACT Guidelines available online. Word length ranges from 1,200 to 2,500. Payment for features starts at $250 per contracted page (plus $75 per for images), depending on the total package submitted (including its quality) and the writer's level of woodworking and writing experience. "All submissions, except 'Out of the Woodwork' columns and 'Tricks of the Trade,' should be preceded by a query. We accept unsolicited manuscripts and artwork, although, if sent via post, they must be accompanied by a self-addressed stamped envelope to be returned. Digital queries are preferred. We try to respond to all queries within 60 days."

NEEDS "Our primary needs are how-to articles on woodworking projects, and instructional features dealing with woodworking and techniques. We rarely publish freelance articles about woodworkers and their particular work. The tone of articles should be conversational and informal, as if the writer is speaking directly to the reader."

TIPS "Write an 'End Grain' column for us and then follow up with photos of your projects. Submissions should include materials list, complete diagrams (blueprints not necessary), and discussion of the step-by-step process. We select attractive, practical projects with quality construction for which the authors can supply quality digital photography."

POTTERY MAKING ILLUSTRATED

Pottery Making Illustrated, 600 N. Cleveland Ave., Suite 210, Westerville OH 43082. (614)895-4213. Fax: (614)891-8960. E-mail: editorial@potterymaking.org. Website: www.ceramicartsdaily.org/pottery-making-illustrated. *Pottery Making Illustrated* provides well-illustrated, practical, how-to instruction for all skill levels on all aspects of ceramic art.

HOW TO CONTACT "We require professional digital images for publication. Digital images should be delivered as uncompressed four-color (CMYK), 300 dpi image files with a minimum print size of 5 inches (preferably TIFF or EPS format). Image files should be burned to a CD and mailed to our editorial offices with your complete submission. Images can also be uploaded to our FTP site. Uploaded files must be stuffed or zipped. Include all captions on a separate sheet of paper. Each image or graphic element must have a caption. Make sure image file names clearly match up with caption numbers. Captions for processes and techniques should describe the activity shown. Captions for finished ware should include: the title, dimensions, specific ceramic medium (earthenware, porcelain, etc.), forming/glazing techniques, cone number and firing process (pit fired, high fire, raku, etc.). Provide a brief 1 or 2 sentence biography about yourself and include an e-mail address, Web address, fax number or postal address if you want direct reader feedback. Our authors have indicated that this has been a valuable tool. If images or illustrations were provided by a third party, include her/his name so proper credit may be published. It is your responsibility to obtain the rights for any photographs, illustrations, or other third-party materials submitted."

TERMS "We ask for exclusive worldwide rights for the text (both print and electronic versions, including but not limited to publishing on demand, database online services, reprints, or books), and

nonexclusive rights for use of the photographic materials in print or electronic media. This nonexclusive agreement allows for the continued use of the photographic material in any way the artist chooses after the article has appeared in *Pottery Making Illustrated*. When your article is published, you'll be paid at the current rate of 10¢ per word for text and $25 per image or graphic illustration."

PRIMITIVE QUILTS & PROJECTS

E-mail: homespunmedia@aol.com. Website: www.primitivequiltsandprojects.com. "A premium quilting magazine dedicated to the primitive quilter, rug hooker, stitcher, and more! Each issue features at least 15 projects from some of the most admired designers in the primitive fiber arts world."

PRIMS

Prims, 22992 Mill Creek Dr., Laguna Hills CA 92653. E-mail: prims@stampington.com. Website: www.stampington.com/prims. "*Prims* exclusively features art inspired by a bygone era. You will find artwork of primitive-, folk-, historic-, and early Americana-style artists that will captivate the imagination and enchant with their simple beauty. The traditional beauty of handcrafted art making includes dolls, paintings, and mixed-media artwork, along with teddy bears in Stampington & Company's unique publication."

HOW TO CONTACT "We prefer submissions of original art. If original art is not available, our next preference is high-resolution digital images (300 dpi at 8½ × 10). If hi-res digital images are not available, we will very rarely consider professional-quality transparencies or color slides. Color-copy submissions are not accepted. All artwork must be identified with the artist's name, address, e-mail, and phone number clearly printed on a label attached to each sample. Inscribe your name and address somewhere on each piece of art. If you desire acknowledgment of artwork receipt, please include a self-addressed stamped postcard. If the artwork is three-dimensional, please attach your identification with a removable string, or pack the sample in a plastic bag with your identification. If you have a unique artistic technique you'd like to share with others, please send samples of your artwork accompanied by a query letter outlining your article idea to the respective managing editor at: Prims, 22992

Mill Creek Drive, Laguna Hills, CA 92653. Managing editors also welcome brief e-mail inquiries."

NEEDS "Managing editors seek first-rate projects and encourage artists who have not published articles before to submit ideas, as editorial assistance will be provided."

TERMS Competitive editorial compensation is provided for all published articles. "We may hold your sample for an extended period of time—9–12 months is common. Due to the large volume of artwork we receive, *Prims* will return only those submissions accompanied by sufficient postage in the form of cash, check, or money order made out to Stampington & Company. We cannot offer delivery confirmation; however, we are happy to put insurance on the submission. If you wish to have your artwork insured for the return journey, please include sufficient funds and indicate your preference in a postcard or letter enclosed with your submission. Please do not attach postage to packaging, and do not send loose postage stamps. Contributors from outside the US, please send cash, check, or money order in US funds to Stampington & Company. For questions regarding your artwork, please send inquiries to artmanagement@stampington.com."

QUICK & EASY CROCHET

Website: www.quickandeasycrochetmagazine.com. "America's no. 1 crochet magazine. Filled with easy-to-follow instructions for crocheted fashions, pillows, potholders, afghans, coverlets, bridal gowns, dollies, and more."

QUICK CARDS MADE EASY

Website: www.cardmakingandpapercraft.com/maga-zine/quickcards. *Quick Cards Made Easy* is packed with stylish card projects, for every occasion, each issue. Published 13 times a year.

QUILT

E-mail: quiltmag@epix.net. Website: www.quiltmag.com. "Published 6 times per year, *Quilt* will fulfill your every quilting need. Each issue is bursting with patterns in a variety of styles for all skill levels. Quilts are showcased in beautifully styled room settings, and clear directions and illustrations accompany each project. Our

talented designers use current fabric collections, so you can create the exact quilt shown, and many projects include kit information for easy ordering."

QUILT ALMANAC

E-mail: quiltmag@epix.net. Website: www.quiltmag.com. "Published each January, *Quilt Almanac* features quilts for all seasons, from traditional to modern, and showcases a variety of techniques. This newsstand-only issue will provide you with inspiring projects to keep you busy all year long. Our designers create both quilts and small projects ideal for newer quilters or for experienced quilters looking for a quick and relaxing project."

QUILTER'S NEWSLETTER MAGAZINE

E-mail: questions@qnm.com. Website: www.quilters-newsletter.com. *Quilters Newsletter* is a specialized publication for quilt lovers and quilt makers. Its domestic and international readership of approximately 200,000 includes professional and nonprofessional quilt makers, quilt collectors, historians, and teachers.

TERMS "Our rates depend on what rights we buy, how much editing or rewriting is required, if you can provide usable sewn samples, and whether we use your photos or do the photography in our studio. We reserve the right to use accepted material in any appropriate issue and for any editorial purpose. For general articles, as well as for each pattern that we develop from a submitted quilt, payment will be negotiated upon acceptance. We make no payment for material used in our News columns or for feature material sent by industry professionals or their representatives that promotes a person, event, or product. Payment for Top Tips used in Short Takes is $25. Payment for showcasing a quilt on our cover and presenting a pattern for a portion of or all of the quilt is $350 plus 10 copies of that issue. Payment for Photo Finish and About Space is $50 and 10 copies of that issue."

QUILTER'S WORLD

E-mail: editor@quiltersworld.com. Website: www.quiltersworld.com. Estab. 1979. *Quilter's World* features classic and current trends in quilt design.

QUILTING ARTS MAGAZINE

E-mail: submissions@quiltingarts.com. Website: www.quiltingdaily.com. "At *Quilting Arts*, we celebrate contemporary art quilting, surface design, mixed media, fiber art trends, and more. We are always looking for new techniques, innovative processes, and unique approaches to the art of quilting."

HOW TO CONTACT Guidelines available on website.

QUILTMAKER

E-mail: editor@quiltmaker.com. Website: www.quiltmaker.com. Quiltmaker publishes 6 regular issues per year, available by subscription (print and digital), at quilt shops and on newsstands.

⟳ QUILTMANIA

Website: www.quiltmania.com/english/home.html. *Quiltmania* is published every 2 months in 3 versions: French, Dutch, and English.

QUILTS & MORE

E-mail: apq@meredith.com. Website: www.allpeoplequilt.com/magazines-more/quilts-and-more.

QUILT SAMPLER

Website: www.allpeoplequilt.com/magazines-more/quilt-sampler.

QUILTY

E-mail: contributors@qnntv.com. Website: www.heyquilty.com. Quilting magazine.

⟳ RELOVED

E-mail: sally.fitzgerald@anthem-publishing.com. Website: www.relovedmag.co.uk. Contact: Sally Fitzgerald, editor. *Reloved* is the exciting new magazine at the heart of thrifting, shabby chic, and upcycling. With an emphasis on breathing new life into old, forgotten objects, it brings a hands-on approach to this thriving pastime.

SAMPLER & ANTIQUE NEEDLEWORK QUARTERLY

E-mail: editor@sanqmagazine.com. Website: www.sanqmagazine.com. *Sampler & Antique Needlework Quarterly* is the premiere magazine for those who look at the handwork from centuries past with a sense of awe, wonder, and inquisitiveness.

⟳ SCRAP 365

Traplet Publications Ltd., Traplet House, Pendragon Close Malvern WR14 1GA, United Kingdom. E-mail: scrap365@traplet.com. Website: www.inspiredtomake.com/zone/scrap-365/home. Contact: Alison Parris, editor. "Published 6 times a year, every issue is 90 pages stuffed with scrappy inspiration. As our strapline suggests, our magazine is aimed at keen scrapbookers who love and live their hobby."

⟳ SCRAPBOOK MAGAZINE

Website: www.papercraftmagazines.com/the-magazines/scrapbook-magazine. *Scrapbook Magazine* is Britain's biggest-selling scrapbook magazine. Published every 6 weeks, each issue shows you the ins and outs for bringing your photos and memories to life through the wonderful world of scrapbooking, allowing you to create stunning and personalized mini works of art using your photos, papers, found objects, and recycled elements.

SEW BEAUTIFUL

E-mail: editorial@sewbeautifulmag.com. Website: www.sewbeautifulmag.com. *Sew Beautiful* is one of the largest, most recognized heirloom sewing titles in the U.S.

⟳ SEWING WORLD

Traplet Publications Ltd., Traplet House, Pendragon Close Malvern WR14 1GA, UK. Website: www.inspiredtomake.com/zone/sewing-world/home. *Sewing World* is a monthly magazine packed full of delicious, contemporary sewing projects as well as fabrics, techniques, products, features, and interviews.

SEW IT ALL

Website: www.sewitallmag.com. *Sew It All* is published once a year in December by Creative Crafts Group. It is a special newsstand issue brought to you by the editors of *Sew News*.

SEW MAGAZINE

E-mail: lorraine.luximon@aceville.co.uk. Website: www.sewmag.co.uk. Contact: Lorraine Luximon, editor. "Inspiration for you, your home, and the little ones—the UK's only sewing magazine that gives you a FREE full-sized dressmaker's pattern every month!"

SEW NEWS

Sew News Editor, 741 Corporate Circle, Suite A, Golden CO 80401. E-mail: sewnews@sewnews.com. Website: www.sewnews.com. *Sew News* is the go-to guide for the most current and relevant information that the sewing world has to offer.

HOW TO CONTACT Query by letter or e-mail; do not send finished manuscripts. Query should consist of a brief outline of the article, a sketch or photo of the intended project, a list of the illustrations or photographs you envision with it, an explanation of why your proposed article would be of interest to the *Sew News* reader, and why you are qualified to write it.

NEEDS Articles should teach a specific technique, inspire the reader to try a project, introduce the reader to a new product or company related to sewing, or inform the reader about current fashion and sewing trends.

TERMS When an article is accepted, you'll be sent an assignment sheet detailing what is expected of you for the assignment and the intended payment (from $50 to $500, new writers generally $50–150, depending on the length and complexity of the subject, and the garment(s), samples, photography, illustrations, or sources to be supplied). After you receive the assignment, please sign and return it within 10 days. If you're unable to meet a deadline for any reason, please inform *Sew News* immediately. Failure to do so will void assignment. All articles, including those specifically assigned, are written "on speculation". All payments will be made upon publication. To receive the full payment suggested in the assignment sheet, the article must be submitted by the specified deadline, include all elements detailed in the assignment sheet, and be of acceptable quality (to be determined by the *Sew News* editorial staff). Payment may be decreased for late arrival, missing elements, or poor quality. *Sew News* reserves the right to return articles for rewriting or clarification of information, return samples for redo/corrections and, in extreme cases, to return them without payment.

SEW SIMPLE

Website: www.sewsimple.com. *Sew Simple* is right in tune with today's younger stitchers.

SEW SOMERSET

Sew Somerset, 22992 Mill Creek Dr., Laguna Hills CA 92653. E-mail: sewsomerset@stampington.com. Website: www.stampington.com/sew-somerset. "*Sew Somerset* represents a new way of looking at sewn art. More than ever before, artists are discovering the joy of combining sewing with mixed-media projects, showing the world that stitches are not just for fabric anymore! In this 144-page publication, readers will find gorgeous photographs, easy-to-understand techniques, and endless inspiration. *Sew Somerset* will help crafters and artists alike learn how to add stitches of varied lengths, sizes, colors, and dimensions into their next project to create a look that is 'So Somerset!'"

HOW TO CONTACT "We prefer submissions of original art. If original art is not available, our next preference is high resolution digital images (300 dpi at 8½ × 10). If hi-res digital images are not available, we will very rarely consider professional-quality transparencies or color slides. Color-copy submissions are not accepted. All artwork must be identified with the artist's name, address, e-mail, and phone number clearly printed on a label attached to each sample. Inscribe your name and address somewhere on each piece of art. If you desire acknowledgment of artwork receipt, please include a self-addressed stamped postcard. If the artwork is three-dimensional, please attach your identification with a removable string, or pack the sample in a plastic bag with your identification. If you have a unique artistic technique you'd like to share with others, please send samples of your artwork accompanied by a query letter outlining your article idea to the respective managing editor at: Sew Somerset, 22992 Mill Creek

Drive, Laguna Hills, CA 92653. Managing editors also welcome brief e-mail inquiries."

NEEDS "Managing editors seek first-rate projects and encourage artists who have not published articles before to submit ideas, as editorial assistance will be provided."

TERMS Competitive editorial compensation is provided for all published articles. "We may hold your sample for an extended period of time—9–12 months is common. Due to the large volume of artwork we receive, *Sew Somerset* will return only those submissions accompanied by sufficient postage in the form of cash, check, or money order made out to Stampington & Company. We cannot offer delivery confirmation; however, we are happy to put insurance on the submission. If you wish to have your artwork insured for the return journey, please include sufficient funds and indicate your preference in a postcard or letter enclosed with your submission. Please do not attach postage to packaging, and do not send loose postage stamps. Contributors from outside the US, please send cash, check, or money order in US funds to Stampington & Company. For questions regarding your artwork, please send inquiries to artmanagement@stampington.com."

SIMPLE QUILTS & SEWING

E-mail: quiltmag@epix.net. Website: www.quiltmag.com. Magazine about quilting and sewing.

SIMPLY CARDS & PAPERCRAFTS

Website: www.papercraftmagazines.com/the-magazines/simply-cards-papercraft. "*Simply Cards & Papercraft* is the UK's most inspirational papercraft magazine full of inspiration for quality cards for every occasion. It's full of the newest techniques, products, and up-to-the-minute ideas."

SIMPLY CROCHET

E-mail: simplycrochet@futurenet.com. Website: www.simplycrochetmag.co.uk. *Simply Crochet* is a dedicated crochet magazine from the makers of *Simply Knitting*, *The Knitter*, *Crochet Today!*, and *Mollie Makes*. Featuring over 20 crochet patterns every month and technical advice, clear instructions, and crochet inspiration, *Simply Crochet* will get you hooked on handmade!

SIMPLY HOMEMADE

Website: www.simplyhomemademag.com. "*Simply Homemade* is a magazine designed specifically for those of us who love crafting and can't get enough of making things."

SIMPLY KNITTING

E-mail: simplyknitting@futurenet.com. Website: www.simplyknitting.co.uk. On sale 13 times a year, *Simply Knitting* is packed with patterns, yarn reviews, knitting tips, and knitting news.

SOMERSET APPRENTICE

Somerset Apprentice, 22992 Mill Creek Dr., Laguna Hills CA 92653. E-mail: somersetapprentice@stampington.com. Website: www.stampington.com/somerset-apprentice. "*Somerset Apprentice* takes its readers by the hand to teach them the fundamentals of creating Somerset-style art—one basic step at a time. Successful artists share their favorite tips and techniques, including layered collage, mixed media, and assemblage art, which are presented through detailed, close-up photographs and clear, concise instructions. Join the pros on a step-by-step journey as they complete an entire work of art! This top-selling magazine has everything you'll need to learn a new craft, fine-tune your technique, and gather inspiration for your creative adventure."

HOW TO CONTACT "We prefer submissions of original art. If original art is not available, our next preference is high-resolution digital images (300 dpi at 8½ × 10). If hi-res digital images are not available, we will very rarely consider professional-quality transparencies or color slides. Color-copy submissions are not accepted. All artwork must be identified with the artist's name, address, e-mail, and phone number clearly printed on a label attached to each sample. Inscribe your name and address somewhere on each piece of art. If you desire acknowledgment of artwork receipt, please include a self-addressed stamped postcard. If the artwork is three-dimensional, please attach your identification with a removable string, or pack the sample in a plastic bag with your identification. If you have a unique artistic technique you'd like to share with others, please send samples of your artwork accompanied by a query letter outlining your article idea to the respective managing editor at: Somerset Apprentice, 22992 Mill Creek Drive, Laguna Hills, CA 92653. Managing editors also welcome brief e-mail inquiries."

NEEDS "Managing editors seek first-rate projects and encourage artists who have not published articles before to submit ideas, as editorial assistance will be provided."

TERMS Competitive editorial compensation is provided for all published articles. "We may hold your sample for an extended period of time—9–12 months is common. Due to the large volume of artwork we receive, *Somerset Apprentice* will return only those submissions accompanied by sufficient postage in the form of cash, check, or money order made out to Stampington & Company. We cannot offer delivery confirmation; however, we are happy to put insurance on the submission. If you wish to have your artwork insured for the return journey, please include sufficient funds and indicate your preference in a postcard or letter enclosed with your submission. Please do not attach postage to packaging, and do not send loose postage stamps. Contributors from outside the US, please send cash, check, or money order in US funds to Stampington & Company. For questions regarding your artwork, please send inquiries to artmanagement@stampington.com."

SOMERSET DIGITAL STUDIO

Somerset Digital Studio, 22992 Mill Creek Dr., Laguna Hills CA 92653. E-mail: somersetdigitalstudio@stampington.com. Website: www.stampington.com/somerset-digital-studio. "*Somerset Digital Studio* showcases some of the best digitally created artwork around, and these breathtaking samples of scrapbook pages, ATCs, and collages will have readers joining in this growing trend of creating digitally altered artwork in no time. Each of the 144 lush, full-color pages found in every issue contain captivating feature articles, a full gallery of digital eye candy, a digital dictionary, software comparison chart, digital tutorial, and more."

HOW TO CONTACT "We prefer submissions of original art. If original art is not available, our next preference is high resolution digital images (300 dpi at 8½

× 10). If hi-res digital images are not available, we will very rarely consider professional-quality transparencies or color slides. Color-copy submissions are not accepted. All artwork must be identified with the artist's name, address, e-mail, and phone number clearly printed on a label attached to each sample. Inscribe your name and address somewhere on each piece of art. If you desire acknowledgment of artwork receipt, please include a self-addressed stamped postcard. If the artwork is three-dimensional, please attach your identification with a removable string, or pack the sample in a plastic bag with your identification. If you have a unique artistic technique you'd like to share with others, please send samples of your artwork accompanied by a query letter outlining your article idea to the respective managing editor at: Somerset Digital Studio, 22992 Mill Creek Drive, Laguna Hills, CA 92653. Managing editors also welcome brief e-mail inquiries."

NEEDS "Managing editors seek first-rate projects and encourage artists who have not published articles before to submit ideas, as editorial assistance will be provided."

TERMS Competitive editorial compensation is provided for all published articles. "We may hold your sample for an extended period of time—9–12 months is common. Due to the large volume of artwork we receive, *Somerset Digital Studio* will return only those submissions accompanied by sufficient postage in the form of cash, check, or money order made out to Stampington & Company. We cannot offer delivery confirmation; however, we are happy to put insurance on the submission. If you wish to have your artwork insured for the return journey, please include sufficient funds and indicate your preference in a postcard or letter enclosed with your submission. Please do not attach postage to packaging, and do not send loose postage stamps. Contributors from outside the US, please send cash, check, or money order in US funds to Stampington & Company. For questions regarding your artwork, please send inquiries to artmanagement@stampington.com."

SOMERSET HOME

Somerset Home, 22992 Mill Creek Dr., Laguna Hills CA 92653. E-mail: somersethome@stampington.com. Website: www.stampington.com/somersethome. "*Somerset Home* magazine beautifully blends 'Somerset-esque' art together with functional, everyday items to add an artful touch of décor. The result is a truly distinctive annual magazine that exemplifies creative living and showcases hundreds of tips, techniques, and charming accents designed to enlighten, organize, and beautify any dwelling place. When you wander through the inspiring pages of *Somerset Home*, you'll be enthralled by room after room of beautiful projects, and inside this inviting 160-page publication, you'll find unique and artistic creative ideas for every corner of your home."

HOW TO CONTACT "We prefer submissions of original art. If original art is not available, our next preference is high-resolution digital images (300 dpi at 8½ × 10). If hi-res digital images are not available, we will very rarely consider professional-quality transparencies or color slides. Color-copy submissions are not accepted. All artwork must be identified with the artist's name, address, e-mail, and phone number clearly printed on a label attached to each sample. Inscribe your name and address somewhere on each piece of art. If you desire acknowledgment of artwork receipt, please include a self-addressed stamped postcard. If the artwork is three-dimensional, please attach your identification with a removable string, or pack the sample in a plastic bag with your identification. If you have a unique artistic technique you'd like to share with others, please send samples of your artwork accompanied by a query letter outlining your article idea to the respective managing editor at: Somerset Home, 22992 Mill Creek Drive, Laguna Hills, CA 92653. Managing editors also welcome brief e-mail inquiries."

NEEDS "Managing editors seek first-rate projects and encourage artists who have not published articles before to submit ideas, as editorial assistance will be provided."

TERMS Competitive editorial compensation is provided for all published articles. "We may hold your sample for an extended period of time—9–12 months is common. Due to the large volume of artwork we receive, *Somerset Home* will return only those submissions accompanied by sufficient postage in the form of cash, check, or money order made out to Stampington & Company. We cannot offer delivery confirmation; however, we are happy to put insurance on the submission. If you wish to have your artwork insured for the return journey, please include sufficient funds and indicate your preference in a postcard or letter enclosed with your submission. Please do not attach postage to packaging, and do not send loose postage stamps. Contributors from outside the US, please send cash, check, or money order in US funds to Stampington & Company. For questions regarding your artwork, please send inquiries to artmanagement@stampington.com."

SOMERSET LIFE

Somerset Life, 22992 Mill Creek Dr., Laguna Hills CA 92653. E-mail: somersetlife@stampington.com. Website: www.stampington.com/somerset-life. "Each issue of *Somerset Life* provides an abundance of inspiring ideas to infuse our daily lives with simple pleasures, art, romance, creativity, and beauty. Stunning photography and insightful and entertaining articles illustrate touching moments captured in poetry and artwork, unique ways to present gifts and treasured items, simple but beautiful remembrances, fresh ideas to elevate the art of letter writing, and many other imaginative ideas to enhance our lives with artful elements. *Somerset Life* will inspire you to make every day extraordinary!"

HOW TO CONTACT "We prefer submissions of original art. If original art is not available, our next preference is high-resolution digital images (300 dpi at 8½ × 10). If hi-res digital images are not available, we will very rarely consider professional-quality transparencies or color slides. Color-copy submissions are not accepted. All artwork must be identified with the artist's name, address, e-mail, and phone number clearly printed on a label attached to each sample. Inscribe your name and address somewhere on each piece of art. If you desire acknowledgment of artwork receipt, please include a self-addressed stamped postcard. If the artwork is three-dimensional, please attach your identification with a removable string, or pack the sample in a plastic bag with your identification. If you have a unique artistic technique you'd like to share with others, please send samples of your artwork accompanied by a query letter outlining your article idea to the respective managing editor at: Somerset Life, 22992 Mill Creek Drive, Laguna Hills, CA 92653. Managing editors also welcome brief e-mail inquiries."

NEEDS "Managing editors seek first-rate projects and encourage artists who have not published articles before to submit ideas, as editorial assistance will be provided."

TERMS Competitive editorial compensation is provided for all published articles. "We may hold your sample for an extended period of time—9–12 months is common. Due to the large volume of artwork we receive, *Somerset Life* will return only those submissions accompanied by sufficient postage in the form of cash, check, or money order made out to Stampington & Company. We cannot offer delivery confirmation; however, we are happy to put insurance on the submission. If you wish to have your artwork insured for the return journey, please include sufficient funds and indicate your preference in a postcard or letter enclosed with your submission. Please do not attach postage to packaging, and do not send loose postage stamps. Contributors from outside the US, please send cash, check, or money order in US funds to Stampington & Company. For questions regarding your artwork, please send inquiries to artmanagement@stampington.com."

SOMERSET MEMORIES

Somerset Memories, 22992 Mill Creek Dr., Laguna Hills CA 92653. E-mail: somersetmemories@stampington.com. Website: www.stampington.com/somerset-memories. "*Somerset Memories* provides a showcase for arts and crafts that feature family photographs and memorabilia. This unique semiannual magazine presents sophisticated scrapbook and journal pages, plus a gorgeous array of paper crafts, fabric arts, memorabilia, and mixed-media art made by our talented readers and contributors."

HOW TO CONTACT "We prefer submissions of original art. If original art is not available, our next preference is high-resolution digital images (300 dpi at 8½ × 10). If hi-res digital images are not available, we will very rarely consider professional-quality transparencies or color slides. Color-copy submissions are not accepted. All artwork must be identified with the artist's name, address, e-mail, and phone number clearly printed on a label attached to each sample. Inscribe your name and address somewhere on each piece of art. If you desire acknowledgment of artwork receipt, please include a self-addressed stamped postcard. If the artwork is three-dimensional, please attach your identification with a re-

movable string, or pack the sample in a plastic bag with your identification. If you have a unique artistic technique you'd like to share with others, please send samples of your artwork accompanied by a query letter outlining your article idea to the respective managing editor at: Somerset Memories, 22992 Mill Creek Drive, Laguna Hills, CA 92653. Managing editors also welcome brief e-mail inquiries."

NEEDS "Managing editors seek first-rate projects and encourage artists who have not published articles before to submit ideas, as editorial assistance will be provided."

TERMS Competitive editorial compensation is provided for all published articles. "We may hold your sample for an extended period of time—9–12 months is common. Due to the large volume of artwork we receive, *Somerset Memories* will return only those submissions accompanied by sufficient postage in the form of cash, check, or money order made out to Stampington & Company. We cannot offer delivery confirmation; however, we are happy to put insurance on the submission. If you wish to have your artwork insured for the return journey, please include sufficient funds and indicate your preference in a postcard or letter enclosed with your submission. Please do not attach postage to packaging, and do not send loose postage stamps. Contributors from outside the US, please send cash, check, or money order in US funds to Stampington & Company. For questions regarding your artwork, please send inquiries to artmanagement@stampington.com."

SOMERSET STUDIO

Somerset Studio, 22992 Mill Creek Dr., Laguna Hills CA 92653. E-mail: somersetstudio@stampington.com. Website: www.stampington.com/somerset-studio. "Paper crafting, art stamping and the lettering arts are elevated to an artistic level in *Somerset Studio*! Come join in the celebration of these popular handcrafting styles by exploring the industry's most trusted and innovative mixed-media magazine, as you learn from fellow artists working with exotic papers, intriguing art stamps, fine calligraphy, and a variety of mediums."

HOW TO CONTACT "We prefer submissions of original art. If original art is not available, our next preference is high resolution digital images (300 dpi at 8½ ×

10). If hi-res digital images are not available, we will very rarely consider professional-quality transparencies or color slides. Color-copy submissions are not accepted. All artwork must be identified with the artist's name, address, e-mail, and phone number clearly printed on a label attached to each sample. Inscribe your name and address somewhere on each piece of art. If you desire acknowledgment of artwork receipt, please include a self-addressed stamped postcard. If the artwork is three-dimensional, please attach your identification with a removable string, or pack the sample in a plastic bag with your identification. If you have a unique artistic technique you'd like to share with others, please send samples of your artwork accompanied by a query letter outlining your article idea to the respective managing rditor at: Somerset Studio, 22992 Mill Creek Drive, Laguna Hills, CA 92653. Managing editors also welcome brief e-mail inquiries."

NEEDS "Managing editors seek first-rate projects and encourage artists who have not published articles before to submit ideas, as editorial assistance will be provided."

TERMS Competitive editorial compensation is provided for all published articles. "We may hold your sample for an extended period of time—9–12 months is common. Due to the large volume of artwork we receive, *Somerset Studio* will return only those submissions accompanied by sufficient postage in the form of cash, check, or money order made out to Stampington & Company. We cannot offer delivery confirmation; however, we are happy to put insurance on the submission. If you wish to have your artwork insured for the return journey, please include sufficient funds and indicate your preference in a postcard or letter enclosed with your submission. Please do not attach postage to packaging, and do not send loose postage stamps. Contributors from outside the US, please send cash, check, or money order in US funds to Stampington & Company. For questions regarding your artwork, please send inquiries to artmanagement@stampington.com."

SOMERSET STUDIO GALLERY

Somerset Studio Gallery, 22992 Mill Creek Dr., Laguna Hills CA 92653. E-mail: somersetstudiogallery@stampington.com. Website: www.stampington.com/somerset-gallery. "*Somerset Studio Gallery* is filled with hundreds of samples of extraordinary artwork presented up close and in detail. Whether your passion is rubber stamping, calligraphy, or paper crafting, the newest *Gallery* features everything you love about *Somerset Studio* in 200 lush pages, including enlightening how-to-articles, beautifully photographed projects, and hundreds of handmade creations by your favorite artists, as well as by you, our talented readers."

HOW TO CONTACT "We prefer submissions of original art. If original art is not available, our next preference is high-resolution digital images (300 dpi at 8½ × 10). If hi-res digital images are not available, we will very rarely consider professional-quality transparencies or color slides. Color-copy submissions are not accepted. All artwork must be identified with the artist's name, address, e-mail, and phone number clearly printed on a label attached to each sample. Inscribe your name and address somewhere on each piece of art. If you desire acknowledgment of artwork receipt, please include a self-addressed stamped postcard. If the artwork is three-dimensional, please attach your identification with a removable string, or pack the sample in a plastic bag with your identification. If you have a unique artistic technique you'd like to share with others, please send samples of your artwork accompanied by a query letter outlining your article idea to the respective managing editor at: Somerset Studio Gallery, 22992 Mill Creek Drive, Laguna Hills, CA 92653. Managing editors also welcome brief e-mail inquiries."

NEEDS "Managing editors seek first-rate projects and encourage artists who have not published articles before to submit ideas, as editorial assistance will be provided."

TERMS Competitive editorial compensation is provided for all published articles. "We may hold your sample for an extended period of time — 9 - 12 months is common. Due to the large volume of artwork we receive, *Somerset Studio Gallery* will return only those submissions accompanied by sufficient postage in the form of cash, check, or money order made out to Stampington & Company. We cannot offer delivery confirmation; however, we are happy to put insurance on the submission. If you wish to have your artwork insured for the return journey, please include sufficient funds and indicate your preference in a postcard or letter enclosed with your submission. Please do not attach postage to packaging, and do not send loose postage stamps.

Contributors from outside the US, please send cash, check, or money order in US funds to Stampington & Company. For questions regarding your artwork, please send inquiries to artmanagement@stampington.com."

SOMERSET WORKSHOP

Somerset Workshop, 22992 Mill Creek Dr., Laguna Hills CA 92653. E-mail: submissions@stampington.com. Website: www.stampington.com/somerset-workshop. "Learn fabulous techniques to help you make breathtaking projects that are illustrated from start to finish. All chapters in this 144-page book include simple stepped-out photographs with clear instructions to help you create exciting projects from some of the finest art and crafting instructors in our industry."

HOW TO CONTACT "We prefer submissions of original art. If original art is not available, our next preference is high-resolution digital images (300 dpi at 8½ × 10). If hi-res digital images are not available, we will very rarely consider professional-quality transparencies or color slides. Color-copy submissions are not accepted. All artwork must be identified with the artist's name, address, e-mail, and phone number clearly printed on a label attached to each sample. Inscribe your name and address somewhere on each piece of art. If you desire acknowledgment of artwork receipt, please include a self-addressed stamped postcard. If the artwork is three-dimensional, please attach your identification with a removable string, or pack the sample in a plastic bag with your identification. If you have a unique artistic technique you'd like to share with others, please send samples of your artwork accompanied by a query letter outlining your article idea to the respective managing editor at: Somerset Workshop, 22992 Mill Creek Drive, Laguna Hills, CA 92653. Managing editors also welcome brief e-mail inquiries."

NEEDS "Managing editors seek first-rate projects and encourage artists who have not published articles before to submit ideas, as editorial assistance will be provided."

TERMS Competitive editorial compensation is provided for all published articles. "We may hold your sample for an extended period of time—9–12 months is common. Due to the large volume of artwork we receive, Somerset Workshop will return only those submissions accompanied by sufficient postage in the form of cash, check, or money order

made out to Stampington & Company. We cannot offer delivery confirmation; however, we are happy to put insurance on the submission. If you wish to have your artwork insured for the return journey, please include sufficient funds and indicate your preference in a postcard or letter enclosed with your submission. Please do not attach postage to packaging, and do not send loose postage stamps. Contributors from outside the US, please send cash, check, or money order in US funds to Stampington & Company. For questions regarding your artwork, please send inquiries to artmanagement@stampington.com."

SPIN-OFF

Interweave Press, 4868 Innovation Dr., Fort Collins CO 80625. E-mail: spinoff@interweave.com. Website: www.spinningdaily.com. "*Spin-Off* is a quarterly magazine devoted to the interests of handspinners at all skill levels. Informative articles in each issue aim to encourage the novice, challenge the expert, and increase every spinner's working knowledge of this ancient and complex craft."

HOW TO CONTACT Guidelines available on website.

THE STAMPERS' SAMPLER

The Stamper's Sampler, 22992 Mill Creek Dr., Laguna Hills CA 92653. E-mail: thestamperssampler@stampington.com. Website: www.stampington.com/the-stampers-sampler. "This delightful magazine provides over 200 cards and stamped project ideas, complete with detailed shots and step-by-step instructions to provide an added dose of paper-crafting inspiration. The artwork contributed by our talented readers is published in full color on gorgeous, glossy paper stock. Newly revamped, this quarterly publication comes complete with a free bonus artist paper and almost 40 more pages of featured hand-stamped projects tucked inside. In every issue, readers will also find a free Tempting Template and unique challenge results to help spark their creativity."

HOW TO CONTACT "We prefer submissions of original art. If original art is not available, our next preference is high-resolution digital images (300 dpi at 8½ × 10). If hi-res digital images are not available, we will very rarely consider professional-quality transparencies or color slides. Color-copy submissions are not accepted. All artwork must be identified with the artist's name, address, e-mail, and phone number clearly printed on a label attached to each sample. Inscribe your name and address somewhere on each piece of art. If you desire acknowledgment of artwork receipt, please include a self-addressed stamped postcard. If the artwork is three-dimensional, please attach your identification with a removable string, or pack the sample in a plastic bag with your identification. If you have a unique artistic technique you'd like to share with others, please send samples of your artwork accompanied by a query letter outlining your article idea to the respective managing editor at: The Stamper's Sampler, 22992 Mill Creek Drive, Laguna Hills, CA 92653. Managing editors also welcome brief e-mail inquiries."

NEEDS "Managing editors seek first-rate projects and encourage artists who have not published articles before to submit ideas, as editorial assistance will be provided."

TERMS Competitive editorial compensation is provided for all published articles. "We may hold your sample for an extended period of time—9–12 months is common. Due to the large volume of artwork we receive, *The Stampers' Sampler* will return only those submissions accompanied by sufficient postage in the form of cash, check, or money order made out to Stampington & Company. We cannot offer delivery confirmation; however, we are happy to put insurance on the submission. If you wish to have your artwork insured for the return journey, please include sufficient funds and indicate your preference in a postcard or letter enclosed with your submission. Please do not attach postage to packaging, and do not send loose postage stamps. Contributors from outside the US, please send cash, check, or money order in US funds to Stampington & Company. For questions regarding your artwork, please send inquiries to artmanagement@stampington.com."

STEP BY STEP WIRE JEWELRY

620 W. Sedgwick St., Philadelphia PA 19119. E-mail: denise.peck@fwcommunity.com. Website: www.jewelrymakingdaily.com. Contact: Denise Peck. Step by Step Wire Jewelry is published 6 times/year by Interweave/FW Media. The magazine is project oriented, with step-by-step instructions for creating wire jewelry, as well as tips, tools, and techniques. Articles range from beginner to expert level. Writers must be able to substantiate that material submitted is an original design, accurate, and must make sure that all steps involved in the creation of the piece are feasible using the tools listed.

HOW TO CONTACT Guidelines available on website.

STITCH

E-mail: stitchsubmissions@interweave.com. Website: www.sewdaily.com. "*Stitch* is a special-issue sewing magazine all about creating with fabric and thread. Yes, it's sewing, but oh so much more. It's loaded with clever projects and modern designs for your wardrobe and home, inspiring designer profiles, plus hot trends, news, and inspiration from the global community of sewing. Whether you're just learning to sew or have been sewing forever, *Stitch* will inspire you to make beautiful things that showcase your unique point of view."

HOW TO CONTACT Guidelines available on website.

STUFFED

Stuffed, 22992 Mill Creek Dr., Laguna Hills CA 92653. E-mail: stuffed@stampington.com. Website: www.stampington.com/stuffed. *Stuffed* celebrates the loveable and huggable creatures known as "softies."

HOW TO CONTACT "We prefer submissions of original art. If original art is not available, our next preference is high-resolution digital images (300 dpi at 8½ × 10). If hi-res digital images are not available, we will very rarely consider professional-quality transparencies or color slides. Color-copy submissions are not accepted. All artwork must be identified with the artist's name, address, e-mail, and phone number clearly printed on a label attached to each sample. Inscribe your name and address somewhere on each piece of art. If you desire acknowledgment of artwork receipt, please include a self-addressed stamped postcard. If the artwork is three-dimensional, please attach your identification with a removable string, or pack the sample in a plastic bag with your identification. If you have a unique artistic technique you'd like to share with others, please send samples of your artwork accompanied by a query letter outlining your article idea to the respective managing editor at: Stuffed, 22992 Mill Creek Drive, Laguna Hills, CA 92653. Managing editors also welcome brief e-mail inquiries."

NEEDS "Managing editors seek first-rate projects and encourage artists who have not published articles before to submit ideas, as editorial assistance will be provided."

TERMS Competitive editorial compensation is provided for all published articles. "We may hold your sample for an extended period of time—9–12 months is common. Due to the large volume of artwork we receive, *Stuffed* will return only those submissions accompanied by sufficient postage in the form of cash, check, or money order made out to Stampington & Company. We cannot offer delivery confirmation; however, we are happy to put insurance on the submission. If you wish to have your artwork insured for the return journey, please include sufficient funds and indicate your preference in a postcard or letter enclosed with your submission. Please do not attach postage to packaging, and do not send loose postage stamps. Contributors from outside the US, please send cash, check, or money order in US funds to Stampington & Company. For questions regarding your artwork, please send inquiries to artmanagement@stampington.com."

TAKE TEN

Take Ten, 22992 Mill Creek Dr., Laguna Hills CA 92653. E-mail: taketen@stampington.com. Website: www.stampington.com/take-ten. From the publisher that brings you *The Stampers' Sampler* and *Somerset Studio* comes a 144-page special issue brimming with card ideas. *Take Ten* offers rubber stamp enthusiasts of all levels great ideas for creating quick and easy cards in 10 minutes or less. You'll find hundreds of full-color samples inside each volume of this unique publication.

HOW TO CONTACT "We prefer submissions of original art. If original art is not available, our next preference is high-resolution digital images (300 dpi at 8½ × 10). If hi-res digital images are not available, we will very rarely consider professional-quality transparencies or color slides. Color-copy submissions are not accepted. All artwork must be identified with the artist's name, address, e-mail, and phone number clearly printed on a label attached to each sample. Inscribe your name and address somewhere on each piece of art. If you desire acknowledgment of artwork receipt, please include a self-addressed stamped postcard. If the artwork is three-dimensional, please attach your identification with a removable string, or pack the sample in a plastic bag with your identification. If you have a unique artistic technique you'd like to share with others, please send samples of your artwork accompanied by a query letter outlining your article idea to the respective managing editor at: Take Ten, 22992 Mill Creek Drive, Laguna Hills, CA 92653. Managing editors also welcome brief e-mail inquiries."

NEEDS "Managing editors seek first rate projects and encourage artists who have not published articles before to submit ideas, as editorial assistance will be provided."

TERMS Competitive editorial compensation is provided for all published articles. "We may hold your sample for an extended period of time—9–12 months is common. Due to the large volume of artwork we receive, *Take Ten* will return only those submissions accompanied by sufficient postage in the form of cash, check, or money order made out to Stampington & Company. We cannot offer delivery confirmation; however, we are happy to put insurance on the submission. If you wish to have your artwork insured for the return journey, please include sufficient funds and indicate your preference in a postcard or letter enclosed with your submission. Please do not attach postage to packaging, and do not send loose postage stamps. Contributors from outside the US, please send cash, check, or money order in US funds to Stampington & Company. For questions regarding your artwork, please send inquiries to artmanagement@stampington.com."

🔱 TEXTILE FIBRE FORUM MAGAZINE

Website: www.artwearpublications.com.au/subscriptions/textile-fibre-forum-magazine.html. "*Textile Fibre Forum* has been in print since the 1980s. It has been under the ArtWear Publications banner since late 2011, with Janet De Boer and Marie-Therese Wisniowski as co-editors."

🔱 THE SIMPLE THINGS

E-mail: thesimplethings@futurenet.com. Website: www.thesimplethings.com. *The Simple Things* is published 13 times a year and celebrates the things that matter most.

THREADS

The Taunton Press, Inc., 63 South Main St., P.O. Box 5506, Newton CT 06470-5506. (800)309-9262. E-mail: th@taunton.com. Website: www.threadsmagazine. com. *Threads* is the trusted resource for both longtime sewers continuing to perfect their sewing skills and new sewers learning the fundamentals.

VINTAGE MADE MAGAZINE

Website: www.artwearpublications.com.au/subscriptions/vintage-made-magazine.html. "This great title is all about the love of vintage. It contains feature articles on dresses, hats, handbags and shoes, designer profiles, and items or places of historic interest. This is mixed with some handy tutorials, such as how to achieve that perfect vintage hairstyle, or make that essential accessory. The feature of each issue is the full-size dress pattern! The dress range is from a 32"–40" bust, with instructions and tips on where to make alterations. This has been multi-sized from a genuine vintage dress pattern."

VOGUE KNITTING INTERNATIONAL

Website: www.vogueknitting.com. "*Vogue Knitting* is the hand-knitting world's style leader and the magazine knitters turn to on a regular basis for inspirational patterns, chic styling, and compelling techniques."

WHERE WOMEN COOK

Where Women Cook, 22992 Mill Creek Dr., Laguna Hills CA 92653. E-mail: wherewomencook@stampington.com. Website: www.stampington.com/where-women-cook. "*Where Women Cook*, is an exciting publication packed to the brim with stunning photographs and heartwarming stories. Creative storage ideas, eye-catching décor, delicious food and drink recipes, and inspirational narratives will keep you intrigued from cover to cover."

HOW TO CONTACT "We prefer submissions of original art. If original art is not available, our next preference is high-resolution digital images (300 dpi at 8½ × 10). If hi-res digital images are not available, we will very rarely consider professional-quality transparencies or color slides. Color-copy submissions are not accepted. All artwork must be identified with the artist's name, address, e-mail, and phone number clearly printed on a label attached to each sample. Inscribe your name and address somewhere on each piece of art. If you desire acknowledgment of artwork receipt, please include a self-addressed stamped postcard. If the artwork is three-dimensional, please attach your identification with a removable string, or pack the sample in a plastic bag with your identification. If you have a unique artistic technique you'd like to share with others, please send samples of your artwork accompanied by a query letter outlining your article idea to the respective managing editor at: Where Women Cook, 22992 Mill Creek Drive, Laguna Hills, CA 92653. Managing editors also welcome brief e-mail inquiries."

NEEDS "Managing editors seek first-rate projects and encourage artists who have not published articles before to submit ideas, as editorial assistance will be provided."

TERMS Competitive editorial compensation is provided for all published articles. "We may hold your sample for an extended period of time—9–12 months is common. Due to the large volume of artwork we receive, *Where Women Cook* will return only those submissions accompanied by sufficient postage in the form of cash, check, or money order made out to Stampington & Company. We cannot offer delivery confirmation; however, we are happy to put insurance on the submission. If you wish to have your artwork insured for the return journey, please include sufficient funds and indicate your preference in a postcard or letter enclosed with your submission. Please do not attach postage to packaging, and do not send loose postage stamps. Contributors from outside the US, please send cash, check, or money order in US funds to Stampington & Company. For questions regarding your artwork, please send inquiries to artmanagement@stampington.com."

WHERE WOMEN CREATE

Where Women Create, 22992 Mill Creek Dr., Laguna Hills CA 92653. E-mail: wherewomencreate@stampington.com. Website: www.stampington.com/where-women-create. "*Where Women Create* invites you into the creative spaces of the most extraordinary women of our time. Through stunning photography and inspirational stories, each issue of this quarterly magazine will nourish souls and motivate creative processes."

HOW TO CONTACT "We prefer submissions of original art. If original art is not available, our next preference is high-resolution digital images (300 dpi at 8½ × 10). If hi res digital images are not available, we will very rarely consider professional-quality transparencies or color slides. Color-copy submissions are not accepted. All artwork must be identified with the artist's name, address, e-mail, and phone number clearly printed on a label attached to each sample. Inscribe your name and address somewhere on each piece of art. If you desire acknowledgment of artwork receipt, please include a self-addressed stamped postcard. If the artwork is three-dimensional, please attach your identification with a removable string, or pack the sample in a plastic bag with your identification. If you have a unique artistic technique you'd like to share with others, please send samples of your artwork accompanied by a query letter outlining your article idea to the respective managing editor at: Where Women Create, 22992 Mill Creek Drive, Laguna Hills, CA 92653. Managing editors also welcome brief e-mail inquiries."

NEEDS "Managing editors seek first-rate projects and encourage artists who have not published articles before to submit ideas, as editorial assistance will be provided."

TERMS Competitive editorial compensation is provided for all published articles. "We may hold your sample for an extended period of time—9-12 months is common. Due to the large volume of artwork we receive, *Where Women Create* will return only those submissions accompanied by sufficient postage in the form of cash, check, or money order made out to Stampington & Company. We cannot offer delivery confirmation; however, we are happy to put insurance on the submission. If you wish to have your artwork insured for the return journey, please include sufficient funds and indicate your preference in a postcard or letter enclosed with your submission. Please do not attach postage to packaging, and do not send loose postage stamps. Contributors from outside the US, please send cash, check, or money order in US funds to Stampington & Company. For questions regarding your artwork, please send inquiries to artmanagement@stampington.com."

WILLOW & SAGE

Willow & Sage, 22992 Mill Creek Dr., Laguna Hills CA 92653. E mail: willowandsage@stampington. com. Website: www.stampington.com/willow-and-sage. "This brand-new publication features stunning photography, alongside recipes for creating handmade items that soothe and replenish both body and soul. In addition to showcasing natural bath salts and soaks, soaps, face masks, sugar scrubs, how-to-use essential oils, and more, *Willow and Sage* magazine highlights the art of presentation—giving special attention to beautiful packaging—and reveals how to create fragrant spa kits and must-have gift bundles for any occasion."

HOW TO CONTACT "We prefer submissions of original art. If original art is not available, our next preference is high-resolution digital images (300 dpi at 8½ ×10). If hi-res digital images are not available, we will very rarely consider professional-quality transparencies or color slides. Color-copy submissions are not accepted. All artwork must be identified with the artist's name, address, e-mail, and phone number clearly printed on a label attached to each sample. Inscribe your name and address somewhere on each piece of art. If you desire acknowledgment of artwork receipt, please include a self-addressed stamped postcard. If the artwork is three-dimensional, please attach your identification with a removable string, or pack the sample in a plastic bag with your identification. If you have a unique artistic technique you'd like to share with others, please send samples of your artwork accompanied by a query letter outlining your article idea to the respective managing editor at: Willow & Sage, 22992 Mill Creek Drive, Laguna Hills, CA 92653 Managing editors also welcome brief e-mail inquiries."

NEEDS "Managing editors seek first-rate projects and encourage artists who have not published articles before to submit ideas, as editorial assistance will be provided."

TERMS Competitive editorial compensation is provided for all published articles. "We may hold your sample for an extended period of time—9-12 months is common. Due to the large volume of artwork we receive, Somerset Studio will return only those submissions accompanied by sufficient postage in the form of cash, check, or money order made out to Stampington & Company. We cannot offer delivery confirmation; however, we are happy to put insurance on the submission. If you wish to have your artwork insured for the return journey, please include sufficient funds and indicate your preference in a postcard or letter enclosed with your submission. Please do not attach postage to packaging, and do not send loose postage stamps. Contributors from outside the US, please send cash, check, or money order in US funds to Stampington & Company. For questions regarding your artwork, please send inquiries to artmanagement@stampington.com."

WOMAN'S DAY

300 W. 57th St., 28th flr., New York NY 10019. (212)649-2000. E-mail: womansday@hearst.com. Website: www.womansday.com. "*Woman's Day* is an indispensable resource to 20 million women. The brand speaks to our reader's values and focuses on what's important. We empower her with smart solutions for her core concerns—health, home, food, style and money, and celebrate the connection she cherishes with family, friends, and community. Whether in-book, online, mobile, or through social outlets, we provide inspiring insight and fresh ideas on how to get the most of everything."

HOW TO CONTACT "Our editors work almost exclusively with experienced writers who have clips from major national magazines. As a result, we accept unsolicited manuscripts only from writers with such credentials. There are no exceptions. If you do have significant national writing experience, and you have an idea or manuscript that you think might interest us, e-mail us at womansday@hearst.com, and please include some of your most recent clips."

☁ WOODCARVING

E-mail: helen.chrystie@thegmcgroup.com. Website: www.thegmcgroup.com. "*Woodcarving's* inspiring features, projects, technical articles and reviews have wide appeal—it is read in 57 countries worldwide. Featuring the work of top professionals and the most talented amateur carvers from around the world, it has a new, picture-led design which offers insight into the process of creating both great and humble carvings."

WOODCARVING MAGAZINE

E-mail: editors@woodcarvingillustrated.com. Website: www.woodcarvingillustrated.com. Magazine about woodcarving.

WOODCRAFT MAGAZINE

P.O. Box 7020, Parkersburg WV 26102-7020. (304)865-5268. Fax: (304)420-9840. E-mail: kiah_harpool@woodcraftmagazine.com. Website: www.woodcraftmagazine.com. Contact: Jim Harrold, editor-in-chief. Estab. 2005. Bimonthly trade magazine. Circ. 115,662. Sample available on request.

HOW TO CONTACT Request via e-mail Accepts unsolicited submissions. Approached by 15 project/pattern designers/year. Has featured projects/patters by Andy Rae, Marlen Kemmet, Craig Bentzley. Preferred subjects: woodworking. Submission format: PDF or DOC files. Include brief description and photos. Submit print-ready photography and step-by-step/assembly diagrams for proposal. Model and property release required. Photo captions required. Submit color photos and illustrations via CD, zip, e-mail as TIFF or JPEG files.

TERMS Send e-mail with project text, concepts, samples, photographs, and website. Keeps samples on file; send business card. Responds only if interested. Will negotiate rights with designers unwilling to sell. Finds freelancers by word of mouth.

TIPS "Read and understand the magazine."

THE WORLD OF CROSS STITCHING

Immediate Media Co. Bristol, 9th Floor Tower House, Fairfax St., Bristol United Kingdom BS4 3DH. Contact: Ruth Southorn, editor. Estab. 1997. Four weekly (13 issues/year) consumer magazine. "*The World of Cross Stitching* is a special-interest magazine focusing on cross-stitch projects with related cross-stitch/needlework-based feature articles for an audience who are primarily women ranging in age from late 20s-early 50s." Circ. 39,457.

HOW TO CONTACT Request via e-mail. Accepts unsolicited submissions. Approached by 4 project/pattern designers/year. Buys 90 project/pattern designs per issue from freelancers. Has featured projects/patterns by Joan Elliott, Maria Diaz, Jenny Barton, Susan Bates, Rhona Norrie, Margaret Sherry. Preferred subjects: cross-stitch. Submission format: JPEG, computer-generated cross-stitch charts. Include concept, sketch, or computer-designed chart. Model and property release preferred.

TERMS Send query letter or e-mail with résumé, project concepts, project samples, and website. Keeps samples on file; provide self-promotion piece to be kept for possible future assignment.

Responds in 1 week. Pays $320 maximum for project/pattern design; $100 maximum for industry related articles; pay also varies based on experience, design complexity, size of design. Credit line given. Pays on publication. Buys publication (digital & print) and syndication rights only. Finds freelancers through agent/reps, submissions, word of mouth, magazines, online. Undergoes technical edit before publication.

TIPS "Definitely read our magazine for indication of current style/fresh feel required. I am interested in a wide variety of design subject themes and techniques (e.g., whole stitch only vs. factional stitch, blackwork/assisi, techniques using specialty threads/metallic thread accents/bead detailing for more complex designs). When contacting me, let me know some details of your typical design style/interests, details of any particular subject areas which you are specifically interested in, with my requirements in mind. It is imperative that I can rely on freelance designers to adhere to our strict deadlines. The majority of our projects are worked on 14-count white aida to suit our audience, however, evenweave/linen fabrics are regularly used too, along with hand-dyed fabrics. Although it is not common for me to accept designs as a result of direct submission, it has occasionally happened. It is more common that I discover a new freelance designer as a result of them getting in touch. When submitting ideas please indicate: 1)a suggestion of the finished design size (stitch count) and suggestion(s) for fabric usage; 2)ideas of color palette to be used, if a pencil sketch only and color submission is not supplied; 3) indication of techniques involved, so that I might get an idea of what experience level of stitcher will enjoy this design; 4)any ideas for possible finishing."

YARN MAGAZINE

Website: www.artwearpublications.com.au/subscriptions/yarn-magazine.html. "Features patterns covering a wide range of skill sets and techniques, from beginner to advanced."

ONLINE COMMUNITIES

The actual act of crafting—working with our hands to create a unique item—can be, by its very nature, solitary. Most of the time, crafting is a one-person job, and working from a home studio can be isolating. That's why it's so important to become part of the craft community. Connecting with other people who understand what you do and the personal toll it can take is valuable for a myriad of reasons. Not only do communities of like-minded people help encourage and inspire one another, they can be a valuable resource when questions arise. It's likely that you are not the first person to have a certain question or run up against a certain problem, and a member of your community will almost always be willing to lend a helping hand or offer an opinion. Remember to give back as much as you take! If you can help out another member of your community, lending a helping hand makes for a stronger group.

In the same way, keep in mind that the very community you look to for advice and support may also be your primary sales demographic! Joining a community as a member first and a seller second (or last!) makes real relationships built on trust—not commerce—possible. Look through the following listings for national organizations and online groups that are applicable to you and your craft, but also look into your local community for small craft groups that can provide in-person interaction. Searching through Meetup.com is a good way to find local groups with similar interests, as well as asking at your favorite craft store. If no groups exist, consider starting your own. Join a guild or take a class at a local shop, and begin building relationships. Soon, you'll know enough people to form a mini group with the exact focus you had in mind.

Break out of your studio every so often and check in with your fellow crafters. They may turn into your biggest supporters and your most reliable market research.

KEY TO SYMBOLS & ABBREVIATIONS

⊕	Canadian market
⬤	market located outside of the U.S. and Canada
⌂	market prefers to work with local artists/designers
b&w	black & white (photo or illustration)
SASE	self-addressed, stamped envelope
SAE	self-addressed envelope
IRC	International Reply Coupon, for use when mailing to countries other than your own

COMPLAINT PROCEDURE

If you feel you have not been treated fairly by a company listed in *Crafter's Market*, we advise you to take the following steps:

- First, try to contact the company. Sometimes one e-mail or letter can quickly clear up the matter.
- Document all your correspondence with the company. If you write to us with a complaint, provide the details of your submission, the date of your first contact with the company, and the nature of your subsequent correspondence.
- We will enter your complaint into our files.
- The number and severity of complaints will be considered in our decision whether to delete the listing from the next edition.
- We reserve the right to not list any company for any reason.

ALLIANCE FOR SUSTAINABLE ARTS PROFESSIONAL PRACTICES

Website: www.artflock.org. Estab. 2008. The Alliance for Sustainable Arts Professional Practices is a coalition of not-for-profit arts institutions in the New York area that share resources, methods, and best practices with artists as they build and manage their professional lives. Membership cost: Annual dues are based upon the organization's current operating budge (see website for details). Membership restrictions: nonprofit organizations offering professional practices programs. Goal/mission: "to identify overlaps and gaps in offerings, assist in inter-organizational collaborations, and to strengthen each individual organization's visibility and outreach to the arts community." Who should join: not-for-profit arts organizations and arts-related businesses dedicated to sharing professional development opportunities and best practice resources with artists in the New York City area.

AMERICAN CRAFT COUNCIL

(612)206-3100. E-mail: council@craftcouncil.org. Website: www.craftcouncil.org. Estab. 1943. National/international guild, professional resource. Membership cost: standard, $40/yr ($55/yr outside U.S.); professional, $55/yr. Membership restrictions: standard, none; professional, craft artists. Goal/mission: "We champion craft." Who should join: students, collectors, scholars, enthusiasts, craft artists. Sells advertisement space on website, in magazine; contact Joanne Smith (jsmith@craftcouncil.org) for advertising rates. **TIPS** "Know the best practices when woodworking. From safety to tool use, to finishes and types of wood. It's important to have a wide range of woodworking knowledge and be able to express it on camera or in writing. Our videos & articles are a great resource for all levels of woodworkers. We have over 400 articles & 400 videos which have in-depth woodworking instructions. We encourage woodworkers to get back in the shop."

AMERICAN NEEDLEPOINT GUILD

(608)443-2476. Fax: (608)443-2474 or (608)443-2478. E-mail: membership@needlepoint.org. Website: www.needlepoint.org. Estab. 1972. National/international guild, online community, online forum, professional resource. Membership cost: $40/yr; Canada/Mexico $52/yr; all other international $60/yr; lifetime

$2,000; international lifetime $2,200. Membership restrictions: none. Goal/mission: "educational and cultural development through participation in and encouragement of interest in the art of needlepoint." Who should join: all stitchers.

AMERICAN QUILTER'S SOCIETY

(270)898-7903 or (800)626-5420. Fax: (270)898-1173. Website: www.americanquilter.com. Estab. 1984. National/international guild, online community, online forum, professional resource. Membership cost: $25/yr. Membership restrictions: standard, none; professional, craft artists. Goal/mission: to provide a forum for quilters of all skill levels to expand their horizons in quilt making, design, self-expression, and quilt collecting. Who should join: quilters. Sells advertisement space on website, in magazine; see website for media kit and advertising specifics.

AMERICAN SEWING GUILD

(713)729-3000. Fax: (713)721-9230. Website: www.asg.org. Estab. 1984. National/international guild, online community, online forum, professional resource, professional networking tool. Membership cost: varies, see website. Membership restrictions: none. Goal/mission: to help members learn new sewing skills, network with others who share an interest in sewing, and participate in community service sewing projects. Who should join: sewing enthusiasts. Sells advertisement space through magazine; e-mail (advertising@asg.org) for rates.

THE ART QUILT ASSOCIATION

Grand Junction CO. E-mail: info@theartquiltassociation.com. Website: www.theartquiltassociation.com. Estab. 1996. National/international guild, professional resource. Membership cost: $25/yr. Membership restrictions: none. Mission/goal: "to explore textile manipulation and diversity of mixed media as an art form." Who should join: those interested in art quilt.

ASSOCIATION OF SEWING AND DESIGN PROFESSIONALS

(877)755-0303. E-mail: admin@sewingprofessionals.org. Website: www.paccprofessionals.org. Estab. 1984.

National/international guild, online community, online forum, professional resource, professional networking tool. Membership cost: varies, see website. Membership restrictions: none. Goal/mission: to support individuals engaged in sewing and design-related businesses, in both commercial and home-based settings. Educating the general public about the unique and valuable services offered by sewing and design professionals. Who should join: sewing professionals. Sells advertisement space in newsletter; e-mail (advertising@sewingprofessionals.org.) for rates or see website.

BURDA STYLE

Website: www.burdastyle.com. Estab. 2007. Online community, online forum. Membership cost: none. Membership restrictions: none. Goal/mission: to bring the traditional craft of sewing to a new generation of fashion designers, sewing hobbyists, DIYers, and anyone looking to sew something. Who should join: people passionate about sewing. Sells advertisement space; e-mail (maryeveholder@comcast.net) for rates or see website.

CERAMIC ARTS DAILY

(614)794-5843. Fax: (614)794-5842. Website: www.ceramicartsdaily.org. Online community, online forum. Membership cost: none. Membership restrictions: none. Goal/mission: "CeramicArtsDaily.org provides a wide array of tools for learning about and improving skills, and a place for artists to display their work and to share ideas and perspectives about how their art and life interact to shape each other." Who should join: active potters & ceramic artists; those interested in learning about ceramics. Sells advertisement space; e-mail (mbracht@ceramics.org) for rates or see website.

CLAYSTATION

Website: www.claystation.com. Online community, online forum. Membership cost: none. Membership restrictions: none. Goal/mission: "to be a social research network for the ceramic arts." Who should join: people with an interest in ceramic arts. Sells advertisement space; see website for rates.

CRAFT & HOBBY ASSOCIATION

319 E. 54th St., Elmwood Park NJ 07407. (201)835-1200. E-mail: info@craftandhobby.org. Website: www.craftandhobby.org. Estab. 2004. National/international guild, online community, online forum, professional resource, virtual classroom, professional networking tool. Membership cost: varies. Membership restrictions: none. Goal/mission: "to create a vibrant industry with an exciting image, an expanding customer base, and successful members." Who should join: suppliers, buyers, industry professionals in craft. Sells advertisement space; see website for rates.

CRAFT BANTER

Website: www.craftbanter.com. Online forum. Membership cost: none. Membership restrictions: none. Goal/mission: "to be a craft forum acting as a gateway to the finest craft-related newsgroups." Who should join: people interested in crafts.

CRAFTSTER

Website: www.craftster.org. Online community. Membership cost: none. Membership restrictions: none. Goal/mission: provide a community for indie crafts. Who should join: people interested in crafts. Sells advertisement; see website for details.

CRAFT YARN COUNCIL OF AMERICA

(704)824-7838. Fax: (704)671-2366. Website: www.craftyarncouncil.com. Online community, online forum, professional resource. Membership cost: none. Membership restrictions: none. Goal/mission: "to provide educational resources." Who should join: yarn companies, accessory manufacturers, magazine, book publishers, and consultants in the yarn industry.

THE CROCHET CROWD

10 Mullen Drive, P.O. Box 473, Walkerton, Ontario N0G 2V0 Canada. E-mail: MikeysHelpDesk@hotmail.com. Website: www.thecrochetcrowd.com. Estab. 2008. Online community, online forum. Membership cost: none. Membership restrictions: none. Mission/goal: "to educate the consumer which leads to confident feel-good buying power from the consumer that benefits distributors & manufacturers."

Who should join: those interested in crochet. Sells advertisement; see website for details.

CROCHET GUILD OF AMERICA

1100-H Brandywine Blvd., Zanesville OH 43701. (740)452-4541. Fax: (740)452-2552. Website: www.crochet.org. National/international guild, online forum. Membership cost: varies. Membership restrictions: none. Goal/mission: to educate the public about crochet, provide education and networking opportunities, and set a national standard for the quality, art, and skill of crochet through creative endeavors. Who should join: all those who desire to perpetuate the art and skill of crochet.

CROCHET ME

Website: www.crochetme.com. Online community. Membership cost: free. Membership restrictions: none. Who should join: those interested in crochet. Sells advertisement; see website for information.

CROCHETVILLE

Website: www.crochetville.com. Estab. 2004. Online community. Membership cost: none. Membership restrictions: none. Who should join: those interested in crochet.

DEVIANTART

Website: www.deviantart.com. Online community. Preferred subjets: art. Membership cost: none. Membership restrictions: none. Goal/mission: "to entertain, inspire, and empower the artist in all of us." Who should join: artists & art enthusiasts. Sells advertisement on website.

EMBROIDERER'S GUILD OF AMERICA

1355 Bardstown Rd., Suite 157, Louisville KY 40204. (502)589-6956. Fax: (502)584-7900. Website: www.egausa.org. Estab. 1970. National/international guild. Membership cost: varies. Membership restrictions: none. Goal/mission: "to promote cooperation and the exchange of ideas among those who are engaged in needlework throughout the world." Who should join: anyone interested in embroidery.

GANOKSIN

E-mail: service@ganoksin.com. Website: www.ganoksin.com. Estab. 1970. Online community, online forum, professional resource. Preferred subjects: gem & jewelry. Membership cost: none. Membership restrictions: none. Goal/mission: "to educate, improve working conditions, and facilitate sharing between goldsmiths globally." Who should join: jewelers, professionals, hobbyists. Sells advertisement on website, e-mail blasts, and online video network; see website for rates.

THE GUILD OF JEWELLERY DESIGNERS

Hockley, Birmingham West Midlands, United Kingdom. E-mail: alan@guildofjewellerydesigners.co.uk. Website: www.guildofjewellerydesigners.co.uk. International guild, online community, online forum. Membership cost: free; various paid options. Membership restrictions: none. Mission/goal: "to help promote UK jewelery designers." Who should join: Jewelery designers based in the UK. Sells advertisement; see website for details.

HANDMADE ARTISTS

P.O. Box 530, Point Pleasant NJ 08742. E-mail: admin@handmadeartistsshop.com. Website: www.handmadeartists.com. Online community, online forum. Membership cost: none. Membership restrictions: none. Goal/mission: "community of people banded together in an effort to support each other and handmade." Who should join: creative people who work with their hands.

HOME SEWING ASSOCIATION

P.O. Box 369, Monroeville PA 15146. Website: www.sewing.org. Online community, online forum. Membership cost: none. Membership restrictions: none. Sells advertisement; see website for rates.

INDIE BUSINESS NETWORK

206-B N. Hayne St., Monroe NC 28112. (908)444-6343. Website: www.indiebusinessnetwork.com. Online community, online forum, professional resource, professional networking tool. Membership cost: varies. Membership restrictions: none. Goal/mission:

to empower and to encourage the success of creative entrepreneurs. Who should join: manufacturers of handmade soaps, cosmetics, candles, artisan perfumes, aromatherapy products, jewelry, baked goods, confections, and other artisnal consumer products.

INSTRUCTABLES

E-mail: info@instructables.com. Website: www.instructables.com. Online community, online forum, virtual classroom. Membership cost: free; paid options also available. Membership restrictions: none. Goal/mission: to share projects, connect with others, and make an impact on the world. Who should join: creative people who make things. Sells advertisement. See website for details.

INTERNATIONAL POLYMER CLAY ASSOCIATION

162 Lake St, Haverhill MA 01832. Website: www.theipca.org. National/international guild, professional resource. Membership cost: varies. Membership restrictions: none. Goal/mission: to educate the public about polymer clay, and to study and promote an interest in the use of polymer clay as an artistic medium. Who should join: those interested in the art of polymer clay.

INTERNATIONAL QUILT ASSOCIATION

7660 Woodway, Suite 550, Houston TX 77063. (713)781-6882. Fax: (713)781-8182. E-mail: iqa@quilts.com. Website: www.quilts.org. Estab. 1979. Nonprofit organization. Membership cost: varies. Membership restrictions: only open to individuals. Goal/mission: "dedicated to the preservation of the art of quilting, the attainment of public recognition for quilting as an art form, and the advancement of the state of the art throughout the world." Who should join: individuals interested in the art of quilting.

JEWELRY MAKING DAILY

Website: www.jewelrymakingdaily.com. Estab. 1979. Online community, online forum. Membership cost: free. Membership restrictions: none. Who should join: those interested in jewelry making. Sells advertisement; see website for details.

KNITPICKS

(800)574-1323. Website: www.knitpicks.com. "From beginners knitting tutorials to advanced techniques, our huge index of free videos and step-by-step tutorials on knitting, crocheting, & other fiber crafts will solve all of your 'how-to' questions."

KNITTER'S REVIEW

Website: www.knittersreview.com. Online community, online forum. Membership cost: free. Membership restrictions: none. Goal/mission: "to provide quality product information to help knitters make informed purchasing decisions and, ultimately, have a more fulfilling lifelong knitting experience." Who should join: serious fiber enthusiasts of all skill levels.

◉ KNITTING & CROCHET GUILD

Unit 4, Lee Mills Industrial Estate, St. Georges Road, Scholes Holmfirth HD9 1RT, United Kingdom. E-mail: secretary@kcguild.org.uk. Website: www.kcguild.org.uk. Estab. 1978. International guild. Membership cost: £25. Membership restrictions: none. Goal/mission: "to share and develop skills, knowledge, and enthusiasm about hand knitting, machine knitting, and crochet." Who should join: all levels of knitters, crocheters, from beginners to professionals.

KNITTING DAILY

Website: www.knittingdaily.com. Online community, online forum. Membership cost: free. Membership restrictions: none. Who should join: those interested in knitting. Sells advertisement; see website for details.

THE KNITTING GUILD ASSOCIATION

1100-H Brandywine Blvd., Zanesville OH 43701-7303. (740)452-4541. E-mail: TKGA@TKGA.com. Website: www.tkga.com. National/international guild, local guild, online community, online forum. Membership cost: varies. Membership restrictions: none. Mission/goal: "representing you and your stitching art to the world." Who should join: knitters. Sells advertisement in magazine; see website for details.

KNITTING HELP

P.O. Box 3306, Amherst CA 01004. E-mail: amy@ knittinghelp.com. Website: www.knittinghelp.com. Estab. 2004. Online community, online forum, virtual classroom. Membership cost: free. Membership restrictions: none. Who should join: those interested in knitting. Sells advertisement; contact sheldon@ knittinghelp.com for details.

KNITTING PARADISE

382 NE 191st St., #74906, Miami FL 33179. E-mail: info@knittingparadise.com. Website: www.knittingparadise.com. Online community, online forum. Membership cost: free. Membership restrictions: none. Who should join: those interested in knitting.

KNITTING UNIVERSE

P. O. Box 965, Sioux Falls SD 57101-0965. (800)232-5648. Fax: (605)338-2994. Website: www.knittinguniverse.com. Online community. Membership cost: none. Membership restrictions: none. Who should join: all levels of knitters.

THE MODERN QUILT GUILD

4470 W. Sunset Blvd., #226, Los Angeles CA 90027. (740)452-4541. E-mail: info@themodernquiltguild. com. Website: www.themodernquiltguild.com. Estab. 2009. National/international guild, local guild, online community, online forum. Membership cost: varies. Membership restrictions: none. Mission/goal: "to support and encourage the growth and development of modern quilting through art, education, and community." Who should join: modern quilters.

NATIONAL ACADEMY OF NEEDLE ARTS

E-mail: membership@needleart.org. Website: www. needleart.org. Estab. 1985. National/international guild, professional resource. Membership cost: varies. Membership restrictions: none. Mission/goal: "to educate and elevate needlework to NeedleART in the works of creative expression known as art." Who should join: those interested in needlework.

THE NATIONAL NEEDLE ARTS ASSOCIATION

1100-H Brandywine Blvd., Zanesville OH 43701-7303. (800)889-8662; (740)455-6773. E-mail: info@tnna. org. Website: www.tnna.org. Membership organization, professional resource, professional networking tool. Membership cost: varies. Membership restrictions: open only to verifiable businesses providing services and/or products for the needlearts industry. Mission/goal: "The National NeedleArts Association advances its community of professional businesses by encouraging the passion for needlearts through education, industry knowledge exchange, and a strong marketplace." Who should join: businesses providing services and/or products for the needlearts industry.

THE NATIONAL QUILTING ASSOCIATION

P.O. Box 12190, Columbus OH 43212-0190. (614)488-8520. Fax: (614)488-8521. Website: www.nqaquilts. org. Estab. 1970. Nonprofit organization. Membership cost: varies. Membership restrictions: none. Mission/goal: "The National Quilting Association, Inc., promotes the art, craft, and legacy of quiltmaking, encouraging high standards through education, preservation, and philanthropic endeavors." Who should join: quilters.

OH MY! HANDMADE GOODNESS

Website: www.ohmyhandmade.com. Estab. 2010. Online community, professional resource. Membership cost: see website. Membership restrictions: none. Mission/goal: "gather makers & entrepreneurs to cooperatively share their knowledge, resources, peer support, and mentorship." Who should join: creative makers & entrepreneurs. Sells advertisement; see website for details.

PALMER/PLETSCH

1801 NW, Upshur St., Suite 100, Portland OR 97209. Website: www.palmerpletsch.com. Professional resource, virtual classroom. Membership cost: see website for details. Membership restrictions: none. Who should join: those interested in sewing.

PINTEREST

Website: www.pinterest.com. Online community. Membership cost: free. Membership restrictions: none. Who should join: anyone.

PRECIOUS METAL CLAY GUILD

Website: www.pmcguild.com. National/international guild, local guild, online community, professional resource, Membership cost: free. Membership restrictions: none. Mission/goal: "to serve as the ambassador of Precious Metal Clay™." Who should join: those interested in working with precious metal clay.

QNNTV

E-mail: customerservice@qnntv.com. Website: www.qnntv.com. Estab. 2007. Online community, virtual classroom. Preferred subjects: quilting. Membership cost: $69.99/yr. Membership restrictions: none. Goal/mission: "A division of F+W, A Content + eCommerce Company, QNNtv launched in 2007 and is your top online resource for quilting videos. QNNtv videos are streamed and available to members worldwide, 24/7, from any computer or handheld device with a high-speed internet connection. The mobility of QNNtv makes it easy to watch the online quilting videos from the comfort of your home or on the go from your mobile device! Whether you want to perfect quilt-finishing techniques, learn how to resize quilt blocks, make a fast, easy quilt, or learn new quilting techniques, QNNtv has all the quilting videos you want and need to improve your skills. You will find quilting videos compatible with your current skill level, from instructors you can trust. Learn from experts like Patrick Lose in Quilting Celebrations, Eleanor Burns in Quilt in a Day, Mark Lipinski & Jodie Davis in Quilt Out Loud, Mary Fons in Quilty, and many many more. If you're ready to propel yourself to advance your quilting skills, sign up for QNNtv with a membership option that's right for you." Who should join: open to all. Hires speakers/lecturers, class teachers, workshop/retreat leaders, pattern creators. Sells advertisement space on website, in newsletter and e-mail blast; contact Cristy Adamski (Cristy.Adamski@fwcommunity.com) for advertising rates.

QUILTERS CLUB OF AMERICA

(888)253-0203. E-mail: admin@quiltersclubofamerica.com. Website: www.quiltersclubofamerica.com. Affinity quilting club, online community. Membership cost: free; $29.95/yr. Membership restrictions: none. Mission/goal: "to help members enhance their knowledge, skill, and enjoyment of quilting." Who should join: enthusiastic quilters.

QUILTING BOARD

E-mail: info@quiltingboard.com. Website: www.quiltingboard.com. Online forum. Membership cost: free. Membership restrictions: none. Who should join: quilters.

QUILTING DAILY

Website: www.quiltingdaily.com. Online community, online forum. Membership cost: free. Membership restrictions: none. Who should join: those interested in quilting. Sells advertisement; see website for details.

RAVELRY

203 Washington St., #244, Salem MA 01970. Website: www.ravelry.com. Online community. Membership cost: free. Membership restrictions: none. Who should join: knitters & crocheters. Sells advertisement; see website for details.

SCRAPBOOKING SOCIETY

Website: www.scrapbookingsociety.com. Online community. Membership cost: free. Membership restrictions: none. Who should join: those interested in scrapbooking. Sells advertisement; see website for details.

SEAMS

4921-C Broad River Rd., Columbia SC 29212. (803)772-5861. Fax: (803)731-7709. E-mail: info@seams.org. Website: www.seams.org. Nonprofit organization, professional resource. Membership cost: varies. Membership restrictions: none. Mission/goal: "to support the resurging US-sewn products industry by using membership networking and collaboration, offering members benefit packages that help control overhead expenses, giving members access to educational programs to help improve the quality and productivity of their companies and the industry as a whole, and keeping members informed about legislation in Washington, D.C., that may impact the industry." Who should join: sewn products manufacturing and contract manufacturing companies and their suppliers.

STUDIO ART QUILT ASSOCIATES

P.O. Box 572, Storrs CT 06268-0572. (860)487-4199. E-mail: info@SAQA.com. Website: www.saqa.com. Estab. 1989. Nonprofit organization, professional resource. Membership cost: varies. Membership restrictions: none. Mission/goal: "to promote the art quilt through education, exhibitions, professional development, documentation, and publications." Who should join: artists, teachers, collectors, galler owners, museum curators, and corporate sponsors.

THE SWITCHBOARDS

Website: www.theswitchboards.com. Online community, online forum, professional resource, professional networking tool. Membership cost: $12/month; $97/yr. Membership restrictions: none. Mission/goal: "TSB is an online hub that plays hostess to crafty and crafty service-related businesses." Who should join: crafters, bloggers, web designers, photographers, artists, coaches.

TEXTILE SOCIETY OF AMERICA

P.O. Box 5617, Berkeley CA 94705. (510)363-4541. E-mail: tsa@textilesociety.org. Website: www.textilesocietyofamerica.org. Estab. 1987. Nonprofit organization, professional resource. Membership cost: varies. Membership restrictions: none. Mission/goal: "dedicated to promoting and exchanging knowledge about textiles." Who should join: those interested in textiles.

WEAVOLUTION

7 St. Paul St., Suite 1660, Baltimore MD 21202. Website: www.weavolution.com. Online community, online forum. Membership cost: none. Membership restrictions: none. Mission/goal: "to have a website exclusively for handweavers where members could post drafts, pictures, details about their projects, and to share ideas and struggles with each other." Who should join: handweavers.

WOODWORKERS GUILD OF AMERICA

Website: www.wwgoa.com. Contact: George Vondriska, managing editor. National/international guild, online community, professional resource. Preferred subjects: woodworking. Membership cost: free or paid; premium membership $29.98/year. Membership restrictions: none. Goal/mission: "to provide our members with the best instructional woodworking videos, articles and plans on the Internet. As well as foster a community where woodworkers can join together to share ideas & experiences." Who should join: woodworkers of all levels. Hires crafters/artisans as speakers/lecturers, blog/online article writers, online video talent. Sells advertisement space on website, newsletter, e-mail blasts; contact Jim Kopp (jimk@wwgoa.com) for advertising rates & options. Site traffic: 10,000 visits per day; 5,500 unique visits per day; 41,495 Facebook fans.

TIPS "Know the best practices when woodworking. From safety to tool use, to finishes and types of wood. It's important to have a wide range of woodworking knowledge and be able to express it on camera or in writing. Our videos & articles are a great resource for all level of woodworkers. We have over 400 articles & 400 videos which have in-depth woodworking instructions. We encourage woodworkers to get back in the shop."

RETREATS

Many crafters realize that the way to make their business a success is through diversification. Focusing on one specific area of sales can limit your potential income. So, when you run an online shop, sell at trade shows, have commissioned work in galleries, and regularly work with a publisher, what's left? Teaching!

While you can certainly find ways to teach locally, many find teaching at art and craft retreats to be a wonderful way to reach new audiences, open up new revenue streams and, in some cases, relax at the same time. This section lists national and international retreats geared towards creative souls. If you haven't considered teaching at a retreat, you really should. These types of events are an investment on the student's part, and you'll find they are very eager learners. Quite often, students attend the same retreat year after year because of the wonderful sense of community and knowledge they take away. If you're feeling adventurous and want to know more about organizing and putting on a retreat of your own, be sure to read Heather Power's article "Hosting Creative Retreats."

But what if you aren't ready to teach your own craft? If you're still growing your skills and expanding your knowledge on a particular subject, then this section is for you, too. Investing in attending a craft retreat centered around your specific medium can be an incredibly rewarding experience. Immersing yourself in your craft can feed your inspiration, develop your talents and foster relationships with fellow attendees that last a lifetime. Take time to research the retreat you're considering taking, talk with other students, and ask about their experiences. When you get there, be open to the possibilities!

KEY TO SYMBOLS & ABBREVIATIONS

☘	Canadian market
⬤	market located outside of the U.S. and Canada
⌂	market prefers to work with local artists/designers
b&w	black & white (photo or illustration)
SASE	self-addressed, stamped envelope
SAE	self-addressed envelope
IRC	International Reply Coupon, for use when mailing to countries other than your own

ADORN ME

Phoenix Rising Productions, P.O. Box 37338, Phoenix AZ 85069-7338. E-mail: info@artunraveled.com. Website: www.artunraveled.com. "Won't you join us for artful days filled with creativity, joy and laughter? Join in the camaraderie and forge lifelong friendships while learning and creating in workshops taught by internationally known artists. With over 50 workshops to choose from, there's something for everyone. This year we've added a few mixed-media workshops, so please check out the workshops page for the daily schedule. Come for one workshop or for many—we hope you'll decide to join us to have the time of your life—art experiences like no other!"

ALABAMA CHANIN

The Factory, 462 Lane Dr., Florence AL 35630. E-mail: office@alabamachanin.com. Website: www.alabamachanin.com. "We provide materials, know-how, local cuisine, and so much more at each of our workshops. Work with our instructors and immerse yourself in slow design and manufacturing."

AN ARTISTS' RETREAT
WITH ANNA RHODES

(206)328-1788. E-mail: annarhodes@anartistsretreat.com. Website: www.anartistsretreat.com. "An Artists' Retreat™ with Anna Rhodes- for the inquisitive beginner, the seasoned artist, and anyone wishing to expand creative potential. This is an in-depth concentrated art course designed to encourage instinctive, confident creativity through developing skill and imagination within a creative community. Students experience the unfolding of their unique style and palette and will have the opportunity to explore the wonders of a wide array of the finest pigments, pencils, papers, and brushes. Through drawing and composing, painting and layering mixtures of mediums, personalized instruction and group discussion, we will use both experimental and traditional techniques to guide our travels through realism, impressionism, and into the realm of magic."

ARKANSAS FIBER FEST

E-mail: arfiberfest@gmail.com. Website: www.arfiberfest.com. Estab. 2007. "This is an annual gathering for knitters, crocheters, spinners, weavers, and all fiber arts lovers."

ARROW ROCK QUILT CAMP

(660)837-3268. E-mail: lblevins@iland.net. Website: www.arrowrockquiltcamp.com. "Arrow Rock Quilt Camp is all about giving quilters a relaxed atmosphere in which they can learn new techniques, eat well, make new friends, and have a good time."

ART & SOUL

Art and Soul Retreats, 30231 SE Wheeler Rd, Boring OR 97009. E-mail: info@artandsoulretreat.com. Website: www.artandsoulretreat.com. Estab. 1999. "Art and Soul is the premier mixed-media art retreat in the United States. We offer an exciting week of classes taught by a select group of professional and inspiring instructors. Our diverse lineup of classes include mixed media, painting, fiber, encaustic, assemblage, metal, jewelry, fabric, and paper art. This event is more then a retreat and learning process, it's an unforgettable time spent with your artistic tribe that will create many happy memories. Art is created, friends are made, joy is everywhere. Join us for an amazing experience that feeds your heart and soul."

ARTISTIC ALCHEMY: A TAHOE RETREAT
FOR CREATIVE SEWISTS AND QUILTERS

Website: www.artisticalchemyblog.wordpress.com. "We come together for this retreat, in a magical spot on Lake Tahoe, to offer you the chance to discover your own alchemy as you explore the concepts and techniques of quilting and clothing arts."

ART IS YOU

E-mail: visuallyspeakingllc@gmail.com. Website: www.eatcakecreate.com. Estab. 2005. "Our philosophy is to create a moment in time where artists, whether they be faculty or students, can come together to share in their passion for creativity. To create, self-nourish, replenish personal creative resources and to nurture not only individual souls but the souls of those around them. Whether creating something is part of your daily routine or indeed the closest to creating has been using a glue stick, there is something for everybody."

ART QUILT SANTA FE

E-mail: aqsf@att.net. Website: www.artquiltsantafe. com. "Art Quilt Santa Fe is a quilt workshop, a fiber art workshop, and a quilt retreat dedicated to supplying a unique Santa Fe experience. We provide workshops that include quilting techniques, fiber art techniques, understanding color and design, working on and creating quilts under the mentoring and direction of experienced nationally known teachers and quilters."

ART RETREAT AT THE DESERT

E-mail: barb@vivimagoo.com. Website: www.vivimagoo.com/prairie. "Just one of a series of art retreats across our beautiful country! This retreat provides little bits of heaven where creative souls can meet, be inspired by each other, create unique art taught by renowned instructors, and return home energized and touched in some way by the experience."

ART RETREAT AT THE PRAIRIE

E-mail: barb@vivimagoo.com. Website: www. vivimagoo.com/prairie. "Our outstanding lineup of instructors inspires our students to create beautiful pieces, and our amazing students create the most warm and welcoming atmosphere to create friendships. We hope you'll join us at the upcoming art retreat at the prairie."

ART RETREAT CAMP

E-mail: susan@artstreamstudios.com. Website: www.artstreamstudios.com/arc/index.htm#. VZK95_lVhBc. "A private rustic island brimming with natural wonder surrounded by crystal-clear waters is nothing short of a breathtaking place to begin. This is the place to restart. To rediscover what is important within you from a place of wonder. The creative you will come out to PLAY. At artstream we take play seriously. We created this intimate summer retreat as a quiet experience for you to breathe in all that nature has to offer. While opening up to the creative play we have in store for you. With kindred spirits. And with expert guides that will help spark discovery through playful processes. It's a deeply refreshing experience unlike any other and we want you to join us on the island this year."

BEAD CRUISE

(269)637-0682. E-mail: humblearts@gmail.com. Website: www.beadcruise.com. Contact: Heather Powers, event promoter. Estab. 2005. "The Bead Cruise is an annual event hosted by beadmaker, designer, and author, Heather Powers. Each year we travel to different locations and on a different ship, which makes it fun and exciting for those joining us again. Our incredible classes have something for everyone: off-loom beading, wirework, bead embroidery, metalwork, and unique bead-stringing projects. Our instructors teach all over the world, including at the biggest beading events in the country. Our cruise focuses on quality classes with innovative designers!"

BEADING BY THE BAY

(269)637-0682. E-mail: info@beadingbythebay.com. Website: www.beadingbythebay.com. Estab. 2008. "Beading by the Bay in beautiful San Francisco. Learn new off-loom seed bead techniques, create beautiful jewelry, and relax the weekend away with accomplished instructors."

BEADS AND COLOR RETREAT

(269)637-0682. E-mail: Beverly@gilbertdesigns.net. Website: www.beverlyashgilbert.com/workshops/ beadscolor2528.html. "Join us for colorful art workshop retreats in Beverly's sun-filled studio on beautiful Whidbey Island. Get your creative juices flowing and join us for the entire retreat, or just a day, filled with beads, color, wine, and food."

BEADS ON THE VINE

2555 Biddle Ranch Rd., San Luis Obispo CA 93401. (805)440-2613. Fax: (866)562-0452. E-mail: info@schoolofbeadwork.com. Website: www.beadsonthevine. com. Estab. 2002. "Experience 3 days of seed bead weaving in California's central coast wine country." **ADDITIONAL INFORMATION** Retreat held in July. Attendance: 48. Class size: 16. Geared towards handmade items. Focus: seed beads. Accepts Visa, MasterCard, American Express, PayPal, check.

BEADVENTURES

Beadventures, Inc., 2415 La Honda Dr., Anchorage AK 99517. (907)258-2331. Fax: (907)258-2332. E-mail: cfrasca@beadventures.com. Website: www.beadventures.com. Contact: Cheryl Frasca, owner. Estab. 1994. "We offer international travel to over 14 countries with many talented teachers and experts in the field of beadwork, beadmaking, fiber arts, and more. Creativity, sparked by culture and nurtured by talented teachers is what Beadventures is all about."

BENEATH THE SURFACE

E-mail: alisaburke@gmail.com. Website: www.shopalisaburke.com/collections/retreats-and-classes/products/beneath-the-surface-2-day-class. "Beneath the Surface is a two class dedicated to designing and creating your very own unique and one-of-a-kind fabric. We will start with the design process and move into all kinds of techniques-screen printing, using dye, resists, painting, printmaking, stamp carving, and LOTS more! After two days of creativity you will walk away with all kinds of new techniques, inspiration, and a STACK of fabric to use in your own creative projects!"

BE PRESENT RETREATS

Website: www.bepresentretreats.com. "The Be Present Retreats are an invitation to pause in your life and gather in an intimate, creative community to explore, create, discover, and soak up the world around you. Each retreat includes creative play + adventures combined with stories and 'being present' exercises to encourage awareness of this moment. At each retreat, you will also be invited to practice self-care to rest and nurture yourself as needed."

BIG BEAR CRAFT COTTAGE

P.O. Box 6436, Big Bear Lake CA 92315. (301)704-1796 or (909)281-4006. E-mail: bigbearcraftcottage@gmail.com. Website: www.bigbearcraftcottage.com. "Unwind from your busy schedule and escape to the beautiful mountains of Big Bear Lake for a relaxing weekend with your friends and family. If you are into hobbies such as crafting, quilting, reading, board games, paper crafts, puzzles and more, we have an all-purpose Craft Room, with ample space personal group gatherings. This is a great place for a girls' getaway weekend!"

BLACK SHEEP GATHERING

P.O. Box 51092, Eugene OR 97405. E-mail: blacksheepgathering@gmail.com; sheepmom@cmc.net. Website: www.blacksheepgathering.org. "The Black Sheep Gathering is an annual event during which participants exchange their knowledge of an appreciation for handcraft fibers and the animals that produce them. Goals: The Black Sheep Gathering strives to provide an environment dedicated to: education, cooperation and participation, an atmosphere of fellowship and fun, and celebrating natural-colored animals and their fibers."

BLUE BIRD LANE RETREATS

20531 S. Yale Ave., Mounds OK 74047. (918)633-6628. E-mail: reservations@bluebirdretreat.com. Website: www.bluebirdretreat.com. "Enjoy the songbirds from the front deck in the Spring or keep cool behind our floor-to-ceiling window views during the Summer heat. Find a rocking chair on the back balcony for the perfect Fall evening, and when the Winter turns frosty, cozy up with a warm cup of coffee in a comfy chair. Choose a relaxing 3-day weekend retreat with friends. Rent the entire facility for a family reunion, or stop by during the week to spend the day cropping. Every visit to The Lane is the perfect escape from the hustle and bustle of daily life."

BROWN BAG RETREATS

The Creation Station!, 252 E. Hwy. 246, Unit A, Buellton CA 93427. (805)693-0174. Fax: (805)693-0164. E-mail: info@thecreationstation.com. Website: www.thecreationstation.com/brown-bag-retreats.htm. "It's a very friendly and fun gathering of quilters/sewers sharing a weekend together. We call it 'Brown Bag' because each retreater brings her/his own project to work on and everyone brings something to share at the Friday night potluck. There are no classes, no schedules to adhere to, no workshop to follow—just you, your sewing machine, your project, and everyone else! Your weekend will be filled with good food, good fun, and good friends— we like to tell people you'll have nothing to do except 'graze and sew' (meaning enjoy the yummy snacks and food and then get back to sewing!)"

☙ CALL OF THE WILD SOUL RETREATS

Website: www.callofthewildsoul.com. "Our retreats illuminate the intersection of the creative + the sacred. We openly encourage self-exploration through acts of wild and bold expression. Our teachers are guides inward; handpicked for their heart-led approach and commitment to soul-archaeology. We are a collective of wild women seeking expanded consciousness, creativity, and community."

CAMP ARTSEEN

E-mail: fun@campartseen.com. Website: www.campartseen.com/summer-art-retreat/art-workshops-at-camp-artseen. "Camp ArtSeen is an annual, weekend art retreat combining the playfulness of summer camp, the inspiration of art school, and the opportunity to just let go. Camp ArtSeen brings together working artists, aspiring makers, and curious creative types to make art and make friends in a beautiful, peaceful setting, far from the hustle and bustle of everyday life. Typical activities include art workshops, yoga, live music, movie night, glow-in-the-dark bocce ball, sunbathing and swimming, hiking, sharing organic meals, and plenty of free time to hike alone or share stories with fellow campers over a glass of wine. "

CAROLINA FIBER FROLIC

411 Pine St., Ft. Mill SC 29715. (803)547-4299. E-mail: jan@carolinafiberfrolic.com. Website: www.carolinafiberfrolic.com. Contact: Jan Smiley, retreat organizer. Estab. 2010. "The Carolina Fiber Frolic is a friendly, welcoming retreat held all day Friday & Saturday, and until noon on Sunday in the North Carolina Mountains. We embrace knitters, spinners, felters, crocheters, dyers, and weavers. The Fall retreat is "all retreat" and people bring their own projects to work on. The Spring retreat also hosts optional classes in a variety of fiber crafts that people sign up for ahead of time and take throughout the weekend. We have a fantastic caterer that supplies our lunches & dinner and the conference center has 2 large double-sided fireplaces as well as wide covered porches with rocking chairs. Evening happy hour & activities, informal but informative after-lunch talks, door prizes, and Fashion Show and Tell round out a full and fun weekend at the Carolina Fiber Frolic."

ADDITIONAL INFORMATION Retreat held in March & November. Attendance: 40-50. Class size: 6-12. Geared towards handmade items. Focus: knitting, spinning, weaving, fiber arts. Accepts instructor applications online. Accepts PayPal, check.

CEDAR CHEST QUILTERS GUILD RETREAT

Website: www.cedarchestquiltersguild.org/retreat. "Experience 4 fun-filled days and nights of classes, trunk shows, meet-and- greet events, and an All-Night Sew with door prizes & drawings all night long. Learn new techniques and tricks from some great local and national teachers to hone your quilting skills and build some great friendships with fellow quilters."

CHERISHED MOMENTS CRAFT HIDEAWAY

(765)628-7235. E-mail: tresha@crafthideaway.com. Website: www.crafthideaway.com. "Everybody needs a little pampering. Gather your girlfriends, sisters, mothers, and come spend a weekend at the Hideaway. Bring your craft projects (or just a book) and unwind from the stress of everyday life. Be a little selfish. It's all about you!"

CHICAGO ART RETREATS

E-mail: info@chicagoartretreats.org. Website: www.chicagoartretreats.org. "The Artist's Retreats are an invitation for artists of all disciplines to rediscover and be inspired by Chicago. Unfortunately, we cannot provide studio space, but you will be able to visit many of Chicago's museums, galleries, and urban treasures; we encourage research; time to be inspired by the cityscape; opportunity to share space and ideas with other artists in residence and artists from Chicago to forge lasting relationships. Salons are held on Saturday evening where residency participants and local artists will meet and talk."

CHICAGO URBAN ART RETREAT CENTER

1957 S. Spaulding Ave., Chicago IL 60623. (773)542-9126. E-mail: info@urbanartretreat.com. Website: www.urbanartretreat.com. Estab. 1984. "We are an oasis of peace and safety in an urban environment on public transportation with a direct route to downtown, plenty of outdoor space to enjoy, an art gallery, art studio, and friendly people. We specialize in working with talented artists and artisans, students who are testing out their artistic/creative abilities, and folks who enjoy a peaceful and satisfying experience. We are located in a real Chicago neighborhood that can be very inspiring. Our nonprofit organization often provides free creative experience for adults to enjoy and learn from where they can relax and be free from judgment. We are known for our artistic bohemian facility and small group workshops with plenty of one-on-one attention."

ADDITIONAL INFORMATION Retreat held weekly on Saturday mornings. Class size: 3–10. Geared towards handmade items. Focus: crochet, weaving, fiber arts, mixed media, paper craft, sewing, jewelry making, painting, collages, assemblage. Accepts instructor applications online. Accepts PayPal, check, or cash.

CHICKEN CREEK HEN HOUSE RETREAT

(918)457-3307. E-mail: darmstrong@lrec.org. Website: www.cchenhouseretreat.com. "The Hen House is a 2,100 sq. ft. constructed (2011) home for 'gatherings, get-a-ways, and special events,' with a focus on quilting and scrapbooking retreats."

CONFERENCE OF NOTHERN CALIFORNIA HANDWEAVERS

E-mail: advisory@cnch.org. Website: www.cnch.org/conferences. "CNCH sponsors an annual conference for handweaving-related fiber arts. In even numbered years, a full conference is hosted, featuring seminars, workshops, exhibits, shows, and a marketplace. In odd-numbered years, an alternative retreat-style conference is hosted, where the offerings vary."

CRAFT CRUISES

Website: www.craftcruises.com. "Cruising with a purpose is about collecting experiences and making new friends. If you have found yourself resisting cruising then you may want to think again. Craft Cruises® is known for having the highest-quality educational programs onboard award-winning cruise lines. Craft Cruises® carefully selects the cruise lines, ships, and itineraries used to ensure each passenger's safety, comfort, and enjoyment."

CRAFTING AT CAMP RETREAT

Website: www.cvillenaz.com/craft. "Our retreat is for women of all ages and experiences who enjoy crafts of all kinds. We get together at the Virginia Nazarene Camp in Buckingham several times a year to spend a weekend laughing, sharing, eating, crafting, and occasionally sleeping. We offer a 6-ft. table all your own, unlimited time to work on your projects (you don't have to sleep if you don't want to), a relaxed schedule with minimal distractions and interruptions. We may play a few games, give away a few prizes, and break for meals and devotions, but our main focus is uninterrupted time to work on your crafting projects. Cost for the retreat is $86, which includes 2 nights lodging and 4 meals, and don't forget that exclusive 6-ft. table."

CRAFTY CHICKS RETREATS

(509)999-6187. E-mail: krystaws@comcast.net. Website: www.facebook.com/craftychicksretreats. "CCR appeals to all kinds of different crafters, like painters, quilters, scrapbookers, crocheters, sewers, beaders, etc. Come relax, laugh, and make memories!"

CRAFTY RETREATS

44 (0)1566 776932. E-mail: info@craftyretreats.com. Website: www.craftyretreats.com. "Crafty Retreats offers exciting residential craft courses on a range of subjects in rural France. Although we are based in Cornwall, United Kingdom, all our holidays take place in our purpose-built center in the Limousin. We hope you will enjoy visiting and learning new skills with us."

CREATE, EXPLORE, DISCOVER

E-mail: sarah@red-line-design.com. Website: www.createexplorediscover.com. "Create.explore.discover is focused on guided hands-on projects and personal interaction with experienced artist-instructors. During the day retreats, in April and September, participants begin the day with a special welcome and 'art-awakening' session. You will then delve into a single-medium series of classes exploring the ins and outs with an expert. Beginners and advanced students alike will discover new techniques and unearth their own personal style. Following your day of creativity, participants and instructors will relax and unwind with an artists' reception and discussion-in-the-round to help participants reflect and appreciate the time spent on *themselves*. During the weekend retreat each participant experiences three unique guided art and creativity workshops, exploring the various art forms and media. The retreat kicks off on Friday evening with a welcome dinner with fellow participants and instructors. Saturday and Sunday mornings begin with a special 'art-awakening' session before your day of classes. On Saturday, an artists' reception and discussion-in-the-round completes the first day of activities, with time to enjoy an evening meal in the historic Lake Tahoe town of Truckee, California. Sunday begins anew with a final workshop to complete your creative journey."

CREATE MIXED MEDIA RETREAT

E-mail: create@interweave.com. Website: www.seattle.createmixedmediaretreat.com. "CREATE Mixed Media Retreat is a 5-day event presented by the editors of *Cloth Paper Scissors*® magazine that gives attendees the opportunity to explore new techniques for their mixed-media artmaking, including sewing, mixed-media collage, album design, jewelry making and art journaling."

CREATIVE PASSIONS CROP & QUILT RETREAT

203 Pearl St., Chesaning MI 48616. (989)845-2159. E-mail: lgreenfelder@hotmail.com. Website: www.creativepassionsllc.com. "Creative Passions is an adult women's retreat, located in the cozy, historical village of Chesaning, Michigan, just off M-57 in southwest Saginaw county. The newly renovated church was built in 1868. It has some original stained-glass windows, as well as natural lighting. It is within walking distance from restaurants and small-town shops. With a ramp into the building and all work areas on the main floor, you can easily wheel in all your supplies."

❥ CREATIVITY ART RETREAT

E-mail: shelley@creativityartretreat.com. Website: www.creativityartretreat.com. "Our retreat brings together some of the most exciting art instructors from across Canada and the States. The Retreat provides an inspiring and safe forum for people to explore and explode their creative juices, be they absolute beginners or experienced artists; and to discover and expand their own individual marks in an atmosphere of community, enthusiasm, and learning."

DOVER QUILT RETREAT

(302)734-0920. E-mail: info@doverquiltretreat.com. Website: www.doverquiltretreat.com. "Leave the solitude of your sewing room and have a great weekend or week-long retreat quilting with your friends at Dover Quilt Retreat. Nestled among Mennonite and Amish neighbors, enjoy the peaceful country setting of Kent County, Delaware."

EVERJEAN QUILT & CRAFT RETREAT

(828)926-1381. E-mail: lapnc@aol.com. Website: www.everjeanquiltretreat.com. "Everjean Quilt & Craft Retreat is a home in the Smoky Mountains set up for quilt retreats and/or whatever hobby you may enjoy. Quilting, scrapbooking, knitting, we have the perfect place for you to plan your private retreat with your friends to meet, create, and complete your projects!"

FIBER RETREAT

E-mail: carroll-bartlettl@missouri.edu. Website: www.sites.google.com/site/fiberretreat2011/schedule-at-a-glance-1/home. "We invite you with enthusiasm and excitement to join us in Jefferson City, MO, to participate in a learning experience with other fiber artists from around Missouri. We invite you to have a good time, make new friends, renew old acquaintances, and learn a new thing about spinning, weaving and natural dyeing, knitting, and crochet."

FIBERS OF FAITH KNITTING RETREAT

(888)863-2267. E-mail: retreats@singinghills.net. Website: www.singinghills.net. "Fibers of Faith Retreats combine Christian women, their faith, knitting, crocheting, and other fiber arts, at Singing Hills Christian Conference Center. Located in central New Hampshire, Singing Hills is easy to get to from all over New England."

FOCUS ON FIBER

Website: www.focusonfiberfloridastyle.com. "Enjoy a true retreat from the frantic fiber world at beautiful Atlantic Center for the Arts in New Smyrna Beach, Florida. Nothing is required of attendees other than they enjoy themselves and renew their spirits. Along with spacious studios specifically set up for computers, painting, dyeing, and sewing, there is room for sculpture, dance, yoga, and quiet spots for reading, writing, and communing with nature."

FRIENDS & FIBERWORKS

E-mail: lisa@friendsandfiberworks.com. Website: www.friendsandfiberworks.com. "Three spectacular days of classes/workshops and FREE demonstrations! Artist and vendors from all over will feature workshops in felting, spinning, weaving, dyeing, knitting, crocheting, and much more!"

GATHERING, THE

85 E. Gay St., Ste. 707, Columbus OH 43215. (614)222-2243. Fax: (614)222-2427. E-mail: admin@isgb.org. Website: www.isgb.org/gathering.html. "The Gathering,, is an occasion to become involved in the glass world and make valuable contacts. There are a wide variety of events at the conference to satisfy many interests. It is an opportunity for attendees to network with each other, gallery owners, collectors, technical vendors, and suppliers. It also gives technical vendors an opportunity to showcase new equipment, tools, supplies, and glass. Through demonstrations, lectures, panel discussions, and more, attendees can learn new techniques and business skills to further their glass bead knowledge."

GRAND OAK RETREAT

10481 Scottsboro Highway, Scottsboro AL 35769. (256)656-8917. Website: www.grandoakretreat.com. "Grand Oak Retreat is the perfect location for your next small group retreat, 24 people or less. Our focus is on crafting groups such as scrapbooking and quilting."

GREAT BEAD ESCAPE, THE

(772)359-0442. E-mail: jenny@thegreatbeadescaperetreats.com. Website: www.thegreatbeadescaperetreats.com. "Our retreat is about learning something new, trying something different, making some wonderful new friends, all while making beautiful jewelry. Most of our classes are perfect for the beginner or someone that wants more practice in a certain area. There will be some advanced classes taught. Our retreat is all-inclusive. One price will cover 5 half-day classes of your choice, all materials, room, and meals. Each class is limited to 6 students."

GRIFFIN DYEWORKS FIBER RETREAT

Griffin Dyeworks & Fiber Arts, 13300 Victory Blvd. #311, Van Nuys CA 91401. E-mail: info@griffindyeworks.com. Website: www.griffindyeworks.com/fiber-retreat. "Griffin Dyeworks sponsors a 3-day fiber retreat in the Los Angeles area. An exciting fiber adventure that will keep you busy all weekend, you'll do the crafts you love, meet local and faraway artists, and learn entirely new skills!"

HEAVENLY STITCHES QUILT RETREAT

(888)863-2267. E-mail: retreats@singinghills.net. Website: www.singinghills.net. "Heavenly Stitches Quilt Retreats combine Christian women, their faith, quilting, and sewing at Singing Hills Christian Conference Center. Located in central New Hampshire, Singing Hills is easy to get to from all over New England."

HISTORY UNWOUND RETREAT

P.O. Box 2381, Yorktown VA 23692. (757)726-7259. E-mail: kimberly@somebunnyslove.com; info@historyunwound.org. Website: www.historyunwound.org. "A 3-day retreat consisting of the education and learning of handcrafting textiles throughout history. A variety of lectures, classes, and demonstrations are held during this weekend."

HOPE HILL RETREAT

(903)583-2814. Website: www.hopehillretreat.com. "Hope Hill Retreat is a shabby chic rural getaway for scrapbooking, crafting, and quilting—nestled amongst several acres of beautiful countryside, 10 miles south of Bonham, Texas. The quiet, country setting provides just the inspiration you need to complete your projects while enjoying the company of your friends."

ISLAND CRAFT ADVENTURES

Website: www.islandcraftadventures.com. "Week-long knitting retreats on beautiful Salt Spring Island in British Columbia, Canada. Stay in a luxuriously rustic farmhouse overlooking the Pacific Ocean, eat fresh, delicious, professionally prepared meals, meet other eager knitters, and knit to your heart's content. What could be better?"

JEWELRY ARTISTS NETWORK RETREAT

(757)726-7259. Website: www.jewelryartistsnetwork. com. "The Jewelry Artists Network Retreat is an annual weeklong retreat held in October each year. For a week a group of artists gather together, sharing a house and creating from morning until late in the evening (or the wee hours of the morning depending on who you are). We share tools and techniques. We share ideas and inspiration. We share meals and a lot of chatter and laughter."

JUST CROP! RETREATS

(714)309-9274. E-mail: justcropretreats@gmail.com. Website: www.justcropretreats.com. "Are you looking for a place where you can work on your scrapbooks/ crafty projects without interruptions from your daily schedules and responsibilities at home? Just Crop! Retreats has just the place for you! We offer you a place where you can work on your projects that you have been longing to do. There are no interruptions from your daily routines or responsibilities that seem to stop you from working on your projects at home."

KANUGA KNITTING & QUILTING RETREAT

Kanuga Conferences, Inc, P.O. Box 250, Hendersonville NC 28793-0250. (828)692-9136. E-mail: info@kanuga. org. Website: www.kanuga.org/conference-calendar/ conference-calendar-details/kanuga-knitting-quilting-retreat. "Learn new techniques from patient experts as you enjoy the perfect weekend escape for knitters and quilters. Experience the casual, friendly atmosphere in the Blue Ridge Mountains that only Kanuga can offer. Knitters and quilters can choose a project to work on during this 3-day retreat. Projects will be offered for beginning to advanced knitters and beginning to intermediate quilters. You are also welcome to bring your own project to work on. In addition to daily classes, there will be get-togethers by the fire, time for hiking to scenic mountain overlooks, and visiting area yarn and quilting shops."

KATHY'S KAPTURED MOMENTS

8050 E. State Rd. 16, Twelve Mile IN 46988. (574)721-6876. E-mail: kbutch622@yahoo.com. Website: www. kathyskapturedmoments.com. "Kathy's Kaptured Moments was designed specifically for scrapbookers. It's the perfect place to kapture the important moments in our lives by recording them in scrapbooks. This retreat's upscale accommodations are also well designed for quilters, crafters of all kinds, and even those who just want to get away with friends."

KEEPING IT CRAFTY RETREATS & MORE

(509)460-2264. E-mail: craftychicks@clearwire. net. Website: www.craftychicksweekendgetaways. com. "Keeping It Crafty Retreats & More (previously known as Crafty Chicks Weekend Getaways) specializes in all-inclusive scrapbooking and craft retreats for women, and is based in the southeast Washington community of the Tri-Cities (Richland-Pasco-Kennewick), Washington. With the inspiration of the mighty Columbia River and surrounded by the lush and beautiful vineyards of the Horse Heaven Hills and Red Mountain AVAs, Keeping It Crafty Retreats offers a unique and memorable experience at every retreat, party, and event. We coordinate the details while you enjoy your weekend, doing what you truly love to do: create!"

KENT NEEDLE ARTS RETREAT

(860)927-3808. Website: www.blacksheepyarnsct. com. "This is a getaway weekend where you can concentrate on developing your skills and taking your needlework to new heights; classes are available at all skill levels. Care has been taken to ensure there is a variety of activities including shopping the local stores, boutiques, restaurants, a special Retreat Marketplace with yarn tastings, and a gala dinner/fashion show."

KNITAWAY

(303)433-9205. E-mail: cheryl@cheryloberle.com. Website: www.cheryloberle.com/Knitaway.html. "Arrive at the Studio on Wednesday afternoon for the introductory get-together and then spend the next three and a half days immersed in the session workshop in my knitting/teaching Studio in the historic Highlands district of Denver, Colorado. I like to think of the Studio as a playhouse for knitters. There's the yarn room, the knitting library, our 'snack time central' kitchen, and the meeting room where we will be sharing and exploring techniques all in one cozy place. With a knitting nest around your chair, a front porch and flower garden to enjoy, and an historic neighborhood to explore, you'll feel right at home."

KNITTER'S REVIEW RETREAT

Website: www.knittersreview.com. "The Knitter's Review Retreat is a special kind of gathering that mixes inspiration, learning, play, and a healthy dose of low-stress downtime with your peers. I take great care in pulling together just the right blend of people, vendors, and activities to create a weekend that leaves you feeling relaxed, inspired, and welcomed as part of a community."

KNITTING AND YOGA ADVENTURES

E-mail: knittingyogi@maine.rr.com. Website: www.knittingandyogaadventures.com. "Organized trips to wonderful locations featuring knitting workshops with nationally recognized knitting designers, yoga classes, massage therapy, and hikes."

KNITTING IN THE HILLS GETAWAY

E-mail: (512)707-7396. Website: www.hillcountryweavers.com/pages/events. "Our retreat will be a time to relax, rejuvenate, and refresh in the beauty of the Hill Country. It will be a time to catch up with old friends and a chance to meet some new ones too."

🌑 KNITTING RETREAT IN IRELAND

E-mail: victoria@ballycastleknits.com. Website: www.ballycastleknits.com/tours.htm. "Relax at the Dunloe, a five-star luxury resort hotel located in Killarney, Co. Kerry. Renew your appreciation for crafting in beautiful places, refresh your knitting skills, and learn some new ones. This is a very ambitious knitting retreat and tour. Everything below is included in your tour pack-

age, but you may want to stay back at the hotel for a relaxing day in our private knitting lounge. Victoria will be your knitting instructor and is a member of several craft guilds. She will be there to help you work on your latest project or to start a new one. We will have a group project to start together as well. If you are bringing a non-knitter with you, consider some of the other activities for him or her—horseback riding, falconry, tennis, golf, hiking, fishing, and exploring."

KNITTREAT

5577 State Rte. 7, New Waterford OH 44445. (330)457-0351. E-mail: knittreat@gmail.com. Website: www.knittreat.com. Contact: Elaine Smith, organizer. Estab. 2013. "Knitting classes, fashion show, and 3 days and nights of fun."

ADDITIONAL INFORMATION Retreat held in August & November. Attendance: 65+. Class size: 20. Geared towards handmade items. Focus: knitting, crochet, jewelry making. Accepts instructor applications online. Accepts Visa, MasterCard, check.

LAKE ARROWHEAD RETREATS

(760)208-5514. E-mail: info@lakearrowheadretreats.com. Website: www.lakearrowheadretreats.com. "Imagine an uninterrupted 48 hours dedicated to the project of your choice. Immerse yourself in your favorite hobby together with friends or come on your own and make new friends! Whether quilting, scrapbooking, beading, or just getting away from it all, our goal is to provide a memorable weekend getaway with great food, good friends, and warm hospitality."

LA-LA LAND CRAFT RETREATS

E-mail: info@lalalandcrafts.com. Website: www.lalalandcrafts.com. Estab. 2012. "Enjoy 3 days full of classes, projects, games, and other events hosted by our talented International La-La Land Crafts Design Team while overlooking the gorgeous California coastline!"

LANTERN MOON RETREAT

7911 NE 33rd Dr., Suite 140, Portland OR 97211. (800)530-4170 or (503)460-0003. Fax: (503)284-6230. Website: www.lanternmoon.com. Estab. 2012. "Connect with your knitting sisters and share your love of the handcrafted arts at the Lantern Moon Retreat. We are heading to a place where the sun shines most of the year . . . central Oregon . . . and a quaint town full of arts & culture, including the internationally acclaimed Sisters Outdoor Quilt Show."

LAVENDERSAGE ART RETREAT

Website: www.janelafazio.com/lavender-sage-art-retreat. "On this retreat: You'll create your own unique sketchbook and fill it with drawings and watercolors and nature prints.You will learn to draw and watercolor and easy printmaking (or strengthen your existing skills) with Jane's gentle, honest, and insightful teaching.You'll experience the charming artsy town of Taos and stay at the restful, historic, and slightly magical Mabel Dodge Luhan Inn. You'll have a week just for yourself, shared with like-minded people."

LOFT ART RETREAT

E-mail: jenn@shurkus.com. Website: www.shurkus.com/artretreat. "Envision walking into a spacious, bright, inspiring loft—this is where you will start your creative journey. During these retreats you will create a unique project. It may be a stack of cards or a mixed-media creation. No matter if you are a card maker, a papercrafter, a scrapbooker, or all of the above, this retreat is for you!"

MAGNOLIA RIDGE HIDEAWAY RETREATS

(608)576-3623. E-mail: mail@bloomingescapes.com. Website: www.bloomingescapes.com/retreat.shtml. "Retreats for scrapbooking, quilting, and stamping in Wisconsin. Scrapbook, quilt, stamp, and craft in comfort for a girls' getaway."

MAINE KNITTING CRUISES

Website: www.mainewindjammer.com/maine-knitting-cruises. "Various events with a variety of instructors throughout the year. Interested in putting together your own knitting or crochet cruise? Have a knitting group you'd like to travel with? The Riggin is available for sailing & knitting charters."

MAKE IT! MARK IT! MASK IT! MIXED-MEDIA MIDWEST - CHICAGO RETREAT

E-mail: registrar@scrap-a-thon.com. Website: www.makeit-markit-maskit-mixed-media.blogspot.com. This is a mixed-media art retreat hosted by artist LuLu Haynes, near Chicago. Ladies of all crafts and levels are welcome to attend.

MEADOWS CRAFT RETREAT , THE

(952)220-5910. E-mail: garden323@aol.com. Website: www.meadowsmn.com. "We have space for 12 crafting guests in a totally renovated 3,000-square foot home set on a 13-acre farmstead. Relax and enjoy rural Midwest America rocking on the front porch, discovering one of the many garden destinations, strolling our meandering meadow paths, or chatting with friends on the patio."

SWANSEN'S KNITTING CAMPS, MEG

E-mail: info@schoolhousepress.com. Website: www.schoolhousepress.com/camp.htm. "Knitting Camp came into being when Elizabeth Zimmermann began teaching a weekend knitting course at an extension of the University of Wisconsin. Elizabeth Zimmermann passed the torch to her daughter, knitting designer Meg Swansen, and Schoolhouse Press now offers 4 sessions Thursday through Monday during 4 weekends in July. (Knitting Camp dates are posted by the end of August each year)."

MEMORY LANE CRAFTING RETREAT

10006 N. Rote Rd., Orangeville IL 61060. (815)868-2363. E-mail: memorylanecr@gmail.com. Website: www.memorylanecraftingretreat.com. "Memory Lane Crafting Retreat is the ideal place to spend time together, enjoying friendship and fun! Whether your passion is scrapbooking, quilting, knitting, spinning, beading, writing, or a girls' getaway, Memory Lane has it all! This is the perfect location to relax, laugh, and make memories. The retreat can accommodate up to nine comfortably between 3 bedrooms and sitting area. The main floor crafting room is a beautiful, south-facing room with plenty of natural light overlooking a pond and the picturesque countryside. Our fully stocked kitchen makes meal preparation easy. If you prefer not to cook, we can provide restaurant recommendations."

MENDOCINO ART CENTER RETREATS

(707)937-5818 or (800)653-3328. E-mail: register@mendocinoartcenter.org. Website: www.mendocinoartcenter.org/workshops.html. "The Mendocino Art Center is a highly regarded artistic and educational institution known for retreat-style classes led by superlative artist-instructors. Approximately 200 2-to 5-day classes are offered each year in ceramics, fiber arts, fine art, jewelry/metalsmithing and sculpture/ blacksmithing."

MEN'S KNITTING RETREAT

Website: www.mensknittingretreat.com. "Letting men gather in beautiful settings and explore their passion for knitting, crocheting, spinning, and yarn. It's not often that men have the opportunity to get together in a supportive and educational environment to learn and ask about all aspects of crafting with yarn, including knitting, crocheting, weaving, spinning, tatting, embroidery, etc. With retreats specifically dedicated to providing workshops and support, the environment created often allows men to experience creativity outside the normal bounds of what they're used to."

MINNESOTA KNITTERS' GUILD YARNOVER

E-mail: sue_traczyk@yahoo.com; tabarrett0261@yahoo.com. Website: www.knitters.org/whats-yarnover. Contact: Sue Traczyk or Tracy Barrett. Estab. 1986. "Each year the Minnesota Knitters' Guild has a day-long event called Yarnover held in the Twin Cities metro area. Prestigious local and national instructors (listed below) teach a variety of courses and fiber vendors fill the Yarnover Market, which is free and open to the public."

MISSOURI BEAD RETREAT

E-mail: mobeadretreat@gmail.com. Website: www.mobeadretreat.wordpress.com. "BR is geared towards attracting new or seasoned artists who enjoy flameworking to make unique, handcrafted items. Flameworking (also called lampworking) differs from traditional glassblowing since a torch is used to melt the glass instead of a furnace. Items made through flameworking also tends to be smaller in scale and more intricate in design."

MOONTIDE LACE KNITTING RETREAT

E-mail: mobeadretreat@gmail.com. Website: www.moonriselaceknitting.com/Moontide.htm. "Join us for a fabulous week spent with fellow knitters in beautiful, serene Wellfleet, Cape Cod. Focus on your knitting and enjoy a lovely beach vacation at the same time. Classroom time is mixed with free time for vacation activities and show/share/knit in the evenings. We stay right by the ocean, in a group of cottages which back up to the National Seashore, the same ones we've been enjoying for years. The pattern for the retreat project will be exclusively available only to the retreat attendees and is a strictly kept secret until the first day of the retreat! You'll advance both your technical skills and your ability to translate your creativity into a knittable piece. There will be approximately 24 hours of instruction at our main cabin which has a large, comfortable classroom."

NEEDLEPOINTER RETREATS, THE

(425)252-2277 or (888)252-9733. E-mail: shop@theneedlepointer.com. Website: www.theneedlepointer.com/stitching-retreats. "We host 3 stitching retreats each year. They are a wonderful getaway weekend! Enjoy a relaxing time of stitching in the company of other stitchers. The retreat is held at The Inn at Port Gardner, a charming, cozy inn at the Everett waterfront marina. Complimentary continental breakfasts are provided by the Inn (for those staying at The Inn). The retreat provides lunch on Saturday, a snack bar of goodies in the stitching room, surprise gifts throughout the weekend, and lots of time to stitch and relax. We have optional classes for you to take at the shop; check our classes page for details."

NEW ENGLAND FIBER ARTS RETREAT

(866)633-6625. E-mail: retreats@medomakcamp.com. Website: www.moonriselaceknitting.com/Moontide.htm. "Come join us for a week of fiber-filled fun in beautiful Midcoast Maine. Whether you knit, crochet, spin, felt, dye, or weave, or if you've always wanted to learn how, this is the place for you! Enjoy the company of fellow fiber enthusiasts while you spin by the fireplace or knit in rocking chairs on the porch of our lodge. Work on a community weaving project throughout the week. Collect natural dyestuffs around camp and dye your own yarn and fiber. Most of all, relax!"

NORTH CAROLINA SCRAPBOOK RETREATS

E-mail: mertful@yahoo.com. Website: www.northcarolinascrapbookretreats.com. "Our retreats were created with you in mind where you can scrap with all your scrapbooking friends orfamily and work on your albums. We have some great scrapbook weekends planned. Our North Carolina Scrapbooking Retreats were created to meet the needs of overworked, stressed-out, seriously addicted scrappers. At our Scrappin' Retreats we give every scrapper a full 54 HOURS of uninterrupted cropping time by offering you these wonderful weekend scrapbooking events in Virginia and North Carolina. We have an atmosphere where you can relax in your jammies, stay up all night giggling with girlfriends, and create fabulous scrapbook pages. Won't you come join us?"

NORTHEAST ART WORKSHOPS AND RETREATS

19 Kettle Cove Ln., Bldg. C7, Gloucester MA 01930. (978)729-4970. E-mail: kmasella@icloud.com. Website: www.northeastartworkshops.com. "Come bring your art, spirit, and creativity to new levels at our relaxed art workshop retreats with kind, generous, accomplished internationally-acclaimed artist instructors who have received the highest levels of honors, awards, and accolades. A uniquely unforgettable art experience of growth, inspiration, laughter, and lifelong friendships—like art therapy, but so much more. Our spacious, well-lit, and comfortable studio is a supportive atmosphere welcoming all ages and levels (adults only during nude modeling) with individual 'play-stations' and other surprises accessible 24 hours—here in America's oldest working Art Colony."

NORTHEAST KINGDOM RETREATS

Website: www.nekretreats.com. "Nestled between the Green Mountains and the Connecticut River in northern Vermont, Vermont's Northeast Kingdom offers breathtaking scenery, outstanding lodging and dining, ecotourism and agritourism, Vermont-made products, a rich diversity of art, and recreational opportunities which have gained the Northeast Kingdom national and international recognition. Vermont's Northeast Kingdom is revered by residents and visitors alike for its lovely countryside, abundant natural resources, and the preservation of traditional landscapes and lifestyles that have made the Vermont experience one to be cherished. Make plans to visit the Kingdom this summer for your Vermont Vacation—take a hike, go for a paddle, hit the links, do some mountain biking, or just relax and get away from it all."

NORTHERN CALIFORNIA KNITTING RETREAT

E-mail: marlybuff@aol.com. Website: www.ravelry.com/groups/northern-california-knitting-retreat. "The Northern California Knitting Retreat takes place at the St. Francis Retreat Center in San Juan Bautista, California. The retreat is organized by a committee of friends brought together by their love of fiber craft and knitting from northern California and by The 2 Knit Lit Chicks and The Yarniacs podcasts."

NORTHERN FIBERS RETREAT

E-mail: info@northhouse.org. Website: www.northhouse.org/programs/events/northernfibersretreat.htm. "What could be better than focusing on fibers in the heart of winter? This event celebrates all manner of fiber arts featuring seminars and class offerings from long-time North House instructors."

OLYMPIA BEAD RETREAT

E-mail: info@teresasullivanstudio.com. Website: www.swantowninn.com/weddings-events/olympia-bead-retreat.htm. "The Olympia Bead Retreat is a fun, nurturing place to stretch your creative boundaries, hone your skills, and develop your artistic voice. This intensive, exhilarating exploration of beadweaving is kept intentionally small-scale, so you receive the attention you deserve."

PINE LILY RETREAT HOUSE

P.O. Box 864, Lacombe LA 70445. (985)768-6069. E-mail: pinelilyretreat@yahoo.com. Website: www.pinelilyretreat.com. "Pine Lily Retreat house is a cozy 2,000-square foot, newly renovated cottage with 3 bedrooms including an *extra large* Craft Room. A fully complimented kitchen ready for you if you feel the need to cook, with a full dining room for group meals."

PINS & NEEDLES RETREAT

(859)986-3832. E-mail: info@fiberfrenzy.net. Website: www.fiberfrenzy.net. "Pins & Needles Retreat is held at Boone Tavern in Berea, KY, and includes knitting, quilting, and spinning."

POSIE PATCH RETREAT

(920)857-4025. E-mail: posiepatchretreat@yahoo. com. Website: www.posiepatchretreat.com. "The Posie Patch Retreat is a fabulous location for your next scrapbooking, quilting, stamping, or craft retreat. You will have 2,500 square feet of space to create to your heart's content in our studio."

🌊 POWELL RIVER FIBRE RETREAT

Website: www.prfiberfest.com. "Powell River, on the upper Sunshine Coast, is hosting the annual Vancouver Island Spinners and Weavers Retreat. Weavers and spinners from the Islands and the Sunshine Coast will socialize and share their skills and stories."

QUILTERS' PARADISE RETREAT: QUILTING BY THE BEACH

E-mail: customerservice@quiltingbythebay.com. Website: www.quiltingbythebay.com. "Join the fun at Quilting by the Bay's Annual Quilters' Retreat!"

QUILTING IN THE DESERT

E-mail: quiltcampretreats@gmail.com. Website: www. quiltcamp.com. "Quilting in the Desert is a 5-day quilting retreat in Phoenix, AZ. We offer 2-, 3-, and 5-day classes for quilters of all abilities and varied interests."

QUILT PLACE, THE

575 Barton Blvd., Rockledge FL 32955. (321)223-9969. E-mail: shop@thequiltplace.com. Website: www. thequiltplace.com. "This beautiful and relaxing spot is on the Indian River in Cocoa, Florida, and is only 3½ miles from the shop in Rockledge. Imagine a relaxing weekend watching dolphins breaching, swimming in the pool, and of course lots of quilting. There will be no cooking, no cleaning, and no interruptions!!"

QUILT RETREAT AT SEA

(210)858-6399. Website: www.quiltretreatatsea.com. "We organize fabulous quilt retreat events, both on land and at sea. Our quilt designer-teachers are chosen for their enthusiasm and experience. They design a new project for our events and you should be able to complete this during our event."

QUILT ST. GEORGE RETREAT

Website: www.quiltstgeorge.com. "We have 23 teachers teaching everything from applique to basic patchwork, wool embroidery, traditional embroidery, quilting techniques, quilt design software, domestic machine quilting, antique quilt lectures, and thread seminars. Come see what all the excitement is about! And did I mention delicious food, fantastic lecturers, Prizes, Button Bingo with Chocolate, and Superior Threads Tours."

RED BARN RETREATS

(866)430-1717. Website: www.redbarnretreats.com. "Tools and supplies are available along with a large, well-lit, private workspace to comfortably work on your photographs, quilts, and sewing projects. Having our massage therapist come during your time has been very popular. An entire weekend for less than $100 per person!"

RED CEDAR HOUSE

E-mail: relax@redcedarhouse.net. Website: www.redcedarhouse.net. "Relax and enjoy a weekend designed just for you to work on your craft or hobby. At the Red Cedar House, you'll find the perfect getaway for scrapbookers, stampers, card makers, quilters, or any craft or hobby group. We're the perfect place for girlfriend getaways. Make memories by creating scrapbooks or quilts for your families to enjoy for years to come. Stay up all night, lounge by the pool, rock on the porch, watch a movie, take a relaxing walk around our property, or have a blissful massage from our massage therapist."

RED DOOR RETREAT

E-mail: reddoorretreat@gmail.com. Website: www. reddoorretreat.com. "An unhosted getaway for quilters, crafters, and other adults wanting relaxing time away."

RED ROOSTER RETREATS

E-mail: info@redroosterretreat.com. Website: www. redroosterretreat.com. "Specializes in crafting getaways for scrapbooking, quilting, and small church groups. Located on beautiful Smith Lake in north Alabama. Maximum group size is 23, minimum is 12. Meals, snacks, work space, and a relaxing atmosphere provided."

REME RETREATS

E-mail: reme@remeretreats.com. Website: www.remeretreats.com. "Borrowing the words of one of our students, ReMe has put the 'Retreat' back in retreats! We specialize in small intimate groups who share a love of creativity, peacefulness, good food, laughter, and desire much more than just art classes (although you will get plenty of those, too!) ReMe is more than just an art retreat, it is a Remarkable, Extraordinary, Memorable, Experience = ReMe."

RIPPLE WOMEN'S RETREATS

(970)349-7487. E-mail: melissa@crestedbuttearts. org. Website: www.crestedbuttearts.org/page. cfm?pageid=34582. "The Crested Butte Wildflower Festival in partnership with the Art Studio of the Center for the Arts brings you 'Ripple: Three-Day Women's Art Retreats.' Retreats in varying mediums are offered each year in March, June, July, and September. Participants are invited to immerse themselves in art surrounded by our majestic mountain scenery in a nonthreatening, relaxing, and pampered environment."

ROCKIN' REALITY CRAFT, FIBER & ART RETREATS

E-mail: rena@rockinreality.com. Website: www.rockinreality.com. "Rockin' Reality Retreat Services hosts the ultimate scrapbook, quilting, and craft retreats in central Texas. Our retreats are held at Rockin' Reality Retreat Center, owned and operated by Rena & Don Cotti."

ROSE VILLA RETREATS

115 E. Grand River, P.O. Box 115, Laingsburg MI 48848. (517)258-1426. E-mail: rosevillaretreat@gmail. com. Website: www.rosevillaretreat.com. "A warm and inviting quilting, scrapbooking, stamping, and general hobby retreat located in the heart of Laingsburg, Michigan."

SANTA BARBARA QUILTING RETREATS

(805)705-5523. E-mail: info@santabarbaraquilting. com. Website: www.santabarbaraquilting.com. "We are a boutique retreat company operating in Santa Barbara County, California."

SCRAPAWAY

168 Point Plaza, Butler PA 16001. (724)287-4311. E-mail: scrpabookstation@aol.com. Website: www. scrapbookstation.com. "This retreat is for ladies who wish to avoid the circus-like atmosphere of large scrapbook vacations or conventions & concentrate on making friends & scrapping the weekend away. At our retreat you'll get plenty of work space! You won't feel like a sardine when scrapping with us."

SCRAPPER'S RX SCRAPBOOKING WEEKEND RETREATS

(321)626-2767. E-mail: tammyandstacy@scrappersrx. com. Website: www.scrappersrx.com. "We provide scrapbookers' a getaway that provides them the environment to preserve their family memories and a place to unwind from everyday responsibilities and truly enjoy themselves."

SCRAPPIN' HOME RETREATS

7433 Spout Springs Rd., Ste. 7433 - PMB 48, Flowery Branch GA 30542. (770)337-2519. E-mail: kare@ scrappinretreats.com. Website: www.scrappinretreats.com/homeretreats.htm. "Scrappin' HOME Retreats are Friday thru Sunday weekends located at our home in Flowery Branch, Georgia. Designed to accommodate up to 12 scrappers, Scrappin' HOME Retreats combines the high standards you've come to expect from Scrappin' Retreats with the affordability of small, intimate weekend retreats."

SEAMS LIKE HOME QUILTING RETREAT

(724)984-1399. Website: www.seamslikehomeretreat. com. "Seams Like Home is a quilting retreat and bed & breakfast located between Uniontown and Connellsville, PA, in a beautiful rural setting that is peaceful and relaxing."

SEASIDE BEAD RETREAT

E-mail: owsky@gmail.com. Website: www.beadelves. com. "Join us in this historic village for beading, fun, and friends, plus delicious food and amazing scenery!"

SEW DELIGHTFUL

(208)731-1391. E-mail: greenetj@msn.com. Website: www.sew-delightful.com. "We offer delightful quilters' retreats!"

SEW MANY MEMORIES

P.O. Box 338, Guttenburg IA 52052. (563)252-2389. E-mail: sewmanymemories@live.com. Website: www. sewmanymemoriesgetaway.com. "Sew Many Memories is an all-inclusive, pampered weekend retreat getaway for quilting or scrapbooking, located in the restored 1885 historic St. Clair hotel in Guttenberg. We are just one block from the picturesque Mississippi River in Iowa's 2006 Most Historic Town! Our weekends are designed to rejuvenate you in a stress-free environment, as we pamper you from Friday night to Sunday noon! Enjoy a favorite pastime of quilting or scrapbooking, or maybe even just time away with friends!"

SEW SOUTH

E-mail: jennifer@sewsouthretreat.com. Website: www.sewsouthretreat.com. "What's Sew South? It's a modern sewing retreat in Charlotte, NC. It's a super fun weekend with friends old and new. It's sewing for the fun of it and making something for yourself. It's dusting off that WIP and having the time to make some headway! It's laughing, chatting, giggling, making connections, being creative, being yourself. It's staying up late or going to bed early, no cooking, no cleaning, no chores—just fun! It's creative, it's inspiring, it's relaxing. It's just the place for you!"

SEWTOPIA RETREAT

E-mail: info@gosewtopia.com. Website: www.gosewtopia.com. "Sewtopia is a weekend where attendees can leave all the stresses of daily life behind to indulge themselves, focus on sewing projects, and get together with friends, old and new. We will strive to do two amazing events each year. The spring event will focus on education and the fall event will be a retreat-style event."

SHEEP IN THE CITY GETAWAY

E-mail: hello@just4ewe.com. Website: www.just-4ewe.com/Sheep_in_the_City/Sheep_in_the_City/Welcome.html. "Come on and join in the fun. Three days of fiber overload, vendors, classes, door prizes, and party fun!! Bring your wheel and or a project to work on, and sit in the fiber circle with other addicts. Spend the day, or the weekend! New Vendors and new ideas."

SHEEPISH IN SEATTLE

E-mail: thetravelingewe@gmail.com. Website: www. thetravelingewe.com. "Join The Traveling Ewe for a weekend of yarn tourism in and around Seattle. Stops include local yarn shops, fiber galleries, and more."

SIMPLY STITCHING

(417)336-5016. Website: www.ceciliassamplers.com/classes.asp. "Simply Stitching is a 'no frills' weekend that you can spend stitching, visiting, shopping, and eating! It will be from Thursday afternoon until Sunday morning. We will include a welcome dinner catered to the conference room on Thursday evening. You will also receive a tote bag and T-shirt to commemorate the weekend. We will offer a 10% discount to all attendees for purchases in Cecilia's Samplers. The cost of the Simply Stitching retreat will be $50 which is payable at the time you make your reservation for the retreat. We'll still have a charity, with a $100 Cecilia's Samplers gift card as a prize. The trading table, the 50% off sale, and Buck-A-Bag fabric will still be included at the retreat. And, as usual, there's always one of us at the conference room with the group to answer questions, give directions, help with needlework questions, and to contact the shop for deliveries to the conference room. You are still welcome to bring snacks for the snack table, too!"

SPRING KNITTING RETREAT IN ICELANDIC NATURE

E-mail: helene@helenemagnusson.com. Website: www.icelandicknitter.com/en/travels/spring-knitting-retreat-in-icelandic-nature/. "This 6-day retreat will take us to the beautiful West of Iceland where the enchanting landscape, the first flowers of spring, the green moss, the utterly cute lambs and kids, the busy bird life, will inspire us as much as the knitting artifacts in the Textile Museum in Blönduós that we will have the chance to visit. Hélène will tell us about the Icelandic knitting traditions with a focus on the famous Icelandic lopi yoke sweater. We will meet with many local crafters, spinners, dyers, and tanners for an unforgettable insight into the Icelandic culture and knitting heritage. This trip does not include hiking but participants will be provided with the opportunity of exploring and taking walks where we will be staying, enjoy some bird watching, or go horse riding."

SQUAM

Squam Art Workshops, 143 Ivy St., Providence RI 02906. E-mail: elizabeth@squamartworkshops.com. Website: www.squamartworkshops.com. "We teach, inspire, and heal. Our community receives encouragement, training, inspiration and experience that expands their creative spirit. We help dissolve restrictions and limitations on the definition of what it means to be an artist."

STITCHER'S GARDEN SCHOOLHOUSE GATHERING, A

A Stitcher's Garden, 7070 Cedar Bay Rd., Fayetteville NY 13066. (315)449-2181. Fax: (315)445-7934. E-mail: jan@AStitchersGarden.com. Website: www.AStitchersGarden.com. Estab. 1999. "We invite you to join us at our Stitching Friends Retreat, meet this talented designer, see her lovely models in person, and spend the weekend with her. She will teach a project that she has designed exclusively for us named 'Fragments From An English Garden.'"

STITCHING AT THE BEACH

E-mail: palsconvention@hotmail.com. Website: www.downsunshinelane.com/beach.htm. "We will be doing lots of stitching, chatting, laughing, shopping, eating, and more! We will be spending 4 days in an oceanfront conference center with our stitching & exchanges!"

STITCHIN' POST'S QUILT TIL YOU WILT BEACH RETREAT, THE

P.O. Box 280, Sisters OR 97759. (541)549-6061. E-mail: stitchin@stitchinpost.com. Website: www.stitchinpost.com/quilt-class-workshop-retreat/quilting-retreats-workshops.html. "Join us for a relaxing weekend getaway at the beach! Bring your sewing, knitting, or reading to the Overleaf Lodge in scenic Yachats, Oregon. Savor the many nearby coastal attractions and enjoy walks along the gorgeous rocky coastline. All of the Overleaf rooms have spectacular ocean views. Take advantage of the Overleaf in-house spa and be spoiled by the 'good fairies' available to help you with your projects. Register early, as this retreat fills quickly! Don't forget to bring an item to share at 'Show & Tell.'"

STITCHTOPIA KNITTING HOLIDAYS

01473 660800. E-mail: enquiries@arenatravel.com. Website: www.arenatravel.com/our-holidays/stitchtopia-knitting-crochet-holidays/view#. "Our knitting holidays, in association with Rowan, combine your passion for knitting with some amazing locations across the world. Each holiday is different, but the focus will always be on perfecting your craft with top experts, lovely hotels, inspiring destinations, and enjoying like-minded company."

STUDIO CRESCENDOH

E-mail: studio@crescendoh.com. Website: www.crescendoh.com/studio_crescendoh. "WORKSHOPS + LECTURES + SPECIAL EVENTS. Half-day, full-day, multi-day workshops, lectures, and special events are scheduled throughout the year. Once you purchase a workshop through PayPal or Google Checkout, you will be enrolled."

SUMMIT SEW & QUILT RETREAT CENTER

(704)682-9567. E-mail: kim@summitquiltretreat.com. Website: www.summitquiltretreat.com. "We offer sew & quilt retreats."

SUPER SUMMER KNITOGETHER

TheKnitGirllls, LLC, P.O. Box 876, Pomona NJ 08240. (662)626-7751. Website: www.supersummerknitogether.com. SSK is a 5-day knitting retreat.

TETON PATCHWORKS QUILTERS' RETREAT

(208)456-2130. E-mail: tetonpatchworks@aol.com. Website: www.tetonpatchworks.com. "Our retreat center is specially designed for up to 8 quilters who want the ideal quilting retreat. The sewing room has 8 quilting stations distinctively designed with the quilter in mind. Each station has its own swivel chair and OTT light to provide true-color illumination. There is enough design wall space for everyone. The 2 spacious cutting tables are complete with large cutting mats and rulers. The 2 ironing stations have their irons ready to go. All you bring is your sewing machine and plenty of fabric!"

CREATIVE SOUL RETREAT, THE

(928)282-3809. E-mail: sac@sedonaartscenter.org. Website: www.sedonaartscenter.org/SedonaArtRetreats. "The Creative Soul Retreat offers a unique tour of self-discovery as you explore a world of creative possibilities. Sedona is known for three things: its beautiful and unique landscape, its art colony atmosphere, and as a place for spiritual retreat. The Sedona Arts Center has wrapped these elements into a unique package where art and self-discovery fuse—creating the opportunity for artists and those who would consider themselves non-artists to engage fully in the experience of art. The retreat program is made of 6 hands-on experiences that become for each participant a personal creative path."

THREADS AND BEDS CREATIVE SEWING AND RETREAT CENTER

(217)431-9202. E-mail: reservations@threadsoftimefab.com. Website: www.threadsandbedsretreat.com. "Our retreat center offers 10,000 square feet of spacious sewing area, comfortable accommodations, and kitchens. Whether you are a single sewer or a group, we have everything you need to plan your next sewing getaway!"

TIMBERHAZE RETREAT

(651)257-1947. E-mail: stay@timberhazeretreat.com. Website: www.timberhazeretreat.com. "Timberhaze Retreat is designed for groups of up to 8 people to stay, relax, create, regenerate, or to simply enjoy spending time together. Our home features a large, well-lit craft room that is set up and equipped with sturdy tables, comfortable chairs, and a design wall (made especially with quilters in mind). The craft room is also an ideal work space to inspire whatever your creative pursuit may be. Alternatively, use the craft room as a meeting space, or for a place to just relax and hang out."

TWO RIVERS YARNS SPRING KNITTING RETREAT

E-mail: mary@tworiversyarns.com. Website: www.tworiversyarns.com. "After a long winter of gray days and cold temperatures, why not treat yourself to a weekend away: meet other knitters, learn something new, and experience the beauty of rural western Maryland. You will enjoy plenty of knitting time, instruction, catered organic meals, plus a soothing massage if you choose. We hope that this will be an experience to rejuvinate your body, mind, and spirit and leave behind the winter blues."

TYLER BEAD RETREAT

(870)615-2072. E-mail: belindajoann@yahoo.com. Website: www.tylerbeadretreat.com. Two-day retreat held in June & November.

UNWIND: A FIBER ARTS GETAWAY IN THE MOUNTAINS

E-mail: sue@unwindgetaway.com. Website: www.unwindgetaway.com. "Come unwind in Blowing Rock, North Carolina! This getaway is not just about education, but about community and relaxing too. Take classes from fabulous instructors. Learn and share with old friends and new. Explore your surrounds, like nearby Grandfather Mountain and downtown

Blowing Rock and the local yarn store, Unwound Yarn. And of course, unwind for awhile in the fantastic Meadowbrook Inn."

VASHON ISLAND SEWING RETREAT

P.O. Box 2143, Vashon WA 98070-2143. (206)567-5039. E-mail: penny@stitchinggirlssociety.org. Website: www.vashonislandsewingretreat.com. Estab. 1984. "Our Retreats are all about sewing, sharing, and having fun: sewing classes, sewing for fun; sharing ideas, sharing projects, sharing inspiration, sharing friendship and good times from sunup to sundown with no interruptions, wonderful food, beautiful scenery, and all the time in the world to sew. Retreaters sleep in cozy cabins nestled in the fir forest or the newer Retreat Center; hike the pebbled paths to the lodges, or around the peninsula loop trail, or down to the salt water beach; dine on the fabulous meals prepared especially for the Vashon Island Sewing Retreat by Camp Burton's Chef."

VERMONT SUMMER RETREATS, THE

E-mail: beth@knittingtraditions.com. Website: www.knittingtraditions.com/workshops/beths-vermont-retreats. "Join us for an extended weekend in August to knit, laugh, and join in camaraderie of the very best kind."

VIRGINIA SCRAPBOOK RETREATS

E-mail: mertful@yahoo.com. Website: www.virginiascrapbookretreats.com. "Our retreats were created with you in mind where you can scrap with all your scrapbooking friends or family and work on your albums. We have some great scrapbook weekends planned. Our Virginia Scrapbooking Retreats were created to meet the needs of overworked, stressed-out, seriously addicted scrappers. At our Scrappin' Retreats we give every scrapper a full 54 HOURS of uninterrupted cropping time by offering you these wonderful weekend scrapbooking events in Virginia and North Carolina. We have an atmosphere where you can relax in your jammies, stay up all night giggling with girlfriends, and create fabulous scrapbook pages. Won't you come join us?"

WHISTLESTOP QUILT RETREAT

Whistlestop Quilt Retreat, 134 Head of Creek Rd., Sweetwater TN 37874. (865)684-6858. E-mail: jodi@whistlestopquiltretreat.com. Website: www.whistlestopquiltretreat.com. "The Whistlestop Quilt Retreat, located in Sweetwater, Tennessee, is a 150-year old farmhouse on 7 acres of picturesque farmland where you can step back in time and gather with friends. Experience Whistlestop with your private group of up to 18 friends, or join us for a Whistlestop Open Retreat, workshop, or class."

WINDY STITCHES RETREAT

(406)539-6144. E-mail: lori@windystitches.com. Website: www.windystitches.com. "Windy Stitches Retreat is a wonderful place where quilters, knitters, scrapbookers, and other crafters can get away and relax in the company of friends. Our 3-bedroom, 2-bath retreat has comfortable accommodations for up to 8 people."

WOODLAND RIDGE RETREAT

Woodland Ridge Retreat, P.O. Box 27, Downsville WI 54735. (715)664-8220. E-mail: dyecandy@gmail.com. Website: www.woodlandridgeretreat.com. "Woodland Ridge Retreat is a creative getaway for quilters, fiber artists, scrapbookers, and artists. Located in the rural village of Downsville, Wisconsin, this idyllic property overlooks the scenic Red Cedar River Valley in the west-central part of the state. Our retreat offers deluxe accommodations and brightly lit gathering rooms. The facility is on one level with ADA-accessible guest accommodations."

WOOLEN WILLOW RETREATS

E-mail: woolenwillowretreats@yahoo.com. Website: www.woolenwillowretreats.weebly.com. "Woolen Willow Retreats hosts retreats each year dedicated to all styles of quilters and rug hookers. Simply click on one of the tabs at the top of the page, and begin your retreat planning!"

YARN CUPBOARD RETREAT

(315)399-5148. E-mail: info@yarncupboard.com. Website: www.yarncupboard.com/festival. "The Yarn Cupboard has many opportunities for instruction with a full roster of classes. We believe at the Yarn Cupboard we go beyond just supplying beautiful fibers or providing help. We are a fiber arts community."

YARNOVER SLEEPOVER RETREAT

(315)399-5148. E-mail: yarnoversleepover@gmail.com. Website: www.yarnoversleepover.com. "Wake up in stitches…. This is a yarn retreat for knitters and crocheters looking for fun classes with fabulous teachers and delicious food."

YOUR TIME ARTS & CRAFTS RETREATS

(763)682-2061. E-mail: yourtimecrafts@gmail.com. Website: www.yourtimecrafts.com. "Your Time Arts & Crafts Retreat is a crafter's paradise. Located in historic Buffalo, Minnesota, just 40 miles from the Twin Cities, our retreat offers the perfect place to visit with old and new friends, share your creativity, have fun,

and enjoy personal time away from home. We offer full-service accommodations in our fully restored home nestled in a quiet and serene small-town village atmosphere."

ZOMBIE KNITPOCALYPSE RETREAT

Website: www.zombieknitpocalypse.com. "ZK is an urban knitting retreat hosted in downtown Rochester, MN. The retreat runs Wednesday afternoon through Sunday midday, with a relaxed atmosphere that encourages knitting, meeting new friends, shopping, and eating great food at the wonderful restaurants centrally located in downtown Rochester. In fact, once you get to the hotel, there is very little need for a car, as everything is within walking distance. While the retreat atmosphere is laidback, there are also many optional opportunities to get involved. You can pack your weekend with as many fun activities as you care to join."

REGIONAL CRAFT SHOW INDEX

Florida

Indiana

Iowa

Kansas

Kentucky

SUBJECT INDEX

ANTIQUES

SUBJECT INDEX

CLAY/PORCELAIN

COLLAGE

CRAFT SUPPLIES

CRAFTING RETREATS

FINE ARTS

FOLK AND NATIVE AMERICAN ART

FURNITURE

GLASS ART

GOURDS

GOURMET/ARTISAN FOODS

GREEN MARKET

HANDBAGS

HOLIDAY/SEASONAL

JEWELRY

KNITTING

MILLINERY

MIXED MEDIA

NEEDLE ARTS

NEEDLEPOINT

PAPERCRAFTING

PERFORMANCE ART

PHOTOGRAPHY

PLUSHIES/SOFTIES

QUILTS AND QUILTING

RAKU

RUBBER STAMPING

RUGS AND RUG HOOKING

SCRAPBOOKING

YARN ARTS

GENERAL INDEX

CRAFT A BETTER BUSINESS!

These ar...   ...m your

FOR INSPIRIN...   ...FTDAILY.COM